Damnatio Memoriae

THEY SHALL NOT BE FORGOTTEN

A study of the Francoist genocide
of Cordoba 1936-1949

Annotated English Translation of
La Victoria Sangrienta by
FRANCISCO MORENO GÓMEZ

by

MAGDALENA GORRELL JAÉN

Towards the retrieval of the Historic Memory of Spain

Damnatio Memoriae Vol. 1 by Magdalena Gorrell Jaén

ISBN 978-1-970072-35-8 (Paperback)
ISBN 978-1-970072-36-5 (Hardback)

This book is written to provide information and motivation to readers. Its purpose is not to render any type of psychological, legal, or professional advice of any kind. The content is the sole opinion and expression of the author, and not necessarily that of the publisher.

Printed in the United States of America.

New Leaf Media, LLC
175 S. 3rd Street, Suite 200
Columbus, OH 43215
www.thenewleafmedia.com

VOLUME I
Victory Without Peace

CONTENTS

TABLES

APPENDIXES

AD LIMINA

Francisco 'Paco' Moreno Gómez has, with notable tenacity, investigated the Francoist repression in Cordoba, the Andalusian province that Franco used to test the efficacy of his program to eradicate the Republican half of Spain who opposed his insurrection. The figures are clear, as Paco Moreno points out: four thousand Republicans slaughtered in the immediate post-war period in Cordoba city alone, as compared to a handful of victims amongst those who supported the military coup. An appalling proportion that did not temper the violence that the rebels had earlier demonstrated in the territory they occupied during the civil war. In Cordoba province, a strong class system that opposed the aristocracy and wealthy landowners and the expectations of the bulk of the working class helps explain why the vengeance of the Falangist upper class fell so heavily upon the Republicans who struggled for a more egalitarian social order.

Even before the fall of the Republican government, the rebels began taking over the entire administrative apparatus of the government in the territories they had conquered, first through extra-judicial executive orders, then by rule of law under edicts from Franco's self-proclaimed government in Burgos directed at creating a new social order for the country. Where there had been collective management systems, the new lords of the manor and the *señoritos* bore down on these latter-day vassals with a re-creation of a medieval form of servitude. The new serfs were not only manual laborers and shepherds, but teachers, doctors, lawyers and numerous other individuals who believed in the democratic ideals of the Republic, even though they might not wear the espadrilles that traditionally shod the feet of the working and farming classes.

With his meticulous investigation, Paco Moreno, demonstrates how the blood bath was programmed from the onset by the military coup led by Generals Franco and Mola, as another way of dominating the people. Part of their plan was to undo everything that had been achieved during the Republic's brief tenure, beginning with the laws themselves. 'Combativeness, propaganda, political activism and ideology' were placed at the service of Spain's *Army of Salvation* and its partners. With this expression, the author draws attention to yet another example of all that he calls 'the use of language as a weapon for mass destruction', the forerunner of a manner of thought that still exists to this day.

Moreno Gómez, a professor for many years until his recent retirement, reminds us of the role of the Church in using virtual machetes to hack a path across a society that was beginning to become secular. A Church that returned to rites and formalities that harked back to the Inquisition as a means of purifying society. Nor did the Church spare the children as it used them as key players for establishing the new National Catholicism, a pillar of the new regime. Paco Moreno reports eyewitness statements that are at the same time both sarcastic and tragic, such as when Ernesto Caballero recalls how whenever a childhood friend swore as they worked, he would look around fearfully, waiting to be struck by the bolt of lightning with which he had been threatened by the nuns who employed the boys. Few priests and nuns did not fit that mold. Paco Moreno recalls the words of one of the few Republican village priests, Marino Ayerra, who was able to escape into exile and who defined those times as 'a new Middle Ages that spreads its dark wings over the homes'. Even more striking is his reflection regarding the militarized and clerical life of those times: "Why did they want the Fascist Party when they already had the Church?"

Prior to examining the events of the immediate post-war, the 'Bloody Victory', he examines the quagmire of indecision by which the National Defense Council (CND), entrusted with negotiating a peaceful surrender, failed to save an immense territory containing half a million troops. In the South of the country, by the end of Franco's infamous 'Victory Walk', army units with thousands of combatants had become an equal number of prisoners.

One satisfaction that the reader gets from this book is how its author speaks loudly and clearly regarding the public historiographic debates of today, putting all who question the existence of the genocide or attempt to sugar-coat the repression, into their place.

Paco Moreno, whose books are examples of thorough research into the violent actions of the fascists who rebelled against the democratic order, does not shirk from using a magnifying glass to divulge, in some detail, the atrocities that were committed. Disgusted with the Church's ongoing syrupy disavowal of the events through its supposed compassion for the dramatic occurrences of the past, Paco Moreno reports cases such as those of the children of the Mayor of Villanueva de Cordoba, executed by firing squad, who were forced to beg in order to survive whilst their mother went into hiding after she was stripped naked and forcibly subjected to the castor oil and shaven head treatment. Paco Moreno does not mince his words as he states that this is an example of the insurgents' intent to shatter the moral fortitude of the defeated, or 'disaffected' as they were called. For most, survival was their sole objective. He does not shrink from shedding light on the innumerable dead from starvation, within and without the prisons and so many other 'rod and thwack' complexes such as the numerous concentration camps.

His asides regarding economic matters are especially relevant. As he says, insufficient importance has been given to the Francoist authorities' abolition of the Republican currency, which forced widespread penury upon the defeated. Still, when all was said and done, this was just yet another feature of the programmed pillaging, first during the war through extra-judicial seizures and appropriations and, when it was almost over, the legalization of the spoils of war rule under the so-called Law of Political Responsibilities. This law was a weapon that would make ghostly appearances, years after the accused had been executed, adding to the misery of their families.

Franco and his fellow fascists were intent at creating a New State where society kneels before the sword and the cross. All means for attaining this goal were acceptable, including weapons of mass psychological destructions such as free rein given to snitches and informers, the use of offensive nicknames and insults in order to convince the persecuted of their own guilt, in addition to the press such as the Cordovan newspaper *Azul* which voluntary collaborated with this mission.

In conclusion, Paco Moreno asks whether the plethora of crosses erected at the Valley of the Fallen and similar shrines and that have populated cities and towns all over Spain from the moment they were occupied by the rebels, are not yet another feature of the anger that the government encouraged against the repressed. These and other public memorials, raised where they are continuously visible to all, remain as symbols dedicated to ensuring the permanency of a memory – the victors' memory. Thanks to Francisco Moreno Gomes' scientifically-led research, we now have a first-class weapon with which to work against the victors' enduring desire to obliterate all recollection of those who perished and to dilute the pain and injustice suffered in silence by the defeated, despite multiple latter-day Francoist attempts to erase their memories and re-write History.

Mirta Núnez Diaz-Balart
Chair and Professor of 20ᵗʰ Century Historic Memory
Universidad Complutense de Madrid

*"The Republic represents the restoration
of all the civic rights to the people,
to every single Spaniard, without hate,
revenge or reprisals, opening the way
for a new judicial era. The Spanish Republic is the home of
Republicans and also of all Spaniards of good will."*

*Antonio Jaén Morente, Cordoba, 16 April 1931 after
proclaiming the Second Spanish Republic on 14 April*

Magdalena Gorrell Jaén Guimaraens, to whom Francisco Moreno Gomes entrusted the task of writing the English version of his investigation into Franco's post-civil war repression of Cordoba city and province, is the granddaughter of Antonio Jaén Morente, one of the celebrated Spanish intellectuals of the 'Generation of 1898'. Scholar, professor, author, diplomat and politician from Cordoba, he devoted his life and work to the history of Spain and to the cause of liberty and justice for all. It is to the memory of this great Republican and to all those who dedicated their lives to the Republic, both in Spain and in exile, that her work is dedicated.

Vila Nova de Cerveira, Portugal, 2019

A VICTÓRIA SANGRIENTA 1939-1945

INTRODUCTION

THE HISTORY OF THE CIVIL WAR. An ongoing Pact of Silence. Sugar-coating the facts, negativism, neo-conservative thought, counter-memory. A 'Third' Spain. … the lies.

The Spanish civil war ended over 75 years ago, and bells celebrating Franco's victory pealed all over the land. This was no Surrender at Breda nor Convention of Vergara.[i] There was no thought of any form of reconciliation. Spain was swept by a whirlwind of repression and revenge, the precursor of a humanitarian catastrophe without bounds as both during and after the war, the perpetrators of the 1936 military coup massacred the best of Spain. Supporters of the insurgent Franco and his military only represented half of the Spanish population; the other half, excluded and repressed at the most productive stage of their lives, barely managed to survive at the feet of a totalitarian New State that swiftly moved to subjugate them as it sank its teeth into a vanquished people that was unable to flee its grasp[ii].

Today, our society knows very little of these events as the impact of that victory has continued to this day to be filtered by an enduring right-wing policy of enforced silence and memory destruction so as to prevent History

---

[i] Two notable historical military treaties in which the Spanish victors were notably magnanimous.

[ii] Of those who managed to escape, hundreds of thousands of Spaniards were lost to their country when they went into exile. Liberty for those who fled to France and were interned there, would be short-lived when they were sent back to Spain.

from attributing any blame on the aggressors of the past. The so-called Pact of Silence is a misnomer, as there was no such pact. What remains is the *desmemoria*, the planned eradication of every memory of that period, because memory itself is accusative. From the end of the civil war to the death of Franco in 1975, including the so-called Period of Transition towards democracy during the 1950s, in schools and universities there was and continues to be no detailed or even superficial teaching of the implications of the 1936 military coup and its consequences. A consequence of the persistence of so many iniquities from the past, nowhere in any field of knowledge except that of the Spanish civil war, do we find such a high degree of academic discord, such confusion in society, so many enduring myths and fallacies, so many ideological influences engulfing the historical reality. The worst of all are the myths and the fallacies used to substantiate an uncompromising objectivity in the most ideological formats possible: an ideology of theoretical neutrality; an ideology that follows the theory of equidistance; an ideology that promotes the theory of equivalency, that 'everyone was the same'; an ideology that considers that there are first class victims (present-day victims of ETA and terrorists - 858 and 191) and second class victims (executed by Francoism, 140,000)... Of even greater concern today is the fanatic dogma, the intractable beliefs of those who refuse to listen to reason, of the crazy men who have never said they were sorry. That is how it all begins: the creation of the most absolute confusion.

As Rogelio López Cuenca stated: "(…) The end result is an embellishment of History, a mythology of the past; an utterly artificial reinterpretation of past events, assembled and beautified as if this were a product that one wishes to sell on the market(...)".[iii] Ángel Viñas has also drawn attention to the same mindset, to the tendency of some sectors to sugar-coat the past and try to sell us a pig in a poke: "If in Hungary or Slovakia, also European Union member states, we note with some concern of instances of whitewashing the Fascist past (...) In Spain, we must not fail to react to the actions of some untrustworthy academics and half-baked, shameless members of the media, lest we suffer that which occurred in Chile where in all seriousness, the official position is to gloss over General Pinochet's dictatorship by describing it as just a military regime."[iv]

In Spain, the fiends responsible for covering up the fascist-totalitarian-dictatorial past have been running loose for some time as they gloss over 'the darkest page of Franco's dictatorship that historiographers have attempted and

---

[iii] *Tesis: Carretera de Almería (1ª Parte)*, (Thesis: Road to Almería – Part I) Internet documentary (available on You Tube).

[iv] Ángel Viñas (Ed.), *En el combate por la historia* (In the fight for History). Pasado & Presente, Barcelona, 2012, p. 24.

are attempting to conceal.[v] Reig Tapia further stated (as did Judge Garzón) that July 18 1936 "marked the beginning of a crime against humanity, whereby Franco and the regime that he fathered were much more criminal than General Pinochet in Chile or Slobodan Milosevic in Serbia (...) Yet, how can one explain that Pinochet and Milosevic are considered guilty of genocide and that the whole world trembles at their crimes against humanity, whilst at the same time there are those who are tearing their hair out in irritation because Franco is being considered in like manner?"[vi]

This and much more form the Iberian pyramid of socio-political contradictions and the mountain of vested interests regarding the Spanish civil war. Although many books and papers have been written on the Francoist repression and these have circulated amongst the minority and a certain elite, the 'new history', the history of the Democracy, has not reached the bulk of the Spanish population. As a result, the wide field of that which is called 'public opinion' continues to reflect a false understanding of the history of Francoism that has remained intact, well and truly wrapped up and unraveled to this day, despite any number of recent studies. Perhaps, if the television media were to have helped us after the death of Franco, at least by airing a modicum of important documentaries or interviews with individuals who had a lot to say, Francoism might have been unmasked as was the 'Jewish case'. In the matter of the 'Spanish case' it has not been so. Spanish mass media (especially television) tirelessly persist in presenting the public with a grand design that might feed their stomachs but not our intelligence. In the case of historic topics – 'our case' – it is not a matter of official censorship but of a self-censorship that has existed since the death of the Dictator. The reporter instinctively knows which topics are well-received and which ones are not, so he is content to ignore 'that which must remain unspoken', without being ordered by anyone to do so. This being so, what has happened had to happen: the false Francoist history continues to be disseminated with impunity and nothing can be done about that. Worse still, the major mass media are in the hands of the many and varied right-wing groups, precisely those for whom Francoism is a sacred creed to be safeguarded at all costs.

Today, well into the 21st century, it has become increasingly difficult to present the Spanish people with a responsible study of Francoist crimes - genocide, crime against humanity, or war crimes - however you wish to call them. In thirty-five years of democracy, the history of the Second Republic and its destruction by the 1936 military coup has been written against the

---

[v]   Alberto Reig Tapia, "La pervivencia de los mitos Francoistas" (The survival of the Francoist myths), Ibid., p. 912.

[vi]   Ibid., pp. 14 and 18.

political tide. Even greater have been the difficulties in unravelling the history of the great Francoist repression during the war and in the post-war period. More than half of the Spanish population have been force-fed a simplistic conservatism and the evident socio-political so-called pact of silence that existed during the period of transition and they are not ready to sit back calmly and receive the historic truth. They show no interest in learning of the humanitarian catastrophe for which Francoism was responsible. No one knows, or wants to know, the full truth of what they were taught (or mis-taught) at school or the information (almost always, misinformation) they get through the media.

> "I have not heard anyone say that we should forget the Holocaust, forget the 'train of death' that went to Auschwitz, forget Pinochet (…) But in Spain, we had to draw a thick veil, forget all our relatives, forget the sufferings and the anguish, and all the rest. Here, I know not why, we are supposed to forget everything, to erase it all and turn over a new page; we are not even supposed to seek those responsible, and they even are against our attempts to obtain closure [exhumation and identification of the dead]."

So spoke Clara González in 2003, whose four uncles lay in the Piedrafita de Babia (León) mass grave.[vii] Clara's aunt, Isabel González, one of those supremely distinguished Spanish women and whose two brothers also lay in that grave, commented in words worthy of a philosopher:

> "What was the purpose of all of this? What good has come from killing these people? What has been the good of these deaths and the deaths of so many others?"

So why the forced oblivion? Just compare the attention paid and the official concern with the recognition of victims of today – the 858 victims of ETA and 191 victims of the 11 March terrorist attack, which is both fair and necessary, with the total amnesia, the *damnatio memoriae*, regarding the more than 140,000 who were executed by Franco? Psychological support to relatives of today's victims is a fair and honorable thing, but what about

---

[vii] Montse Armengou and Ricard Belis, in the documentary entitled *Las fosas del silencio* (The mass graves of silence). Televisión de Catalunya, 2003, 30'. The subject is the disinternment of 7 bodies in the Piedrafita de Baia mass grave, among which, both González brothers, Clara's uncles.

the psychological support to the relatives of yesterday's victims who still seek closure? Surviving families such as Clara González's who will never forget:

> "The Falangistas celebrated their killing those who lie in the mass grave by forcing my mother [Isabel González, whose brothers had just been shot], who was known to be a good cook, to prepare them a meal, and my aunt Asunción and another of my mother's sisters-in-law to play the tambourine and entertain them whilst they feasted on some of the family's lambs they had also slaughtered."[viii]

The history of Spain is truly very complicated. Little tolerance is to be expected in the general socio-political climate through which this work hopes to open a way forward. Teaching the Spanish people their 20th century history is difficult as it is a two-fold problem: those who do not know on the one hand and those who do not want to know on the other. Although people may talk about the many cases of genocide throughout history, they never speak of the Francoist genocide, mention of which has been vetoed until today by its perpetrators. Despite this, as historians attempt to reconstruct these events, they are striving to create a public record. The history is there and the deeds are there.

The following work was governed by the historian's three fundamental principles: truth, accuracy and documentation. Since 1978, Moreno Gómez has engaged in his project of reconstructing the details of the great Francoist repression, first in the city of Cordoba, and in his latest books, as it was applied throughout the province of Cordoba as a whole. On these pages, he set down, in black and white, the results of all that he has researched, that he obtained from written sources, that he was told first-hand by victims, from witness accounts. You could say that this is his narration of everything that he has seen and heard in the voices, the files and the faces of the victims and their families.

First, however, Moreno Gómez addresses the great labyrinth of present-day hostility towards the history of the Francoist repression: the fanaticism of those who do not wish to know (as well as those who throw stones at historians for various reasons). He totally agrees with Sánchez Ferlosio who stated that "You cannot convince anybody of anything."[ix] Perhaps one might

---

[viii] Ibid. The author's interviews with Asunción Álvarez, Isabel González and her niece, Clara González.
[ix] Rafael Sánchez Ferlosio, Interview in *EL PAÍS*, 22 May 2007.

convince 22nd century readers, when through information and culture, the Spanish people have espoused the reality of the facts.

To begin with, Spanish historians of the civil war need to accept that they have a problem with the political right-wing's extremely conservative stance that has been handed down without interruption by the Francoists. The intractability of the Right against any research into the history of the civil war inspired an ad hoc publication led by Ángel Viñas: *En el combate por la historia* (2002).[x] The purpose of this closing of ranks is not difficult to detect: it is a question of preventing people from knowing exactly what occurred under Franco, a project to destroy all memory of that time, to throw more soil over the graves of the victims and to wipe out more than half a century of Spanish history. The Spanish right-wing (political Right – entrepreneurs, financial institutions; social, judiciary, military, ecclesiastic, mediatic and academic Right) are determined to erase the recent past: *Delenda est historia.* There are a great many right-wingers and moreover, they are at the heart of the present Government, which is why historians must investigate and write against a tide of disapproval. What is surprising is that the political Left is also failing to make the grade. Spanish social-democracy has been seriously negligent when it comes to assuming the historical truth.

Unlike some European right-wing groups, the Spanish Right lacks the minimum antifascist traditions of the French so-called civilized Right, inherited from Charles de Gaulle. The Spanish Right not only lacks an anti-fascist tradition as it also lacks a democratic tradition. Put to the test during half a century of thralldom and travesty under the self-styled parties of change, when a true democracy worthy of its name arrived in Spain for the first time in 1931, followers of the Spanish Right (especially in the military barracks, casinos and church vestries) dedicated themselves to boycotting the Second Republic until they were able to demolish it following the 1936 military coup. When that democracy was restored in 1977, the Right imposed conditions of impunity, self-amnesty and forgetfulness of the past, creating Francoist gallows under which a perplexed, weak and disoriented Left was forced to march. Today, the Spanish right-wing groups turn a deaf ear to the international organizations that are demanding compensation for a past defiled by 140,000 murdered or 'disappeared' individuals. They take no notice of the mechanisms of so-called 'transitional justice' or 'universal justice' under International Law, as endorsed by several United Nations bodies. During the past year (Fall-Winter, 2013-2014), no less than three UN bodies called Spain to task for neglecting the issue of the disappeared and for neglecting to pay due attention to the victims and/or create a Committee

---

[x]   Ángel Viñas. *In the fight for History.* 2002

of Truth. On each occasion, the governing right-wing party has mocked these bodies, replying to their comments with a jingle praising the 'model' transition and the 'reconciliation' falsehoods, curtly shooing them away like so many pesky flies.

In addition to the Report from the UN Commission against Torture (November 2009), there are other reports that need to be mentioned. Following a week-long visit to Spain, the UN Working Group on Enforced or Involuntary Disappearances published a Preliminary Report September 30 2013.[xi] The Working Group reported that, in Spain, there had been grave and widespread violations of human rights during the civil war, citing provisional figures of 114,226 disappeared and 30,960 children stolen under Francoism ('systematic sequestration of children'). Commenting on the lack of links and communication between victims' groups and the state authorities and the 'lack of any national plan for the search for disappeared persons,' the Working Group declared that it was "a matter of urgency that the Government begin a search for the truth, and in particular, make of the establishment of the fate and whereabouts of the disappeared persons, an immediate priority." The Working Group also noted that mapping of the mass graves was not yet complete and that there remained "other important challenges," including "the lack of any law on access to information and the difficulty in accessing the archives", among others. The politicians of the ruling PP party coldly showed the UN commissioners the door. Is there anyone brave enough to put Rajoy to work searching for victims of Francoism in the fields, along the roads and in the ditches of Spain? On October 13 2013, a mass beatification of 522 Francoist 'martyrs', was attended by Government ministers, yet today when one tries to obtain recognition for Republican 'saints', whenever the same civil authorities can throw stones and garbage at these, they do so.

On 3 February 2014, at the end of his official visit to Spain, Pablo de Greiff, UN Special Rapporteur on the promotion of truth, justice, reparation and guarantees of non-recurrence, spoke of his findings. He stated that the victims and their associations with whom he had been in contact felt that they were insufficiently recognized and listened to. A primary target of his statement was the Amnesty Law of October 1977, that he said was a breach of international conventions to which Spain was a party, such as the International Civil and Political Rights Pact, whose Article 2.3 prohibits amnesty for serious violations of human rights, signed by Spain on 28 September 1976 and ratified 27 April 1977, before the enactment of the Amnesty Law that,

---

[xi] UN Committee on Enforced Disappearances, Working Group report on Spain, A/HRC/27/49/Add.1.

in Spain, is taken as the law that puts an end to the matter[xii]. (I would add, like similar laws in South America, almost all of which have been abolished, albeit not in Spain. In other words, the so-called 'model transition' in Spain was no model anywhere.) De Greiff clarified that although the Amnesty Law suspended penal responsibility, what it could not shelve was an investigation of the acts, at the very least. He showed his concern for the Government's failure to update the map of the mass graves of the disappeared in Spain (the figure still stands at 2,382 mass graves found, containing some 45,000 individual remains). As regards the pillar of truth, in reality, there has never been an official policy in this respect. The archives continue to hold dossiers classified as confidential on the grounds of the right to privacy, documents that are inaccessible to the international entities that wish to consult them on the grounds of the right to the truth.

De Greiff continues, listing a whole series of incongruences in Spain: the Law of Historic Memory did not rescind the sentences handed down by the Francoist courts, contrary to that which was done in Germany, for example, nor has there ever been any mention of restoring the personal property that was seized by Francoists. Francoist signs and symbols continue to be displayed all over the country. He added that they had received ambiguous information regarding the way that the civil war and the dictatorship were taught in schools. Lastly, among other points, he refers to the undermining of the legislation that governs the Spanish courts' application of International Law. (Here, Moreno Gómez mentions something that he referred to elsewhere, and that is that the Spanish courts are schooled on the fringes of modern International Law, and that they function within a kind of judicial autocracy clearly inherited from Francoism, totally secluded within the country's borders from the outside world.)

In defense of those judges who have not lost a sense of what is right and proper, Joaquín Bosch, speaker for Judges for Democracy, deserves a special mention for the article that he published on the Internet, entitled 'Ten things you should know about the crimes of the Franco regime.'[xiii] Despite this, one reads the most incredible claptrap about the victims of Francoism. An example of this are the events in the Provincial Court of Cordoba, in the Dorado Luque Case, when the Court of Appeals rejected Appeal 355/2006 against the sentence of the 2nd Court (3.651/2006 of 11 August) disallowing any official criminal responsibility. The Court justified its ruling for the sake of reconciliation, citing an agreement of a Parliamentary Committee

---

[xii] *Lei de punto final.*
[xiii] Joaquín Bosch, "Las diez cosas que deberíass aber sobre los crímenes del Francoismo." *Diario Público.es,* Madrid, 19-10-2013.

dated 20 November 2002, devoid of any force of law, according to which one should avoid any kind of initiative that might "reopen old wounds or stir civil confrontation". To make matters worse, also according to the Court, "Argentina was a military coup; in Spain, it was a war." The sentence further contained such an amount of legal nonsense, bar-room chatter and topics and fallacies about the civil war, that it appears that no one was able to comprehend the gravity of exactly that which is going on in the Spanish legal system today, which astounds foreign observers.

It is no secret that the Spanish right-wing experienced democracy without even barely absorbing any of it. The right-wing has never condemned Francoism, two out of three right-wingers continue to defend the 18 July 1936 insurrection, they voted against the Law of Historic Memory and, when the right-wing was recently elected to the Government, they left it without a budget, they continue daily to tarnish the memory of the Second Republic, they have forever erased its name from the Transition and the Constitution, they persist in the slander with which the Francoists demonized the Second Republic... Moreno Gómes states he has never forgotten a statement he heard at a meeting in Huesca: "The French Right, from de Gaulle onwards, has always maintained an antifascist tradition, contrary to the Spanish Right, which has never adopted such a position because it is a readaptation of Francoism."

Given such a background one cannot be surprised that the anti-memory movement has erupted so aggressively in Spain. (In the Fall of 2013, he was stunned to hear of a public jumble sale of fascist memorabilia in Quijorna, Madrid, under the approving eyes of the local Lady Mayor.) In early February 2014, *Fachas*[xiv] destroyed several monuments that had been erected to fallen Republicans on the Ebro battlefields: the monument to the 43rd Division, the one dedicated to General Líster... In Cantabria, Fachas destroyed a monument to the guerrillas, the monument that Jesús de Cos cared so much for. In Fuente Palmera (Cordoba), they decapitated the monument to Captain Ximeno.

A politician from Galicia recently declared that "if Republicans were executed, it was because they must have done something". At about the same time, a high-ranking member of the Partido Popular (PP), Rafael Hernando, referred to the Second Republic as "the Regime that ended up with a million dead" and soon afterwards astounded everyone by declaring, on television, that "some people only think of disinterring their relatives when there are subsidies on offer". The PP speaks out daily in open contempt for the victims of Francoism. Another PP leader, Jaime Mayor Oreja, speaks of the "the

---

[xiv] A colloquial expression used to describe right-wingers of every size and shape.

extraordinary tranquility of life under Francoism". Matters are no better nowadays. April 22nd there is a celebration in Burgos to pay homage to a war criminal, General Yagüe, the butcher of Badajoz, in outright contempt for the law, with the profanity of despots and the obstinacy of fanatics acting without impunity.

Major German attacks on Republican Spain
during the Civil War (1936–39)

Note number of major concentration/refugee camps (red, encircled on map), especially along the French southern border with Spain.

Key

Initial Nationalist zone – July 1936	Major Land battles
Nationalist advance until September 1936	Naval battles
Nationalist advance until October 1937	
Nationalist advance until November 1938	German bombed cities
Nationalist advance until February 1939	
Last area under Republican control	Concentration camps
Main Nationalist centres	
Main Republican centres	Massacres
	Refugee camps

I

FORTY YEARS OF OPPRESSION AND RETALIATION LIFE AND PROPERTY: SPOILS OF WAR

FRANCO's 'VICTORY WALK'. HALF OF SPAIN IN CHAINS. EARLY FEATURES OF THE FASCIST VICTORY. RETURN OF THE DEFEATED. HUMILIATION AND CONFISCATION.

Democratic Spain falls into the clutches of the fascist victors. Extra-judicial economic repression: widespread pillaging and plunder. Confiscation of property registers. Hunger as an instrument of oppression and genocide. The Law of Political Responsibilities (LPR), another 'official' form of economic repression.

> "... There is nothing worse than the pairing of the barracks mentality with that of the sacristy, since traditional uncouth Spanish Catholicism can hardly be considered Christian..."

Unamuno, last public speech Salamanca, 12 October 1936

Franco's Victory Walk

Franco's *Paseo de la Victoria* heralded the end of the civil war March 26 1939, a so-called walk as there was no fighting, no significant offensive action of any kind by the rebel forces. Throughout history, all wars have ended with a decisive battle, except for the Spanish civil war. Historically, this may never have been the case, but in Spain it now happened. This was not the fault of the fighting population but of the professional military leaders and their fellow Coryphaei whose defeatism at the end sold out the Republic as did the rebel Nationalists who rose against it in 1936. At the end of the conflict, the eternally clear-thinking Juan Negrín, last Loyalist Premier of Spain who presided over the defeat of the Republican forces, bade farewell to Juan Simeón Vidarte, a fellow politician, with the following words: "*Go without fear, because there is no instance in history when an army of more than half a million men has surrendered without a fight.*"[1]

Franco set March 25 as the deadline for the *Consejo Nacional de Defesa* – CND[i] to surrender the Republican Air Force. However, as some of the planes had flown out of the country and several pilots delayed meeting these demands, not a single plane landed in Burgos on that date. Major Segismundo Casado Lopez who had meanwhile assumed command of the Republican Army in an attempt to negotiate a ceasefire, called Franco frantically, imploring, whining and promising that the Air Force would be handed over the next day. Franco, turning a deaf ear to these histrionics, declared that as certain, actually non-existent, negotiations had failed, nothing but an unconditional surrender was acceptable and he was ordering his Army to begin the Paseo de la Victoria. Casado was told that every town and village in the country should fly a white flag if they wished to avoid the consequences of continued action by Franco's air force and artillery.

As promised, Franco's Victory Walk began at dawn March 26. The Republic was no more; it had been stabbed to death by treason and Franco, with his self-appointed Army, proceeded to take possession of a no longer existent entity. Beginning in the south, the Francoist Nationalist Army crossed the unmanned lines in the region of Peñarroya. The Moroccan Army, under General Yagüe (responsible for the slaughter at Badajoz), set off in the west near Cordoba and the Andalusian Army, under General Muñoz Castellanos in the region of Espiel and the port of Calatraveño. These troops were joined by the Cordoba Army Corps under General Borbón and the Extremaduran Army led by General Soláns. The army marched in the region of Hinojosa and El Viso towards Santa Eufemia and Almadén, and on the right, towards Pozoblanco and Villanueva de Cordoba. The frontlines had totally disappeared. Companies, brigades and entire divisions abandoned their weapons and wandered all over the place as the Republican troops attempted to make their way back to their home towns. This was an extraordinary phenomenon of the en masse disbanding of an entire army. White flags flew from every town and village tower as far as the eye could see. Resignation and anxiety reigned in constricted chests. When Franco heard of the 'sightseeing' nature of the walk on that day, he promptly ordered another wiping-up operation throughout the province of Toledo, towards Mora.

The same day, the Moroccan Army marched through the towns of Hinojosa del Duque, Belalcázar, Fuente La Lancha, Villanueva del Duque, Villaralto and El Viso. The 24th Division, under the command of Colonel Rodríguez de la Herranz and Lieutenant-Colonel Manuel Vázquez Sastre entered Belalcázar. Although the majority of Republican troops in this sector

---

[i] National Defence Council, a military junta under Juan Negrín, formed in order to negotiate a peace deal.

had fallen back towards Santa Eufemia, at the end of the day a light column of Francoist troops reached this village and accepted the surrender of 5,000 soldiers in the region. It is said that some troops shot their rifles upwards into the air as a symbolic act of defiance, before throwing down their weapons.

A long walk home

The Andalusian Army continued its march from the small port of Calatraveño during the morning, entering the towns of Alcaracejos, Añora, Dos Torres and … Pozoblanco! The Nationalists were finally able to enter Pozoblanco, but this time without a fight.[ii] Here, they captured all the equipment, supplies and files belonging to the Republican 8th Army Corps and took 3,100 prisoners. The *Los Jubiles*, civilian freedom fighters who formed an illustrious guerrilla corps that fought alongside the 88th Republican Army Corps, retreated into the Cordoba hills, taking with them many weapons, including mortars, the army gave them, declaring "We shall not surrender nor shall we leave Spain."

All the regiment's units were ordered to retreat to Puertollano and all the senior officers, to Torrecampo. Ildefonso Castro who had been appointed commander of the 8th Army Corps during the last days of the war, left with Major Emiliano Mascaraque Castillo[2], another 8th Army Corps senior officer, intending to go to Ciudad Real in hopes of getting away during the first few days. They spent the night under a heavy snowstorm and arrived in Puertollano by car on the 27th, where they fell into the hands of Falangistas and were imprisoned. A few days later they were transferred to Ocaña penitentiary.

The National Defence Council that appeared to have been created with the sole purpose of saving half of the defeated Republic from being hunted down, both civilian and military, proved to have been a colossal failure. The Nationalist Air Force was making its last bombing attack on Pozoblanco, whilst in Villanueva de Cordoba, it was a case of every man for himself. Several leftists had been arrested by Falangistas near the San Rafael flour factory where they were taken. Rafael Rodriguez, nicknamed *Tres Cuartos* and who had had a bit too much wine to drink, boasted, somewhat audaciously, that he was the Mayor of the town. Claiming that he had to go to the toilet, he escaped through the back door and joined his family in Villanueva de Cordoba.

[ii] The medieval city of Pozoblanco remained fiercely loyal to the Republic throughout the civil war, defeating several attacks by General Queipo de Llano's Nationalist troops in March 1937.

On March 23, already, Lieutenant Lorenzo Cepas Rico[iii], a communist from Villanueva de Cordoba, desperately tried to save himself from the approaching enemy and to obtain help to rescue Villanueva's Communist Municipal Authorities[iv] who had meanwhile been jailed by the Nationalists. After obtaining a safe-conduct pass to travel from Puertollano to Villanueva, he immediately went to Pozoblanco to see the 8th Army Corps' quartermaster, but the officer in charge of transportation refused to give him some trucks. He returned to Villanueva and obtained help from the 114th Brigade in the form of 35 soldiers and their lieutenant and two trucks. The evening of March 26, they immediately left the Las Navas farmhouse where they were staying, to attack the Villanueva jail where his comrades were being held. They entered the town at dawn but before they arrived at the jailhouse, they ran into Vilches' wife who told them that the 8th Army Corps' quartermaster had already been there and had released the men who then left on the road to Conquista.

They drove to Conquista where they found a train packed with people that was going nowhere. They drove around town all day without finding José Caballero and the others. Hearing that the Nationalists had entered Villanueva and were advancing towards Cardeña, and afraid that their retreat might be cut off, they drove out of town down the airport runway as far the railway station and from there, to Puertollano. In the town square, they ran into two fellow communists from Villanueva who refused to join them, claiming that a new front was about to be created in the Sierra Morena. They continued on the road to Cartagena.

In Damiel, the Officer in Charge, a doctor who was preparing to surrender his command to the Nationalists, refused to grant them a safe-conduct pass and some gasoline. Another communist from Villanueva, Francisco Copado, tried to intercede for them but was turned down and urged them to get away from there as quickly as they could. Lieutenant Rico decided to act and, drawing his revolver, obtained the safe-conduct pass and the gasoline at gunpoint. In Manzanares, a company of Nationalist *Guardias de Assalto*[v] barred the way, again forcing them to resort to gunpoint – revolvers

---

[iii] Lieutenant Rico was interned in the North African concentration camps and only returned to Villanueva with the Democracy where he slowly recovered his health and enjoyed a well-deserved respite from so much misfortune. Had Moreno Gómez just decided to speculate on what Rico might have related when he returned home on a stretcher, and analyzed his memories from a distance as others do, they would have been lost to History as later, it would have been too late. It is remarkable how in these days, so many other historians and universities yawn with boredom at any mention of this kind of research.

[iv] Gabino Cabrera, Madero, Bartolomé Caballero, José 'Carnes', Vilches and Francisco Sánchez Muñoz, among others.

[v] An elite armed urban police force, similar to Pretorian Guards.

and machine guns. In Albacete, both trucks broke down but fortunately they were able to join a small convoy led by an Infantry Lieutenant. In Murcia, another armed control point, this time accompanied by some civilian Falangistas. They slowed down, pretended to stop and stepped on the gas at the last moment and drove off at full speed.

Finally, they arrived at the port of Cartagena, on the south-eastern coast, where they hoped to board the *Campido*, an oil tanker that was waiting to take as many as it could to safety. After some difficulty getting safe-conduct passes for their group of some 50, they managed to get on board just as the ship was raising its anchor. Lieutenant Rico was the last one to board and not too soon. As they sailed off they could see Falangista flags flying all over Cartagena.

Everyone set off in an attempt to go home, some went north, some went south, east, west shedding bitter tears as they bade farewell to good companions through hardships and suffering. Everyone from a same town or region got together to form groups for the walk home. Lieutenant Carbonero, three officers from his company and some countrymen began walking and did not stop until they reached Salvañete, where they received a hunk of bread each, only stopping in Cañete to rest at 4 p.m. and eat some of the bread and a little salt cod they had brought with them. White flags flew in every village they passed and everywhere, dirty, ragged, limping, exhausted and starving men with backpacks were going from door to door begging for something to eat.

Nightfall and they continued walking, forming a line with the strongest in front and the weakest at the end, as they fell behind, until they reached Pajaroncillo. Just before they entered the town, they bought a flock of sheep from some shepherds so that when they reached the town, the people could cook them some food. They expected to run into Nationalist troops at any moment and had no idea how they would be received. They found a haystack and slept there until 5 a.m. March 30, when they continued to Carboneras, hoping to find a train for Cuenca.

When they arrived at the station, soaking wet and very tired, they found it full of soldiers so they had settled in a goods wagon. People were already saying that the Nationalists had arrived in the town, but none were visible. The next day, Lieutenant Carbonero and his companions decided to continue to walk as far as Cuenca. Five or six kilometres before Fuentes, it began to pour and then snow heavily. Finally they arrived in Fuentes where they were warmly received at the first house they knocked.

Dawn April 1 was splendid and they continued to walk to Cuenca, when they met the first soldiers sporting red and yellow Nationalist armbands and Nationalist *Guardia Civil*[vi] at the station closest to Cuenca. Several trucks laden with soldiers overtook them and, as they passed, greeted them with the Falangist salute.[vii] When they finally arrived at a control post, a civil guard and several soldiers stopped them and asked for their documents. As they had none, they were told to stand at the side of the road where others were already waiting. At 2 p.m., a guard arrived, ordered everyone to fall in and then marched them across all of Cuenca, to the Seminary. Feeling more cheerful, they had no idea what awaited them.

After waiting more than three hours at the entrance to the Seminary, they fell into groups of 100 and went in. They were hungry but found out that they would not be fed. April 2 came and went and they had not a bite to eat all day. That night, a few groups of 20 got some food but it quickly ran out. Again, they went to bed without eating, suffering a gnawing hunger. Finally, April 4, at noon, they were fed some lentils and a piece of a bread roll that had been cut in four.

And so the days passed until the officers in charge began taking statements, after which some were given leave to go home. Those who had been officers were taken elsewhere, some say to Zaragoza. The rest left in small groups until about 900 of the approximately 2,000 they had numbered at the beginning, were left.

April 24 they were told that those who remained were to be taken to a concentration camp in Corunna, Galicia. When the train on which they travelled arrived ear Ponferrada, a small mining town, the workers and the women looked at them with pity and gave them some bread. They got off the train at Santiago de Compostela and started walking. Outside the station, the bulk of the local population were waiting for them. Some women cried and others gave them a bit to eat when the officer was not looking. They marched on until they reached a village call Labacolla, the site of the concentration camp.[3]

It is through accounts such as these that Moreno Gómez presents us with a vivid understanding of what the 'Black Week' of victory meant for defeated Spain. Casimiro Jabonero's sufferings were those of all who returned home after the defeat. When they arrived at their destination, almost none had time to embrace their families as they were immediately interned. For many, their future was a case of *Vae victis!*

Meanwhile, March 26 the Nationalists pressed forth with their military success as Falangistas, militiamen, legionnaires and Moroccan troops trekked

---

[vi]   Civil Guard. Spanish paramilitary police.

[vii]   The Francoist salute, identical to the Nazi salute, where the right arm is raised outstretched and the had is open flat, palm facing downwards, often referred to by Spaniards as a "salute in the Roman manner", i.e., like one of Caesar's centurions.

across the North of Cordoba province countryside, hunting their quarry like so many birds of prey. The Francoist military issued a Press Release on that day, stating that entire *Rojo*[viii] battalions with their Commanders had raised the white flag of surrender to Franco's forces; 10,000 being the number of prisoners and individuals who turned themselves in.

From Pozoblanco, troops of the 60th Francoist Division, under Lieutenant-Colonel Aguilera, arrived in Añora. Others from the 115th Division entered Dos Torres, where Aguilera was confirmed as military commander, a position he held until some days later he was replaced by Juan Benítez Tatay, the militia commander who ordered the first blood bath.

Azul, the Francoist newspaper of Cordoba, published numerous illustrations of the Fascist parade through the semi-destroyed streets of Pozoblanco lined with locals saluting in the Roman manner, and multiple photographs of an open-air mass celebrated to purify the town from the so-called *Red filth*.[ix] Priests as distinguished participants in the front rows, mobilizing the masses in aid of National Catholicism.[4]

Francoist Air Force Operational Reports[5] also say something about the events of March 26:
at 4 p.m.:

- [Republican] cars and trucks at km. 36 on the road from Alcaracejos to Pozoblanco. – Seven Rojo trucks from this village to Villanueva de Cordoba and an ambulance going the other way. Our troops at 1 km. to the east of Villaralto. No traffic of any kind on the road from El Viso to Pozoblanco; likewise, regarding the villages of Añora, Dos Torres and Pedroche.

and again at 5 p.m.:

- El Viso, 2 kms to the north, has been occupied and overtaken. Our troops are 1.5 kms south of Pozoblanco and advancing. Our troops are visible in Hinojosa del Duque. 30 trucks, apparently belonging to the Rojos, are travelling in this direction on the road from Santa Eufemia to Almadén.

---

viii *Rojo*, or red, meaning all Republicans or members of any left-wing party who supported the legal Democratic regime and therefore, were not loyal to Franco's *Causa General* manifesto or to his regime.

ix *Azul*, Cordoba, April 1 & 2 1939.

The Victory Walk continued on March 27. At the same time that the Nationalist troops reached the village of Almadén, a detachment from the Andalusia Army Corps (the 40th Division, under Colonel Badía) set off from Pozoblanco. At noon, these troops entered the regional capital, Villanueva de Cordoba. That morning, the last Republican leaders had rushed to apply urgent safety or salvation measures to protect the mostly communist population from the cruel persecution that threatened them.

Laura Contreras, a teacher at the Villaviciosa School, and Maria Josefa López ran to get the keys to the Communist Party Headquarters where they burned the lists of members in the files. They then went to the Antifascist Women's Centre where other comrades had done the same. The Villanueva communist leaders that had been freed from jail were waiting for them outside Conquista. Bartolomé Nieto and Laura were told to go to Puertollano and then to Ciudad Real. They set off on foot but when they passed a river near Puertollano, Laura was so exhausted that she felt like killing herself.

In Puertollano, they got a train to Valencia that was so filthy they became infested with lice. During the entire trip, Laura saw many people commit suicide by jumping onto the tracks. At Valencia railway station, they met a communist leader from Villanueva de Cordoba, Gabino Cabrera, who was thinking of going undercover in Valencia. They decided to go back to their home towns and hide nearby in the Fuencaliente Sierra mountains. In the end, they did not dare to do so, so that night they returned to Villanueva and took refuge in Gabino's house. Later, Laura walked along across the fields and handed herself in to the authorities in Villaviciosa.[6]

These were not isolated experiences. The Republican half of Spain was overwhelmed with similar fears and exploits. Everywhere, there were signs of what was to come.

At 2 p.m. on March 27, after an airplane inspection and confirmation that a white flag had been hoisted in the town tower, Nationalist troops entered Villanueva de Cordoba on the road from Pozoblanco and on the road from Obejo. There were several columns from the 60th Division under Colonel Baturone, a Falangista deputation from López Tienda and half a brigade of regular troops, among others. They had left Pozoblanco at 10 A.M. and halted in Los Barreros, to confirm that there was no opposition to their advance. The Moroccans marched on one side of the road and Baturone's Infantry, on the other side. As soon as Baturone arrived, he set up his headquarters in Emilio Reina's house on Calle Herradores. Soon afterwards, General Queipo de Llano himself arrived, accompanied by Commander Ampliato, head of the Secret Service; they left a few hours later as they had another appointment in Almadén. It was a cold Spring day and had snowed. Captain Ignacio Pizarro, of the Guardia Civil, was appointed military commander of the town. He set up his headquarters and the Military Court at the renamed *Plaza del Generalissimo,* number 9.[x] That day, 750 Republican military prisoners and their commanding officer, Lieutenant Domingo Muñoz Sánchez, surrendered in Villanueva, as did a communications company, a squadron of foot soldiers and a Workers Brigade.

Francoist Air Force Operational Reports[xi] for March 27: beginning at 10:30 a.m., reads:

- Our troops can be seen at km. 87 on the road from Pozoblanco to Villanueva de Cordoba. Nothing is moving in this village. In Pedroche, 200 metres from the town, on the Pozoblanco road, there are two large calibre guns to which a white flag is attached. There is no change to the lines in Santa Eufemia; a column is marching towards there on the Las Pilillas road. There is no movement at all for 4 kms from km. 101 onwards. Before Almadén, there are groups of militia waving white flags making their way there and to Almandines. There are 15 carriages at the railway station that crosses the road to Almadén. There are 90 carriages and two engines at the Almadénejos railway station.

at 11 a.m.:

- The village of Pedroche is occupied as are 2 kms beyond it; troops continue to march towards Torrecampo; troops are also advancing from Dos Torres towards El Guijo. Troops SW from Santa Eufemia are advancing to the NE. A column of tanks and trucks are advancing on the Pozoblanco road towards Villanueva de Cordoba; they are some 8 kms from that village and we note many people appearing peaceful. All the farms are flying white flags and so is the village of Alamillo.

at 12 noon:

- Cover given to the 4th and 5th Squadrons that are bombing the Almadénejos railway station.[xii] The bombing over, we reconnoitred

---

[x] This square, renamed in honour of Franco, lives on in the nightmares of the families of victims of the reprisals who were taken to those headquarters where they lost their skins, quite literally.

[xi] Ministry of Defence. Ibid.

[xii] *Author:* presumably attacking the 90 aforementioned railway carriages.

the front, noting a column of trucks advancing on the road to Almadén, in the Santa Eufemia sector. To the East of that road our troops are advancing, in such a way that we presume they are not finding any resistance. Another column, further East, is advancing towards the River Guadalmez. Our troops have occupied the villages of Villanueva de Cordoba and Pedroche. The population in the village of Torrecampo are waving white flags and the people in the neighbourhood are waiting for the arrival of our troops.

at 6:30 p.m.., the last report of the day:

- We recognize Adamuz, still not occupied by our troops from the Villafranca sector, who remain in their positions. Near the port, our troops are marching on the road from Villanueva de Cordoba to Adamuz, towards the latter. A column is leaving Villanueva on the road to Venta de Cardeña; the vanguard is about 1 km from there. Conquista appears deserted. Torrecampo is occupied by our troops and San Benito likewise. Our troops from Santa Eufemia have occupied Alamillo and another column, coming down from the mountains, has overrun it to the East.

Even as the Francoist *Regulares*[xiii] entered Villanueva de Cordoba on the last day of the war, there was no stopping the looting and raping. In other words, the violent and repressive practices of the Nationalist troops as a whole, most especially the Moroccan troops, occurred everywhere during the occupation of every town and village without exception, at the beginning, during and at the end of the war. A tragic example of this occurred in Villanueva, March 27 1939, when the Moroccan troops, marching down the road to Obejo, passed the La Atalayuela farm, stopped and raped a woman named Catalina Maestre whilst they held her husband at gunpoint.[7] Near the village, they killed a man who had no idea of what was going on, Pedro Capitán Moreno, and they threw his body into a well where he was only discovered some three weeks later. The Arabs were apparently trying to steal his livestock. For some other reason Moreno Gómez was unable to ascertain, two Moroccans were shot and buried next to the washing tanks, near the beginning of the road to Cardeña.

In another incident, a family from Almodóvar del Rio – men, women and children – had taken refuge on a farm near La Charquita, a couple of kilometres from that village. Two Moroccan soldiers went there with obvious

---

[xiii] *Regulares.* Professional or career soldiers. Not conscripts.

evil intent. One of the men saw them coming and hid; the other man, Miguel Claus Salado, did not, either because he could not hide in time or because he stayed to protect his four children. The Arabs arrived and held him at gunpoint whilst they raped his aunt and another woman. As the Arabs left, they shot Miguel Claus and he died in his sister-in-law's arms.[8] Other eye-witnesses attested that the Nationalist troops spent those days looting, not just the towns and villages, but all the surrounding farms as well. Others arrived at the La Alcarria farm, which belonged to Luna Gómez Rodríguez, and took everything they could lay their hands on, including her sewing scissors.[9]

The victorious troops continued their advance during the afternoon of March 27. At 5:30 p.m., troops of the 102nd and 112th Divisions, under Colonel Castejón (the butcher of Puente Genil), entered Cardeña. Elsewhere, the 105th Cadiz Battalion under Commander Luis Gómez entered Torrecampo, and we know from another Air Force report that they were greeted by an excited crowd saluting with raised right arms and shouting Viva Franco!

March 28, Nationalist troops marched from the area of the Guadalquivir River and Villafranca towards Adamuz, 'cleaning up' the hills from the Guadalmellato River to Montoro as they went and taking several thousand prisoners that they rounded up in Adamuz. (A photo in the Cordoba *Azul* newspaper shows the prisoners being marched down one of the streets.) Many of the regular army soldiers whose looting and misdeeds mentioned earlier converged that day in Villanueva de Cordoba.

Conquista was the last village in the province of Cordoba to be visited by such 'illustrious' conquerors, was occupied March 28 by an Infantry unit under the command of Second Lieutenant Valderramas. These troops also marched through Azuel, whilst other units marched from Cardeña as far as Marmolejo, Andújar and other towns in the neighbouring province of Jaén. 450 Nationalist prisoners captured by the Republican army during the last battle in January, the battle of Cordoba-Extremadura, were freed in San Benito.[10]

General Yagüe arrived in Almadén, which had been occupied March 27 and his troops entered Puertollano March 29. Republican Artillery Major Blanco Pedraza, previously an enthusiastic *Casadista*[xiv] from Villanueva de Cordoba, was entrusted with negotiating the surrender of the town. At the last minute, his assistant José Arévalo Toril, stripped him piece by piece of his insignia as the Nationalist troops arrived at the railway station in carriages

---

xiv *Casadistas.* Supporters of Sigesmundo Casado, a socialist Army officer, who as a member of the National Defense Committee (CND), advocated negotiating a peaceful surrender with Franco in an attempt to avoid reprisals. Franco, who was only interested in an unconditional surrender, made false promises, ignoring Casado and the CND.

Blanco himself had ordered. Even though Blanco, when negotiating the surrender, had begged that only Spanish troops should occupy Puertollano, Yagüe sent the train back full of Moroccan troops. So much for Franco's promises to the Casadistas.

The Republican leader of the Extremadura Army Corps, General Escobar (later executed) and a senior officer, Enrique Ruiz-Fornells, were captured in Almadén. By then, there were more than 60,000 military prisoners from the region of Cordoba, Almadén and Puertollano. Added to these, were hundreds of civilians considered hostile to Franco, the so-called 'disaffected' or Rojos, were being crammed into every kind of building, warehouses, yards, convents and especially the Puertollano bullring.

The truth is that the war was not over for anybody. For some, the enormous task of victory and vengeance, persecution and vigilance, coercion and anger had just begun. For others, hunger, overcrowding, torture, death, the destruction of their homes, exile, illness and despair, awaited them. The long dark night of Francoism was just beginning, impelled by something much greater than vengeance alone: the planned extermination of an entire people. There can be no sweetening of the pill or denying of the facts. The fog of times past cannot erase the crimes against humanity. The reality was what it was, as Herbert R. Southworth wrote: "You were right, gentlemen, it was a crusade, but the cross was a swastika."[11]

The documents and photographs of those tragic days cannot be ignored nor must they be forgotten. One well-known, albeit unsourced, photograph shows a line of haggard, defeated soldiers, marching under white flags of surrender. On April 1, *ABC* of Seville printed photographs of Queipo de Llano, the Andalusia and Extremadura war criminal, proudly walking down the streets of Almadén. The same day, this newspaper also published an image of thousands of prisoners being marched to a concentration camp, along the road towards Peñarroya-Pueblonuevo. According to Carlos Menéndez[12], one of the prisoners who walked from Alcaracejos to Pueblonuevo, people everywhere lined the streets shouting Viva Franco! as they raised their right arms in the Roman salute. How many closet Falangistas came out during those and the coming days? Several months later, on October 3 the Bishop of Cordoba, Adolfo Pérez Muñoz, appears in photos saluting with his right arm raised. To this day, the Spanish Catholic Church still gives little or no indication that it may be critical of, nor does it express its regret at what happened then. The Church remains unwilling to ask for forgiveness when faced with its scandalous identification with Fascism. In September 1971, a synod of bishops and priests proposed that the Church publicly ask for forgiveness because in those days they did not know how to be true 'ministers of reconciliation'. The motion was rejected because it was not approved by the statutory two-thirds majority of those present.

Half of Spain in chains

Prisoners, thousands of prisoners everywhere, half Spain was under arrest. That was Franco's Spain: boundless humiliation and wire fencing. It never occurred to the victorious *Nuevo Estado*[xv] that there could have been any form of reconciliation – a concept that has been discussed to exhaustion until it has become meaningless. In fact, there was no reconciliation, nor could it ever have been achieved: from the onset, the plan was to *exterminate* a people, the reason why the military coup was conceived and launched. Without an extermination, the military coup lost its purpose. The three parties to the coup (found in military barracks, the casinos[xvi] and church sacristies) demanded a plan that would 'exterminate, cleanse, disinfect and massacre' all the Godless', everyone who was 'anti-Spain', every Freemason, Marxists, Anarchist and all the promoters of laicism, modernity and 'dissolutionary' ideas. The Church considered that all non-Catholic ideas, ostensibly those of the Republican democracy were dissolutionary. On the other hand, the unholy tripartite did not consider the Nazi, Falangista or Francoist ideas, nor the Roman salute that the hierarchy of the times exhibited so vigorously, could be considered to be the slightest dissolutionary.

The number of prisoners in Francoist hands was beyond belief and unique in the History of Spain. Added to the aforementioned 60,000 prisoners, were the troops captured at the Caceres-Badajoz-Toledo front (a region known as the Siberia of Badajoz).

Units of the regular Army, such as the one in which Corporal José Pérez Navarrete. A conscript from Pozoblanco served, were left without direction when the war ended. His unit was sent to the village of Alcaudete de la Jara, where they remained until Mach 28. Confused, the soldiers stood down and everyone was sent on his own way. Corporal Navarette and several comrades reported the next day to the so-called Nationalist Army in the village of Espinoso del Rey where they went from the frying pan into the fire.

About 4 p.m. on the last day of the month, they were informed that they belonged to the Rojo Army and that there were some 7,000 of them. Without their having had anything to eat, they were herded onto trucks, driven across hills and mountains, places totally unknown to them, until at 2

[xv] Franco's New State.
[xvi] Not to be confused with gambling casinos. Generally, gentlemen's clubs frequented by the wealthy and upper classes of society, often described as *señoritos*.

a.m. the next day they arrived at Casa de la Jaeña. More dead than alive, they were led at dawn to a nearby farm that was surrounded by wire. They were stacked there like espadrilles on shelves, and there they remained four days, without food or water.

Looking like skeletons, they were then taken to a nearby farm when they were told that as 'Marxist prisoners' they would be placed in a concentration camp. They were fed very little food every 24 hours and they lost all hope of ever returning to their homes. April 21, they were issued travel passes and released to make their way to the Calera railway station and home by train.[13]

This description of the La Jaeña concentration camp at Aldeanueva de Barbarroya, Toledo, has not been previously mentioned in studies of this period. Located in the middle of the fields, Republican prisoners were kept totally isolated from the neighbouring villages. All the officers in the camp were quickly separated from the rank and file then taken to Talavera, where they were summarily executed. The railway station mentioned in the above account is the one at Calera y Chozas, Toledo.

All over Spain, never-ending lines of exhausted prisoners, wearied by despair and hunger, were marched along country roads and down village streets; more than 40,000 in the Centre of the country and a similar number on the Levante [xvii] front. There is no denying the numbers. Nevertheless, when Negrín told Juan Simeón Vidarte that never before in History had an army of half a million men surrendered without a fight, he failed to say whether this number included those who had already fled to France or not.

At least two to three hundred thousand Republican combatants fell into Francoist hands. When you add the astronomical number of civilians who were wandering all over Spain and were being arrested right, left and centre during those days, as well as the great many regular soldiers and other combatants who managed to make their way home only to be immediately imprisoned, the total number of prisoners goes through the roof. Thus, the expression 'Half Spain in chains' or better still, the title of a recent television documentary: *Spain, an immense prison*.

Never in the History of Spain has there ever been such a humanitarian catastrophe. Under Franco, all historical statistics were outstripped, everywhere and in every possible scenario. That is why, when Moreno Gómez speaks of the concept of crimes against humanity, genocide or extermination, he is not exaggerating the reality, contrary to today's efforts by today's heirs of the victors who persist in belittling, or declaring off-limits the mention, let

---

[xvii] *Levante* is the name by which the eastern region of Spain, along the Mediterranean coast, is known.

14

alone the study, of the repression that, under Franco, can be compared to that under Hitler and Stalin.[14]

The astonishing number of prisoners in Cordoba province alone, were sent mainly to three partially-destroyed villages enclosed by ditches and wire fencing: Valsequillo, La Granjuela and Los Blázquez. There were others in the region of Peñarroya-Pueblonuevo. After the fall of the La Serena pocket (summer, 1938), many more were captured in Fuenteobejuna, in Cordoba capital and elsewhere in the province. According to López Rodríguez, the first lot of prisoners taken at the La Serena pocket totalling exactly 6,280, were not sent to the Castuera concentration camp it was not yet completed, but to Campillo and Guareña and then, to camps in Mérida (3,605), Fuenteobejuna (481), Cordoba capital (2,194) and Almendralejo.[15]

The camps in Valsequillo, La Granjela and Los Blázquez began to fill up after the defeat following the Republic's defeat in its last battle at the beginning of February 1939, the battle of Cordoba-Extremadura that resulted in almost 6,500 prisoners. Another 700 were interned in Almendralejo and Fuenteobejuna as well as La Isla in Huelva. The Nationalist army expected to capture such an enormous number of prisoners that in March 1939, the military headquarters began rushing to complete the Castuera concentration camp in Badajoz, which was not complete until the day on which war ended, when there was a new flood of prisoners. Then followed the flood of prisoners as war ended. López Rodríguez further reports that in the immediate post-war period, an additional 7,500 were imprisoned in Valsequillo, 8,153 in La Granuela and 1,342 in Los Blázquez, although these numbers rose and fell from one day to another.

The last days of the war, many combatants from the area North of Cordoba fled towards Puertollano and Ciudad Real, as well as to other locations in La Mancha, such as Almadén, where they were eventually captured. A small concentration camp in Chillón held 750 prisoners and another one in Almadenejos, over 1,000.

Extra-judicial violence was the norm during the Victory Walk. The unmitigated account of a war crime, by a soldier of the 41st Republican Division in Extremadura, Albino Garrido, has recently come to light, been recorded and can be listened to on the Internet.[16]

"On March 28 1939, once we had laid down our weapons, the officers of the 41st Division decided that a committee should be sent to contact the Nationalist troops that were entering Extremadura from the North. The men entrusted with negotiating this delicate 'surrender' were a Captain (a physician, head of the 66th Brigade Hospital), a Militia

Lieutenant and several other soldiers, of which I was one. They presented themselves to Lieutenant Colonel Francisco Adame Triana, commander of the 2nd Regiment of the 19th Nationalist Division, who was arriving from North of Badajoz".

Taking the Captain and the Lieutenant aside, Colonel Adame asked the Captain why he had not gone over to the Nationalists. He replied that it was difficult, that he was engaged in medical treatments and that he was born in Murcia. Next, Adame asked the Militia Lieutenant which academy he had attended. He replied that he had not attended any military academy, that he was a member of the Militia. 'Ah so', replied the officer:

> 'Therefore, you are a Lieutenant of the People's Army.' Without another word, Adame turned to the Nationalists and called out: 'Aim! Fire! That is how we do justice in Nationalist Spain.' The bodies of both negotiators were left where they fell. I and the other members of the group were sent to Pantano de Cíjara concentration camp, near Castilblanco, and later to Castuera."

There were many tragedies in the manner by which the Spanish Falangistas handled their victory. Moreno Gómez was able to record the details of a few such crimes during the first days, but the majority, almost all, remain forever unknown. One largely forgotten crime devastated the Republican Navy when March 5 1939 Admiral Miguel Buiza Fernández-Palacios fled the naval base in the port of Cartagena that was under heavy attack, which a view to saving as much of the fleet as he could. He made his way to French Algeria which he knew was tantamount to handing the fleet over to Franco as a few days earlier the French Government had recognized the Burgos Government as the only legal Spanish government. Denied entrance to Oran, the French authorities directed it to the Tunisian port of Bizert (a French protectorate) where it arrived March 11 and was interned by the French. Except for a few sailors who on board the several ships on guard duty, the remainder of the crew sked for political asylum and were interned in a nearby concentration camp. When Admiral Francisco Moreno arrived in Bizerte April 14 to take command of the now-Nationalist Navy, the French authorities polled the Republican crew. Of the 4,000 naval personnel, 2,350 decided to return to Spain, almost all Senior Staff Officers and a great many crew, especially machinists. Unfortunately, as the 'Hounds of Victory' were baying for blood, Admiral Moreno ordered the summary slaughter of 50

Republican sailors who had decided to return to Spain. The remainder were disembarked in Cadiz, where they were sent to Rota and other concentration camps in that province.

Early features of the Fascist victory

Falangista flags fluttered victoriously all over Cordoba province. A first report after the end of the March 1939 Victory Walk was of a burst of looting by the victors, a precursor of the unbridled seizure of the spoils of war that would soon loom over the defeated. No sooner did the troops enter the towns and villages, that they attacked the military stores whose guards had disappeared. In Pozoblanco, the victorious soldiers did not wait a minute before plundering the goods. They even left an amount to be shared amongst the 'new' merchants.[xviii] In Villanueva de Cordoba, the contents of the great La Alpujarra warehouse, as in many other towns, were seized. The most important confiscation in the region was the recently harvested grain and all the livestock kept on Cabañeros farm, belonging to some 40 collective farms in Los Pedroches, March 26. Days later, Nationalists seized a large number of animals also belonging to Los Pedroches collective farmers that were being kept at El Yegüerzo farm in Cardeña.

Bartolomé Cabrera Peralbo, a member of the UGT trade union, who was responsible for caring for the livestock, was totally helpless to prevent the seizure. The military commander of Cardeña summoned him and ordered him to hand over all the weapons on the property, reminding him that he would be responsible for everything there was, even if he had to go and get it himself. He replied that there was nobody there who controlled anything, that they had had some two hundred suckling pigs, each weighing about 50 pounds, but that two days previously soldiers had shot them and taken them away. The goats that they had disappeared and, of the breeding rabbits, only the metal cages remained. The soldiers had taken all their food stores. They opened the wine store and spent all day removing bottles and demijohns, saying that it was wine for the Administrative Officer's wine cellar.[17]

When the soldier arrived at the Villanueva collective farms in Loma del Caballero, Manuel Bustos Badia[18] tells how everyone became afraid and went home leaving the livestock behind, except for his father who refused to abandon the animals. Two Falangista henchmen, Fresco 'El Tirador' and Mariano 'El Gitano' arrived and, on Torrico's orders, took all that was left".

[xviii] Falangistas and other friendly civilians who had seized premises belonging to defeated Republican shopowners.

As the Nationalist troops took a town or village, they seized many types of collective ventures, both agricultural and livestock, that they then handed over to traditional gentlemen farmers, primarily major landowners, who returned to the land after having absented themselves from Cordoba and Seville for the past three years. They brought with them a new rural Fascism and the return of the old ways and customs of deferential day labourers that had prevailed under the monarchy.

In Cordoba capital, right-wingers and municipal authorities could not contain their joy when March 28, Eduardo Valera Valverde, the new Governor of Cordoba, inflamed with the spirit of Francoism, addressed the people of Cordoba in celebration of the new *Duce*, or *Caudillo*'s, occupation of Madrid. His speech was published in its entirety in the local newspaper, *ABC*.[19]

At the beginning of April, the Falangista Cordoba authorities took symbolic possession of the towns and villages in the North of the province (Los Pedroches district), by making the rounds of the region with a retinue comprising Governor Valera; the provincial head of the Falange (FET and JONS)[xix], Fernando Fernández de Córoba; the president of the Provincial Appelate Court, José Aguilaz; and the Inspector of Health, Luis Nájera, among others.

Days before, March 28, Los Pedroches was visited by the Social Welfare caravan bringing some snacks and light supplies for the civil population. When they arrived at Alcaracejos, they found the town deserted and partly destroyed. They then went on to other towns, such as Almadén. There were quite a few such expeditions during the first few days of the conquest, directed at gaining some sympathy from the unfriendly and apprehensive civil population. An example of this occurred when Nationalist units approached Madrid in November with the statue of Saint Rafael they had taken from Cordoba[xx] to preside over a celebratory open-air mass planned for San Bernardo square and some trucks full of melons and watermelons for the populace. Madrid, however, was still resisting so they were forced to cancel the mass and return the statue to Cordoba, under a pouring rain, leaving the melons and watermelons to rot.

[xix] FALANGE ESPAÑOLA DE LAS JUNTAS DE OFENSIVA NACIONAL-SINDICALISTA. Union of the Committees of the National Syndicalist Offensive in Spain, coalition of right-wing fascist parties in Spain, the sole legal party under Franco

[xx] The statue of Saint Rafael, patron saint of Cordoba, is jealously protected by the Cordovans as a symbol of their leadership and power over the centuries of which they are so proud. Taking it to Madrid to preside over a Francoist mass was both an insult to Republicans in both cities as it was an affirmation of Francoist power over the nation.

The last few days of March 1939 were bitterly cold – it snowed around Los Pedroches – as Nationalists prepared for the 'Holy Week of the Victory' (April 2, Palm Sunday to April 7, Holy Friday). House searches, arrests, first interrogations, beatings and floggings, and the other usual Francoist practices were the norm everywhere, clearly part of a planned, not 'improvised' shedding of blood, as some have written without justification.

Later, Moreno Gómez shows how Franco liberally applied the so-called extra-judicial *Lei das Fugas*[xxi] throughout the recently conquered Centre-South region during the months of April and May as part of these Fascist Easter Victory celebrations. Again, this was the affirmation of the alliance of the sword and the cross: two faces of the same coin. Gunpowder and incense, as Hilari Raguer wrote.[20]

With victory, National Catholicism exploded across the country in all its 'glory'. The clergy resumed the splendour of the beginning of the century and they strutted down the streets in front of their congregations, entertaining cheers, hymns and a multitude of celebratory acts: *Te Deum laudamus*, alleluias and thanksgivings. During those dramatic early days, crowds gathered on the streets primarily for military or religious reasons, attracted by the parades or processions or a combination of both.

Men clothed in black cassocks, with wide-brimmed hats and flowing capes returned to the social and political centre stage after three years' absence with unusual force. Falange flags hung side-by-side with religious banners. Open-air masses were celebrated everywhere, always with a strong military presence, resounding with the hymns and Vivas! proper to the moment, embellished with all the symbols of a Fascist state soaked in holy water, contrary to the pagan versions seen in Germany and Italy. This was, without a shadow of a doubt, the most fanatic Holy Week in Spanish history.

Today, it is difficult to find eye-witness descriptions for the many kinds of memories of that period. Certainly in Cordoba, where on Palm Sunday, the Church organized a picturesque pilgrimage to Fuensanta Church to give thanks for the victory. In Alsasua, Navarra, however, we do have the account of Father Marino Ayerra, one of the few priests who rejected the military coup and the ensuing slaughter.[21]

[xxi] Law of Escapes. Prisoners were taken out for 'walks from which they never returned. These walks were known as *paseos*, the tongue-in-cheek name given to the extra-legal execution of prisoners or captives. Guards, leading prisoners from one jail to another, would drop back a distance and on the pretence that the prisoners ahead were 'escaping', shoot them in the back. Another practice was for members of a firing squad to loosen their captives' bonds and remove their blindfolds, then turn around pretending to give them a chance to get away. As the captives fled, they were shot by the whole firing squad. Anyone who survived received a 'mercy shot' in the back of the head. This was in total violation of the Geneva Convention, which Franco in any case, did not recognize.

In his book on his experiences in Alsasua, Fr. Ayerra tells of a great manifestation that the Nationalists organized in Alsasua to celebrate Franco's victory, to the overwhelming joy of a few and the stifled, concentrated pain of almost all the population, already subjugated and again bound in chains. It is his description that a new Middle Ages had spread its dark wings over their homes.

> "In Alsasua, as everywhere, the hills echoed with pealing bells and the sound of fireworks, calling all the neighbouring villagers to attend. A military band led the triumphal march, beginning at the Military Headquarters then into the parish church where a thanksgiving *Salve Regina* was sung. The cortège then went up and down the streets of the town until it arrived at the church of the Capuchin monks where the *Salve Regina* was again sung. The procession then returned to the starting point - Military Headquarters - where the Military Commander gave a closing speech."

When the procession arrived at the parish church, a few steps in front of the Military Headquarters, Fr. Ayerra felt compelled to say a few words to everyone who was present:

> "By all means, *pax vobis, pax vobis*, for all. Let us celebrate the triumph of Christ and not the triumph of the Passion. Let this be our motto, therefore, not the *vae victis*, the woe to the vanquished of usual fights between brothers (…) There is no need for me to remind you of the nobility of the Spanish and Christian knight who, when facing his defeated enemy, raised his sword and saluted him. Honour and glory to the victor and glory and honour to the vanquished!"

The religious cortège left the parish church and followed the procession around the village. Ahead, members of the public sang Nationalist and Militia hymns. Behind, military, civil and religious authorities followed. As the procession arrived at the church of the Capuchin monks, a tall, imposing Capuchin monk came out under a rain cloak. At the end of the hymn to the Virgin Mary, he turned towards the crowd and in a loud, bombastic voice, addressed the assembly:

"The God of the Armies has triumphed once again. Does this mean that the war is over? Absolutely not! The life of Man is a permanent state of war against the enemies of God, subjugated, yes, but rebellious, always ready to rise again, to mutiny… No! The war is not over. We are always at war… To you, yes. *Pax vobis*… But to the others?… *Non est pax inpiis!* No peace of any kind for the unGodly!…"

The Capuchin monk's speech was a brutal response to Mariano Ayera and in tune with what every member of the Spanish clergy, and the victors as a whole, were preaching at the moment. There was to be no pardon. This was the voice of the exterminators, at its most evident and brutal. The fact of the matter was that 99.99% of all Spanish clergy identified themselves with the Capuchin monk who so strongly criticized Father Ayerra's pacifying words. On this day, no other cleric in victorious Spain dared speak out in such a manner or express such an opinion, just this humble Basque parish priest in Alsasua in the Catholic province of Navarra.

In the other half of Spain, the defeated population cried in secret, leaving their children bewildered as to their overwhelming sadness. As one older gentleman said, one of the saddest memories he had of the end of the war, when he was only eight years old, was hearing his grandmother cry all night as trucks full of victorious soldiers passed their house, at the entrance to Tarancón, Cuenca, all night.[22]

The first Francoist town councils, or *Ayuntamientos*, were quickly created and the first Mayors bore surnames belonging to the great landed gentry. In Pozoblanco, the first Mayor was Antonio Herrero Martos, a wealthy rancher. In Villanueva, it was the no less wealthy land mogul Antonio Casimiro 'El Niño Herruzo' Herruzo Martos during the summer of 1939 after which some were replaced by medium-sized landowners.

The new town councils were set up as was the norm in a militarized State, under the aegis of the military authority from whom all legitimacy issued. Captain Casas Ochoa of the military judiciary was responsible for the mountain villages. The new councillors 'swore upon their honour to faithfully carry out their respective functions with zeal, austerity and energy, taking inspiration from Nationalist Spain and General Franco's regulations then sent telegrams of congratulations to Franco, Queipo de Llano and other Nationalist leaders. The first proposal every new council unanimously approved was to purchase portraits of General Franco and José Antonio Primo de Rivera, the dictator, and a crucifix. This was immediately followed by the decision to proceed with the utmost urgency to purge the Town Council of Republicans, to banish them from the town and to replace the entire staff, from the porter to the highest ranking employee. In each council, this extensive, huge and almost unprecedented purge would be supervised by one of the new councillors who was appointed to manage the disciplinary proceedings.

Consultation of the Minutes of Meetings of the Cordoba province town councils, immediately draws attention to the avalanche of claims from Falangistas for municipal jobs, based on allegations of being ex-prisoners, ex-combatants, relatives of *caídos*[xxii], war wounded and other similar entitlements. At the same time, these job seekers attempted to add to the 'merit' of their claim by pointing out how cruelly they had dealt with the defeated when doing house searches, detaining individuals and detailing the first beatings they gave in improvised prisons, military headquarters or Nationalist barracks. The new national sport became to down a couple of drinks, go down to the town jail and beat up some prisoners.

Positions in the municipal police were filled by the most unsavoury individuals. Never before had these guards enjoyed such extra-judicial power and been given such a carte blanche, as in the first post-war period. So much so, that in La Rambla, the first depositions from defeated returnees were taken by the head of the municipal police. In Villanueva de Cordoba, the head of the municipal police, Bartolomé 'Berenguer' Cepas Díaz, became one of the nightmares of the entire neighbourhood and especially by those deemed to be 'disaffected'. This was also true of others such as Vicente 'Salado' Muñoz Fernández (whose brothers were among the caídos) and Diego 'El Chunga' Cachinero Torralbo who, with his cruelty, had already surpassed himself as a member of the recently created Military Police, under the tragically infamous SIPM[xxiii] Lieutenant, Leopoldo Mena. According to the municipal Minutes of July 14 1939, when applying for the job El Chunga alleged in his favour that he was both a veteran and a wounded soldier.[23] Another infamous municipal policeman was Emilio 'El del Lunar' Santofimia because of his crazy methods. It is interesting that he, as well as the job-seeker before him were both defectors from the left. Many of the newly-employed also had prior criminal records such as Berenguer who had served as a guard with Torrico and had been jailed before the war for having killed a hunter in the countryside.

Within the context of post-war rural Fascism, rural policemen also played a significant role because of their past connections with the large landholdings. They actually became material executors of the repression and the punishments as they helped the Guardia Civil. This was the murky

---

[xxii] *Caidos* or 'fallen'. Generic Designation for everyone who was killed while serving in the Nationalist Army or died for the Francoist cause. Hence, the *Los Caidos* national monument outside Madrid.

[xxiii] *Servicio de Información y Policia Militar* – Military Intelligence and Police Service.

world of informers who cropped up like poison mushrooms all over the place, including the capital, that Moreno Gómez had studied since 1985. There is absolutely nothing new in the topic that was recently addressed by Óscar Rodríguez Barreira in his work on the phenomenon of the informers.[24]

The victorious town councils, in addition to their major role in the flowchart of the repression (gathering and supplying information, classifying individuals, etc.), were also responsible for managing the pensions allocated to widows or relatives of municipal employees who had fallen during the days of the rebellion. They went even further paying past due salaries to Falangista municipal guards and employees who had been employed since the summer of 1936. When relatives of employees who had been purged by the Francoists dared to ask for any back pay, the managers denied these requests that they deemed inadmissible.

As a whole, the first view of the victory was of a country festooned with the paraphernalia of public acts, military homages and parades, blessings of flags and victors, processions and calls for revenge, and clergy and military speaking in a single voice, during a month of April crazed by triumphalist paroxysms. Even Francesc Cambó whom nobody could suspect of leftist sympathies exclaimed in amazement that "Spain had become a permanent celebration of victorious power, a shameless exhibition of revenge and vendettas."

Adding insult to injury, on the anniversary of the declaration of the Second Republic, April 14, Cordoba's Town Council organized a homage to the eccentric Falangista General Millán Astray, consisting of the gift of a one-metre-tall image of the Sacred Heart of Jesus, handed to him by the Mayor of the provincial capital, José Maria Verastegui. 'A roué in penitent's clothing,' as the poet Antonio Machado might have described him.[xxiv]

April also witnessed the *delirium tremens* of the victors and Franco's triumphal walk around the capitals of Andalusia. Saturday April 15, Franco arrived in Seville, the parting shot of a magnificent tournée in praise of his base - his 'loyal' multitude. The other multitude would be sent to the dungeons. The central act of the tour was the great victory parade that was celebrated in Seville, Sunday 16, a key date in the Regime's first steps because as the victors paraded, Vatican Radio transmitted Pope Pius XII's message of blessing to Franco and the heroes of the victory.

The April 16 celebrations in Seville were a Nationalist military highpoint. The magnificent parade, down Avenida de Mayo, was led by General Yagüe (the butcher of Badajoz) at the head of the Moroccan Army Corps. Next came, the Extremadura Army Corps, led by General Soláns,

---

[xxiv] Antonio Machado. Eminent Spanish poet and writer 1879-1939). Republican intellectual.

followed by the flag bearers of the *Falange Española*[xxv] and the *Requeté*[xxvi], led by Coronel Redondo; the Granada Army Corps with its commander, General González Espinosa; and the Cordoba Army Corps under General Borbón. These were followed by the Andalusia Army Corps led by General Muñoz Castellanos and Colonels Castejón (the butcher of Puente Genil) and Baturone (the butcher of Palma del Rio). Next came other units, Artillery, Air Force, etc. Taking the salute, Franco's slight silhouette, accompanied by Queipo de Llano (who would not be "Viceroy" of Andalusia for much longer), the Minister of Government, Serrano Súñez[xxvii], assorted Sevillian leaders and authorities, both civil and ecclesiastic. The Archbishop and other members of the hierarchy, stood with their hands raised in the Falangista salute as the bells of the cathedral pealed.

Despite all the pomp and circumstance, the Seville parade was but a pale image of the magnificent May 19 Victory Parade in Madrid, with its march-past of 120,000 soldiers, Moroccans, legionnaires, Guardia Civil and an 'entire cortege of knights and paladins', a remarkable display of military force that Rubén Darío[25] might have chosen for his poem, "Triumphal March".

Back in Andalusia, Franco was cosseted and revered for three days in Seville before continuing his triumphal tour across the region. At the same time, the Law of Fugitives began to be applied without distinction throughout the villages and across the fields of the Cordoba hill, against the first defeated individuals captured by the Francoist troops.

On the afternoon of April 18, pealing bells announced the dictator's arrival in San Fernando (where dozens upon dozens of sailors had been executed) and in Cadiz capital; April 19, Malaga (where 4,000 victims have been recently exhumed from mass graves in San Rafael cemetery alone); April 20, Granada (where García Lorca lay in an unmarked grave in Viznar). At noon April 21, the victorious cortege made a symbolic visit to the La Cabeza Sanctuary, before entering Jaen, the city Queipo del Llano had bombed. That same day, at 5:30 p.m., Franco was acclaimed in Tendilla Square in Cordoba capital by a huge crowd of Falangistas and right-wingers, both local and many others brought in from surrounding villages, arms raised in the Falangista salute. The Tendillas shook with the noise of the Falangistas, who were hoarse from so much shouting.

Franco, who would stand impassively on the bloody pedestal of half a million dead and another half million exiled, thousands of homes demolished and thousands of families destroyed and a democracy in shreds, was

---

[xxv] *Falange Española*, or *Falange* for short. Coalition of right-wing fascist parties in Spain.
[xxvi] *Requeté*. Paramilitary Carlist Militia, part of Franco's coalition during the civil war.
[xxvii] Franco's brother-in-law.

acclaimed in Cordoba by his followers with the customary hymns and *Vivas!* The provincial authorities of Cordoba had earlier gathered to welcome him in Villa del Rio, where the dictator first set foot in Cordoba province. The Mayor of Cordoba and General Borbón waited on the riverbank in Alcolea to receive him. Cordoba, the martyred city, was about to become the private hunting grounds for the military governor Colonel Ciriaco Cascajo Ruiz, Bruno Ibáñez Gávez – *Don Bruno*, Luíz Zurdo, Father Ildefonso Hidalgo and friar Jacinto de Chucena.

Franco's high-pitched voice[xxviii] rang out shrilly from the balcony of the Góngora Institute, the humiliated seat of the intelligentsia, whose Director and Professor, the distinguished Antonio Jaén Morente, was at that moment somewhere on the Pacific Ocean on his way to exile in Ecuador. Next to him, General Queipo de Llano referred to 'criminal Marxist bombing' despite the fact that it was he who ordered the bombing of Jaén on April 1 1937, killing 155 people in a single day, more than all the casualties of the Government bombing of Nationalist positions in the capital throughout the entire war. Following the bath of the crowd, the dictator went for refreshment to the mansion of the Duke of Hornachuelos, José de La Lastra y Hoces, who was taking up his position as a Military Prosecutor at summary court martials.

After Seville, April 24 Franco returned to Burgos, the seat of his Government until October 18 when Franco moved into the El Pardo royal palace in Madrid. These celebrations marked the end of the wartime Francoist government of the city and province the Nationalists had occupied during the war, as military officials were replaced by other high-ranking officers whose experience and inclination was apparently more suited to the methods of the repressive government that followed the surrender of the Republican forces. Those were tough times for justice, for common sense, for cool heads.

Queipo del Llano's days as Lord of Lives and Properties were numbered. Franco relieved him as Commander in Chief in July and on the twentieth of that same month, appointed General Andrés Saliquet Commander of the II Region in his stead, on the pretext that the butcher of Andalusia and Badajoz should enjoy a 'well-deserved rest'. His farewell was set for July 18, the date chosen by the *ABC* newspaper of Seville to honour his retirement by publishing an insufferable poem by Luis Pérez Solero which had been earlier dedicated to General la Casa González Byass.

[xxviii] Franco, considered to be the most inarticulate of all the fascist leaders of the time because he was unable to utter eight sentences in a row, spoke in a high-pitched and choppy manner.

'What a seed
the General has sown
in the city of Seville!
How he has converted the evil
that suffocated the people
to well-being and affection!

Today, the child
who had been so forgotten,
shall enjoy entertainment and joy
thanks to Don Gonzalo.
Make the child laugh;
a child who laughs, is not bad!

When he becomes a citizen
in this new-born Spain,
he will remember what
Gonzalo Queipo de Llano is doing today,
which is to give bread with one hand
and justice, with the other.'

Colonel Ciriaco Cascajo remained for a while as military governor of Cordoba although despite his 'achievements' as the butcher of several thousand individuals in the capital, among other nefarious deeds, he had to wait a long time to reap the reward of a promotion to General, which he only received February 28 1939. The servile nonsense began immediately afterwards when a public subscription was raised to buy him his General's sash. This subscription was considered closed much later, in October, after 24,000 pesetas had been raised. In addition to a villa in the heart of Cordoba capital, a gift from Cordoba right-wingers in 1936, he received many other gifts. Everywhere, people sang the Colonel-General's praise and generosity, his 'blood accomplishments' and his role in the military coup.

The *ABC* of Cordoba, a city of beggars, orphans, hunger, imprisoned and misery, celebrated the events of July 18 1939 by publishing a passage from a particularly pathetic speech of Cascajo's in which he extolled the innovations he claimed the new Regime had introduced to Cordoba during the three years since the beginning of the war: soup kitchens for the needy, a profusion of Social Welfare dining rooms for children and adults; a special kitchen for diabetic, a charity dining room equal to the finest in Spain, a sanatorium to treat tuberculosis such as was not thought of during the many years when it could have been built; three groups of cheap houses for labourers and workers where 200 families could live in comfort and health; a model children's crèche: and in addition to all this, the unlimited amount of help given to ex-combatants and to the families of those who died in battle...

Meanwhile, the last few months of the war brought several changes to the military and civil leadership of Cordoba. Brigade General Francisco Formoso Blanco replaced Cascajo as military governor November 23. The civil governor, Valera Valverde, was replaced earlier, August 30, by another career military officer, Artillery Captain Joaquín Cárdenas Llavaneras. The Mayor, José María Verastegui, was replaced November 6 by the well-known Cordoba politician, José Tomás Valverde Castilla who, having trained under the Primo de Rivera dictatorship, was a staunch supporter of Calvo Sotelo in 1936. His term of office in Cordoba after the war was brief, as he resigned as Mayor on November 28 to become Civil Governor of Seville. The position of Mayor of Cordoba was handed on to Manuel Sarazá Murcia, who had served as Mayor earlier during the tragic days of 1936 and during the 'Terror of Don Bruno',[xxix] the leading war criminal and genocide in this provincial capital city.

In the end, the first view of the victory was that of a country enveloped by an intense wave of patriotic euphoria, Falangista parades, open-air masses, widespread detentions and accusations, executions and starvation in the jails. On the other hand, festivals promoting Social Welfare, long queues for any kind of food and public subscriptions of all kinds, such as one for the reconstruction of the La Cabeza Sanctuary. Every town and village was busy erecting monuments and crosses to the Nationalist caídos. In Cordoba capital, a cross to the fallen was placed on the Malamuerta Tower, which was odd because the only fallen in Cordoba were 4,000 Republicans who were assassinated.

In towns all over the province, such as Fernán Núñez, victory parties were celebrated with barrels of wine, fireworks and marching bands, regardless of the cost of these festivities during this time of extreme poverty and suffering.[26]

[xxix] Bruno Ibáñez Gálvez. Lieutenant-Colonel of the Guardia Civil appointed by Queipo de Llano as Head of Public Order in Cordoba and who with his reign of terror during his short tenure in office, was responsible for no less than four thousand executions in Cordoba and numerous imprisoned or diappeared. Upon his departure to a new posting, 'Don Bruno' stated that he could claim no merit for his achievements – he simply limited himself to signing the lists that were presented to him by his deputies and by the clergy.

Return of the defeated. Humiliation and confiscations.

"The absolute secrecy surrounding the repression during forty interminable years, together with the cynical declarations of pro-Francoist leaders as they deny the most evident realities, still leave seeds of doubt in some minds regarding the dramatic truth."

Sócrates Gómez, *Tiempo de Historia,* January 1980.

1. Democratic Spain falls into the clutches of the fascist victors.

No sooner had Franco declared victory that there was no doubt as to what awaited the return of the defeated to their home towns. The Spanish countryside became peopled by terrified individuals, itinerant families, an indescribable coming and going of the population, some searching for a safe haven, others walking non-stop, without respite, towards the homes they had long ago abandoned. The few working vehicles, trucks and trains were crammed with thousands of Spaniards; women, old people and children walked for miles to the limit of their endurance, painting an unbelievable panorama of pain, fear, dark forebodings – a human catastrophe that is difficult to reconstruct today given the very few historians who are willing to undertake this task.

One of the victorious government's more astute stratagems were the general instructions encouraging all the defeated, combatants or not, to return to their home towns (where they could be more easily hunted down). The only breath of hope that the defeated clung to was the fabrication that victorious Francoists spread everywhere: 'He whose hands are not sullied with blood has nothing to fear'. The truth would soon become apparent as the ruse was visible to all. The fact is that this never was a tacit, unspoken fallacy. Franco himself openly used the 'hands not stained with blood' sophism in his bare-faced statements to the world. Franco, who wanted to appear to be complying with the 1929 Geneva Convention, which only permitted enemies to be punished for 'ordinary crimes' and not for 'political transgressions', nor even for 'rebelling' as this was not contemplated as a crime in cases of civil war. He wanted to show the world that he was pursuing criminals and not politically-motivated individuals. This was yet another example of how Franco manipulated the people and used language as a weapon of mass destruction. Hence, Paul Preston's sound judgement in his book on Franco: *The great manipulator.*[27]

The month of April 1939 saw a constant coming and going of trucks laden with soldiers and endless columns of defeated combatants on foot guarded by the victors, railway stations packed with people, both civilians and ex-combatants downloaded from some goods wagons to be loaded onto others towards multiple destinations. All the defeated tried to avoid going through town centres because of the open animosity of the victorious franquistas and the new authorities, eager to punish every republican they could lay their hands on. Ex-combatants particularly suffered the ill treatment meted out in the towns by the same people who had previously respected them when they were the ones with guns. It was the unhappy return, in humiliation, both for civilian refugees and ex-combatants who had been surprised by the end of the war in distant battle fronts and were considered pariahs everywhere they went. The pain of the return, worse than the difficult moments of the evacuation months or years earlier, was instinctive in nature: a search for the natural sanctuary of one's fatherland.[28]

Still, the defeat was so overwhelming, the victors so vindictive and ruthless, that for the defeated, there no longer was any kind of fatherland, neither large nor small. Moreno Gómez remarked that although there have been defeats throughout history, he could not recall a single one where there was so much planned revenge, not just against ex-combatants but worse, against the entire civilian population that did not support the victorious regime. Even at the end of World War II in Europe, although there were reprisals against the leading defeated elite, there were none against the civilian population.

When the ex-combatants returned to their home towns and their families, they were faced with many tragic situations that break one's heart, such as when José Manuel Matencio who, with a companion, after taking almost a month to get home, hiding during the day and walking at night. That night, not long after he arrived, his young sons hearing a noise in the kitchen got out of bed and went to see what it was. There, they saw two men whose unshod feet were bandaged with bloody rags. One of them, was crying because they did not want him to touch them as they did not recognize him.[29]

It was not just ex-combatants who were returning home, but also the thousands of families who had earlier fled the fighting and taken refuge in Republican-held territory. Elisa Carillo's family returned to Posadas by train from Argamasilla de Calatrava, Ciudad Real. As they got off the train, the village schoolmaster, a Falangista, recognized her father and called out to the Guardia Civil: "Fine fish we caught tonight! For now, handcuff him!". They quickly took him away, first to Cordoba jail then to jail in Palencia. From there, the family was notified that he had died 'of a heart attack'.[30]

Returning families had harrowing experiences, as was the case of Francisca Adame's family that had also taken refuge in Ciudad Real and was returning to their home in Posadas where her father felt they would be safe from the authorities who were looking for him. They got as far as a little village, Miguel Turra, 4 kms away, where they joined other refugees and that night the war ended.

At daybreak, a Guardia Civil and a priest came accompanied by a woman crying out: "Long lie Christ the King!" and a truck full of Moroccan soldiers. They were sent to a house for refugees where they remained several days with nothing but lentils to eat. As the villagers passed on their way to an open air mass that was to be held in the village hall, they yelled: "Make the refugees come out! Make them come out!" Francisca was chosen to come out and they shouted *Cara al sol! Cara al sol!* But she did not know what they meant.[xxx]

Finally arriving by train in Posadas, they were greeted by a couple of Guardias Civiles shouting: "Refugees over here; refugees, here!" Francisca's uncle who was waiting for them took the family to her grandmother's house but her father and all officers of rank were taken aside. They were told that a ship was coming for them but when they got to the port of Alicante, no ship had arrived. They were taken to a cinema and then to a prison camp. Half of the men died in that camp and the remainder were shuttled from one camp to another – San Fernando Fort, Santa Barbara Castle, Elche, until they were brought to Cordoba to be tried by a military court. [31]

Rafael Garcia Contreras described his father's return to Pedro Abad in April 1939 because his father believed the Caudillo's words that no one whose hands were not sullied with blood could return home. They left by train in a cattle wagon from Rus, Ciudad Real, and made their way to their house to find that only the walls and the street door remained standing. His father threw his kit bag to the ground and hugged his mother and sister who were crying.

There was no time for anything else. Behind them stood two Guardias Civiles who took his father away to their barracks where he received beating after beating and was tortured, which left him with a large wound in his back. One day, Rafael's aunt carried him in her arms so that he could see his father as he was taken from the barracks to the jail. He was dripping blood all over his body. November 20, after his wounds had healed, they took him back to the village and shot him against the Pedro Abad cemetery wall.[32]

Many people made their way back on foot, walking all or part of the way. Bartolomé Marín, from La Rambla, found himself in Valencia at the

---

[xxx] *Cara al Sol* (Face to the sun.) The title of the Spanish Falange party anthem.

end of the war and he walked back as far as Jaén where he obtained a safe-conduct pass in Ubeda. A truck took him to Bujalance. From there, he again walked, to La Rambla.[33] Still, many others did not choose to return to their home towns: many people of little political importance remained in Madrid, Valencia and other towns, working at whatever they could, always keeping their thoughts to themselves.

In Fernán Núñez, as Arcángel Bedmar writes, victory parties were celebrated with barrels of wine, fireworks and marching bands, regardless of the cost of these festivities during this time of extreme poverty and suffering.

After the July 25 1936 slaughter of so-called anarchists in the village of Fernán Núñez at the hands of the Spanish Foreign Legion[xxxi], refugees from the violence, and there were a great many, escaped along the usual route for these country villages: after briefly wandering through fields and farms (El Alcaparro, etc.), they ended up making their way to Espejo and Castro del Río, Bujalance (to join the Andalusia-Extremadura Republican forces), and eventually to villages in Jaén and also to Manzanares, another CNT-National Workers Union sanctuary. Arcángel Bedmar Gonzálvez says that 42 of them were lost forever in battle.

The refugees who survived returned under appalling conditions, packed in all kinds of transport, dirty and dejected, dragging their few belongings. Their condition was so bad, that April 17 1939 the head of the Provincial Board of Health, informed its branch in Fernán Núñez of the high incidence of scabies and other parasitic afflictions of the skin among those who were returning from the Red Zone, ordering it to take all appropriate measures to remedy the situation.[34]

At least 1,500 people – 440 women, 271 men and 688 ex-combatants and an indeterminate number of children under the age of 16 – returned to Fernán Núñez. Many others were unable to return in the early days, either because there were interned in concentration camps, jails or forced labour battalions, all over Spain. It was a dramatic number of returnees for a village of only 11,000 inhabitants. To these figures, we need to add the numbers for all the other towns and villages in Spain to get an idea of the indescribable extent of the internal migration.

Bedmar adds that, upon their return, many discovered that their relatives had either taken their own lives or had died during their extended absence, as occurred to Andés Osuna Sánchez who had fled and been imprisoned after

---

[xxxi] Fighting on the Nationalist side, the Spanish Foreign Legion had a reputation for brutality that, in the early months of the civil war, was used to intimidate and terrorize the opponents of Franco's uprising, particularly anyone professing to be communist or socialist or a member of a trade unions, all whom Franco labelled anarchists.

the war, returned to find that his wife, Ana Creso Rosal, had hung herself, aged 45, in January 1937.

Furthermore, when the refugees returned to their homes, they usually discovered that their homes had been ransacked by Falangistas who had seized all their furniture and other household goods. They could not complain. They had to suffer in silence and go out and beg for references from members of the regime (persons of 'recognized solvency'), in order to obtain the release of their fathers, husbands, sons or brothers from the concentration camps or temporary jails in which they had been interned. Sadly, those references were frequently denied them.

As far as acts of humiliation are concerned, the mothers of twelve neighbours in the village of Santa Cruz who had been assassinated during the first days of the coup, were put to sweeping the town square. What a far cry from what we can 'psychological support for victims' that is so widely offered victims of violence today, or the so-called 'request for forgiveness to victims' families'. In those days there was only one kind of therapy for relatives of the victims: humiliation, degradation, castor oil and shaven heads. In the same village of Santa Cruz, Falangistas shaved the head of an elderly lady named Benilde, a cousin of the Mayor's, stripped her naked and forced her to drink castor oil, just because she dared to ask for the return of a bed. She died a few days later. When the relatives of Juan José Gómez Gálvez (four children and their sick mother) returned from Torredelcampo, Jaén, where they had taken refuge, they found their house was occupied by a Falangista. He finally gave them a room in which to live, but he continued to occupy the building as if he owned it. Such was the so-called behaviour beyond reproach of these persons 'of good standing' and of 'recognized solvency'.

The punishment and extermination program was terrible and unbearable. The victorious Right, traditional *Defender of the Family*, had no qualms in destroying thousands upon thousands of homes and families all over Spain. When victory was declared, the Francoist population began to mistreat all the refugees they could find. They kicked the refugees out of their homes or any shelter they had been able to find and left them to fend for themselves outdoors, without the slightest sign of charity or love for one's fellow man that was so vigorously preached by Catholics. For example, many individuals and families who had fled Montilla in July 1936 returned during that tragic month of April 1939. The Gómez Márquez family and others who had taken refuge in Jabalquinto, Jaén, and were housed in the local barracks were forcibly ejected by a shrieking crowd of Catholic Francoist women. They spent three days outdoors, without any shelter and at the mercy of the elements, until they were able to get on a filthy goods train that returned them to Montilla.[35] The Ruz Morales family took four days to arrive on a goods train from Murcia. Like these, thousands more painful examples.

There are notable examples of the great unofficial confiscation or economic oppression (plundering and looting, to call a spade a spade) of Montilla that affected the people much more than the later official economic repression under the Law of Political Responsibility. To be a Falangista or member of the local militia was very profitable in those days. Since 1936, the Francoist town council in Montilla had assumed the extra-legal management of the property belonging to all those who had earlier fled the hostilities. A local Bureau was set up to make an inventory of their assets and property, so that when the refugees returned, they found that their homes had already been plundered by the Falangistas and all their furniture and chattel gone. As regards urban or rural real estate, most of these properties were lost forever to their lawful owners. The Bureau expropriated ex-Mayor Manuel Sánchez' house on Calle Ciprés and a bar belonging to his family. Socialist Gregorio Sánchez lost his house on Calle Las Prietas and some land, although in the case of the land, thanks to an influential relative he was able to recover it after some lengthy negotiations. Josefa Martinez, who had been widowed during the war and had no means of living when she returned, appealed to the municipal police for the return of a vineyard she had rented in 1936. In reply, she was beaten and called a whore, with total disregard for the fact that she was accompanied by a young child. For many years after the war, the municipality seized the crops that the family of Rafael García Espejo who had gone into exile, grew on his farm, El Barrizal.

Although some returnees arrived in Montilla on foot, the majority did so in 'third class carriages', to use Antonio Machado's expression. Guardas Civiles and armed Falangistas were posted on station platforms, to hunt and capture. The most appreciated prizes were leftist leaders and senior and administrative officers of the recently-defeated Republican Army. These would be led with cheers and shouts of delight to the Nationalist Army Headquarters on Calle Ancha or to the Francoist Guardia Civil barracks where they were subjected to a first interrogation, the first beatings and humiliations.

Many ex-combatants returned by means of safe-conduct passes from the innumerable concentration camps all over Spain. If they did not, the Falangistas would go looking for them. A committee of guards and Falangistas eagerly did the rounds of the Alicante jails and camps on fishing expeditions. This was how they were able to capture and bring back Juan Cordoba Zafra and Manuel Alcaide Aguilar, commanders of the Republican Army, the last democratic Mayor of Montilla, Manuel Sánchez Ruiz, and city councillor Francisco Merino Delgado whose tragic fate will be described further ahead.

Returned men had to comply with two requirements as soon as they arrived. First, they had to go immediately to the Guardia Civil and present themselves for a first interrogation (for some unknown reason, the first interrogations in La Rambla were handled by the head of the municipal police). That done, almost all were sent to the improvised jail that had been set up for this purpose, which in Fernán Nuñez was the village cinema which began by housing some 200 prisoners. Again according to Bedmar, Fernán Núñez prison guards amused themselves by beating the prisoners with rods. One day, in front of all the prisoners, they beat three by breaking a chair over their heads: Amor Jiménez, Pedro Antúnez and Antonio Naranjo. When the prisoners were taken from the jail to the barracks to make further statements, the Guardia Civil beat them again. On other occasions, prisoners would be taken out of the jail and set to clean the streets. That and many other humiliations, acts of degradation and aggravation, all calculated to make life unbearable for the defeated.

In his study of Lucena[36], Arcángel Bedmar records 27 prisoners who, in July 1940, were transferred to the Montilla jail and later, to Cordoba. In the latter prison, 4 of the almost 1,000 who died of starvation in the 1940s were from Lucena. It would appear that the final number of Lucena prisoners was not higher because of the 132 executions involved in the 'total cleansing' of the town in 1936. In April 1939, a concentration camp in Lucena held 305 prisoners, not necessarily all from Lucena. On the other hand, amongst the arbitrary actions of the victors, there is the case of Antonio Fuillerat Carrasco, a socialist from the village of Jauja who travelled to Lucena from Manzanares concentration camp in April, was court-martialled and curiously, absolved. When he returned to Jauja, he was beaten several times by the Falangistas. According to his grandson Rafael, "weakened by the beatings, upsetting experiences and a disease that he contracted when harvesting rice, he died young, aged 41 years".[37]

At least eight ex-combatants who returned to the tiny village of Montemayor during that black Spring. Antonio Jiménez Marín, who like others had left to fight for the Republic and ended up in exile in France in Barcarés concentration camp. June 1939 he decided to return to Spain, turned himself in in Montemayor, was tried in Cordoba and sentenced to 30 years in prison. José Carmona Aguilar, a Lieutenant in the Militia, was sent to Barcarés camp in France, returned and was sent to the Lacolla Workers Brigade. Other Montemayor Barcarés inmates included José Luque Solano whose father obtained his release, and Rafael Moreno Llamas and Antonio Nadales Luque who were also released.

Applications for the release of prisoners were usually successful, but only insofar as they were to swell the ranks of the Forced Labour Brigades or Disciplinary Worker Soldiers Brigades, such as Brigade 51 of Oyarzun (Guipúzocoa), where Antonio Nadales was received by Franco's New Spain. Although José Francisco Luque Moreno[38] was also released thanks to his family's efforts, he was unable to return from France until June 1940. In Spain, he was warmly welcomed at Miranda de Ebro concentration camp by Ángel Carmona Jiménez, eminent Montemayor school teacher who had had a brilliant career during the war at the heart of the FETE-UGT[xxxii] labour union. A friend of Modoaldo Garrido, before the war he had taught at the famous Academia Espinar in Cordoba. Lastly, among the residents that Montemayor lost into exile, special note is made of the great combatant, Alejandro Cabello Sánchez. Severely wounded in the war, he ended up as a brilliant university professor in Hungry and in Cuba. If Franco's military coup could cause such damage in tiny Montemayor, imagine its total impact on every town in Spain.

When the defeated returned to the hamlet of Rute, they were greeted by the sounds of the victors' marching bands. However, no sooner did the menfolk arrive, after thousands of trials and complicated ways and by-ways, that they had to follow the usual procedure: a first deposition before the Guardia Civil and a first report regarding those considered to be hostile to the regime, the so-called disaffected. Those who did not immediately land in jail were not free: they had to report every evening at 8 p.m. to the doors of the Guardia Civil barracks, answer the roll call and sing *Cara al Sol*.[39] The Fascist population delighted in watching the 'red rabble' bite the dust. Sundays, they had to attend the noon mass at the church of Santa Catarina so that they could be purified of 'dissolutionary ideas'. At the end of the war, Las Palomas anise factory was used as a temporary prison to house some 80 prisoners who were put to work repairing the Carcabuey road.

This sample of the sufferings of the Cordoba country folk would not be complete without mention of the case of the defiant city of Baena, the subject of an extensive study by Arcángel Bedmar. The Military Historical Archives (AHM) contain a file for this town of great conflicting passions, listing the names of prisoners from the Red Zone calculated as at least 2,174. This indication of the great many persons forcibly displaced following the military coup in the villages is yet another example of this authentic humanitarian catastrophe. As usual, the returnees were required to present themselves to the Guardia Civil barracks or to Army Headquarters, for a first interrogatory deposition.[40]

---

xxxii FEDERACIÓN DE TRABAJADORES DE LA ENSEÑANZA-UGT. Federation of Teaching Professionals – General Union of Workers.

In Baena, the prisoners were interned in the jail on Plaza Vieja and in Tercia jail, together with prisoners from Albendin, Valenzuela and Luque. In February 1940, they were transferred to the Santa Maria de Scala Coeli convent in Castro del Rio that held 1,500 prisoners. In October of the same year, prisoners from all over the province were packed into Cordoba's New Prison, where there was a real extermination. Prisoners were not held for long periods of time in any of the great Francoist prisons, but frequently moved from one to another, the cynically so-called 'penitentiary tourism'. One can follow the tracks of these unfortunate men from every town in Cordoba province, in and out of Franco's prisons, all over Spain.

In Baena, as everywhere else, the prisoners were systematically beaten for the amusement of Falangistas, either in the prison itself during interrogations or in the barracks during a summary proceeding. Without a doubt, the Francoist Guardia Civil were the great specialists in beatings and torture. Bedmar describes the agony of a prisoner who survived being interrogated and being held for four hours on his knees, a garrotte around his neck, whilst they beat him on his back. A member of the Zarabanda family, whom they had hung by his arms while he was tortured, was unable to withstand the pain and later died in the hospital. José Tarifa Gálvez, who drafted an appeal to the Cordoba Judge Advocate in July 1940, explained that 'The [accused's] entire deposition is totally false; he was forced to say this in the Guardia Civil barracks whilst they beat him with a rod'. Such cases of unbearable torture led to many suicides, as we shall later see.

No less than 172 of the defeated from Baena were sent to forced labour in the Workers Brigades or the Disciplinary Worker Soldiers Brigades (Los Pastores, Algeciras; Los Barrios, Cádiz; Melilla; Tetuán; at the Labacolla airfield, where there were many from Albendín, etc.). At least two from Baena died in the Melilla or San Roque Brigades. Thirteen from Baena died from starvation in Cordoba jail. These included: Antonio Romero León (his brother José was executed in July 1936), José Padillo Rojano (his brother Juan was a victim of the Nazis in Gusen, 1941), Antonio Arroyo León (his son Antonio Arroyo Rodríguez committed suicide in Tremp jail in 1939 and his other son, Manuel Arroyo Rodríguez, was executed in 1943).

There are numerous examples of how entire working-class families were destroyed time and again by the so-called Defenders of the Family who took communion daily and beat their chests in repentance for their sins. It was cynicism and cruelty raised to the nth degree, a thorough repression at multiple levels, one that too many historians are still not taking seriously, engrossed as they are in refuting undeniable facts. No matter how one looks at it, this was a programmed, systematic extermination.

When they could, the imprisoned wrote heart-rending letters to their family, thanking them for their efforts to send them clothes and food whenever they could, as without them, they felt it would be impossible for them to go on. Similar letters to the one that 43-year-old Joaquin Moreno Muñoz, imprisoned in Cordoba, sent his family February 1942:

> "My dear parents and brothers… Mother, I received everything that you say you sent me, as you do not know how well I have been and that I am better from the weakness that I had. If you can continue to come or send me clothes and what food you can, I will be better off; if you cannot, it will be impossible for me to go on… You have no idea how pleased a prisoner is to know that he is remembered, more so in the circumstances in which I find myself; nobody knows that better than one who has to endure these situations and how they devour you. Tomás of my heart: do whatever you can, both for the sake of my health and to relieve me of this unbearable burden…" Worse was yet to happen to him one month later. March 10, he was taken to San Rafael cemetery in Cordoba and executed. [xxxiii]

A look at the National Institute of Statistics records for the 1930-1940 decade in Baena shows that whilst the number of widowers rose 16.3%, which was in agreement with the rate of population growth, the number of widows rose 46.15% (588 in all), witness to the extent of the extermination of the men from that town by execution or acts of war.[41]

There were hundreds of thousands such tragedies all over Spain, as we are now learning of in a great many recent televised documentaries dedicated to recovering the historic memory of Spain and to countering the prevalent historically correct discourse on the basis of the truth as related by eye-witness reports of survivors. A frequent complaint referred to the prison chaplains whom most considered to be nasty and malicious. They said the chaplain would tell them that they were evil and that they were redeeming their sins by doing forced labour. Still, they kept quiet and did their best to raise each other's morale and never lose their dignity.

[xxxiii] Copies of this and many other letters from prisoners are reproduced elsewhere.

"In one way or another they wanted to exterminate you, either by firing squad, by starvation or forced labour... The priest was evil, very evil, he was a Francoist. He would tell us that we were redeeming our sons with our work. We had to listen to all of this and keep quiet. We were the evil ones... But we never lost our dignity: whenever we could, we raised each other's morale... They were unable to destroy our morale, they couldn't."[42]

José Espejo Ruz and Jesús Maria Romero Ruiz recently published two interesting studies of the effects of the Francoist repression.[43] The latter's work is particularly important as it gives details of the first depositions of the 583 returnees who were interrogated when they returned to La Rambla in 1939: 297 interrogated by the Guardia Civil; 286 interrogated by the head of the Municipal Police. A number of women and under-age children must be added to that total. Although some of these may be duplicates, the list is an eloquent sample of the great many people in the South of Spain who fled the rebels in 1936 and the great many who were forced to return in humiliation in 1939 and were subjected to the strictures of the Francoist extermination program.

We can draw many conclusions from these interrogations. More than a thousand residents of La Rambla fled to the Republican zone upon the outbreak of the civil war. Entire families and many workers from a same farm frequently formed groups who walked or rode animals together. One returnee who was interrogated stated that he was part of a group of 150 farm workers on Mina de las Puertas farm who, with their families, set off on foot towards Espejo, taking 20 horses with them, walking all night until they reached Castro del Río. The route was similar for everyone: they first went to Espejo that was packed with a multitude of country folk. One interrogation revealed a curious fact, that in order for them to be given food in Espejo, they had to be carrying a rifle. Then, onwards to Castro del Río, Bujalance. From there, they split up: some to villages in Jaén province; others, to Villa del Río, Montoro and Andújar. Many went on towards Ciudad Real, Manzanares, and quite a few reached Madrid. Some enlisted as volunteers in the several Republican militia regiments, whereas others worked in orchards, made charcoal, or laboured in the El Centenillo mines whilst they waited to be called up by the Republican draft.

The massive displacement of country folk towards loyal villages was not always totally voluntary. Tenant farmers were reluctant to abandon their farms, orchards, melon patches and crops, or their farming implements. Some did leave voluntarily, primarily because they knew that if they stayed, they would be imprisoned. Modesto García, a volunteer runaway, stated that when the rebel movement broke out on August 16 1936, he was in a field watching his father's goats. His brother came and told him that a municipal policeman had stopped by the house with orders for him to present himself at the Guardia Civil barracks. He decided to go to the red [Republican] zone and he left that same night for Castro del Río.

The interrogations further revealed just how active patrols of armed militia were when it came to recruiting farm workers would not otherwise have left of their own accord:[44]

- Antonio Álvarez declared that on December 22 1936, two paid militia arrived one night at Zueros, a charcoal-workers' shanty, and told those who were there to go with them as life was good in the red zone. So they all did: four men and two families, arriving in Linares where they continued to work as coalmen.

- Alfonso Lucena said that when the red forces retreated from the Torres Cabrera railway station, a red Cavalry Patrol dragged several of them towards the unliberated zone, to Andújar and Marmolejo.

- Antonio Osuna described another case regarding coal workers, this time from Las Pilas farm, where four militiamen arrived on horseback and took him and his family, to Espejo.

- José Pérez stated that says that he left August 1 1936 with his mother and one of his sisters, abandoning a melon field that he had in Pobletes.

- Antonio Romero declared that whilst he was working on Miguelo Farm, two armed militia appeared and forced him and three others to follow them to Montoro October 23 1936.

- Juan Toledano tells how he was working one night on a melon patch he shared fifty-fifty with Pastoseco, when a patrol appeared, none of which were known to him, and forced him to go to Espejo, Andújar.

- Sebastián Trócoli said that he was working in his uncle's melon patch in Tentecarretas, near Montalbán, when a patrol arrived including El Confitero, El Tropillo and others he knew, ordering them to go to Espejo. However, he was unsupportive of their cause so in January 1939 he went over to the Nationalists who received him, not in a hotel as he expected, but in the La Aurora (Malaga) concentration camp.

- Cristóbal Villegas declared that finding himself in a watermelon patch that he and his father worked in Los Arenales, La Rambla, a patrol of ten to twelve armed men appeared on horseback and forced them to go with them.

- Another individual interrogated tells how, when he was travelling from Fernán Nuñez along the road to La Rambla, he met a group of men whom he did not know because they were not from his village, and who forced him to follow them to Espejo.

Residents of La Rambla whose lives, homes and farms had been destroyed as a result of the military coup, enlisted in great numbers in the Jaén, Ciudad Real and Madrid militia units (at the end of 1936 these became Mixed Brigades). A noteworthy example is the men who went to Madrid to enlist in the Cordoba Volunteer Battalion (about twenty) that had been created by the distinguished Member of Parliament Antonio Jaén Morente, under the command of his nephew, Antonio Jaén Romero. A large part of this battalion was later incorporated in the 103rd Militia Battalion (MB) and another part, in the 40th MB. Elsewhere, many enlisted in the so-called Torres Battalion, from Valdepeñas, commanded by Carlos Cornejo, from that town, and later incorporated in the 2nd MB. Others joined the Montilla Company that soon became the Second Battalion of Jaén, later the 92nd MB. Many from La Rambla enlisted in several other battalions of Jaen Militia, including the famous Garcés Battalion, later to become the 73rd MB. In the latter, however, the great majority of recruits came from Montilla and Espejo and, especially, from Villanueva de Cordoba, the birthplace of this famous unit.

Everyone who returned from France ended up in one of the concentration camps in the North. In two or three cases, the returnees were immediately sent to Workers Brigades.

Most who returned to La Rambla in April 1939 and the following months had previously been issued safe-conduct passes and recently released from concentration camps all over Spain. Others had passes issued by Workers Brigades, town military headquarters, and some, by Falangista mayors or leaders. One is astounded by the great many concentration camps in Spain through which the wretched ex-combatants of La Rambla passed before they were released: no less than 50, located in the north, south, east and west of the country. Considering that this was the case of a single village, just imagine the incredible hodgepodge of prisoners from all over the country who were enduring the chaos and suffering of this humanitarian catastrophe without equal in the history of Spain. (Table 1. List of Francoist concentration camps housing + 500 prisoners from La Rambla village in 1939.[xxxiv])

In every town and village, the first examination of all the returnees required the interrogator to do the following: confirm the safe-conduct pass; summarize the declarant's passage through the Republican zone; list the military units to which he belonged; record the names of fellow countrymen with whom he was in contact in the other zone and to provide the following information regarding them: what bloody deeds does he know they committed, what does he know about them, which ones died in battle, which ones got married and where, which ones held a rank of some kind or who were political commissars, and so forth.

Consequently, the massive volume of information from the interrogations provided the Francoists with more information about the Republican zone than the Republicans themselves. On that basis, they were able to target their persecution directly to their prey and tailor its harshness to their victims.

One ex-combatant who returned to Villanueva de Cordoba was Militia Captain Pedro Torralbo Gómez, who had walked there from Jaén. According to his son José's account, when his father left Cazorla he went to Jaén. Unable to find his family, he walked to his village. It took him several days to do so because he had to keep hiding in the hills. He hid in the well-known Calcetas market garden, near the railway station, whose owner was brave enough to send a message to his wife. She met Pedro in the orchard, bringing him civilian clothes so that he could change out of uniform. Pedro Torralbo had intended to take to the hills and join Julián Caballero's guerrillas, but as he was preparing to take refuge on El Minguillo farm where one of his uncles was the manager, he was spotted by Juan Grande, the forest ranger, who turned him in. So began Pedro Torralbo's calvary: Villanueva jail, relentless torture, Burgos prison and finally, a firing squad in Cordoba June 3 1941.[45]

The Cordoba hills, where the Los Pedroches township was still smoking from the last shots from the trenches, resounded with the cunning proclamations[46] of a devious *Caudillo* intent on capturing Rojos.

All lies. A ruse for internal consumption and to feed the hypocritical international image of a 'magnanimous' Caudillo who only killed common

---

[xxxiv]   The numbers in brackets on the Table refer to prisoners identified in a specific camp. In 1938, more than 170,000 defeated Republicans were imprisoned in Francoist concentration camps all over Spain. In 1939, this number rose from between 367,000 to 500,000 inmates in more than 180 temporary and permanent concentration camps. In 1946, 137 forced labor and concentration camps were still operational, housing 30,000 political prisoners. The last concentration camp, in Mirana del Ebro, was closed in 1947.

criminals and no one who might be guilty of political transgressions. Western Europe believed, or appeared to believe it. Such are the eternal mechanisms of the *real politik*. Franco, with his wily proclamations, was like a fox: he attempted to captivate the chickens with promises of generosity and good will. In the hundreds of personal interviews carried out over many years, survivors repeatedly mentioned how they had fallen for Franco's lies and their great disillusionment when the torture and death sentences began to rain upon them.

> **IF YOUR HANDS ARE NOT STAINED WITH COMMON CRIMES. COME. FRANCO OFFERS YOU PEACE, WORK, BREAD AND JUSTICE.**
>
> **IF YOU HAVE NOT COMMITTED ANY CRIMES, YOU HAVE NOTHING TO FEAR. NATIONALIST SPAIN IS FAIR AND GENEROUS.**
>
> **NATIONALIST SPAIN PROTECTS THE PRISONER WHO HAS COMMITTED NO CRIMES.**
>
> **NATIONALIST SPAIN OFFERS YOU BREAD AND A PARDON. WHAT ARE YOU WAITING FOR? WE OFFER YOU CAUDILLO FRANCO'S GENEROSITY.**

In a letter to Moreno Gómez, Pedro Donaire, who fought in Cordoba and in Madrid before enlisting in the elite urban police force, described how he was taken in by the victors' subterfuge and false promises for returnees. He had ended the war in Barcelona and fled to France where he was treated badly by the French, and as he had had no news of his wife and children, his parents and brothers and sisters for almost three years, he decided to return to Spain. He knew that his hands were not sullied with blood and believed that if he did go back he would be welcomed with open arms by the Francoists. Together with his commanding officer, several Lieutenant Colonels and other Republican military commanders, they decided to return to their Fatherland together.

After they handed themselves in, they were taken to San Sebastian and then to Burgos where they were assigned a Military Judge. Transferred in a cattle wagon on a goods train to Barcelona, they were briefly court-martialled. One of the Colonels who was sent with them, Torres Iglesias, was immediately executed. The others were sent to a concentration camp where as prisoners of military significance, they were candidates for the death penalty.[xxxv] So much for the value of the Caudillo's word of honour.[47]

In actual fact, although the percentage of individuals implicated in 'blood' crimes was minimal as few were officially recorded as such, in more than half of Spain, the number of persons murdered by Franco's regime can be counted in the thousands in Navarra, Soria, Zamora, Galicia, Baleares, Canary Islands, and so forth. As other authors have said, the matter of 'crimes' and 'blood' was nothing more than double-talk employed by Francoists to draw the wool over the eyes of the credulous, both within and outside Spain. What the regime intended was not to eliminate non-inexistent 'common criminals' but instead to eradicate the very social foundation of the Republic - its authorities, leaders and politically-aware citizens. It intended to wipe out all ethereal manifestations of revolution, no matter how far-fetched, as an excuse for abolishing the democratic Republican regime and all that it stood for: modernity, reformism and laity. Once that had been achieved, the regime would proceed to build a New totalitarian State on the blood-soaked land, a New Spain, one that was National Catholic or National Unionist, and to restore the privileges enjoyed in the past by the military, the Church and the bourgeoisie, especially the major agrarian landowners.

Earlier, Moreno Gómez described the flood of prisoners in the North of Cordoba province at the end of March 1939, following the beginning of the 'Victory Walk'. We saw how part of the 8th Army Corps of the Republic fled towards Almadén-Puertollano-Ciudad Real. Another part filled the countless jails that were created in the towns and villages and the concentration camps in the Cordoba hills: Valsequillo, La Granjuela, Los Blázquez, Cerro Muriano and a few more. A very few scattered vehicles were able to escape at full-speed across La Mancha province, towards Alicante, only to be captured by Italian troops and interned in the bullring, in Santa Barbara castle, or in Albatera concentration camp.

The first days of the victory, Francoist Military Police spread throughout the recently conquered towns and villages, accompanied by its Information Service (SIPM) that had under its command the 'Cleansing' or 'Information' Committee, setting up regional headquarters in the larger towns and branches

---

[xxxv] Illustrates the remarkable naivety even of Republican Military Police commanders and officers who returned from France apparently unaware that all the officers of the defeated Army were interned in concentration camps where they were classified as group C prisoners and whose military significance alone ensured that they were candidates for the death penalty. Not to mention the fourth group of prisoners, lesser ranks classified as group D, who were accused of crimes for which only 2 or 3% were sent directly to the firing squad, and those classified as group B (disaffected of no political significance), who were also summarily shot.

43

in the smaller villages. In the North of Cordoba Province, the Military Police Headquarters were in Pozoblanco. In Villanueva de Cordoba, there was a branch commanded by the terrifying Lieutenant Leopoldo Mena, notorious in the village as the SIMP Lieutenant who killed several individuals by beating them with rods. In those days, the Military Police and its Information Committee were assisted by a host of unscrupulous individuals that the victory drew from the sewers of society and whose names live on in the *vox populi*. In Pozoblanco, these included: Francisco *El Muleta* Ballesteros (strongman for Antonio Herrero, a wealthy landowner), Juan Andrés *El Pichón* Dueñas (who ended up throwing himself under a train), the security guard – *Guijuelo,* and the infamous Teodoro Valero (deputy to Lieutenant Pepirillo), among others. Particularly hated in Cordoba capital was the disreputable Velasco. He, like so many others, had a miserable end. The oppressors use of this scum and then cast them aside.

On March 27 1939, the SIPM began to pack the prisoners into the most inhospitable places in Villanueva de Cordoba: the anti-aircraft shelter that had been dug in the main square, Pepe Barrón's factory yard, Romo's house on Calle Herradores and Ángel Díaz' fenced-in yard outside town, next to the Ramírez factory. The latter, a temporary holding camp, held several hundred men prisoner without any provisions for several days, except for that which some families were able to bring. The convoys for La Granjuela and for Castuera in Badajoz province left mainly from here. The permanent, albeit improvised, jails in the village were located in the Municipal Depot, Juan Herrero's house on Calle Conquista and the Fuente Vieja schools.

In Pozoblanco, May 1939, the jail at number 40, Calle Dr. Rodríguez Blanco was used first as a prison for women and later, until the end of the year, a prison for both sexes. The main prison was the Prisión del Partido, which according to the attending physician, Juan Redondo Muñoz, housed 990 prisoners in 1939. In 1940, they numbered 313 (many had been sent to the capital), and 336 in 1941, according to his records for the number of vaccinations against typhus and smallpox. His notes also mention that between 1939 and 1940, 105 Republicans were shot in Pozoblanco, an extremely low and inexact number, particularly as Dr. Redondo appears not to have taken note of the 100 prisoners who 'passed' between April and May 1939.[48]

Then began the reprisals. In Villanueva de Cordoba, on April 19, Diego - *El Chunga* took Manuel Cruz - *El Pichaco* prisoner at his house; the next morning, he appeared to have been shot, along with another five individuals, under the extra-legal Law of Fugitives that in those days was applied at full speed, right, left and centre, in the villages of Los Pedroches district. This was a first 'shock of the violence' that was to come. Not the 'improvised repression' that Sánchez Marroyo[49] mistakenly called it, because nothing that

44

occurred under Francoism after July 18 was improvised; everything had been planned, very carefully planned indeed.

The hunt and capture of the defeated continued in Villanueva. Another of the first persons arrested by El Chunga was a member of the Villalteño family, Francisco Rubio, who had returned sick from the front. El Chunga dragged him out of bed and had him taken to jail on a stretcher. El Chunga also arrested Juan Gómez Luna, brother-in-law to the Villalteño sisters. All those arrested were executed.[xxxvi] Later, El Chunga and his cohorts went for Fructuoso Prieto, who had been identified as a communist and was hiding in his house. They threatened his wife until he came out of hiding and gave himself up. They arrested socialist Cecilio Ruiz at the farm where he was working. These hatchet men then roamed the streets threatening the wives of Rojos. El Chunga went to Calle Lepanto, to the house that had belonged to the Communist Member of Parliament, Adriano Romero (imprisoned in Ciudad Real) and threatened to shoot his sister Dolores if she dared to show herself at the front door.[50] He then walked right up Francisca Cabrera in the street, shouting: "Where are your brothers? They are going to die with their boots on." Her brother Gabino Cabrera, a Captain in the 73rd Militia Battalion, was beaten to death a few days later.

The police, the Guardia Civil or the Falange in every town and village in the province waited for the returnees (both those who were travelling without documents and those who had safe-conduct passes from the concentration camps). They waited for them at the railway station and at the bus stops and took them directly to jail, without giving them time to see their families. On the day that Fernando Carrión, ex-Mayor of Peñarroya for the Popular Front, arrived, he found the military police waiting for him at the railway station. He was nevertheless able to get away and see his children, to whom he said goodbye because 'it was the last time they would meet'. He later handed himself in to the police, was sentenced to death, but managed to survive.

The well-known Joaquin Gómez Tienda, nicknamed *Transio*, a trade union leader from Baena and an altruistic and messianic person, symbol of the agrarian utopia in the South, attempted to take refuge in Úbeda (Jaén). He was soon discovered by Falangist Lieutenant Mariano Ariza who ordered him to present himself in Baena. So he did, to his misfortune. No sooner

---

[xxxvi] Visit by Moreno Gómez to the Villalteño family home on Calle Torrecampo, in Villanueva, during the 1980s, where he met with two despondent women in black, (all the men in the family had been executed after the war), who told him this story. Both have since died, taking with them the few eye-witness reports that the author was able to save, when it was still possible to do so, despite all the supposed facilities for researchers during the transition period. The silent despair of those two women was the scar they bore of the genocide.

did he arrive than he was tied up. He asked that he be allowed to see his parents whom he had not seen for three years. His request was refused. The day that he was captured was celebrated by the local fascist population, notably by a school teacher, Fernando - *El Carlista*, who organized a children's demonstration calling for his death. He was executed June 22.

The ex-Mayor of Fuente Obejuna, Agustín León, tried to hide in the village of Albó (Almeria). Four months later, he was informed upon by local Falangistas and taken to his home town where he was executed November 6 1939, under the attentive eye of the bloodthirsty SIPM Lieutenant Flores.

From these and other eye-witness accounts Moreno Gómez was able to reconstruct some interesting facts that do not appear in the written summaries of the official 'interviews', painful accounts that so clearly represent the tragic inner history of the towns during the operation for the hunt and capture of Rojos.

Undoubtedly, at the end of 1939, many returning defeated were encouraged to return home by Franco's promise of a pardon to all whose hands were not stained with blood, and that somehow, they would be able to return to their pre-war life. When Rafael Bedmar Guerrero arrived in Puente Genil, he saw to his surprise that the Guardia Civil was controlling all the exits from the railway station and that everyone coming from 'the other' Spain was being arrested. Aware that his appearance had greatly changed during the past three years, he calmly walked over to one of the guards who did not recognize him, and asked for directions to the Town Hall. He walked down the road to his home without raising suspicion.

Arriving home, nobody expected him, not his mother who broke into tears as for the past three years she did not know whether he was dead or alive. She told him that his brother Manuel had died fighting on the Jarama front, and set about preparing him a meal. Rafael had not yet finished eating when two Guardias Civiles knocked at the door. Without a bye-your-leave, they entered the house and arrested him and took him to their Headquarters. So much for the promised pardon.[51]

A brother of Adriano Romero's, Member of Parliament, Antonio Romero, walked back to Villanueva de Cordoba from the Granada front over several exhausting days. As he approached the village, he heard of the cruel treatment that the defeated were being subjected to and decided to hide on a farm. Several months later, September 24 1939, he undertook a daring cross-country trip on foot to France. He was incredibly lucky as he crossed the border November 8. He was still alive not long ago when he told Moreno Gómez his story. Like his, there are numerous unforgettable accounts of the hardships endured by the thousands of ex-combatants who travelled along roads and cross country during those months of 1939, as they made their way back to their home towns or attempted to hide as well as they could.

2. Extra-judicial economic repression. Widespread pillaging and plunder

Now follows a brief overview of the outrageous phenomenon that was the extra-judicial widespread direct seizure of belongings and pillaging that the victors engaged in from the first day of the war against the property and assets of everyone whom they classified as *disaffected*. The volume of this widespread theft is not recorded, obviously because direct theft, like torture, is never recorded. Although the recent claims of the Historic Memory Movement have been directed at the damage done to the lives of the victims, they are forgetting the damage against the property and the economies of those very same victims. It is very well to clamour for 'truth, justice and reparation', but we must not forget to call for the recovery and restitution of the victims' material property. The latter not only lost their lives, they and their families also lost their property and their savings and were reduced to begging, to suffering in abject poverty.

In cases of transitional justice (or in the absence of any such justice, as in Spain), account is also taken of the mechanisms of restitution, as we have seen in South Africa or in Germany, where the Courts ruled against enterprises that became rich from slave labour. In Spain, however, there has been an absolute impunity regarding the perpetrators of those crimes, the authors of the mass thefts and those who became rich by employing slave labour. The reality of the widespread plundering carried out by the authors of the military coup and the victors can only be very loosely inventoried through the eye witness accounts of the victims or their relatives; that is what Moreno Gómez proposed to attempt to do next.

The legion of those who persist in refuting the events that occurred under Franco and who continue to infest Spanish society and some academic circles, must know that the crime of genocide, as defined by Raphael Lemkin, does not refer solely to the crime of exterminating human groups (blood crimes) but to many other crimes as well, such as "actions taken to ruin the economic existence of the members of a community".[52] In his famous work, *Axis Rule,* Lemkin lists eight methods of genocide: "political, social, cultural, economic, biologic, physical, religious and moral."[53] Of these, Franco committed six of them in full, including the economic genocide of his political opponents. Lemkin further goes into great detail to explain his concept of genocide: as a "coordinated plan of different actions intended to provoke the disintegration of the political and social institutions, culture, national feeling, religion and separate economic existence and the destruction of personal safety, liberty, health, dignity, as well as the life of any individuals who belong to those groups". A perfect description of the great Francoist repression. Also of great concern to Lemkin was the impact of acts of genocide against life, liberty and property, [54] the three pillars of the devastation that Franco wrought, with malice aforethought, upon those he defeated.

Lemkin's expectations were shattered at the Paris Convention for the Prevention and Sanction of Genocide under United Nations resolution of 9 December 1948 (*Resolution 160 A, III*). Only 'ethical and religious' criteria were approved. France at least tried to include 'opinions' as a criterion. Following pressure from the USSR, the 'political' criterion was eliminated. Pressure within the USA delayed this country's signing the Convention until 1988. It is a known fact that genocide is the work of the states, which is why so many took care not to 'get their fingers burnt'. That which was approved, was approved, but it is Lemkin's thoughts and doctrine that interest us, as well as everything that he wanted to teach the world in terms of 'universal justice' regarding intra border massacres and acts of 'barbarism'. Therefore, to Spanish negationists of today, Moreno Gómez says: "If you care to look at the history of the civil war and its aftermath seen through Lemkin's eyes, you will find it increasingly difficult to continue to deny the Francoist crimes of genocide. Furthermore, denial *per se*, is also a form of genocide, according to Gregory H. Stanton, both the contemporary denial of the facts and the denial after the facts."[55]

Today's historians and promoters of the Historic Memory of Spain now have to do some basic field work. Curiously, oral testimonies are the only documents that can put us on the track of the Francoist plundering as we cannot expect to find this information among existing written documentation. José Francisco Luque Moreno, a historian from Montemayor, has contributed some very interesting data regarding the direct confiscation. This looting that we call 'unofficial', 'direct' or 'unregulated' extra-judicial economic repression was no more than theft by the fistful, an amassing of perceived spoils of war. An example of this are the several residents of Montemayor who returned to their homes in 1939 to discover that all their household belongings, carts and livestock had all been plundered.[56]

One of so many similar cases occurred in the village of Castrillo de la Vega, Burgos, after José Brizuela's father was assassinated and his family was forced to hand over 400 kilos of the wheat they had harvested that summer to the same people, he told Mirta Núñez, who murdered his father July 29. His 10-year-old brother and himself, aged only 7, had helped in that harvest.[57]

The humiliation of the returned, the ransacking of their homes and the pillaging of their belongings was not a sporadic event; it was widespread practice and those who fought it often suffered the consequences. Francisco

Poyatos, a Cordoba attorney, kept written records of some cases of this pillaging in the immediate post-war period such as this one in Adamuz when he was consulted by a neighbour from the Cordoba hills, to no avail:. One of these cases refers to Adamuz:

— 'I have a very handsome mule. The local boss insists that I must sell it to him. I flatly refused and he replied with threats. Can he force me to sell it to him?'

— Not at all, I said. That gentleman cannot seize your mule."

A few weeks later, he heard that the neighbour who consulted him had been executed."[58]

All legal niceties went by the board when local Falangistas in a town cast their greedy eyes on a disaffected person's goods and property. Spring 1941, Manuel Cañuelo and Juan Medina, two left-wing scum in El Viso, Cordoba, decided that they would confiscate a shepherd's hunting dog. They then followed this up by taking his sheep and his house. The shepherd, aware that harassment and beatings at the barracks were liberally applied to anyone who objected to such acts, and that individuals were freely arrested on the slightest allegation of plotting with the guerrillas in the hills, decided that he had no choice but to do just that. He grabbed his 16-year-old son and fled to the hills. This son, José Murillo, became the famous guerrilla *Comandante Rios*. Musé Murillo Alegre, his father, was later captured in 1946 and he hanged himself in Cordoba prison.[59]

Not even the clergy were exempt from temptation as was the case of a priest who lived in the same building in Madrid as Dr. Joaquim Sama Naharro, who when he was allowed out on parole from prison, was punished to 250 kms distant. The director of the prison in Cordoba, a very shrewd man, told Dr. Sama that it appeared that someone was coveting his apartment. How right he was. The greedy priest denounced Dr. Sama to the authorities and gave them some very damaging information regarding him and his family. That was all it took.[60]

In Cordoba, Dr. Sama Naharro gave Moreno Gómez an example of how even the family of a disaffected person who had been executed was not exempt from the threat of a seizure. When Manuel Fernández Contreras, a barber who was a member of the Izquierda Republicana was executed in Pozoblanco, the local fascist seized his house. Fortunately, however, as the house was in his wife's name, she was later able to get it back.

The same was not the case of Bartolomé Cabrera Peralbo, who told Moreno Gómez that one day his family was left with only the clothes on their backs after their house was ransacked, emptied and they were kicked out. He was told that they looted the house because Bartomolé himself had seized it. One day, he ran into Juan Félix *El Pichón* Dueñas and he was wearing Bartolomé's trousers and his fur jacket… His wife desperately tried to get them to return her stocking machine and her daughter Maria's sewing machine, but although she was assured they would get them back, nothing happened. Juanito Garcia told my wife that he would talk to Antonio Bautista and if he agreed, her machines would be returned to her. Nothing happened."[61]

Other times, more than greed, rivalry between village tradesmen appeared to play a part. Francisco Pino, the head of the Falange in Villanueva del Rey, Cordoba, seized his rival's bakery and soon afterwards, the other village baker who also owned a flour factory, Francisco Vizuelte, appeared shot, apparently in order to get rid of the competition.

The total lack of compassion for the families of the executed was notable and widespread. It mattered not that a widow and her children might find themselves without a roof over their heads after her property was seized. José Torralbo Rico recalls when in 1939, after his father Militia Captain Pedro *Quadrado* Torralbo Gómez was executed in Cordoba, his mother left their home in Jaén where they lived while he was on military duty, to return to her parents' house in Villanueva: de Cordoba. They left in a hurry, leaving her household goods behind. José mother managed to come to an arrangement with someone she knew who owned a truck and who agreed to help her bring back everything she had left. When they got to the house, it was empty. It had been thoroughly looted and not a handkerchief was left. Beds, clothes, blankets… they took it all. The family was not only left without anything to eat, they did not even have clothes to wear, nor beds to sleep in, nor blankets to keep them war. From then onwards, they slept on a pile of straw in his grandparents' attic.[62]

The epidemic of seizure and plundering got totally out of control as every possible event or act on the part of a disaffected family was an opportunity for graft, not to say, the outright theft of goods and property. In Pedroche, a family appealed to the head of the Falange for a reference so they could get their son out of a concentration camp. The Falangista agreed but only on the condition that they hand over a pig they had fattened for slaughter.[63] Then there was the case of Manuel Cañete Esteban, a land worker and treasurer of the Workers Centre in La Rambla who, with two other prisoners, was taken away in a truck on a *paseo* on 6 September 6. In desperation, he managed to jump out of the truck and run off, but he was caught and shot in an olive grove. The Falange seized a plot of land he owned in Montalban; his family was unable to get it back.

Beatriz Blancas Pino from Adamuz, sister to the famous guerrilla leader nicknamed *Veneno*, told how after her father's death, Señoritos from the village entered her mother's house and raided it of everything of value - several silk Chinese shawls, her father's dress suits and other valuables they said now belonged to them, including properties she had inherited from my grandmother - a three-storied house, olive groves and fields, goats and sheep. When she went to pay her taxes hoping to keep her property, they threatened to arrest her. She lost everything.[64]

Like the above tales of the pillaging and ransacking, too many others such as those of Juan *El* Escribano from Villanueva, Matías Romero Badía, also from Villanueva de Cordoba, Juan A. Velsasco Diez from El Saucejo, Josefa de la Fuente from Cabezas de San Juan and the poet Juan Ramón Jiménez, in Madrid, and so very many more, remain to be told. Sadly, as time passes, few of the older survivors are still with us and too many of their children are still afraid of talking of their families' experiences.

Fortunately, thanks to the birth of the Movement for the Historic Memory of Spain and its multiple branches throughout the country, more and more people are coming out with their memories. When Moreno Gómez attended a Historic Memory Conference in Seville November 24 2012, he was able to obtain numerous first-hand depositions of unrelenting suffering and theft. As a veteran of these conferences, Francisca Adame said: "The post-war period was much worse than the war. The books do not tell what we went through; you had to have lived it. I do not want to die without getting it all off my chest."

A television documentary filmed in several small villages of Navarra was clearly directed at calling attention to the extra-judicial economic damage suffered by Republicans and from which the authors of the coup reaped many benefits. The documentary also contains very clear oral testimonies of the suffering in Lesaka, Peralta, Murchante, Lerin, Larraga, Sartaguda, Carcar, Castejón and Burgi, first-hand depositions of great historical value. All are heart-breaking, but none quite so much as the following ones:[xxxvii]

[xxxvii] Oral testimonies recorded in the above documentary: Fernando Gurrea (Lerin), Gloria Villafranca (Peralta), Josefine Campos (Peralta), Pedro Lantz (Lesaka), Josefina Lamberro (Larraga), José Jarauta (Murchante), Justino Berrozpe (idem), Antonio Bartos (idem), Félix Moreno (Sartaguda), Julio Sesma (idem), Paz Moreno (idem), Laureano Socarro (Carcar), Josefina Jiménez (Castejón), y Vicente Lacasia (Burgi).

- "The Guardia Civil came for my father, but he had already fled. A few days later they returned at night with a truck and took my mother, who had a baby in arms, and until today...

- "They came to my house at 2 a.m. and ordered us to open the door, if not, they would break it down. My sister said that she also wanted to know what they were doing to my father. 'Right you are, get dressed!' She got dressed and went with them. We have not seen either of them since."

- "The gang went around the town, leading women whose heads they had shaved, making them shout 'Long live the whores that we are!' They took the children out of the schools so they could watch and applaud. They shaved the head of one woman whose husband was imprisoned and forced her and her young children to drink castor oil. My mother had to go begging and we had to go to the Social Welfare office and beg the soldiers for bread".

The same documentary mentions the frequent cases of forced labour in Falangista homes, villages and country houses: "People who were considered to be Rojos, who had escaped from 'the truck'[xxxviii] were housed with right-wing families or on farms..." 'You will go here, you will go there...' where they were forced to work for no pay, harvesting and threshing the grain... When leftists were sent to work at the airfield, they did so for free..."

From Barcelona, Moreno Gómez received Antonio Reseco's report on the tragic fate of his maternal grandfather and the family's possessions, in 1940.[65] Juan Rivera, who owned a brickworks in Belmez, spent the war in the Republican zone because he had been elected Deputy Mayor by one of the Republican parties. When he returned to Belmez after the victory and was arrested, he was charged with being 'a communist', to be eliminated and 'informed that all his properties should be given to deserving individuals in the village.' Juan was court-martialled in Fuente Obejuna and executed in Hinojosa del Duque May 25 1940. He was also condemned under the Law of Political Responsibilities and his family was fined 100 pesetas.

As a rule, all working families' homes, especially those who during the war had gone to the Republican zone, were looted by Francoists who seized their furniture, household goods and other belongings, as this book

---

[xxxviii] Referring to the *paseo* truck on which Falangistas loaded the men they captured and took away, usually to prison and often summarily executed under the Law of Fugitives.

repeatedly describes. Faced with all these accounts, it is incomprehensible how today, those who like to sweeten the pill when speaking of the Regime, can continue to spout their shameful, false version of the events, without ever having come into contact with the victims or survivors of the great plunder.

To make matters worse, if possible, on top of it all the Church and its defenders were always present to 'bless' the booty and lend their support to Francoists and Falangistas, totally in disregard of the Sixth Commandment *Thou shalt not kill.* They also ignored the Eighth Commandment *Thou shalt not steal.* The Ninth Commandment *Thou shalt not bear false witness against your neighbour,* of course also fell by the wayside. None of the Francoist courts-martial, especially, paid heed to the latter. The Tenth Commandment *Thou shalt not covet your neighbour's house, your neighbour's wife, nor his male servant, nor his female servant, nor his ox, nor his donkey, nor anything that is your neighbour's,* fared no better. 'National Catholicism and the Ten Commandments': what a ground-breaking subject for a Ph.D. thesis this would be.

There can be no doubt that the victors saw themselves up as legitimate proprietors of lives and property. Quite literally. Consultation of the residency registers was the order of the day. Pairs of Falangistas, municipal police or the usual opportunists, felt free to knock at every door. When someone was taken away under arrest, the looters entered his house, taking everything they wanted: pots and pans, food, beds and mattresses. When the first executed individuals fell wearing new clothes or new shoes, the members of the firing squad took their victims' clothes and shoes. When they met one of their victim's widow in the village square, they would jeer at her: 'Just you wait. Tomorrow you will suffer the same fate as your bastard husband!'.[xxxix]

3. Confiscation of Property Registers

From July 17 1936 onwards, the perpetrators of the military coup and the victors "unofficially" began an impressive amount of extra-judicial direct confiscation, the out-and-out theft of property belonging to Republican families, which was undoubtedly much greater than the "official" plundering by means of the confiscation of Property Registers[xl] during the war and the Law of Political Responsibilities, during the post-war period. Nonetheless, this was a three-pronged economic cataclysm: simple looting and ransacking by opportunists, expropriations to finance the consolidation of the New State

---

[xxxix] Tragic anecdote based on real facts, often repeated in Cordoba villages.
[xl] List of Republican individuals and corporate owners of property.

and the regime's intent to apply an economic punishment to the defeated to force them to succumb.

When addressing the question of Franco's economic annihilation of his enemies, we are again reminded of Raphael Lemkin, the great authority on crimes against humanity, who listed 'actions undertaken to ruin the economic existence of the members of a community' as one of eight types of genocide.[66] The Confiscation of Property Registers, however, was not just created for repressive purposes, but for another reason: to help finance the cost of the war.

Nowadays, there is a greater penchant for studying only the regulations and the legislation instead of supplementing this knowledge by going into the field and obtaining first-hand accounts. Of note is something that is evident: that the great looting cataclysm, from the first day of the uprising, began well before the official rules for it were laid down. In other words, the rules were published as a form of retrospect benediction. To begin with, General Queipo de Llano's extra-judicial edicts in Andalusia were published well before the normative edicts were drafted in Burgos. Queipo's <u>Edict Number 13 (August 18 1936)</u> instituted the '<u>Confiscation of property belonging to instigators of violence, propagandists and rebels</u>'. Days earlier, the <u>Civil Government of Cordoba (August 10 1936) published a list of Entities</u> (union, artistic, pharmaceutical, recreational, etc.) '<u>that are voluntarily disbanding themselves' and will be putting their property at the disposal of the Army of Spanish Salvation</u>, as the Governor sarcastically put it.[67]

Those were the days of uncontrolled pillaging and endless 'patriotic' subscriptions that Moreno Gómez described in his 2008 book.[68] It was not just the humble families of the disaffected who suffered but also the regime's loyal supporters who were continuously called to donate gold and jewels, make multiple patriotic subscriptions, adopt the one single dish meal a week and the day 'without dessert' regimes, and so forth. An outburst of calls for donations that were unsupportable for some and ruinous for others. Those were the days when the Nationalist military were the protagonists of the great robbery and many of its leaders made their fortune during those tragic years. Just where did all those donations of gold and jewels, monies and seized belongings go?

With <u>Edict number 34 dated September 11 1936,</u> Queipo de Llano ordered that the money and property obtained in the recently-occupied towns and villages must be handed over to the military authorities. Property belonging to individuals who were considered liable under Franco's Edict of War, was to be preventatively seized by the military authorities. Consequently, as the rebellious troops advanced, their successes in the field resulted in the thorough looting of homes abandoned by fugitive Republicans. Here again,

Queipo de Llano acted extra-judicially in advance of the Burgos edict that was only published as <u>National Defence Council Decree number 108 on September 13</u>.

The entire 'official' Francoist pillaging setup derives from this Decree 108, according to which the seizure of property would apply to all the belongings of the Republican political parties and of trade unions in general (who owned a substantial amount of real estate) and most especially to all disaffected persons or entities opposed to the Movement. Management of the plundered goods was entrusted to the military officers involved in the revolt and who were granted full powers over lives and property. In fact, Decree 108 set the official stamp on this means of financing the war, the building of the New State and of enrichening many individuals. Decree 108 was later amended and expanded as <u>Decree-Law of January 10 1937</u>, which created the Central and the Provincial Committees for the Administration of Seized Property.

The self-styled 'Viceroy' of Andalusia, General Queipo de Llano, did not cease his flood of edicts for expropriations. Edict 29 dated 2 September ordered the local Guardia Civil commanders to post a list of the names of the 'instigators of the present rebellion', with a view to freezing their bank accounts. In <u>Edicts 49 dated November 5 and 57 dated December 29</u>, Queipo attempted to be as specific as possible regarding the targets of his pillaging by referring to militancy, sophistry, political and ideological activism,[69] in other words, the entire gamut of Republican action.

José Francisco Luque Moreno has studied some interesting aspects of the great theft in the village of Montemayor under the so-called Confiscation of Property Edicts, where the seizure of property also included the revocation and holding back of all kinds of payments owed to the individuals on the register. For example, at least 20 mules were seized in the village, with the approval of the village Military Command and the provincial Agricultural Recovery Committee, and handed over to the town council who took them to Mingo Hijo farm where they were sold at auction in September 1939. There was the case of Gabriel Gómez Marín, arrested at the beginning of the municipal detentions, who lost the contents of his house in Calle Feria, the grain he had harvested and his land. He was able to recover part of his property during the post-war period, thanks to some influential family contacts.[70]

The Confiscation of Property Edicts in Montemayor affected no less than 428 individuals (many more than the Law of Political Responsibilities that in this village was only applied to 71 persons). From December 1936 onwards, the local military commander was ordered to take charge of all the material goods belonging to individuals on the register: beds, tables, chairs, mattresses, clothes, sundry belongings and sewing machines, as well as all livestock. Large warehouses were built to store the booty. The little that escaped storage, was sold at public auction. Palma Garrido, a private tutor who owned a tobacconist's shop, provided one of hundreds of examples of this expropriation of property: he was placed on the confiscation list, his shop was seized by the local authorities and given it to the widow of a Guardia Civil.

An August 21 telegram from the Civil Governor ordered the Mayor and the Commander of the Guardia Civil in Montemayor to seize the livestock on the farms that had been split up under the Agricultural Reform. October 8, the same Civil Governor asked for a list of all seizable rural properties. 33 orders for seizure were issued. At the end of the war, when the returnees arrived in Montemayor only very few of the legal owners were able to recover their property which they did with great difficulty and over a long period of time.[71]

The case of Natividad Rodrigo, daughter of a couple from Burgos who were executed in Villanueva de Odra on September 2 1936 has only recently become known. They had been taken in a raid of 18 persons who were said to have 'disappeared', leaving behind three children, including Natividad who was 5 years old at the time. May 1937, her father, Restituto Rodrigo was ordered to appear before the Confiscation of Property Court, although he had been dead for eight months. The procedure for legitimizing the looting of his property had begun: first, he was given ten days to appear before the Court. Meanwhile, the authorities took out information regarding his political behaviour from the mayor, the municipal judge and the parish priest. The reports were inevitably negative: 'he was a leftist', 'he participated in a First of May rally', 'he voted for the Popular Front at the last elections', 'he expressed himself against the Movement and he was considered to be a member of the Socialist Party'. The next step was the valuation of the property, which in his and his wife's case consisted of one house, several farms, a market garden and all kinds of household goods, valued at 1,279 pesetas. All the property was embargoed in 1939 and given to a relative who had meanwhile become a member of the Falange.[72]

These were the usual procedures for the confiscation of property by the aforementioned Central Committee for the Administration of Confiscated Property (Decree-Law of 10 January 1937) and its Provincial Committees, presided by the Civil Governor, with an army officer as prosecuting judge. In this way, Republicans not only lost their lives or their freedom, they also lost their belongings that went to swell the pockets of the victors.

Rich pickings were the bank accounts that were confiscated or frozen. According to Central Committee data, between July 1936 and March 1938, the Francoists filed 75,000 indictments against persons whose bank accounts were ordered to be attached, in 15 provinces alone. Another 100,000 indictments were expected from another 20 provinces.[73] Equally valuable was the real estate that was seized from Republican political parties and syndicates and that usually ended up in the hands of the Falange (more than 33 buildings in Cordoba province).[74] The management of the entire setup was always left to the military.

This mass confiscation of real estate and other assets, farms, industries and businesses, was very profitable for the military raptors. In Toledo, for example, half of the rural property was confiscated.[75] Many lowlifes supported the new regime solely because it enabled them to steal businesses, trade, property and personal belongings, even if killing was involved, as in Fernán Núñez (Cordoba), where Fernando Valle Luque and his wife Maria Antonia Jiménez were murdered August 16 1936 for their shop. This wartime chapter about the wanton confiscations is just one that illustrates how under Francoism, military coup, Crusade and armed robbery all come together as one.

According to Barragán Moriana, in Cordoba province, Montemayor was the village that suffered the most from the Confiscation of Property Edict, which he reports as 410 indictments, although Luque Moreno raises this to 428. This was followed by La Rambla, with 300; Fernán Nuñez, with 286; Espiel, 262. 16 Cordoba villages suffered more than 100 indictments each.[76]

The Cordoba Provincial Committee for Confiscations was presided by the Civil Governor, Valera Valverde, a reactionary who had an intriguing history during the Republic, as he was implicated in the 1932 failed uprising against the government led by José Sanjurjo. The Prosecutors for the military were: Clemente Heras, Pedro Herrera, Antonio J. Rueda Roldán and Luis Estrada Pérez.

Antonio Barragán Moriana unearthed the early confiscation proceedings against several distinguished Cordoba Republicans, such as Antonio Jaén Morente, Member of Parliament for the Popular Front, prosecuted with a devilish rhetoric by Pedro Herrera on November 2 1936: '... resident in this capital and cursed son of the same, Antonio Jaén Morente, resident at Calle Juan de Mena number 6...'. Also indicted was Antonio Jaén's personal secretary, the physician Mariano Moya Fernández who accompanied Antonio Jaén when he was appointed Ambassador to Lima (Peru) in 1933. Mariano Moya was saved by a miracle, despite having been indicted and banished to Burgos in 1936. Judge Enrique Poole Escat, was another of those prosecuted because they were 'friends of Jaén Morente and frequented his office, as well as followers of the politics of the Republican Left'. The list of those indicted under the Confiscation of Property edict was later expanded to include the elite of Cordoba Republicans, upper middle class, middle class and notables:

attorneys, physicians, professors, political leaders and so on, such as Rafael Castejón (also banished from Cordoba in 1936), Juan Díaz del Moral and many others.[77]

When the <u>Law of Political Responsibilities was published February 9 1939</u>, all the indictments under the Confiscation of Property Edict pending at the end of the war were transferred to the jurisdiction of the new law and would continue to be prosecuted until the LPR was repealed December 12 1966.

The grand finale of the victory celebrations was illuminated by these repressive precedents. More than ever, from the end of the war onwards, the victorious Francoists would assume their ownership of lives and property and implement a new repression, a form of multi-repression that ensured that the defeated would be hassled from all sides. In addition to the aforementioned wartime economic repression and the one that was expected during the post-war, life became insufferable for the defeated who were surrounded by a tremendous vacuum. The outlook for those who belonged to the so-called other half of Spain was so bad that all who could, emigrated.

The end of the war also marked the creation of yet another instrument with which Francoists would humiliate the Spanish people: the mortification that was forced upon the prisoners who had been detained en masse and who packed the several concentration camps in Cordoba and Castuera, and their families who had to seek references of good behaviour in order to obtain the safe-conduct pass without which a prisoner would not be set free. Each reference had to be signed by at least two right-wing 'guarantors' of a prisoner's character. The safe-conduct pass was compulsory for everyone who left his home for a walk, who travelled or even left the camp to go and work in the neighbouring fields. Once, when in a fit of rage the Falange representative confiscated the inmates' passes, harvesters and olive growers could not go out into the fields and these local labourers lost the few days of casual work they had. Furthermore, even the simplest bureaucratic act required the presentation of a *good conduct certificate*, signed by the parish priest, a representative of the local Falange and the municipal police or local Guardia Civil post, the three power brokers of National Catholicism, the National Syndicalist Revolution that swept the country. In other words, unadulterated social control. Francoists believed that half of the population was a suspicious mass that had to be quarantined. Not for days, but during years.

There now arose another major problem, the one faced by the young men who were being conscripted into the military service and who had to obtain a favourable classification from the Local Recruitment Boards whose primary mission was to define the recruits' character in light of the

Glorious National Movement. After a usually cursory examination, the young men were classified as either loyal or disaffected. The latter were forced to purge themselves of all leftist tendencies by serving in one of the *Disciplinary Battalions of Worker Soldiers*. The Enlistment Boards comprised a President (the Mayor), a representative of the Falange, another ex-captive, a representative of the military authorities, and two manual labourers. The supreme authority was always military. Not only had the New Spain had been converted into one huge prison, it had now also become one huge military barracks.

In additional to the usual general harassment, the defeated population were now faced with the drama of how to survive in a clearly hostile environment, which led to multiple desperate situations (suicide, emigration, begging). Those whose names had been placed on a blacklist were forbidden to work and were excluded from everything. There was no place for the defeated in Franco's Spain. All of this formed the kaleidoscope of the multi-repression, a form of genocide that was not simply limited to bloodshed, killing and physical destruction, but especially directed at propelling placing half a country, a complete social class and an entire defeated sector into the eye of a doctrinal hurricane. Multi-repression consisted of much more: of eliminating almost all due process of law, all the chances of survival, the right to food and the right to work, of depriving the defeated of their freedom and throwing them into jail, denying them their Fatherland and forcing them into exile, abolishing the rights of parents over their children, besieging the defeated on all sides and destroying every glimmer of hope. From the moment the military uprising began July 17 1936, ethnic cleansing and extermination in Spain could be summarized as the exclusion of half the Spanish population, not just physically but in every other possible way, solely because of the people's political ideas and social standing.

4. Hunger as an Instrument of Oppression and Genocide

Returning to the doctrine of Raphael Lemkin, the father of the theory of genocide, and the formulate his condemnation of barbarous crimes (i.e., genocide), among the several criminal features to which he draws attention, he includes 'actions to ruin the economic survival of the oppressed'.[78] He later added 'economic genocide'[79] and drew attention to the elemental rights to 'life, liberty and property'.[80] If Moreno Gómez repeatedly refers to Lemkin, it is because nowadays negationists obstinately continue to refuse to admit to the several aspects of Francoist criminality. Furthermore, when it comes to introducing extreme hunger as a feature of the defeated's existence, something more sinister becomes apparent. Hunger was an example of modern Fascist methods for obliterating an individual's personality, a prime instrument of psychological and ideological destruction.

From time immemorial, oppressors have known that one of the most effective instruments for breaking down a people's moral integrity, perhaps more than taking away their freedom or their life, is to reduce them to extreme poverty and destitution. A person who finds himself totally insolvent automatically becomes bereft of all ideology and is unable to think of anything else other than his sustenance. Extreme poverty is an instrument for humiliating and controlling people. The collected letters from the great poet, Miguel Hernández, subjected to starvation in jail, especially in 1941, only mention food, he writes begging letters to all and sundry, he only thinks of food, and never refers to either poetry or literature that were his passion.[81]

Following the Nationalist military victory, the defeated learned what hunger truly is, in its most literal meaning, as we shall see later in Chapter 6 when Moreno Gómez addresses the lethal hunger in Francoist prisons. Meanwhile, Francoists had become the owners of lives and property and they forced their victory on the population with successive extra-judicial bouts of confiscation and pillaging.

There is a terrible economic reality that studies of the post-war period have paid little attention to: the abolishment of the Republican currency and its extremely serious economic consequences. With victory, Franco enacted the worst of all possible penalties: with a single stroke of his pen, the population was left penniless. No less than 13,251 million pesetas of Republican currency, plus another 10,356 million on deposit at banks, were declared null and void. A sum total of 23,607 million pesetas was no longer legal tender. [82] In one fell swoop, the defeated were left them without a centavo and left to beg. This marked the beginning of the abject poverty and indescribable hunger that, aggravated by many other adverse circumstances, would torture the defeated population.[xli]

The repressive methods of absolute impoverishment were widely practiced by European Fascists during the 1930s and 1940s. Suffice to recall the skeletal images of the Nazi victims, transported by machines like so many bales of hay, to the mass graves. These skeletal victims of Hitler and of Franco remain a permanent burden on History's conscience, if one accepts that

---

[xli] In order to give the reader an idea of the values in terms of the 1936 peseta and the extent of the economic consequence, the 2017 USD value is indicated in brackets at the current exchange rate. The peseta values were converted into USD as 1$=9.41 PTA in 1939 and into their equivalent USD amount in 2017, at https://,dollartimes.com/inflation/inflatio. php?amount=1&year=1939.

History has a conscience. For those who do not, was penury just yet another stratagem like so many others, all that was done to further the interests (*real politik*) of the powers-that-be. It is interesting to note that the tragic year of 1941 is notorious as the year when the greatest number of persons died from starvation, both in Nazi concentration camps and in Franco's prisons. The Jewish case and the Spanish case (the one that nobody talks about) coincided in 1941. During this year, hunger as an instrument of oppression and genocide caused inconceivable suffering in Spain and in Germany. Nazis and Francoists, fraternally united by a common denominator, *mutatis mutandis*.

In addition to the genocide in Francoist prisons, hunger became one of the horses of the apocalypse that Franco released upon all the defeated in Spain. It was not enough for the dictator to defeat his opponents; they also had to bite the dust, emaciated by hunger, yet another a link in the chain of humiliation to ensure that his opponents would not raise their heads 'for thirty years'. The repressive poverty began with *the total confiscation of property* (direct seizures, sentences for the confiscation of property and the Law of Political Responsibilities), followed by the *absolute exclusion from employment* whereby the defeated were prohibited from accepting any public job, from applying for teaching positions, from owning any kind of businesses (considered spoils of war by the victors), not forgetting the *blacklists* by which anyone who had not humiliated himself sufficiently according to the strictures of National Catholicism, could not even obtain work as a day labourer.

Considerable work remains to be done to quantify the total number of dead from starvation in Franco's Spain. I can, however, affirm that every town and village in Cordoba province, without exception, has lists of persons who 'died from starvation', in varying numbers - half a dozen here, a dozen or more there, depending on the location - during the entire post-war period and especially 1945-1946 – the 'years of hunger'. Moreno Gómez regrets that when he was doing field work in Cordoba in 1978 and 1979, he only took note of violent deaths, neglecting to note these side effects of the repression. Nevertheless, Moreno Gómez delves into the memories from his own childhood that remind him of those tragic days, as do others who come from country towns. He remembers the great many poor who begged on the streets in every town, a phenomenon that only began to disappear during the 1960s. He remembers the great many people who roamed the fields searching for acorns and all kinds of oddly edible greens - hedge mustard, wild spinach, purslane, thistles, cress, leeks, nettles, dandelions… and vegetables - turnips, radishes, beans, vetch, in an attempt to stave their hunger. All of this was forbidden by the Guardia Civil who posted guards at the entrances to the villages. They searched everyone who arrived, confiscated their sacks, bags or back-packs and gave them a beating. Those victims were the 'itinerant carpet sellers'[xlii] of yesteryear, society's poor that governments like to exhibit to 'show' that there exists a rule of law.

Moreno Gómez recalls his childhood in Villanueva de Cordoba:

"We who come from country villages, I repeat, have the good fortune of possessing memories, memories that are surely alien to city people. I still have my ration card, dated 1948. I am not trying to teach anybody anything, more so because my personal memory dates from the 1950s and not the terrible 1940s.

Still, I remember that my family, of modest means, never had desserts after meals. A box of oranges was only taken to the farms on days when the pigs were slaughtered. The rest of the time there was no dessert other than what we could gather from our orchard, almost always only in summer (plums, figs or watermelons). It was much worse for anyone who did not have an orchard. In the Fall, we had quince. Other fruit, such as bananas, were an unattainable luxury. We sometimes sold old tools to be able to buy some bananas. ~

What can I say about milk? Milk in cartons was an invention of the 1960s. In my home, when the cow or the goat gave birth, we had milk; if not, which was most of the year, there was none. More peculiar still was the matter of coffee, which people today will remember was known as 'good coffee' and that in my house was only purchased on the days of the pig slaughter or when the sewing woman came. The rest of the year we drank 'coffee' made from toasted barley and was nothing more than black, hot water. During the war and post-war years, everybody drank barley coffee for breakfast, the same as in the prisons. It is hard to imagine this today, in these days of a consumer society.

If this is what I can dredge from my childhood memories of the 1950s, almost during the 'fat cow' days of the Regime, what can it have been like immediately after the war? If a child of the 1950s can remember the pain of that terrible austerity, even when his family fortunately had some

---

[xlii] The expression 'itinerant carpet sellers' alludes to the droves of North African indigent travellers who went from door to door in Southern Europe during the 1960s and 70's, selling cheap homemade carpets as a way of making a living.

land and an orchard, what kind of miserable existence was it like for all those who had not even the smallest plot?

I remember often being told of people who died from starvation: their bellies swelled from eating boiled greens without olive oil, and they died. If I have brought up these snippets of memory it is because I sometimes read dissertations written by young people of today on the daily life under Francoism and they sound like travel postcards from Lapland, not fascist Spain."

A recent eye-witness account of the first years of the 1940s and halfway through the decade, describes the hunger in the villages of Cordoba as a public disaster, at least among the people who were furthest from the Regime and as such, did not share in the victory pie. During the 1940s, the Campiña countryside of Cordoba, on the left bank of the Guadalquivir, with single crop grain farms, had very few left-overs and even less to trade, contrary to the hillsides north of Cordoba, with its meadows, oak groves, abundance of orchards and vegetable gardens, green fields and fruit. Because of this, during that decade, families from villages in the Campiña would walk for days until they reached villages in the hills, and knock on the doors of huts and farms, begging for food. Around 1946, a family, possibly from Villa del Rio, arrived at the old Venta Velasco, Villanueva de Cordoba, farm, and knocked at the swineherds' hut where Petra Romero Huertas lived. The family of strangers included the father and a young woman of some eighteen years of age, thin as a rake, almost naked as she only wore a humble overall. Petra Romero asked them in and gave the young woman some underwear and other clothing. The young woman's appearance was extremely pitiful. They left, saying that they were heading for Conquista. Petra Romero asked them to stop by the hut on their return. A few days later, they did, but the father was alone: his daughter had died and he had buried her in Conquista. I went to the Civil Registry but could find no record of her death. Perhaps it was not recorded before the family returned to its home in Campiña. [83] That is how one died of starvation in Franco's Spain. Ana Tudela reports that in the province of Jaen, the infant mortality rate in 1942 was as high as 30%, because of the chronic hunger and malnutrition.[84]

Many villages set up hostels, ramshackle buildings that housed dozens and dozens of destitute families who tried to live as they best could, combing the countryside or begging for alms. Villanueva de Cordoba sheltered a great many poor families in Los Bretes (a group of schools)S during the 1940s. The villagers considered 'the groupies', as they called them, to be outcasts.

Franco even invented concentration camps for those who had been banished from towns and for beggars. The years of 1941-1942 (the years of the Spanish Auschwitz), saw the creation of the Las Arenas (La Algaba, Seville) concentration camp, that housed some 300 prisoners employed in digging a canal between La Algaba and Guillena and other slave labour, of which 144 died of starvation. They were not shot. They simply starved to death.[85]

Forcing the defeated to endure the most absolute poverty was a major operation as Franco wanted to ensure that defeated Spain should be left with empty stomachs, because when a person is starving, he thinks of nothing else except food. With hunger as a tool, one can eliminate all aspirations, abolish all ideals, obliterate all political thoughts. All this embellished with a cynical paternalism reinforced by total humiliation, leads human beings to believe that their very survival is a gift from the tyrant. The humiliated give thanks to the dictator, not just for the crust of bread they receive, but also because he has allowed them to live. The life of the defeated becomes the victors' act of charity. When State-programmed violence, fear and poverty appear, it is Fascism rearing its ugly head.

This was a campaign to harass and humble the defeated, to force them to pass under the Francoist gallows of charity and alms-giving. The Falange and the Church behaved as if they were the maestros of that terrible, out-of-tune orchestra, through Social Welfare, Catholic Action, Delegate Committees for the Imprisoned, etc. At the same time that they dispensed charity, they increased their power over the Rojos. For all of these reasons, the great economic repression, expressed as poverty and destitution, gave the victors magnificent results in terms of the social control of the defeated.[86]

We are reminded of the great misery of the people, when we recall the story of the ex-Mayor of Villanueva de Cordoba's children, forced to beg in the streets without their mother knowing, whilst their father, Julián Caballero, fought the rebels as a guerrilla leader in the Sierra Morena. Just this image of the impoverished family of a man who had played such an important role during the Second Republic was sufficient to fill all the local National Catholic leaders with delight. The destitute families in the North of Cordoba invented a solution to help them care for their children: they fostered them out to neighbouring farms where they would tend the livestock in exchange for food and perhaps, some clothing and shoes also.

There was a counterpoint to the people's miserable existence during the post-war that was as picturesque as it was dramatic: the *estraperlo*, or black market, which in turn was a consequence of the rationing. A black marketeer could either operate as a wholesaler or as a small retailer. The poor frequently went to the latter as their only salvation. That rationing could not provide sufficient food for everyone is demonstrated by the fact that the consumption of black market staples such as sugar, vegetables and olive oil increased three-fold during that period. As expected, this activity was prohibited under an October 23 1941 law, with punishments that went as far as the death penalty, but as usual, the truth of the matter was that those who bore the brunt of the repression were the small retailers and very rarely, the wealthy wholesalers. On October 27 1941, a military court was set up in each province to prosecute crimes of hoarding, hiding and sale of products at exorbitant prices. There were cases where some black marketers were condemned to three months' service in Forced Labour Battalions. In October 1940, the government created the Tax Inspectorate, to pursue black market crimes and hoarding, but it was unsuccessful.

A ministerial Decree of May 14 1939, created the ration card that was first given to the family as a whole. The purpose was to enable families to acquire rationed staples at a set price, which they could do only at the specific shop to which they had been assigned.[87] It became rapidly evident that there were insufficient rations to meet the demand, which gave rise to the quaint method of a black market where people paid exorbitant prices for their goods. For example, a kilo of sugar that cost 1.90 pesetas when rationed, could cost as much as 20 pesetas on the black market. A litre of olive oil, 3.75 pesetas when rationed, could cost up to 30 pesetas on the black market. What happened then? The needy became black marketers who traded in a very small way, constantly pursued by the Guardia Civil. Men and women would take advantage of short train runs to go and find goods to sell. On their return, before they reached the stations where the Guardia Civil was always waiting, they would toss their sacks out of the windows and later go back and pick them up. If they were caught by the Guardia Civil, not only would they lose their goods but they would be given a good beating. There were identical controls at the entrances to each town and village for those who went into the fields to forage for food. It frequently happened that the wives of Guardias Civiles would keep part of the goods their husbands seized and do some black market trading of their own with persons in their confidence. The municipal police also participated in this curious trade. Sometimes, they would come to an agreement with the black marketers and share goods that could be seized. The following sign was posted in one of the cemeteries: "If you are not a black marketer, Falangista or clergyman, I'll be waiting for you here this winter". From the heights of power, the Regime's leaders also lined their pockets.

People would store goods with which to speculate and so would merchants, so that when the tax inspectors came by there was a mad rush to cover up or hide products; even so, the inspectors themselves could be easily bought. Tobacco was rationed on June 9 1940 and quickly entered the black market. Moreno Gómez remembers watching his father sow tobacco in the vegetable patch, next to the pimentos, and then dry it in a room on the farm. There was a special ration card for tobacco, for males. There was another ration card for bread. Milk became a luxury good, to such a degree that <u>Decree of June 16 1943</u> banned the consumption of milk in cafés, bars and restaurants. It was like a pharmaceutical product. It was no wonder that the prison staff stole milk that was destined for the Cordoba Provincial Prison by the jug, as they did other foodstuff. At the end of the day, the prisoners were only left with rotten turnips.

An <u>April 5 1943 Decree</u> officially created the individual ration card, although this had been in existence since the previous year, according to a newspaper's sarcastic message to hungry Spain: 'The individual ration card will prevent the wastage of three million rations'.[88] At the time, there were 27 million ration cards in Spain, one for each member of the population. As so it went for this wretched country, resigned to bread and onions, until the end of May 1952 when rationing was abolished and the market for staples was liberalized.

In Cordoba, in 1941 the Civil Government published the regulations and prices for rationed goods almost every week in the press. Black market goods arrived in Cordoba mainly by train, hidden in the locomotives by the engine drivers. Generally speaking, the majority of the engine drivers collaborated with the black marketers in the trains that arrived at dawn. They knew that many poor people, war widows and proscribed individuals of all kinds, could only survive thanks to this trade. Before the trains entered Cordoba, the drivers would throw the goods outside the windows for the black marketers who were waiting at previously agreed spots (Las Margaritas level crossing, La Residencia bridge, in Cercadilla, Viaducto, Santos Pintados, etc.) to pick up. The station itself was strictly controlled by the Guardia Civil who, climbed on the train and searched it thoroughly before passengers were allowed off. Those who were caught with food were arrested and taken to the Tax Inspectorate where their goods were seized, they were fined and mistreated (head shaving and doses of castor oil were the order of the day). Although all this could provide excellent subject matter for today's investigative cinema, Francoism and all its cesspits are mostly ignored by Spanish film-makers. There is still a lot of fear.

In Cordoba capital, one of those who hunted black marketers was Moreno, a municipal policeman who specialized in catching those who brought goods in by train, and who sewed panic in the queues for rationed goods by confiscating women's ration cards for the slightest reason. Likewise, Ballesteros, a corporal in the Guardia de Assalto. Mothers with their children queued since dawn, taking charcoal burners with them to keep warm.

Ballesteros would appear, confiscate the ration card from whoever he felt like, and use it for himself. If a woman refused to hand it over, he would beat her to a pulp; if a merchant protested, Ballesteros would threaten to close his shop. In the case of female black marketers, he would be even harsher: he would arrest them, beat them up, fine them and most especially confiscate everything they had, which he kept for himself. On other occasions, if a woman wished to avoid complications, she would be forced to choose between giving him half of her goods or have sex with him. If she refused, he would have her arrested, shave her head, strip her naked, purge her with castor oil and send her down the street. He particularly liked to have sex with minors, for which he was disciplined.[89] Another Guardia Civil in Cordoba, nicknamed *El Dino,* terrorized female black marketers whom he took to the La Calahorra post, purged them with castor oil and took their goods. He applied all sorts of torture to the men. In the middle of this Francoist *Patio de Monipodio,* or conglomerate of persons with unlawful intentions, there appeared a grotesque 'benefactor' in the person of Ramón Risueño Catalán, Civil Governor and sworn enemy of the black marketers in Cordoba. Because he ordered that the goods that were seized should be shared among the beggars and the needy and because he did not beat the female black marketers or dose them with castor oil, these women began to think of him as a saint.

The same corruption and outrages repeated themselves in town after town. Still, the persecution must not have been considered all that important as the press only published the so-called 'crimes of hoarding' that were punishable by death and where the sentence could not be reduced by hard labour, such as that of the two individuals who were arrested in Montemayor for 'contraband in olive oil and chick peas'.[90] At the end of 1941, Nicolás Ramírez was arrested in Peñaroya after he was found to have an illegal warehouse containing 250 Litres of olive oil that he was selling at 9 pesetas per Litre, when the legal rate was 3.70 pesetas.[91] Nonetheless, the most widespread black market activities in Southern Spain involved the major landowners who produced wheat and olive oil. Although the entire harvest had to be declared to the National Wheat Board, they only declared part and diverted the remainder to the black market, where it was sold at much higher prices. It is calculated that in all of Spain, from 1940 to 1955, 28.45% of all the wheat grown and at least 15% of all the olive oil produced were sold on the black market.[92] In Cordoba, the local press published a scandalous report for all of Spain, whereby 405.268 prosecutions for black marketing, mostly wheat and olive oil, were filed up to October 1943; 50% of all individuals charged were found guilty and the remainder absolved. Moreno Gómez has fond memories of going as a child with my mother to buy some olive oil at a black marketer's house: we were shown to a back room where our two small pitchers were filled.

Black marketeering may have been a popular ploy for alleviating the misery, but nothing in any way as severe as the great corruption of the Regime, which few have studied. As Ramón Garriga said, jail and the firing squad are reserved in Francoist Spain as punishments for all crimes, with a single exception: financial scandals involving the State. Franco, whose conscience is burdened with the execution of professors and physicians for the sole reason that in their youth they were Freemasons, has tolerated his associates', including some of his closest collaborators, trafficking in the well-being of the population.' [93]

In conclusion, and returning to the subject of misery in general, the exploitation of poverty under Francoism is nothing more than one of the defining elements of Fascism: 'total misappropriation', both material and moral, to quote Ricard Vinyes.[94] If we speak of Francoist prisons, total misappropriation was practiced to the full and targeted three fundamental needs: food, hygiene and health. Nazism added a last, terribly symbolic, feature, nudity. Skeletal and naked, the human being retains a single possession: the breath of life. Franco contented himself with shaving his prisoners' heads, but he made them die of hunger in droves, especially in 1941. 'Misappropriation', or in other words, moral and material confiscation of food, hygiene and health, was practiced by Francoism in the prisons and on the streets, always with a view to destroying the identity of the defeated, their personality and their dignity. A defeated person was either transformed or eliminated. This was one of the several features that linked Francoism to European Fascism.

5.   The Law of Political Responsibilities (LPR).

The instigators of the coup and their accomplices especially, were chiefly motivated by two events: the proclamation of the Second Spanish Republic on April 14 1931 and the triumph of the Left in the February 16 1936 legislative elections. Francoism was dedicated to erasing those events from the Annals of History and wiping all reference to them from the face of the Earth.

When Franco signed the Law of Political Responsibilities (LPR) February 9 1939, he sent a clear sign to the Republicans of what was coming. To begin with, this law confirmed that there was not even the remote possibility of an armistice, a fact that would prove to be such a disappointment to Colonel Casado and all those who were blinded by the Caudillo's supposed 'generosity of spirit'. From that moment onwards, there could be no other prospect than a future of unrestrained reprisals and revenge.

To begin with, the LPR was another turning of the screw in the punishment and reprisals against Franco's political opponents. Secondly, it provided an impetus to his determination that no one should escape the strictures of the New State. Thirdly, it was a reminder and an example, in case anyone had not yet taken due note of the wartime imprisonments, tortures and firing squads. Fourth, it provided a doubly effective mechanism for obtaining funds for building the New Totalitarian State at the expense of 'all those who contributed to create or aggravate subversion…'. Effective retroactively to October 1934 (Article 1), the LPR was an unacceptable judicial aberration in that actions that were legal until then, were now penalized, posthumously if necessary. Lastly, Article 3 of the LPR ratified all the prosecutions and expropriations under the Confiscation of Property decrees.

Under the new law, everything was arbitrary and extra-judicial, not to say illegal. The LPR was designed to demolish, punitive and economically, the very bowels of the Republican half of Spain, by ascribing a kind of collective guilt to "all those who contributed to the triumph of the Popular Front in the 1936 elections; those who later supported and defended it, and lastly, who once the Nation had taken up arms in July 1936, tried and continue to try to create obstacles to our National Movement (…). 'Clearly, there was nobody like the Spanish Right able to use our language quite so cynically as a weapon of mass destruction.[95]

Up to 17 supposed political responsibilities were identified in the LPR, some in specific detail, others so totally indiscriminately that they could be applied to almost everybody.[96] Those who had fled Spain were given a deadline of only two months to return and turn themselves in. Three types of penalties were set forth: a) economic sanctions; b) possible exile or banishment; and c) possible disentitlement. In other words, extreme sanctions could entail the confiscation of all a victim's property and he could even be stripped of his citizenship.

At first, prosecution for political responsibilities was based on sentences handed down by courts martial. A summary of the sentence was sent first to the Regional Political Responsibility Courts and then to the Provincial Courts (Special Hearings or Courts). Prosecution could also be initiated on the basis of denunciations from private individuals or Francoist authorities. The procedure was grounded on three principle reports: from the Mayor (usually the local head of the Falange Española), the head of the local Guardia Civil post and the parish priest.) That the latter report is included is particularly significant as it demonstrates the active role of the Church in the repressive machine, a truly serious matter regarding an institution that preached a mission of fraternity and charity to all people, without exceptions. In reality, the Inquisition was riding again, this time on the back of Francoism. Together with other features, this was National Catholicism.

The LPR was another of the New State's wide-reaching phenomena against the masses, one that was predominantly dedicated to repression. Francoism's sole expertise was in the field of military disciplinary mechanisms: mass imprisonments, mass court-martials and mass Political Responsibility judicial procedures. This explains the unmitigated chaos in processing the three phenomena. There had to be continuous reprieves in the jails; the courts-martial were overwhelmed (in the 1st Military Region, Madrid, alone, 300,000 individuals were tried, even though many charges were collective); and then there was the processing of the indictments under the LPR, another typical log jam of the times, which is why there had to be an end to the indictments, as they did on April 13 1945.

Needless to say, the military were the leaders of all these repressive initiatives. The government created the National Court of Political Responsibilities (presided by Enrique Suñer), 18 Regional and their respective Provincial PR Courts. For each court and likewise, the Court for the Repression of Freemasonry and Communism, there were always three Presiding Judges: a military commander, a civilian magistrate and a high-ranking member of the Falange. These courts, contrary to the practice in Germany and Italy, were always subordinate to the military, with the consequent feelings of resentment among the judiciary.

An important legal date was the publication of the <u>Order of September 23 1939</u>, by which all the cheap housing belonging to leftist cooperatives became the property of the National Housing Institute. Equally, if not more surprising, was the handing over to the Falange, of all the buildings belonging to trade unions (more than 33 buildings in the province of Cordoba alone).[97]

Because of the chaos resulting from the back-up in prosecutions under the LPR, that law was amended on <u>19 February 19 1942</u> so that only financially solvent individuals would be arraigned, leaving out all those whose property was worth less than 25,000 pesetas [$45,820]. The effect of this was immediate: 75% of all indictments were withdrawn between 1944 and 1945.[98] The reform of this law also lightened the load of the Seville Regional Provincial PR Court, which handled all the LPR prosecutions, as these cases were transferred to the Provincial Courts. In January 1943, the Cordoba Provincial PR Court dealt with no less than 10,500 indictments (distributed among the 17 Magistrate Courts of the judicial districts). Furthermore, the repressive madness was so schizophrenic that the same person could be indicted by three different courts: a Military Court, the Court of Political Responsibilities and the Court For the Repression of Freemasonry and Communism.

The fund-raising reality of the LPR did not, in any way, meet expectations because almost all of the labourers and peasants who were sentenced to pay a 100 peseta fine (many of whom were also executed by firing squads) were insolvent or impoverished. Even such a small sum could prove ruinous to a working class family as on the whole this was equivalent to one month's wages (6 or 7 pesetas was the average daily wage in 1940). During those onerous years, the Official Bulletin for the Province of Cordoba published extremely long lists of persons fined under the LPR, usually for 100 pesetas each.

The bulk of the economic repression, however, was borne by the Republican political, intellectual and academic elite, most of whom had had brilliant careers and who, in the case of Cordoba, represented an entire generation, wiped out by Francoism and the Church. They decapitated the thinking heads and destroyed a century's worth of culture.

According to Barragán Moriana's extensive research, 98 persons were sentenced in Cordoba to pay more than 1,000 pesetas [$1,825] each, whilst 567 were each fined 1,000 pesetas [$1,825] or less. There was only one exorbitant fine (125,000 pesetas [$300,000]), the one levied against Dr. Vicente Martin Romera, Socialist Member of Parliament for the Frente Popular, who was executed soon after the military coup. His widow had to pay the fine in order to obtain free use of her property. It is worth noting that these economic sanctions did not just punish the individuals who were prosecuted as they were frequently executed by firing squad, but their heirs as well. The family of Blas Infante, executed on the orders of Queipo de Llano in Seville, was ordered to pay his 2,000 peseta [$3,665] fine. Masons, in particular, were usually sentenced to pay extremely large amounts.

In addition to the astronomic fine that Dr. Martin Romera was sentenced to pay, there were others. The family of Antonio Fernández Carretero, school teacher of Villaviciosa, executed, had to pay 10,000 [$18,250] pesetas. The family of José Alcalde Machuca, an attorney of Espiel, executed, had to pay 15,000 pesetas [$27,375]. Alfredo Herrera Siles, physician of Posadas, shot when the Francoist troops entered that town, was fined 5,000 pesetas [$9,125[, which his family paid. Antonio España Ocaña, a Republican icon and a Mason in Palma del Rio who fled into exile, was fined 1,500 pesetas [$2,737], although we do not know whether this was paid so that his family could have access to his estate, or not. A picturesque individual, Máximo Muñoz López, expert quantity surveyor of Conquista, married in Hinojosa del Duque and who played quite a leading role in Los Pedroches during the war, fled to exile in Mexico owing a 15,000 pesetas [$27,375] fine.

Antonio Hidalgo Flores, businessman of La Rambla, a Mason, executed in 1936 (it is said that someone had eyes on his business), was fined 2,000 pesetas [$3,665], which his family paid. The Masons from Lucena who were a breath of fresh air in the middle of the overpowering stench of clerical incense that imbued everything, who followed brilliant careers and who were all executed in 1936, were also fined: Javier Tubio Aranda (250 pesetas [$457]), Domingo Cuenca Navajas (150 pesetas [$273]), José López Jiménez (200 pesetas [$366]) and Anselmo Jiménez Alba (100 pesetas [$182]). One of the Masons in Cordoba capital, Vicente Lombardia Pérez, executed in 1936, was fined 500 pesetas [$910].

Indictments and prosecutions of all sorts rained upon the distinguished Professor of Cordoba and Republican politician, Antonio Jaén Morente, also a Mason, who escaped into exile in Ecuador. He was first prosecuted in Cordoba under the Confiscation of Property Order in 1936; then in Madrid both under the Law of Political Responsibilities and by the Court For the Repression of Freemasonry and Communism (in which he was sentenced to 20 years and 5 days in prison). In the case of his fellow politician, a member of the Republican Left, Ramón Rubio Vicente, vice-president of the Red Cross in Madrid during the war, the Francoists dismissed the charges against him because he 'corrected his mistakes' by handing over the Red Cross funds when the Francoists entered Madrid and by having saved many right-wingers. Another so-called 'Red Angel'.

Jesús Hernández Tomás, Communist Member of Parliament for Cordoba, suffered the wrath of the Francoists despite his being a very junior member of Parliament, as he was condemned by the Court of Political Responsibilities to pay a million pesetas in fines and banishment for 15 years, all which was in vain because he was already living in exile. Pedro Rico López, another junior Member of Parliament for Cordoba and Republican Mayor of Madrid, was fined the highest amount we know of: 10 million pesetas [$18,250 million].[99]

Ramón Carreras Pons was one of those individuals who people now enthusiastically describe as belonging to the 'third Spain'. Professor at the Public School for Teachers, supporter of Leroux and ex-Member of the Constitutional Assembly, he found himself in Madrid in the middle of the war and decided to go to France with his family. He was discovered in La Junquera (Gerona), arrested and tried in Barcelona for attempting to flee and sentenced to pay a 2,000 peseta [$3,665] fine. Another ex-Member of the Constitutional Assembly, socialist Juan Morán Bayo, was prosecuted under the Confiscation of Property Edict in 1936 and the Court of Political Responsibilities in 1940. He left politics in 1936, but the authorities did not consider him sufficiently repentant and fined him 1,000 pesetas [$1,825].

Nationwide, according to information from the Courts, more than 114,000 LPR indictments were dismissed in mid-1941 (only 38% of the total were sentenced). The authorities had calculated that the LPR could affect a quarter of million Spaniards. There is another summary report, cited by Manuel Álvaro Dueñas, that states that 'in the two years during which the Courts were operating, the judges ruled on 38,035 cases. 87,231 remained pending, and 101,440 were dismissed, which represents a total of 188,671 indictments, which if dealt with at an average rate of 19,027 per year, would take nine years and ten months to process'.[100]

As regards Cordoba, based on data published in the Official Bulletin of the Province, Barragán Moriana[101] calculated a total of 6,454 prosecutions under the Law of Political Responsibilities in the province, the following being the most affected judicial districts: Fuente Obejuna (1,150), Montoro (881), Pozoblanco (808), Posadas (614), Hinojosa del Duque (607) and Cordoba capital (544).

In the beginning, the Regional Court of Political Responsibilities in Seville had its headquarters at Calle Amor de Dios, number 18. The Court's services were reorganized after the 1942 reform and many procedures were decentralized to the Provincial and the Magistrate Courts. In 1943, 17 judicial districts were given added jurisdiction in these matters. A consultation in the judicial district of Pozoblanco in 1980, showed more than 600 such indictments that were later filed in the Province of Cordoba Historical Archives. The following case is an example of an indictment that was brought before the Regional Court and where the sentence under the Law of Political Responsibilities was handed down two years after the victim had been executed.[102]

Clearly, the dimension of this brutal economic repression, added to the other repressive mechanisms and measures masterminded by the military, is insane. This was not a productive Spain, but a bureaucratic Spain, in which the military, the Falange, parish priests and a legion of public servants spent day after day preparing and filing indictments with which to prosecute defeated Spaniards. One wonders whether there ever could have been such an extensive repressive and bureaucratic lunacy in old Europe during the other post-war periods.

Presiding Judge: Don Rafael Añino Ilzarbe
Members of the Court:
Don Francisco Diaz Plá, Don Tomás Martin de Barbadillo.
SENTENCE

In the city of Seville, the twenty-fourth of January, nineteen hundred and forty-two. Case number 3,672, Regional Court of Political Responsibilities, before the Provincial Court of Cordoba, against EUGENIO JURADO POZUELO, deceased, aged 32 years, married, carpenter and resident in neighbouring Villanueva de Cordoba.

PROVEN: That the Permanent Council of War for the region, meeting in Villanueva de Cordoba, in an indictment under the terms of the National Movement, pronounced a sentence on 13 March 1940, approved 23 April next, by which Eugenio Jurado Pozuelo, author of a crime of joining the rebellion, was condemned to death, and executed. The accused owned no property, he left a four-year-old daughter, and his widow, who also does not own any property, lives from her employment.

OUTCOME: The legal formalities were observed.

CONSIDERING THAT in the case of Eugenio Jurado Pozuelo, the proven facts represent a serious breach of political responsibilities, as set forth in Item a), Article 4, Law of 9 February 1939.

CONSIDERING THAT there are no attenuating circumstances.

Examined: Articles 8, 10, 12 and 13 of the aforementioned Law, and other applicable legislation.

IT IS THEREFORE DECIDED THAT we must and do condemn Eugenio Jurado Pozuelo to pay the sum of one hundred pesetas. The Provincial Instructor of Cordoba is hereby ordered to notify his widow and her daughter, of this ruling.

THE ABOVE BEING OUR RULING, we so order it and affix our signatures in witness thereof.

Rafael Añino, Francisco Díaz Plá, Tomás Martín Barbadillo. (signatures)

Secretary (signature illegible)

Source: Regional Court of Political Responsibilities, Seville, January 14 1942. Document given to Moreno Gómez by Eugenio Jurado's family.

Endnotes for Chapter I

1   Juan Simeón Vidarte, *Todos fuimos culpables*. (We were all guilty), Barcelona, Grijalbo, 978. Vol. 1. p. 923
2   Emiliano Mascarasque Castillo. 1985. Interviewed several times by Moreno Gomes in Pozoblanco.
3   Casimiro Jabonero. *Diário del soldado republicano Casimiro Jabonero. Campo de prisioneros de Lavacolla, Prisión de Santiago de Compostela, 1939-1940*. (Diary of Casimiro Jabonero, a Republican soldier. Lavacolla concentration camp. Santiago de Compostela Prison – 939.1940.) Ed. Victor Manuel Santidrián Arias, Ayuntamiento, Santiago de Compostela, 2004, pp. 93 et al.
4   *Azul*. Cordoba, April 1 & 2 1939.
5   Historical Archives of the Army of the Air (AHFA). Ministry of Defence, Madrid. Archive A2035.
6   Laura Contreras, September 1980. Interviewed by Moreno Gómez in Villaviciosa, to whom she later also wrote several letters.
7   Members of Catalina Mestre's family eyewitness reports to Moreno Gómez.
8   Miguel Ángel Peña Muñoz. Letter to Moreno Gómez, in which he states that the victim was his grandmother's brother-in-law and that he died in her arms.
9   Luna Gómez Rodriguez. Interviewed by Moreno Gómez in Villanueva de Cordoba.
10 *Diario de Operaciones del Ejército del Sur* (Daily Operations Report of the Army of the South). Serviço Histórico Militar, Madrid; *Partes oficiales de Guerra, 1936-1939*, Vol. I, Ejército Nacional (Official War Reports, 1936-199, Vol. I, Spanish Army). Serviço Histórico Militar, Madrid, 1978, 2 Vols.; General José Cuesta Moreno, Deputy to General Queipo de Llano in Sevilla. Documents. *Hechos ocurridos en los pueblos de la provincia de Cordoba* (Events in towns and villages of the province of Cordoba). Serviço Histórico Militar, Madrid.
11 Herbert R. Southworth. Myth of Franco's Crusade. Translated into Spanish and French. (Paris, France, Ruedo Ibérico, 1963).
12 Carlos Menéndez Viñuela. 1982. Interviewed by Moreno Gomes in Dos Torres.
13 Corporal José Pérez Navarrete's eye-witness acount appears in his unpublished *Diário de la guerra* (War Diary) dated 30 November 1939, Pozoblanco, which was shown to the author by his son, José, December 2013.
14 Gabriel Jackson. Quoted in *Una inmensa prisión. Imágines contra el olvido* (An immense prison. Images against oblivion). Documentary produced and directed by Carlos Ceacero and Guillermo Carnero. 2005. (Impulso Records, 2006).
15 Antonio D. López Rodríguez. *Cruz, bandera y Caudillo. El campo de concentración de Castuera* (Cross, flag and Caudillo. Castuera concentration camp). Badajoz, Ceder-La Serenam, 2006, pp. 98 and 169.
16 Albino Garrido's oral testimony can be heard on YouTube, as part of a 2011 documentary on Spanish TVE2 by Juan Sella and Rafael Robledo, *El pesadillo de Castuera Badajoz* (The nightmare of Castuera Badajoz), which includes multiple visual recordings of oral testimonies of survivors and relatives of disappeared prisoners at this concentration camp., Uploaded 25 January 2014 by CGT

Barcelona to https://youtu.be/MAtWuuQbbQM. Garrido was also interviewed by Luís Sánchez and María Ángeles Hernández, on Cadena Sur, Avila Television following the publication of his book: *Une longue marche. De la répression franquiste aux champs français* (A long march. From the Francoist repression to the French camps). Translated into French by his son Luís Garrido (France, Privat, 2011), later published in the original Spanish. Lleida, Milenio, 2013.

[17] Bartolomé Cabrera Peralbo 1981-1985. Interviewed by Moreno Gómez several times in Pozoblanco.

[18] Manuel Bustos Badia. 15 July 2002. Interviewed by Moreno Gómez in Villanueva de Cordoba.

[19] *ABC,* Cordoba, 29 March 1939. Eduardo Valera Valverde had previously served as a Republican governor in 1931. He was later implicated in the *Sanjurjada* uprising in Seville.

[20] Hilari Raguer, a monk in Montserrat (Barcelona) is one of today's most astute researchers into the Church's role under Franco. Hilari Raguer. *La pólvora y el incienso. La Iglesia y la guerra civil española (1936-1939),* (Gunpowder and Incense. The Church and the Spanish Civil War (1936-1939). Barcelona, Península, 2001.

[21] Marino Ayerra Redin, a Basque parish priest who rejected the military and the role of the Church in the slaughter that followed, fled to exile in Uruguay in 1939 and in 1940 moved to Argentina. In 1958 he published a book on his experiences in Alsasua, Pamploma 1936-1939. *Maldito seais! No me avergoncé del evangelio* (Be damned! I was not ashamed of the Gospel). Buenos Aires, Periplo, 1958.

[22] José Manuel Matencio. 2010. Eye-witness account reported in: *Minutes of the I Jornadas para la Recuperación de la Memoria Histórica* (I Conference on Recovering the Historic Memory). (Posadas, City Council).

[23] Minutes of the Meeting of the Villanueva de Cordoba City Council, 14 July 1939.

[24] Óscar Rodríguez Barreira. 2013. *El franquismo desde los márgenes* (Francoism from the edges). (University of Lleida).

[25] Felix Rubén Dário (1867-1916). Nicaraguan poet, father of the Spanish-American literary movement known as *modernismo.*

[26] Arcángel Bedmar Gonzálves. *La campina roja. La repressión franquista en Fernán Núñez (1936-1943)* (The Red countryside. The Francoist repression in Fernán Núñez). Lucena (Cordoba), Librería Juan de Mairena, 2003, p. 67.

[27] Paul Preston. *El gran manipulador. La mentira cotidiana de Franco* (The great manipulator. Franco's daily lie.) Barcelona, Ediciones B., 2008.

[28] Antonio D. López Rodríguez. *Cruz, bandera y Caudillo. El campo de concentración de Castuera* (Cross, flag and Caudillo. Castuera concentration camp). Badajoz, Ceder-La Serenam, 2006, pp. 98 and 169.

[29] José Manuel Matencio, Ibid.

[30] Elisa, Carillo, p. 85

[31] Francisca Adame in: Mirta Núñez Diaz-Balart et al… *La gran repressión. Los Años de plomo del franquismo* (The great repression. The sombre years of Francoism).

Madrid, Flor del Viento, 2009, pp. 74-75.

[32] Rafael García Contreras. *Sussurros de libertad. Memorias.* (Whispers of freedom. Memories). Cordoba, Puntoreklamo, 2008, pp. 21-23.

[33] Jesús Maria Romero Ruiz. *Recuperación de la memoria histórica de La Rambla* (Recovering the historic memory of La Rambla). (La Rambla, City Council, 2010), p. 201

[34] Arcángel Bedmar Gonzálves. *La campiña roja. La repressión franquista en Fernán Nuñez (1936.1943)* (The red countryside. The Francoist repression in Fernán Nuñez). Lucena (Cordoba), Librria Juan de Mairena, 2003, p. 71.

[35] Ibid. *Los puños y las pistolas. La represión en Montilla (1936-1939)* (Fists and revolvers. The repression in Montilla (1936-1939). Cordoba, Ed. Lucena, 2009, p. 102.

[36] Idem. *República, guerra y represión. Lucena 1931-1939* (Republic, war and repression. Lucena 1931-1939). Lucena City Council, 2010, pp. 218 et al. Revised edition.

[37] Idem. *República, guerra y represión. Lucena 1931-1939* (Republic, war and repression. Lucena 1931-1939). Lucena City Council, 2010, p. 224. Revised edition.

[38] José Francisco Luque Moreno, *Montemayor, 1900-1945. Cuestión social, República, Guerra y Represión* (Montemayor, 1900-1945. Social Issue, Republic, War and Repression.= Cordoba, Provincial Council, 2011, pp. 231 et al.

[39] Arcángel Bedmar Gonzálves. *Desaparecidos. La represió franquista en Rute (1936-1950)* (The disappeared. The Francoist repression in Rute (1936-1950). Lucena, Cordoba, Rute City Council, 2004, Vol. 2, pp. 84 et al.

[40] Arcángel Bedmar Gonzálves. *Baena, roja y negra. Guerra civil y represión (1936-1943)* (Baena, red and black. Civil war and repression). Lucena, Cordoba, Juan de Mairena, 2008, pp. 113 et al Revised edition 2013.

[41] Ibid. p. 138.

[42] Television Documentary. 2007. *Desafectos. Esclavos de Franco en el Pirineo* (The disaffected. Slaves to Franco in the Pyrenees). Regarding a Workers' Battalion in El Roncal-Salazar, employed in the building of a road between these two towns, 1939-1941. Un-named survivors' oral testimonies.

[43] José Espejo Ruz. *Memoria fértil* (Fertile memory) & Jesús Maria Romero Ruiz. *Recuperación de la memoria histórica de La Rambla* (Recovering the historic memory of La Rambla). La Rambla, Cordoba, City Council, 2010.

[44] Jesús Maria Romero Ruíz. Idem. Some examples of the La Rambla interrogations, transcribed and published by that author.

[45] José Torralbo. Interviewed by Moreno Gómez in Villanueva de Cordoba.

[46] Alberto Reig Tapia. *Ideología e historia. Sobre la represión franquista y la guerra civil* (Ideology and history. The Francoist repression and the civil war). Madrid, Akal, 1984. Excellent compilation of proclamations.

[47] Pedro Donaire Leal. November 27 1986, Seville. Written eye-witness account sent to Moreno Gómez.

[48] Pozoblanco Municipal Archives, document provided courtesy of Fernando López.

49   Fernandi Sánchez Marroyo, Professor of Contemporary History, University of Extremadura.

50   Dolores Romero. Interviewed by Moreno Gómez during the 1980s in Espejo, where the family moved permanently because after being released from jail, they were banished from Villanueva. It would be impossible to gather all these reports today. The transition period forced historians to lose no less than 30 years of information, to History's misfortune.

51   Rafael Bedmar Guerreiro, November 1983. Unpublished memoires. He later self-published a second version of these: *1936 – Memorias de una guerra* (1936: Memories of a war). Cordoba, 2007, p. 45.

52   Rafael Lemkin, *Special Report presented to the 5th Conference for the Unification of Penal Law in Madrid. (14 -20 October 1933).*

53   Idem. *Axis Rule in Occupied Europe: Laws of Occupation - Analysis of Government - Proposals for Redress.* Carnegie Endowment for International Peace, Washington, D.C., 1944, Part II, chapter IX.

54   Idem. "Genocide", *American Scholar,* April 1946.

55   Gregory H. Stanton. 1998. *Stop Genocide.* (Yale University Center). Translated by Diana Wang and presented as *Ocho estados de genocidio* (Eight stages of genocide) at the US Department of State, Washington, D.C., 1996. Gregory Stanton is the founder (1999) and President of Genocide Watch and the founder (1999) and Chair of the International Campaign to End Genocide.

56   José Francisco Luque Moreno. Ibid.

57   José Brizuela. In: Núñez Diaz-Balart, Mirta et al. Ibid, p. 179.

58   Francisco Poyatos López. *Recuerdos de un hombre de toga* (Memories of a man wearing a jurist's robes). Cordoba, 1979, p. 151. Self-published.

59   José Murillo Murillo. Numerous interviews with Moreno Gómez in Madrid.

60   Joaquim Sama Naharro. Summer 1983. Two morning-long interviews by Moreno Gómez, in Cordoba. He was exceptionally clear-minded and didn't mince his words.

61   Bartolomé Cabrera Peralbo. November 21 1985. Interviewed by Moreno Gómez in Pozoblanco, and subsequent interviews.

62   José Torralba Rico. *Vidas secretas. Memòries d'un militant clandestí.* (Memoires of a clandestine militant). Mansesa, Barcelona, Centre d'Estudis del Bages, 2009, p. 32.

63   Antonio Bautista Romero. December 27 1985. Interviewed by Moreno Gómez in Cordoba.

64   Beatriz Blacas Pino. May 10 2002. Interviewed by Moreno Gómez in Valencia.

65   Antonio Reseco Rivera. Letter from the victim's grandson, sent Augus 26 1989 from Barcelona.

66   Rafael Lemkin. *Axis Rule*, op. cit.

67   Antonio Barragán Moriana. *Control social y responsabilidades políticas. Cordoba (1936-1945)* (Social control and political responsibilities. Cordoba (1936-1945). Cordoba, El Páramo, 2009, pp. 119 et al. This study includes a list of the "economic" edicts on pp. 315-316.

68   Francisco Moreno Gómez. *1936: El genocidio franquista en Cordoba* (1936: The

Francoist genocide in Cordoba), Barcelona Critica, 2008.

69 Antonio Barragán Moriana. Ibid., p. 125.

70 José Francisco Luque Moreno, Ibid., p. 261.

71 Antonio Miguel Bernal, José Luis Gutiérrez Molina, Fernando Romero and Cecilio Gordillo et al.. *Proyecto Rapina* (Robbery Project). (Seville, January 23 2011). Investigative project created in Seville by the Recovery of the Historic Memory of Andalusia Group, with a view to studying the thefts, confiscations and seizures by Francoists beginning July 18 1936.

72 Natividad Rodrigo. Testimony collected in Villanueva de Odra by the Recovery of the Memory of Andalusia Group under the Robbery Project. Published by Patricia Campelo in: 'Sin muertos, tampoco hay culpable' (If there are no dead, there also are no guilty persons). In: *Memoria Pública*, March 27 2012.

73 Manuel Álvaro Dueñas. 'Control político y represión económica' (Political control and economic repression). In: Núñez Diaz-Balart, Mirta et. al. Ibid., p. 260.

74 Barragán Moriana, A.. Ibid., pp. 204-206.

75 Dueñas. Ibid., p. 261.

76 Barragán Moriana, A. Ibid., p. 164.

77 Idem., p. 145.

78 Rafael Lemkin. October 1933. Vth International Conference for the Unification of Penal Jurisprudence, Madrid.

79 Idem. *Axis Rule in Occupied Europe*, Columbia University Press, New York, 1944.

80 Idem. "Genocide", *American Scholar,* April 1946.

81 Miguel Hernández. *Obra completa. III Prosas. Correspondencia* (Complete work. III Prose. Correspondence). (Madrid, Espasa-Calpe, 1992).

82 Ana Tudela. "Hambre, cartilla y estraperlo: España no come escrúpulos" (Hunger, ration cards and black market: Spain does not eat scruples). Published on the Internet at www.Publico.es April 2 2009.

83 Petra Romero Huertas. Eye-witness report recorded by her son Bartolomé Pozuela, Summer 2011, in Villanueva de Cordoba.

84 Ana Tudela, op. cit.

85 Maria Victoria Fernández Luceño and José Maria Garcia Márquez. *Fallecidos en el campo de concentración de Las Arenas (La Algaba, Sevilla)*, (Deaths in the Las Arenas, La Algaba, Sevilla, concentration camp). *El Mundo*, Seville, 2013.

86 Mirta Núñez Díaz-Balart, Ibid.

87 Franciso Moreno Gómez. *Cordoba en la posguerra (La represión y la guerilla, 1939-1950)* (Post-war Cordoba. Repression and the guerilla, 1930-1950). (Cordoba, F. Baena, 1987),. 296 et al.

88 Newspaper *Cordoba*, May 10 1942.

89 Interviews collected in Cordoba with the assistance of Rafael González Roldán and numerous correspondence with Moreno Gómez.

90 *Cordoba*, 28 September 1940

91 *Cordoba*, 4 December 1941.

92 *Nueva Enciclopedia Larousse. (*Barcelona, Plante, 1980). Vol. 8.

93   Daniel Sueiro and Bernardo Días Nosty. *Historia del franquismo* (The history of Francoism). Madrid, Sedmay Ediciones, 1977, p. 239.

94   Ricard Vinyes. "El universo penitenciario durante el franquismo"(The prison universe during Francoism). In: *Una inmensa prisión* (An immense prison). Barcelona, Crítica, 2003, pp. 170 et al.

95   Antonio Barragán Moriana. Ibid., p. 186.

96   César Laiana Ilundáin. Oral testimony. Basque Documentary. Ibid.

97   Antonio Barragán Moriana. Ibid., 315 & 204-206.

98   Idem, 237.

99   Idem, p. 304

100   Manuel Álvaro Dueñas. "Por derecho de fundación: la legitimación de la represión franquista" (Rulings of the courts: the legitimation of the Francoist repression). In. Núñez Diaz-Balart, Mirta et al., Ibid., p. 124.

101   Barragán Moriana. Ibid., p. 254.

102   Regional Court of Political Responsibilities. Seville. January 14 1942. Document given to the author by Eugenio Jurado's family.

II

CRUSHING THE VANQUISHED (A) - A CRIME AGAINST HUMANITY. THE CONCENTRATION CAMPS ANTE-ROOMS OF THE MULTI-REPRESSION: ARRESTS, SUICIDE, THE CHURCH AND NATIONAL CATHOLICISM

THE CONCENTRATION CAMPS: FIRST CIRCLE OF THE FRANCOIST HELL. ANTEROOMS OF THE MULTI-REPRESSION:
Hunting and capturing *Rojos*. Suicide, the last resort against Fascism. *Los Caídos* in the line of duty for God and Spain. The Church at the root of the New Totalitarian State. Religious manipulation of children. National Catholicism at war with Education.

> "*Those whom you now see exhausted, battered, angry, downcast, unshaven, filthy dirty, destroyed, are nevertheless - don't forget it son, never forget it, no matter what happens – Spain's finest, the only ones who truthfully rose without anything but their bare hands, against Fascism, against the military, against the all-powerful... each in his own way, to the best of his ability...*"

(Max Aub, *Campo de los almendros*, 1968)

The Concentration Camps. First Circle of Franquista Hell

The penal universe was the hub of the fascist repression and in the descent to the Francoist hell, the concentration camps formed the first great circle around this hub. The defeated suffered a first traumatic shock when they were confronted with the strictures of the New State and a second one when they learned what their role was to be under the new regime first, as captives in the concentration camps and later, as prisoners in the jails, where they were subjected to indescribable suffering, a tragic ordeal of the kind that is universally recognized as a crime against humanity. The Rome Statute of the International Criminal Court defines a crime against humanity as 'an act committed as part of a widespread or systematic attack against any civilian population, with knowledge of the attack,' namely 'Imprisonment or other severe deprivation of physical liberty in violation of fundamental rules of international law'[1] and other acts.

History tells us that mass concentration camps were invented by an associate Fascist regime in Germany following Hitler's rise to power in 1933, when Dachau and Buchenwald became operational. In June 1935, the number of 'political' prisoners in Germany rose to 23,000 but dropped to 11,265 at the end of 1938. Following a process of admissions and releases in which they were involved, before and after this date, the number of socialists or communists totalled 150,000.[2] These numbers pale in comparison with the half a million individuals 'concentrated' by Franco in 1939 alone.

Franco is most often ranked as the leader in the fraternity of 20th century European tyrants. The repressive philosophy was the same: the terrifying texts of Generals Mola and Queipo and other high-ranking Nationalist military officers were fully comparable to Hitler's tirades against Jews and Communists.[3]

Especially interesting is what Eric Hobsbawm had to say regarding the purely political nature of the Rome-Berlin-Madrid Axis repression, one that had nothing to do either with 'common crimes' or 'political crimes of rebellion'., in that socialists and communists knew that the principle objectives of a fascist regime was to exterminate them. This was why, when the wolves of the fascist regime were set against them, the first concentration camps in the Third Reich would be designed as a place where communists could be safely kept under lock and key."[4]

Although the fascist repression in Spain was a solely political extermination, Franco took this one step further. To the eradication of his political opponents, he added the punishment and humiliation of an entire defeated army.

The dark phenomenon of mass imprisonment, with the attending grief and suffering, facilitated several Francoist objectives following the defeat of the Republican army. To begin with, it enabled the extensive classification procedure by which Franco would be able to obtain a census of his political enemies. Next, it served as an instrument that provided various means for attaining other objectives directed at promoting the moral defeat and 'cleansing' of everyone who did not support the movement, those whom it designated as disaffected:

physical destruction: punishment, torture, starvation and, in many cases, death by firing squad;

political destruction: eradication of the entire political or trade union education dating from the beginning of the 20th century and that a great part of the social base of the Republic had acquired by means of a great many struggles and many doctrines; in other words, the annihilation all the disaffected in the country;

moral destruction: through terror, by which a defeated individual is pushed to the limits in situations intended to destroy a person's coherence, his dignity and self-respect; to force the prisoner or the incarcerated to negate his inner self and abjure his principles. In quite a few cases, Francoism managed to do this. In many others, when faced by truly indomitable spirits, it did not; and

repudiation and reconversion: the nature of which was clearly ecclesiastic and inquisitorial. The practice of repudiation was instituted by the Church during the Inquisition in the *autos de fe*: if the prisoner abjured his 'heresies', he was put to death before he was burned at the stake; if he did not, he was burned alive. The Church had considerable experience in repudiations, torture, reconversions, atonements and crucifixions, an entire range of evil practices that were resurrected in 1939. In effect, the Church and its chaplains who worked in dozens in all the centres of confinement, were totally involved in fulfilling this fourth objective. Their goal was to force the prisoners, not just to express their love for the Caudillo and Totalitarian Spain by using the Fascist salute, singing Fascist hymns and revering the Francoist flag, but also to embrace the principles of National Catholicism by way of the sacraments, compulsory attendance at Mass, confession, taking communion and participating in other religious ceremonies.

The extent of this *physical, moral, ideological and religious assault* was terrible for those against whom it was directed, some hundreds of thousands of men who came from another, totally antagonistic world. Never, during the expelling of the Jews and the Moors, and all others whom fanatic Spain banished from within its borders throughout History, never were so many persecuted by the Church and Francoism in such a terrible manner as were the Republicans.

As stated earlier, the concentration camps were the first encounter the defeated had with Fascist Spain, camps like those that the Nazis had employed since 1933 to segregate and terrorize their opponents, the starting point for the chain of repression. Furthermore, not only was this a form of administrative criminality that was an integral part of a Government project, the proceedings themselves were unlawful. Hundreds of thousands of men were confined without having committed any crime, without having been lawfully indicted, without having been sentenced by any legitimate court of law.[i] The entire population of the camps was not a population of prisoners

---

i   The decrees and laws enacted by Franco's regime to justify its actions, were a mockery of the true meaning of due process of law and thus should be considered illegal and illegitimate.

83

serving sentences for crimes; they were there simply to be purged of their 'disaffection' with the regime.

The number of concentration camps in Franco's Spain rose rapidly throughout the entire war. The first camps were officially created by a 5 July 1937 Order from the Secretary of War of the self-appointed Burgos Government. By the end of that year, Franco had already taken 106,822 captives.[5] The Concentration Camps Inspectorate was created in 1937 and placed under the command of Colonel Luis de Martín Pinillos. If we add the number of camps created in March, April and August 1938 (especially in Northern Spain, which had already succumbed to Franco) to the existing camps, we arrive at a total of 72.[6] In July 1938, the number of incarcerated totalled more than 166,000.[7] In February-March 1939, the number of prisoners in concentration camps rose to 367,000, to which we must add the 140,000 men taken captive at the end of the war, after the so-called Victory Walk. All these numbers add to a final count of *507,000 individuals incarcerated in concentration camps in April 1939*, but the actual final figure was undoubtedly greater. Joan Llarch reports a total of 700,000.[8] Nonetheless, we can estimate that more than half a million men were held captive during the month of Franco's victory, a shocking number. Furthermore, if to this total we add the more than 270,000 (underestimated) individuals incarcerated in Franco's prisons in January 1940, plus those who came and went afterwards, *Franco's Spain incarcerated a million men and women*, not at any given date, but at successive periods during his reign. Spain had become one immense jail. It was as if the order of the day was: 'Everybody, off to jail'.

Javier Rodrigo computes the final number of permanent concentration camps in Spain at 104, plus numerous temporary camps, for a total 188.[9] This number, however, is not complete as some camps were left out and must be added. For example, there was a temporary camp that he did not include in Paseo de la Estación, Villanueva de Cordoba, containing 1,000 prisoners and two more in Cuenca: one at the site of the Seminary, containing more than 2,000 inmates, and yet another one in La Serrería. There may be more.

During the war in Cordoba province, concentration camps were created in Fuente Obejuna, Cerro Muriano (listed by Joan Llarch as containing 15,000 ex-combatants, although a Jesuit priest whose work he quotes, Fr. Delgado Iribarren S.J., says that this was the maximum capacity of the camp, not that this was the actual number of inmates), Montilla (600), Aguilar de la Frontera (300), Cabra (300), Lucena (300) and Cordoba capital (600 inmates).[10]

At the end of the war, the larger concentration camps in Cordoba province were located in Valsequillo, La Granjuela and Los Blázquez. When they began to overflow, the great majority of Cordovan prisoners were sent to the notorious Castuera camp. In an earlier book on post-war Cordoba[11], Moreno Gómez referred to a total 5,000 prisoners in the Valsequillo concentration camp and 21,000 for all three camps: Valsequillo, La Granjuela and Los Blázquez, a number taken from the work of Fr. Delgado Iribarren S.J., also quoted by Joan Llarch in 1978[12], but still an estimate.

More recently, Antonio D. López Rodríguez published documented data in his magnificent book on Castuera.[13] He states that in the immediate post-war period, 17,000 men were imprisoned in the three Cordoba province concentration camps. They came mainly from Cordoba capital but also from Badajoz. They also came from elsewhere, such as the humourist Miguel Gila From Valsequillo who ended up in La Granjela and who stated in his memoires that there were 12,000 inmates in La Granjuela who were taken from the camp every day to where they had to go and dig. Only after they had finished their work, were they given their only meal of the day: two sardines, an ounce of chocolate and two figs.[14]

According to López Rodriguez[15], the Nationalist Army Corps of Extremadura and Cordoba, stirred by the 'sweet trumpet sounds of victory', captured 62,9000 prisoners (37,000 in Extremadura and 25,000 in Cordoba province). The 60th Division took charge of the prisoners in the North of Cordoba: 7,500 in Valsequillo, 8,153 in La Granjuela and 1,342 in Los Blázquez. This shows just how enormous these concentration camps were. The number of inmates varied greatly as many were vetted and others shifted out elsewhere several times a day. For example, 10 May 10 1939, 2,500 prisoners were transferred from Los Blázquez to Valsequillo. At times, La Granjela held as many as 20,000 inmates.

This was just one aspect of the great humanitarian catastrophe created by Francoism and the regime's avowed intention that no one should be allowed to escape its net. Nobody could ever have imagined just how brutal the victorious armed forces would be. Today, although the academic world avoids discussing the great repression, the historical facts are undeniable, even when they are manipulated. That a country should tolerate this is totally inexcusable. Today, as the victors continue to demand respect for their fallen, it does not occur to anybody to ask for forgiveness for yesterday's victims.

López Rodriguez also tells of the huge number of prisoners captured by the Nationalist Tagus-Guadiana Group of Divisions. A tragically spectacular scenario; half of Spain imprisoning the other half, the so-called 'magnanimous' doing of the Caudillo. On April 5 1939, these Divisions had more than 32,000 rank-and-file soldiers in custody (45,000 twenty days later), plus an additional 18 commanding officers, 700 general officers, 93 administrative officers and sundry non-commissioned officers.

In Badajoz, not including Castuera, on April 22 1939 there were 12,000 prisoners in the so-called Extremaduran Siberia: 3,874 in Caserio Zaldivar and Casas de Don Pedro; 4,290 in Siruela; 651 in Fuenlabrada de los Montes; 502 in Castilblanco; and 2,543 in Palacio del Cijara. In the case of Siruela, in accordance with the segregation and exclusion orders of the moment, the prisoners were removed from within the town and packed into the neighbouring farms of Las Lanchas and La Pachona. The purpose of this major 'disinfection' was to 'quarantine' them to forty years, not forty days, seclusion.

Let us return to Cordoba province. The La Granjela camp was swamped with wave after wave of incoming prisoners. Survivors of this period who have been interviewed all agree that they suffered considerably more from hunger during those days, than from the cold. The victors sent no supplies of any kind to the camps for several days. The first week was one of total fasting. Several days later only, the prisoners received a bit of bread and the famous can of sardines. As Miguel Regalón told Moreno Gómez,[16] he and three companions were captured in Regalón, where they remained for three days, without any food. Afterwards, marching under a heavy guard, they arrived in Pueblonuevo del Terrible. They spent a night in an old, damp house and the next morning, still without any food, we were marched to La Granjuela where they were given a bread roll and a can of sardines to be shared among four of us and then ordered to dig a two and a half metre-wide ditch around the town, surrounded on both sides by barbed wire. We began eating wild grass and carob bean flour. The victors often did not send any food to the camps for weeks on end. Juan Pulido Cantador also told how when he was taken to La Granjuela at the end of the war, they were kept without food for the first six days. When the first food arrived, there was such chaos that the guards sprayed the inmates with their machine guns and some died.[17]

In addition to the lack of food and forced labour, the prisoners were subject to visit from local Falangistas who would come to the camp with orders permitting them to remove individuals who, after they left the camp, were tortured and shot." In a later letter, Miguel Regalón added that in Paraleda, Los Blázquez and Valsequillo, where he was also interned, Falangistas from Pueblonuevo, la Añora, Dos Torres and El Viso, would present themselves to the head of the camp with authorizations to remove inmates whom they would take to the neighbouring hills and shoot. Whenever they could leave the camp to gather firewood for the kitchens, they saw the dead and the dying, and once, three hanging from an oak tree."[18]

One of the most descriptive testimonials of the prisoners' lives in the concentration camps is that provided by Jose Maria Carnicer who was taken prisoner at the end of the war and ended up in Castuera, a humiliating hell like so many other camps, where he was interned for three months until he was released on a good behaviour document his father obtained for him, June 1939.[19]

Castuera consisted of a large yard with, in the centre, some flagpoles where the flags of Spain, the Carlists and the Falange, waved. The inmates' huts were arranged around the yard. On one side, the kitchen and on the other, the latrines, which were no more than trenches that the inmates had to dig beforehand. If they needed to go to the toilet at night, they had to call the guard and a soldier with a fixed bayonet would accompany them. The camp was surrounded by a double row of barbed wire, a trench 3 metres deep and 6 metres wide, then another double row of barbed wire. And finally, all around the camp, machine gun posts.

At sunrise, reveille and the inmates had to fall in immediately in front of their hut; if they did not, the sergeants would enter through the windows and lash them with whips. Once they had fallen in, they were made to sing the hymn of the Legion, of the Falange and the *Oriamendi*[ii]. They were then marched out of camp, two by two: on one side of the gate there was a mountain of pickaxes and on the other, a mountain of shovels. There they remained doing forced labour until noon, when they returned to camp to eat.

Depending on the day, they got either cold or hot food. Cold food was a small can of tuna. When it was hot food, they went to get it, two by two, and were given a ladle of water and some chickpeas. In the evening, they got either cold or hot food, the opposite of what they had been given at lunch. As far as bread was concerned, they were given less than half a roll; every hut was allotted 30 or 35 rolls, but as there were 80 of them, they each got less than half a roll.

As far as personal hygiene was concerned, they were never given any water in which to wash and as most of them had no razors, they just let their beards grow. As they could not wash their clothes, they were a mess. As far as bugs were concerned, in addition to being abundant, there were all kinds and colours. One of their pastimes was racing body lice.

When we first arrived at the camp, the guards were Falangistas. When we went out to work, there was a guard for every 8 prisoners. In addition to making sure that we did not escape, another one of their duties was making sure that we did not sleep on the job. These guards always carried rifles. A

---

ii The March of Oriamendi. The hymn of the Carlist movement.

month or a month and a half later, the Falangistas were replaced by soldiers, and we all benefited from that."[20]

These, and more, personal testimonials and letters regarding the horror of the concentration camps, especially the largest, Castuera Valsequillo, La Granjela and Los Blásquez, are reproduced in their entirety in Appendix I. In every one, the author speak of the agony of their capture and transfer to the camps and the humiliation and mistreatment they suffered once they got there, especially the filth and the hunter.

Other Cordovans were distributed amongst concentration camps elsewhere in Francoist Spain. In Albatera, Alicante, the following began their ordeal, with no hope of salvation: Miguel Ranchal, socialist, Mayor of Villanueva del Duque (later executed in Barcelona); José Cantador Huertos, another socialist from Villanueva who had served as secretary to the Carlota town council, executed in Paterna; Francisco Jiménez García, communist, Mayor of Espejo, broken by torture, committed suicide when imprisoned in his town jail.

So it was throughout Spain. Delegations of Falangistas, Guardia Civil and extremists hunted down Republican leaders from their towns. They cast their nets far and wide, just to punish them. The Republicans who remained would fall little by little.

A Falangista delegation went to the Alicante concentration camps in search of some 'heavy weights' from Montilla. There, they captured two Militia commanders - Juan Cordoba Zafra and Manuel Alcaide Aguilar, as well as Manuel Sánchez Ruiz, the Mayor, and Francisco Merino, a town councillor, among others. They took Francisco Hidalgo from Santa Barbara castle.[21]

One of the many disappeared in Castuera was the Mayor of Zafra, José González Barbero. No sooner was he imprisoned in the concentration camp that Falangistas from Zafra discovered his whereabouts and sent a party to the camp to get him. They removed him from the camp and executed him in a neighbouring field around April 29 1939. He remained 'disappeared' as his family was never informed of hat had occurred, until his death was recorded in the Zafra Registry of Deaths only some ten years later.[22]

The lunatic persecution and frenetic hunt was so brutal and schizophrenic that 500 defeated from a single Cordoba village, La Rambla, were released from no less than 50 different concentration camps all over the country, most of them during the Black Spring of 1939. The abridged list of camps from which almost one hundred of the released were removed is an indication of the enormity of the repressive neurosis, as you can see in Table

1. List of Francoist concentration camps housing prisoners from La Rambla village during 1939. The numbers in brackets refer to prisoners identified in a specific camp. In 1938, more than 179,000 defeated Republicans were imprisoned in Francoist concentration camps all over Spain. In 1939, this number rose from between 367,000 to 500,000 inmates in more than 180 temporary and permanent concentration camps. In 1946, 137 forced labour and concentration camps were still operational, housing 30,000 political prisoners. The last concentration camp, in Miranda del Ebro, was closed in 1947.

When the prisoners were released and allowed to return to their home towns, as usual they had to present themselves at the local military or police headquarters for a first interrogation and show the safe-conduct pass issued by the concentration camp from which they had been released.

The notorious concentration camp in the South that most interests us here, is Castuera (Badajoz). The victors began building this camp during March 1939 as soon as they began to get an idea of the huge number of persons they would be imprisoning. So high was this early number, so great the unexpected need for a large camp, that the bells of victory were still pealing yet the camp was only half built. was not particularly crowded as camps go, as on April 22 1939 it housed 6,000 inmates, although more than 20,000 prisoners passed through it between April and September. López Rodríguez says it contained 84 sheds, but some eye-witnesses said there were as many as 92. It was built out of sight of the city of Castuera, in accordance with the rules for segregating and separating the townspeople from the camps so that punishments could be carried out of sight of any possible witnesses, just like the Nazi camps. Two images were posted all over the camp: the crucifix and the flag.

Overcrowding, torture, starvation, infrahuman conditions, physical and verbal violence, bad weather, terror, removals and firing squads, were the norm and attest to the severity of the repression. This degree of punishment was much greater than anyone could have imagined, it terrified the inmates and there were desperate attempts to escape.

It is important to remember that these inmates were not common criminals, they had not been charged with any crime, nor had they been sentenced by any court of law. They were quite simply 'the enemy', the 'disaffected', whose disaffection began here as they came into contact with the terror, with the Francoist intent to destroy their self-esteem once they had been defeated by the insurgent military, Franco's desire to imprison the entire Republican Army.

Because these inmates were irregular and unlawful prisoners, they were considered exempt from all formal rules and guarantees under law. In other words, they were subject, without recourse, to the unconditional and arbitrary whims of those who held them captive. The most heartless hardened criminals were placed at the head of the camps. This was nothing new as since 1936, this was the usual Francoist practice when appointing local military commanders and others responsible for keeping the peace.

In Castuera, in keeping with the dictum of 'power to the most criminal', the newly-appointed head of the camp was Ernesto Naverrete, Guardia Civil commander in Fuente de Cantos and who in 1936 had already ordered the extra-legal execution of 307 individuals.[23] That this kind of criminality was approved under Franco and encouraged by the Falange, is confirmed by the numerous promotions and rewards that Navarrete obtained throughout his career, including his promotion to Brigadier General in 1957 and his being decorated by Franco with the Grand Cross of Saint Hermenegildo.

Navarrete's policy in Castuera was to let Falangistas do whatever they wanted, although he was never loath to roll up his sleeves and, given half a chance, beat inmates half to death. He himself programmed the removals and the disappearances. Under Francoism, every missing person was considered a 'disappearance'. In the beginning, Falangistas were the first to go to the camp looking for fresh meat. When the Guardia Civil took over the job, they became the actual executors of the *paseos*[iii] and of the disappearance of inmates whose bodies 'fell' into the wells of some of the surrounding mines, the Somoza and the Gamonita. López Rodríguez states that all the camp's files have disappeared. The Civil Registers are also totally mute as to the extra-legal executions by firing squad that were frequently carried out in the municipal cemetery, yet another example of the Francoist 'disappearance' strategy. Today, those who persist in denying that Nationalist Spain did not shoot anybody, that individuals whose names are missing from the records just 'disappeared', demand proof in the form of lists or records when they know full well that none exist. As if the people of Badajoz, who have already suffered so much, needed any more aggravation, the leader of this pack, a fervent supporter of National Catholicism, author of countless articles and a Church historian, is Father Martín Rubio who was born in Castuera. still has to contend with Martín Rubio.[24]

The camp's very first task was to make a general classification of the prisoners, the first step in the general census of the repression. Prisoners were divided into four categories: A, B, C and D. The first two groups were considered 'recoverable'. Group C consisted of Republican leaders

---

iii Executions under the unlawful Law of Escapes.

and officials, administrative officers, and political and trade union leaders. Prisoners in Group D were those also accused of presumed criminal acts. Groups C and D were sequestered in a separate shack (number 70 say some, number 80 say others) and subject to 'removals' and to 'disappearing'. On occasion, the latter inmates might be removed by the Guardia Civil and taken to their home towns where they were court-martialled[iv] and in most cases, shot by a firing squad. Neither was life a bed of roses for Group B inmates as they provided the cannon fodder for the beatings, punishments, starvation and sufferings that often also resulted in their death.

Antonia González and Pablo Ortiz, Instituto de Zafra teachers, presented the extensive and extremely informative testimony of a survivor, Rafael Caraballo Cumplido, at the 2003 Barcelona Congress on Concentration Camps and the World of the Penitentiary in Spain during the Civil War and under Francoism.[25]

At the end of the war, Rafael Caraballo Cumplido was imprisoned in Siruela church and then sent to Castuera April 13, 1939. The first things he reported, were the beatings, such as the ones that broke the Mayor of Puebla de Alcocer's spine, and random shootings such as that of a young man in his hut whose mother had come to see him. He jumped through one of the windows at the back of the shed to give her a letter but he was seen by a Legionnaire who shot him in the back. As they watched. He died where he fell.

Rafael bitterly commented on the Church's role in the middle of this inferno whereby Mass was said in the camp and everyone had to attend and sing at least five or six hymns. When one of his companions complained that he didn't give a damn whether he lived or not, one of the Siruela priests commented that they should all envy those who were killed.

As to the behaviour of the guards... there was a winch next to the command post where the inmates went to make depositions, and it was used as a gallows where many died. The guards would get drunk and enter the huts, pick some of them out and take them away, beat them with rods and bring them back in pieces. Some were so unmercifully beaten, it would have been better if they had been killed. Navarrete, the Commander, turned a blind eye. When the camp was dismantled around February 20 1940, the prisoners were sent either to Castuera or Herrera el Duque, then Puebla de Alcocer, to one after another. Rafael was only nineteen years old at the time.

Earlier, Moreno Gómez mentioned how the only way that a prisoner could be released from a camp was by providing good behaviour letters

---

[iv] These courts were always military, regardless of whether the accused were military or civilian, not lawfully constituted civil courts of law.

of reference from persons of recognized standing in his home town. The following is an early example of one such reference:

> "*The undersigned hereby declare that Rafael Cabrera Caballero, resident in the neighbourhood of this city, is a person of guaranteed probity regarding the noble cause of the Nacional Sindicalista,[v] law-abiding and possessed of an exemplary conduct. The trustworthiness of all this information is confirmed by the fact that his relatives have suffered great losses and that they decry the atrocities committed by the Rojos. In witness thereof, we sign this declaration in Pozoblanco, April 2, 1939.*
> *III Year of the Triumph.*
> *Signed: Antonio Moreno Muñoz and Antonio García.[26]*

Later, the format of the reference became more technical and required confirmation by the local triumvirate who controlled the lives and the property of the people: the commander of the Guardia Civil, the Falangista mayor and head of the FET-JONS, and the parish priest. If a prisoner was unable to obtain the reference and could not work in the fields, he would be sent to one of the multiple forced labour battalions where he faced years and years of hard labour with a pick and shovel.

When writing this, Moreno Gómez wondered whether today's readers might think he was exaggerating the Church's involvement, but the fact is that young as he was at the time, he remembers having to go the parish priest to get a Certificate of Good Behaviour for some primary school activity. He also remembers his mother having to pay the priest to get permission to eat meat during Lent (streaky bacon and blood sausage, the only meat we had at the time). These and many other facts are true, no matter how long ago they occurred and how much negationists try to get us to disbelieve them. Because memories are often clouded by the fog of time, before writing of such events authors should perhaps begin with a warning: These descriptions of the past are so strikingly painful that they may hurt some people's feelings.

April and May 1939 were the most terrible months in Castuera concentration camp, as they were everywhere in Franco's Spain. Included with his descriptions of the beatings, removals of individuals from hut 80 and the disappearances, Antonio D. Lopez Rodríguez[27] describes an execution at the camp in May 1939 that Benjamín Gallardo has never forgotten. At 11h in the morning, some persons who were on their way to visit prisoners crossed

---

[v]   National Trades Union.

the path of the 'truck of death' that was taking some prisoners from the camp. The truck stopped next to the Somoza mine, a few kilometres from the camp. The prisoners got off the truck, the guards shot them and threw their bodies into the mine shaft. The unfortunate accidental witnesses who had hidden themselves, got away as soon as they could and fled in terror to Benquerencia.

There is another thing that must not be forgotten. Under Franco, it was the families who were generally considered responsible for providing food and care for the prisoners, not the State. Many relatives of the camp inmates from Cordoba, Extremadura and other towns and villages, made superhuman efforts to travel to the camps to see their kin. This explains the numerous humble families, who from 1936 onwards, could be seen travelling from jail to jail with food for their relatives. The number of these travellers rose dramatically during the first post-war period. One of the great tragic spectacles of Spain under Franco was of hundreds of women in mourning, often accompanied by young children, walking up and down roads towards the prisons and the camps. Prisoners who were unable to get support from their family usually did not live to tell the tale, as the weak broth of nettles, turnips or carrots that the victors fed the prisoners provided very little sustenance.

More about this later, but for the moment, suffice to imagine the sight of people of all ages, sizes and shapes, trekking around the Castuera concentration camp trying to see and give something to their relatives. Here, too, punishment and repression was extended to the families as the jailors took advantage of the situation. Wardens and guards promised to hand over food, clothes or money to the prisoners, in exchange for sexual favours from their relatives at night-time. Falangistas and drunken soldiers did what they wanted with the families who spent the night camped around Castuera. López Rodriguez tells of an interview with an individual who had been a Falangista guard and who, when remembering how they treated the women who visited the prison, broke into tears.[28] At last! A Falangista who showed some remorse over what he did. Still, a river of tears is not enough to atone for that great humanitarian catastrophe.

To give one an idea of the widespread ill-treatment, López Rodríguez records Ángel Sánchez Santos' heart-rending eye-witness account.

Angel was only eight years old when he accompanied his mother to the camp one day as she took some cigarettes and oranges to his father. The camp was surrounded by a double row of barbed wire and a trench. About 8 metres in all. At that distance they communicated by calling out to the prisoners on the other side, but because of the combination of the sound of voices and the distance, they practically could not hear each other. Because he was so little, he scrambled under the first row of barbed wire, crossed the trench, and then crawled under the second row with the items they had brought his father. As he was returning and had already gotten past the first row of wire, a field guard appeared with a revolver and a whip and he began to beat Ángel. The field guards were close to each other on the inside and there were more guards on the outside. The man still could not forget the way that the bastard beat him. He was enormous, he was nicknamed *Mulato* or *Javilla* and he was from Zaamea de la Serena. He came at the boy with his whip and beat him furiously until he almost lost consciousness. His father, stood there on the other side, watching everything, unable to speak out. Ángel was finally able to get back to his mother. He supposes that the things he had managed to give his father were taken away from him later. But what he wanted to tell López Rodrigues was about the beating that Mulato gave him. If that is what they did to an 8-year-old, what were they doing to those whom they held captive?

Numerous oral testimonies and eye-witness accounts and other observations clearly demonstrate that the concentration camp guards executed and 'disappeared' many more inmates than one believes or have been spoken of. In Castuera and everywhere else, witnesses all agree that prisoners were frequently called out from the huts and most simply disappeared, although we know that many of these were executed, as witnesses outside the camp have attested. How can one compute this slaughter? In towns or villages, where people knew each other, Moreno Gómez and other researchers have been able to compile incomplete lists of names not recorded in the Civil Registry. But in the camps, in chance or unknown locations, where not even the prisoners knew each other, they cannot even begin to make these lists, especially as the Francoists erased all traces of their actions wherever they could and Civil Registries do not mention these deceased. For now, however, we must agree that it has been clearly established that countless inmates were slaughtered in Franco's concentration camps, especially during April and May 1939.

Anterooms of the multi-repression

> *"What is incredible is that this can continue, that these assassins of the devil are allowed to remain unpunished… That for almost forty years they have tormented the Spanish people, without any shame or humility. The historical verdict shall be terribly severe."*

> *Olof Palme, 1975*[29]

1. Hunting and Capturing *Rojos*

After so many years of loss of memory and induced amnesia, of dismemory, very few Spaniards today really know what the military coup was all about, what the war was like, nor what Francoism stood for. Flipism and Carlism wagered on forgetfulness, the so-called fallacy of progress: look to the future and forget the past. With so much emphasis on forgetfulness, Spaniards are left with very little on the horizon for the future and almost nothing regarding the past. Dismemory explains why today nobody really knows who who was and why so many action groups and individuals are striving to restore those memories today.

Francoism made its mark on our history and it did so in a terrible way, at the cost of the humanitarian catastrophe that Moreno Gómez is at such pains to reconstruct. Francoist terror was no less that what is said about it; it was so much more than that.

"We must kill, kill, kill. Do you know that? Our program consists of exterminating one third of the male population of Spain."

Thus spoke the aristocratic Lieutenant-Colonel Gonzalo de Aguilera y Munro, 11th Count of Alba de Yeltes,, one of Franco's press officers, a man who knew very well what Franco thought and said.[30]

Earlier, we discovered what Francoist concentration camps were like and the first shock with which the defeated were confronted upon their return home at the end of the war. Right-wingers who were arrested by the Republican government following the uprising (the role of the *chekas*[vi]), never suffered such torments, nor anything that came even remotely close. The phenomenon of the concentration camps the Francoists employed as a means for their repression was, alone, a thousand times worse than the comparatively few Republican arrests in 1936. On its own, however, the tragedy of the camps is too great to enable a proper comparison of both sides' actions. With victory, Franco and his supporters had only just begun to put his formal program into effect. The Falangistas had become so involved in implementing the first part of Franco's agenda - eradication of all who opposed Francoism - that they eventually realized that they were neglecting

---

[vi] The *checkas* were extra-legal courts set up by some left-wing political parties and trade unions and although responsible for the deaths of many right-wingers during the first months following the coup, were falsely accused by Francoists of having assassinated hundreds of thousands of individuals in areas of the country that did not support the 18 July 1936 military coup.

all the plans they had laid for the National Trade Union Revolution, the so-called Glorious Revolution.

The Francoist victory bells were still ringing throughout the country when the incitement "**Go hunt and capture Rojos**" rang in everybody's ears. The victors, inflamed with a desire to exterminate their opponents, did not even stop to savour their victory; they directed all their energy to setting the slaughter in motion. The persecution that followed was intensive and merciless.

The media in 1939 and 1940 provided the public platform for this persecution mania. Every day, the Falangist press, most especially *ABC* of Seville and *Diário Azul* of Cordoba,[31] published detailed reports of arrests in the towns and villages of Cordoba province. This showcasing acted as an unrelenting advertising campaign for the regime, whose effect was to add fuel to the repressive machine everywhere. Such a spectacle of accusations, denunciations and captures would certainly not have occurred or been permitted in the Republican press during the period immediately following the coup that Francoists called the red terror, when tempers ran high. Yet another of the many differences between the two regimes. On the contrary, in 1939 the Francoist campaign of punishment and extermination was carefully expanded and orchestrated by the press that, against the name of every individual arrested, added a list of supposed crimes, none of which had been either corroborated or judged in the Courts. One Francoist juridical irregularity was the flouting of the rule of the presumption of innocence unless proved otherwise, as individuals were considered guilty from the onset just because they belonged to a Republican political party.

The *Diário Azul* newspaper of Cordoba could not contain its delight at the continuous arrests, as when it headlined the May 5 1939 news item rejoicing at the capture of Alfredo Caballero Martínez, ex-councillor for the Frente Popular in Cordoba, ex-director of the Metalworkers Trade Union and provincial secretary of the PCE[vii] since October 1936. Remarkably, such was the chaos in the implementing of the repression, that Caballero was one of the few who escaped being executed. Two days later, the paper reported on the execution by firing squad of the past commander of the Garcés Volunteer Battalion, Manuel Palos Cosano, another ex-director of the Metalworkers Trade Union.

These news items were not in the least informative; they were entirely accusatory. Rather than just informing its readers, the Francoist press cheered and encouraged the repression. Just look at how *Diário Azul* reported actions

---

[vii] *Partido Comunista de España.*

in Castro del Rio, bad-mouthing, if not out rightly slandering, those who had been arrested:

The Castro del Rio Guardia Civil has arrested the following noteworthy extremists who continue to speak their minds after returning from the recently liberated zone:

- Francisco Carpio Algaba, age 25, bachelor. Used violence to force several landowners to give him great sums of money and later voluntarily joined the 85th Red Brigade.

- Gabriel González García, age 38, member of the CNT union. Enlisted with the Rojos and arrested José Puebla Centella, whom he tied up hands and feet, robbed and imprisoned.

- José Rinoso Ortega, age 32, secretary and member of the CNT. This individual, under the orders of the Red Council of War, was commander of the fighters at the Bujalance-Baena crossroads barricade. He later became a member of the Andalusía-Extremadura Red Militia, with the rank of Lieutenant. On October 21 1936, he and his fellow fighters[viii] attacked Castro del Rio, entered the town and got as far as Calle Casas Nuevas.

- Rafael Navajas Rosa, age 30. Enlisted with the Red Army and was appointed responsible for the stolen cattle that he later sold for 69,000 pesetas. Enlisted in the 215th Red Brigade that was garrisoned on the Teruel front...”[32]

On other occasions, the headlines reflected the newspaper's disrespect for the prisoners and its support of the widespread practice of informing on individuals, a practice fanatically followed by the entire right-wing sector of society:

PINKO DENOUNCED
José Payán Porcel informed the Commissariat of an individual named Francisco Landauro García, age 41, who, according to the informer, carried a rifle in the service of the

---

[viii] The official Francoist report described them as guerrillas, although there were no 'guerrillas' at the time, just volunteer fighters who attempted, unsuccessfully, to liberate Castro del Rio from the Francoist troops who had taken the town.

Red cause at the beginning of the Movement in the village of Villaharta, which required his wearing Republican badges on the lapel of his coat. He has been placed at the Civil Governor's disposal."[33]

As a result, simply because he was wearing Republican badges, Francisco Landauro began a long ordeal of imprisonment and torture. His ultimate fate is unknown.

Another article appeared in June announcing that Falangista services in Cordoba capital had captured an anarchist from Torres Cabrera. Manuel Lucena Padilla was accused of having entered Torres Cabrera with 50 militiamen, pillaging the town and arresting Juan Bautista del Rosal Luna whom they killed down by the river, near Santa Crucita.[34]

The *ABC* daily newspaper of Seville was, like all the Francoist press as a rule, as every bit as engaged in publishing news reports of these tragedies. The following article was headlined in April 1939:

IMPORTANT ARRESTS

Cordoba, 21. The Information Brigade of the FET-JONS has been doing a praiseworthy job of performing law enforcement services of great importance.

Police officers Crespo and Pinazo arrested an individual named Joaquín Moreno Herencia, born and resident in Castro del Río, who is charged with having been President of the Trade Union Party before the beginning of the Glorious Movement. In this position, he dedicated himself to all kinds of pillaging and arrests of noted individuals, among them the Inspector of Security and the government delegate in that town, Sebastián Velasco, who as the object of the Red fury, was tormented and assassinated. Joaquín Moreno Herencia was Head Executive of the Grocery Store Committee.

Also worthy of note is the aforementioned brigade's arrest of the female President of the Libertarian Youth of Cordoba, Consuelo Fernández Sánches, 'The Cordovan Pasionaria'."[35]

In May, *ABC* Seville published the news that the Information Brigade of the FET-JONS had arrested Manuel Bellido Moreno, a high-ranking member of the Republican SIPM[ix] active in the Southern zone, between Porcuna and Villa del Río. He, Rafael Galesio, Pedro Sánchez and Ramón Cano Moya, were together accused of having murdered Lieutenant Colonel Luís Pastor Coll, commander of the Nationalist 1st Regiment of the 34th Division.[36]

A few days later, *ABC* Seville reported that the Falange Brigade had arrested a common criminal, Manuel Velasco *El Espartero* Muñoz, who had killed a neighbour in 1934 and was serving a sentence in Ocaña in 1936. Also arrested was Francisco Jurado *El Recovero* Gutiérrez, accused of participating in the incidents at Belalcázar as a Lieutenant in the Republican Militia. The same newspaper continuously published similar news reports, especially regarding events that occurred in Cordoba province, but goodness knows why only here, as identical hunt and capture programs were actively pursued in every Spanish province.

October 31 1939, the examining magistrate in Peñarroya determined that Juan Peñas Pérez, from Hinojosa, was guilty of 'belonging to the 193rd Brigade of the Marxist Army', and Pablo Herruzo Nogales, of belonging to the 69th Brigade.

The hunt and capture Rojos syndrome continued to inflame Francoists during the entire Year of Victory. December 1939, *Diário Azul* reported that Lisardo Cano Fernández, age 32, from Pedroche, was arrested in Cordoba capital for having participated in the murder of Antonio Cabrera, a priest from Pedroche.[37] These kinds of unfounded accusations were consistently made against prisoners.

In a news report regarding Villaviciosa, the paper reported that Rafael Cuevas Alcaide was arrested for having escaped from Pozoblanco jail where he was being held. Taking advantage of the dark and the rain, he went to his family's house in Villaviciosa, but the Guardia Civil found out and he was captured.[38] The commander of the post at the time was Sergeant Romualdo Reyes who in 1936 had led the insurrection in Adamuz. When the uprising in the village was quelled, Cuevas was released from jail.

December 19, the paper published, with its usual delight, the capture of Miguel Justo Sánchez Garrido, age 33, who had been a member of the local War Committee and had fled into the countryside. Rural Policeman José Hernández received a reward for capturing him. Miguel Justo ended his days viciously tortured and facing a firing squad in the Pozoblanco cemetery yet his Civil Registry record states that he died of a brain haemorrhage.

This family was one of those which suffered the most in Pozoblanco. His father, Justo Sánchez, was shot under the Law of Escapes on 6 June. His sister Josefa lived for two years under a sentence of death. His wife Juana

---

[ix] *Servicio de Infomación e Policia Militar* – Military Police and Intelligence Corps

Serrano León was condemned to 12 years in jail. His brother-in-law Juan Cuijo González fled to France but was captured by the Nazis there and transported to Mauthausen concentration camp where he died. The only members of his family who remained at liberty were Miguel Justo's mother and his baby daughter, although his mother was stripped of all her property and household goods.

Also published that December was the chief of police in the capital, José González Lara's announcement that Bernabé Cano Delgado from Adamuz had been arrested because he had killed the village telephone operator's son at the beginning of the war.[39]

Municipal Police and Falangistas competed with each other in hunting and capturing Rojos, flinging accusations right, left and centre to improve their standing with the regime and receive medals and rewards. The Falange group in Cordoba capital and the Police Commissariat worked without respite. Policemen Aparicio Romero, Heredia Espinosa, Ruiz Molina, López Linares and González Lara, to mention but a few of the more notorious, laboured night and day to ensure that no eminent Republican remained hidden in the city. At the end of the year *Diário Azul* published all sorts of libel and insults against José Álvarez Torquemada, a Cordovan mechanic who, after having fled Cordoba in 1936, had helped Antonio Jaén Morente organize the Cordoba Volunteer Battalion in Madrid.[40]

The climate of persecution continued with the same intensity in 1940, in keeping with the regime's ongoing extermination program. January, *Diário Azul* published the arrest of Rafael Muro López – *Carasucia* (the repressors always enjoyed giving nicknames to those they captured), a Freemason and member of the JJ.LL,[x] born and resident in Cordoba, on the grounds that he had been involved in burning the altars in San Agustin Church on the evening of July 18 1936, a fictional event that is not recorded anywhere. He was also accused of supposedly having killed Dios Rios, a Guardia Civil, on Calle Empedrada, before the war. He was arrested by a municipal policeman, Rafael del Olmo Garcia.[41]

October, the paper headlined the news that a high-ranking Marxist in Belalcázar had been captured. This was no less a person than Antonio Vigara Regidor, schoolmaster and ex-president of the *Casa del Pueblo*[xi] who had been living in hiding in his own house for the past year and a half. Vigara Regidor was one of the great intellectuals who helped create the Republic, a wise and venerable man, whose only crime was his ethos. He was arrested

---

[x]   JJ.LL - *Federación Ibérica de Juventudes Libertarias* [Iberian Federation of Libertarian Youth].
[xi] Socialist community social club.

by a municipal policeman, Fernando Ballester, at the height of the plague of informers and accusers. Lieutenant Ortega and Sergeants Escobar and Rodrigues were sent to capture him, on orders from the Spanish Legion which at the time was garrisoned in that town. The right-wingers in Belalcázar could not contain their delight.[42]

November, more news from Belalcázar. The police in Cordoba arrested Higinio Amaro *El Mocho* Rodriguez for committing blood crimes in Belalcázar. In August 1939, after right-wingers in Belalcázar launched a series of attacks and counterattacks in support of Franco, Republican troops were sent down from Madrid to quell the uprising. Although there were many dead on both sides, no fewer than 158 victims were Francoist insurgents. As a result, the Falange accused the entire Republican sector in the town, almost without exception, of blood crimes.[43]

In 1941, we note yet another example of the hunt and capture of the defeated, with the report of the arrest in Jaén of 'the head Rojo in Peñarroya, Eutimio Romero González, President of the Communist Party', who was accused of every killing in the mining zone.[44]

While the press was launching its propaganda campaign proclaiming Francoist successes in arresting the defeated, the military government published numerous judiciary decrees and edicts threatening to declare that all the defeated were to be treated as rebels. In effect, the BOPC[xii] records dozens upon dozens of subpoenas from the military courts that were operating in Cordoba capital and province during 1939 and 1940, as well as numerous search and capture warrants from examining magistrates and military judges throughout the province.

March 13 1940, the examining magistrate in Fuenteobejuna, Eloy Garcia Pérez, issued a warrant for the search and capture of Manuel Caballero Pizarro from the village of Cuenca, a village in which Francoists had previously killed a great many people in 1936. The examining magistrate of Cordoba city, Fernando Sepúlveda Courtoy, issued a similar warrant for José Martinez Santiago from Posadas. This individual, another of the lay Republican saints, had served as town councillor in 1931 and Mayor in 1936, was a member of the Unión Republicana and highly respected Master of the Abril Masonic Lodge in Posadas. In other words, his entire curriculum made him a perfect candidate for the National Catholicism scaffold. Already in October 1936, when Guardia Civil Lieutenant Colonel Bruno Ibáñez was subjecting Cordoba to a bloodbath, another crime against humanity, the Catholic newspaper *El Defensor de Cordoba* came forward to add fuel to the fire of extermination with this headline: 'Freemasonry, that is the enemy'.[45] *Don Bruno*, as he was

---

101

infamously known, took note and liquidated every Mason he could lay his hands on.

In El Viso, José Romero Peñas, the local examining magistrate, ordered the arrest of several individuals who had escaped from Santa Eufemia, including Manuel Fernández – *El Secretario*, Norberto Castillejos – *Veneno* and Luis Blanco Martín, who had fled to the mountains where they survived until after 1947.[46]

Earlier, August 4 1939, the examining magistrate in Belalcázar, Manuel Márquez Rubio, exhausted himself ferociously issuing warrants and searches all over the place when many prisoners he had condemned to death escaped from the Divina Pastora school in Belalcázar, where they had been imprisoned. What followed could have been a scene from a movie. Fifteen escaped, three died whilst escaping, and another was captured (he was later shot in November). The remainder fled to the hills and some became famous for their anti-Francoist activities during the following years.[47]

The judge continued to hunt high and low for Dionisio Castellano *Zabarza* García, Luís Hidalgo *El Huevero* Escribano, Eduardo Bejarano *El Portugués* Medina, Artero Paredes *El Fiscal* de la Cruz and Ángel Torrico *Nene de la Carmela* Garcia. These men did not go like so many sheep to the slaughter; they paid dearly for their lives.

One of these, Ángel Torrico's story could be the subject of another movie. On the evening of September 28 1947, his group of guerrillas was surrounded by the Guardia Civil in the las Hoces mountains of El Viso del Marqués (Ciudad Real). During the fight, all except one (*Pedro el Cruel*), were fatally wounded. When Sergeant Ruano rapidly moved closer to his prey to watch them die, Ángel Torrico, although already in his death throes, summoned enough energy to shoot and kill the bloodthirsty Ruano. Both died: executioner and victim. At least this Republican was avenged in death.[48] Not content with this bloodshed, the Belalcázar judge continued with his hunt for Manuel García *Quivicán* Peco and Francisco Paredes *El Bizco* de la Cruz.[49]

In Obejo, warrants were issued August 9 1940 against two members of the Barrios family: Bartolomé Barrios Herruzo and Luciano Sánchez Barrios. In Villaviciosa, Julio Nevado Martínez and Gabriel Pozuelo *El Gato* Expósito, were subpoenaed September 11 1940. Meanwhile, many of the hunted who could, fled to the hills.

The brutal pursuit of the defeated by Francoists led many individuals to take extreme measures for survival, such as those who camouflaged their and their family's identities and lived under assumed names during the forty years of the dictatorship. Such was the case of the ex-president of the Villaralto War Committee, Manuel Muñoz *El Preso* Sánchez, an active leader of the local

Socialist Youth who had been imprisoned after the October 1934 strikes, and released from prison after the Frente Popular elections.

Villaralto Falangistas searched high and low, without success, for Manuel Muñoz after 1939, but because he had obtained false documents for himself, his wife and son and they were living in a discreet and nomadic fashion. They first went to Los Blázquez where they worked making charcoal pellets, then they traded tobacco on the black market. Finally, they settled as farmers in the province of Malaga until the whole family moved to Salamanca, where Manuel Muñoz died. Shortly before he died, he revealed the family's true identity to his children. His widow and children returned to Villaralto after the death of Franco, to join relatives and obtain correct identity documents.

A similar case was that of the only survivor of the *Los Jubiles* voluntary militia unit, José Moreno *El Quincallero* Salazar, born in Bujalance, an 18-year-old youth who managed to escape from prison in Cordoba capital not long before he was scheduled to be hung by pretending to be one of the bricklayers who were working there. In 1987 Moreno Gómez found him in Osa de la Vega, Cuenca, where he was living under the pseudonym Antonio Pérez Sánchez. They met and he recounted his experiences; his oral testimony is recorded in Moreno Gómez' book on the guerrillas.

2. Suicide, a last protest against Fascism

The relentless harassment of the defeated also fostered another tragic phenomenon: suicide as a last resort against Fascism. One of the consequences of the defeat and the wave of repressive measures was the considerable rise in the number of suicides, which is estimated at some 30% above the average for previous years. Moreno Gómez remembers that at the beginning of the 1950s there were frequent reports of people committing suicide by hanging themselves or throwing themselves down wells. Today this is almost an unknown fact.

The dictatorship's incarceration of half of Spain, exclusions of all kinds, the social vacuum, the beatings and humiliating situations, the lack of any means of survival, the absence of a future and the drama of broken families, painted such an unbearably gloomy picture that a good many people were driven to take their own lives, not only during the hard times immediately following the defeat, but for decades afterwards, during the 1940s and 50s, until the explosive phenomenon of mass emigration provided an escape valve.

Many suicides occurred during the first weeks of victory as a last protest against Fascism, because of the despair of having been defeated and the impossibility of finding a means to leave the country. Everyone has heard of the shocking scenes in the Port of Alicante where numerous ex-combatants, officers, administrative officers and Republican authorities preferred to shoot themselves rather than fall into the hands of the Francoists. Many witnesses have told how every so often you would hear a shot on the quay and someone would fall lifeless to the ground.

Later, as defeated soldiers and civilians painfully made their way back to their hometowns during the Black Spring of 1940, many contemplated suicide – as the witnesses Moreno Gómez interviewed told him. Others did so, jumping from bridges, throwing themselves on train tracks or with the last bullet in their guns. Those who had suffered reprisals from left-wingers in times past never had to endure such terrible moments, more evidence that there can be no comparison between either regime's reprisals.

From the very beginning of the insurrection in 1936, the family dramas that the advent of Francoism created in many homes added to the number of suicides, principally in Andalusía. In his book on the Francoist genocide in Cordoba[50], Moreno Gómez tells of Manuel Landrove Pouzo and Manolo Reyes. Landrove, a municipal employee belonging to the UGT, was executed by firing squad in Cordoba, September 3 1936. After returning home from the cemetery where she had gone to recognize his body, his widow hung herself but not before she had hung each of her three children. A similar act occurred with the widow of Manolo Reyes, an elegant gypsy of Cordoba who was executed because he was recognized in a photo with Fernando de los Rios. Dr. Carlos Zurita, who was acting as a coroner at the time, told Moreno Gómez that at the cemetery, that woman looked at them with a hate that he will never forget. The day after her husband was shot, he learned that she had hung herself, after first hanging each of her seven children, one by one.

Although Moreno Gómez did not wish to make an exhaustive study of this subject in the province, he felt that some stories were necessary to give readers an example of the extreme despair that engulfed the disaffected during the immediate post-war period, when the greater number of suicides occurred in the homes and jails in the province and in the capital, a direct consequence of the brutal repression and torture meted to the imprisoned, particularly to individuals of some consequence in pre-civil war Spain.

24 April, the Communist leader from Villanueva de Cordoba, Gabino Cabrera Expósito, Captain in the famous Garcés Volunteer Battalion and member of the War Committee in 1936, committed suicide by throwing himself down a well at Number 5, Calle Iglesia (known as La Preturilla, later Bar Balagón, today a supermarket), that served as headquarters for the Nationalist SIPM and the Guardia Civil. Corporal Martínez Galiániz was the commander of the post. That evening, broken by ten days of savage beatings while yet again waiting for his turn to be beaten again, he dragged

his bloodied body towards a well in the patio and threw himself down it. His widow, who was still living in 1987, told Moreno Gómez that when she and the family went to the cemetery to recognize his cadaver, his body was an entire wound. He had been hung from his feet and his screams could be heard outside, in the street.

Gabino's sister Francisca was arrested because she left her house dressed in mourning; they shaved her head and forced her to drink castor oil before releasing her.[xiii]

Francisco Jiménez García, Mayor of Espejo in 1936 and a communist who was highly respected by the workers before and during the war when he belonged to the Villanueva de Cordoba Provincial Committee of the PCE. When Franco declared victory, he was arrested in the Port of Alicante and sent to Albatera concentration camp. Falangistas from Montilla and Espejo went there to get him. February 27 1940, he was subjected to continuous and terrible beatings in Espejo jail that he took his own life, although some witnesses say that he was beaten to death with sticks and then hung to simulate a suicide. One of his torturers was known by the nickname of *Mata alcaldes*, meaning 'Killer of Mayors'.

In Pozoblanco, Aniceto Villarreal Jurado, ex-councillor for the Frente Popular, was one of the Republicans most sought after by the Falangistas. They were unable to capture him alive because he first committed suicide by tying himself to some rocks and throwing himself into the cemetery water tank. In reprisal, they shot his brother Eleuerio and his nephew Pedro Villarreal Moreno.

Another famous case in Pozoblanco was that of the Republican doctor Rafael Bueno Roldán, age 53, who died in the local jail November 13 1939, after refusing medical assistance. Officially, he died from septicaemia. He had been condemned to death.

In Dos Torres, another much hunted individual was Eulalio *El Preso* Medrán, for his anti-insurrection activities in 1936. He evaded capture July 14 1939 by taking his life in a small hut on the edge of the town. In Puente Genil, Francisco Delgado Morales slashed his wrists in jail, but they stitched him up and then shot him November 6 1939.

Fear of the influence of the Church often heightened the feeling of despair such as when Bartolomé Rey Torres hung himself August 1 1939

[xiii] Francisca Cabrera. When Gabino's sister discovered that a historian was writing on these subjects, she frequently visited Moreno Gómez and spoke freely about the events during that period, no matter how great the suffering she and her family endured. She belonged to that class of defeated whose moral integrity remained strong and could never be discredited, no matter how much the victors tried to erase the historic memory of the times. Moreno Gómez is honoured that she attended the launching of the his first books.

because he was terrified that he would suffer reprisals for having participated in the burning of the San Sebastian Religious Brotherhood's flag three year earlier.

In Castro del Rio, where the CNT was dominant in the pre-war government, the number of prisoners tortured and executed created such a climate of terror that I know of at least three suicides in the local jail between 1939 and 1940. Felipe Agulera Arroyo, a farm worker, committed suicide May 11 1939 by putting his head into a prison latrine; either that or he collapsed in the latrine, head first, after a session of torture.

There were several executions in Castro del Rio at daybreak December 5 1919: six prisoners, led by Manuel Castro Merino – *El Abogado de los pobres* Merino[xiv], were shot against the cemetery wall. One prisoner, Francisco Torronteras Garcia, who had also been condemned to death decided that he preferred to die in bed, so he cut his wrists with a razor during the night. His body was found the next morning. Another suicide, José Sánchez, put an end to his life and to the torments he had been suffering by throwing himself down a well in the Las Monjas Convent prison August 28 1940.

In Villafranca, Francisco Jurado Fernández, one of the great heroes of the Republic and member of the Villafranca Volunteer Battalion, chose an extreme means to end his life. He had decided that the only way to end the beatings he was regularly receiving was to pretend that he was fleeing the guards as they were leading him to another interrogation. When in the middle of the morning June 9 1939 he was on his way to make yet another statement and receive the subsequent beating, he ran down the street, handcuffed, knowing that there was no possible salvation for him. There was none; they shot him in the back under the Law of Escapes.

Not all took their lives in prison. In Añora, Antonio *El Zumbo* Oviedo, was repeatedly summoned to make statements at the Guardia Civil barracks and then beaten, until one day, after receiving yet another summons, he hung himself in his bedroom at home.

When another member of the Villarelteño family in Villanueva de Cordoba that had suffered so greatly, Hilario Gómez Luna, returned home in 1946 under parole, he found himself unable to bear the loss of so many members of his family: his son was in jail, his father had been executed as had two of his brothers and a brother-in-law. It was just too much for a human being to bear. He took his life.

The Cordoba Provincial Prison was a cemetery of living men. Examination of the list of prisoners who died from starvation and privations (no less than 756 individuals died in this way, 25% of the prison population

---

[xiv] Affectionaly known as 'the people's lawyer'.

in the 1940s), indicates that several bear the hallmarks of suicide. This agrees with eye-witness reports of prisoners taking their own lives by hanging themselves or leaping off the top floor of the jail onto the gallery below. Unfortunately, the inability to contact relatives of the deceased makes it impossible for Moreno Gómez to confirm the accuracy of the following 'official' causes of death given, adding to the infinite number of unknown tragedies for which there is no closure.

- Francisco Priego Parado: fracture of the top and base of the skull, August 20 1941

- Bernardino López Morales, from Villanueva del Duque: skull fracture, April 1 1943

- Joaquín Garcia Lázaro, from Adamuz: rupture of the liver and pulmonary injury, October 17 1944, possibly indicative of torture as the contributing cause.

- Rafael García Gutiérrez, from Villanueva de Cordoba: skull fracture, April 11 1945

- Francisco Romero Paredes, from Belmez: fracture of the spine, June 7 1946.

Although there were other frustrated suicides in Cordoba prison, such as Juan Sánchez Pozuelo, from Villanueva de Cordoba, who after being condemned to death, threw himself from the top floor, did not die from the fall and was still executed by firing squad. It was not unknown for the prison authorities to issue their own version of an inmate's death, preferring to call it suicide to cover up their own culpability. In Almodóvar del Rio, the official version of Ángel Plazuelo Lozano's death in 1939 was that he committed suicide by throwing himself down a well. According to fellow prisoners however, he died from a beating and his body was then thrown down the well to simulate a suicide. Years later, there was a similar official version for the death of Vicente Mudarra Cañete, from Almodóvar, ex-Socialist councillor in 1931, who committed suicide in the Dueso, Santander, jail by throwing himself off the fourth-floor gallery. However, whether this was suicide or murder remains as much of a mystery today as it was then, because he was scheduled to leave prison on parole only a couple of days later.[51]

Alluding to a case outside Cordoba province, there is the tragedy of José Gómez Osorio, the last Republican Governor of Madrid, who was executed in February 1940. His entire family - wife and children - among these the well-known socialist Sócrates Gómez, were imprisoned in different jails. No longer able to bear such misfortune, his 19-year-old younger sister took her own life.[52]

Moreno Gómez hopes that this small, but significant sample, will give readers an idea of the number of lives that were lost in Spain from suicide, so damaged were the minds of those who took their lives because of the military coup, the war, the extermination, the terror and the unbearable living conditions that Franco's military forced upon the defeated and their families. It seems that the Four Horsemen of the Apocalypse had been sent against half of Spain. We only have glimpsed the tip of that monumental iceberg. History will never be able to describe its true magnitude.

3.   *Los Caídos* – Fallen in the Line of Duty for God and for Spain.

The 1939 orgy of repression was fuelled by another vindictive ingredient, the battle cry: ***Caídos por Dios y por España, ¡Presentes!*** All those fallen in the line of duty for God and Spain. Present arms! There undoubtedly also existed a component in Franco's plans demanding a furious vengeance that was more Judaic than evangelic in nature.

Even so, one must be careful and not make assumptions because the Francoist repression was so much more than a matter of revenge. In the first place, because the persecution had been programmed from the very beginning, before there was anything to avenge. Nothing had occurred in more than half of Spain - Galicia, Navarra, Soria, Zamora, Salamanca, the Canary Islands, etc., that had to be avenged, yet these regions were not exempt from the extermination. The Francoist repression clearly pre-dated any feeling of revenge and was at the margin of any vengeance, and if there had been occasional incidents in some places that could be used by Francoists as a pretext for getting even, so much the better for the program.

During the post-war period, banners calling for revenge for those who had fallen in the line of duty for God and for Spain, were part of the Francoist propaganda paraphernalia and were waved in profusion on every public occasion. Here, too, there is another aspect that needs to be made clear: the term *Caídos* represented all the Francoists who had died for the Nationalist cause in battle, as well as in every way as right-wing victims of Republican, or Rojo, actions against Franco and the regime. There was no reason to include Heaven in their cry, but as Francoists started the fire and there was a risk that some of them might be singed, it was wise to include the religious aspect. Just in case. After all, one cannot expect to launch a military coup where everyone is unscathed.

Peter Anderson, at a recent conference, defended a thesis according to which the repression and punishment were a consequence of the existence of Caídos (which he mis-translated as *martyrs* instead of *fallen*, as martyrs was not the standard interpretation of the term in those days).[53] According to Anderson, the repression was accomplished in revenge for and fuelled by memories of these 'martyrs'.[xv] This conclusion, although applicable within the confines of his study, could lead to historical misinterpretation because Anderson's work did not contemplate, let alone explain, the Francoist extermination on dates and in places where there were no Caídos (Galicia, Castilla la Vieja, Navarra, Canary Islands). Such an oversight could mislead one to conclude that first there was a Republican repression, the cause, followed by the Francoist repression, the effect thereof. In fact, the Francoist repression was planned to cover the entire country, with or without any Caídos, as occurred in numerous towns and villages where the Left never bothered anyone belonging to the Right.

The truth is that it was exactly the other way around. There is no possible hypothesis that can excuse Francoism from its nature as the aggressor or deny that at all times, all supporters of the Republic were the prime target of Francoist aggression. True, there were victims on both sides, many more on one than on the other, but there is only one reason for that: this was a military coup. Had there been no coup, there would have been no battles, no dead, no fallen or Caídos, on either side.

True, in some places the Francoist repression was more ferociously enforced than in others, as it was fuelled by the funerals and memorials to their fallen. There were numerous post-war exhumations and reburials, with the ceremonial transfer of coffins from one place to another, all of which excited the Francoists and added an emotional aspect to the repression, but only in some places. Undoubtedly also, post-war calls for punishment from angry relatives of Caídos served to expand the vindictive social base of Francoism, those who were accomplices in the general repression. The repression was orchestrated from above and from below; it was the widespread phenomenon of social complicity that totalitarian regimes always encourage.

Celebration of the memory of the Caídos became an instrument of unification between the affected base and the supporters of the totalitarian State. It created a network of demagogic loyalties, rooted in the heart

---

xv Anderson's study of part of the Pedroches district, Cordoba province, in villages where some Francoists died as a result of the so-called Rojo terror which to a certain extent influences his conclusions. Despite the misnomer, this is not to say that the work itself does not address some very interesting issues that are worthy of reflection.

of Francoism, ready to attack the demonized defeated with full force and from every direction. It was a gigantic culture of punishment, not one of forgiveness, that eventually superseded the official program of extermination that had been the fundamental principle of the fascist Movement since 1936.

So that the repressive impetus should not flag as time passed, what better than to continuously remind the people of the Caídos. Immortalize the memory to perpetuate the punishment *'So that the death of so many will not have been in vain; Always alert and vigilant, in memory of the Caídos'* as Spaniards were repeatedly told. Memory that called for revenge. On the other hand, today we ask for a democratic memory: *truth, justice and reparation* was the call raised by Carlos Jiménez Villarejo and others in Madrid, September 19 2012, in the presence of ex-Judge Baltasar Garzón, in an appeal for the creation of a Committee of Truth as recommended by the United Nations.

Reactionary Spain, that for decades fuelled the memory of its fallen with a spirit of revenge, today cries out with prejudice as the heirs of defeated Spain attempt to disinter existing and newly-discovered mass graves and bury their dead. Closure in the name of a Democratic Historic Memory. The Church also adds to the intolerance of any memory of the defeated every time it evokes the memory of the *Caídos* and calls for them to be beatified and canonized. The Roman Book of Saints is a constant exercise of memory.

Nowadays, society and some general public appear to believe that although memory of some is welcome, remembrance of others is not. Post-war reprisals were verbally fuelled by continuous allusions to 'victims of Rojo brutality'. In Cordoba capital, José María Herrero was the single victim of the Right, (as compared to 4,000 loyalists murdered in the city by the insurgents). The Cross to the Caídos on the La Malmuerta tower is a monument to the only Caído in the city. Inside the Mezquita-Cathedral one can still see a large stone plaque bearing the names of 102 members of the clergy 'murdered by Communism' in the province. Many years had to pass before the first loyalist Walls of Remembrance, engraved with the names of several thousand individuals murdered by Francoism in Cordoba, could be erected in 2011 in both the city's cemeteries.

The post-war Francoist press marked the anniversaries of the 1936 anti-insurgency fighting in the province by publishing elaborate obituaries with the names of Caídos. These occasions were celebrated everywhere with outdoor memorial masses perfumed by gunpowder and incense - the crucifix and the sword – and presided over by local dignitaries: Movement leaders, the Mayor, representatives of the Falange, the armed forces and the Guardia Civil, clergy, the local military commander... The twelve o'clock Sunday mass in San Mateo Church in Lucena was a great Nationalist spectacle: first came the military parade (volunteers, Guardia Civil, Falangistas, municipal police and paramilitary militia), followed by a band playing martial tunes, everyone singing *Cara al Sol* and *Oriamendi* and shouting Viva! to the Virgin of Araceli, the awesome pomp and circumstance of the Church. Again, the crucifix and the sword, the scent of gunpowder and incense, bonding with a common purpose. The most surprising was that when the religious processions left the church in Lucena, the population greeting them with the raised arm of the Fascist salute; anyone who did not do so was strong-armed by believers or Falangistas. Of all the priests in ultra-Catholic Lucena, all of whom were able practitioners of the Fascist salute, one who stood out was Federico Remoro who served as chaplain in the Fascist militia and, with a revolver tucked under his belt, participated in patrolling the streets.[54]

Meanwhile, many towns and villages were busy erecting monuments to their Caídos. July 17 1939, the Pozoblanco Town Council voted to 'erect a monument to the martyrs of the Red Horde'. September 1940, construction began on a huge mausoleum in Villanueva de Cordoba, budgeted at 80,000 pesetas, under the direction of a committee presided by Bartolomé Torrico.[55] November 1941, in Palma del Rio, another wealthy landowner, Félix Moreno Ardunuy, inaugurated a great monument to 42 victims of the Right, paid for out of his own pocket. He probably did so to salve his conscience as it was he who August 27 1936 ordered the machine gunners on his property to mow down more than 200 loyalist townspeople who were imprisoned there. Similar monuments were inaugurated in 1941 in Pedroche, Montoro, Hinojosa, and elsewhere, most of them in the North of Cordoba province, a region that had been a Republican stronghold. In the rest of the province, where Francoism rule had prevailed since the first day of the insurrection, the monuments were erected earlier. In Montilla, a Cross to the Caídos was placed on Calle Obispo Pérez Muñoz in 1937. May 1939, Salesian monks from Montilla inaugurated the Cross of Student Caídos, inscribed 'Don Bosco Alumni - Martyrs to God and to the Fatherland.'

The year of the victory, 1939, was marked by a constant to and fro of bodies, of Nationalist exhumations and re-burials. The body of Captain Cortés in La Cabeza Sanctuary was disinterred at the end of May 1939 and re-buried with a solemn mass and military honours in Andújar. In October, it was the turn of the remains of General Sanjurjo that were carried in triumph to Burgos. The most elaborate of all these ceremonies was the transfer of the remains of the dictator, José Antonio Primo de Rivera, Father of the Falange, from the cemetery of Alicante to the El Escorial monastery. His coffin was carried on the shoulders of Falangistas, who travelled on foot non-stop, day and night, in the Nazi manner. As the cortège passed through the towns, it was greeted with scenes of extreme fanaticism and raucous cries for vengeance. Republican prisoners were taken from the jails and executed by out-of-control firing squads.

In Belmez, June 2 1939, there was an impressive funeral and re-burial of the remains of 41 Caidos who were disinterred and brought from the neighbouring town of Belalcázar where they had been 'assassinated'. Placed in ten coffins, a prayer vigil was organized in City Hall. The re-burial, a crowded affair, was presided by the local authorities, military and Falangistas. Later, when the regime started executing Republicans from Belmez, they were taken to Belalcázar cemetery where they were shot by firing squads as a ritual of revenge. Similar vindictive acts occurred in other places as well, such as Santa Eufemia, where Republican prisoners were executed in a mine in Agudo (Ciudad Real) that had served as a prison for some right-wing individuals in 1936.

Another packed funeral was celebrated 3 October 1929 in Villanueva de Cordoba for 20 individuals whose bodies were transferred from the cemetery in Jaén where they had been shot in 1936. The prayer vigil was held in the church of Cristo Rey Convent, as the main parish building had been turned into a warehouse and market during the war and had not yet been restored to its former use. A Jesuit priest from Villanueva, Fr. Bernabé Copado, ex-chaplain attached to Lieutenant Colonel Luis Redondo's Nationalist paramilitary militia, celebrated the funeral, a vivid demonstration of National Catholicism. Fr. Bernabé led the funeral cortège all the way to the cemetery where he pronounced a heated patriotic-religious speech in the manner of an avenging angel. The fanatic priest, an enthusiastic Francoist activist, closely followed the extermination of Republicans in Villanueva and more than once attended Francoist Council of War meetings at the Casino, together with landowners and army and Guardia Civil officers, as they drafted the blacklists of those who were to be executed. He did not even lift a finger to save a first cousin of his, Francisco Copado. The executions that had been programmed in the Council of War commenced a few days after the mass funeral in Villanueva. According to Catalina Cantador, whose father was executed by firing squad, the day they brought the remains of those who had been previously buried in Jaén was a day of panic for the families of the defeated prisoners who they tortured all through that night.

In Villa del Rio, the victors forced several of the defeated to dig up the graves of some right-wing Caídos, according to José Luís Torralba who told Moreno Gómez the story of his father, Bartolomé Torralba Pastilla. The war over, he handed himself in to the local authorities knowing that although he would be arrested as he had served as an ambulance driver, he was not overly concerned because as his conscience was clear that his hands were not bloodstained, he would be pardoned. The victors, however, treated him mercilessly, beating him daily until his body was one entire sore. He was forced to dig up the dead that the anarchists had killed in Villa del Rio with his bare hands, no tools whatsoever, whilst they whipped him, under the full sun, without a drop of water the whole day. Four months later, a compassionate soldier from his village arranged for him to be transferred to Cordoba Prison where he was executed June 8 1940.[56]

Likewise excited by the spirit of exalting the memory of the dead, the press echoed repeated calls for revenge without quarter and no justice for the defeated. Feliciano Delgado, member of a reactionary family from Balalcázar, published the following article in the Cordoba press:

> "Anniversary. Three years ago, on a hot August day, the Marxist beast entered this town of Balalcázar, annihilating everything in its path… People of Belalcázar… do not forget the lesson, if you find yourselves possessed of envy, ineptitude or despicable thoughts, ignore them and join your *Caídos* and shout: 'Long live Spain! Long live Christ the King! Martyrs and heroes, present arms!".[57]

Causa General Decree of 26 April 1940 instructed the Ministry of Justice to determine the political responsibilities of the Frente Popular Government and to initiate criminal proceedings against the 'subversive forces that in 1936 openly acted against the existence and the essential values of the Fatherland, fortunately saved *in extremis* by the Liberating Movement.'[58] The Causa General archives, consisting of thousands of reports from municipal authorities throughout the country, contain lists of alleged crimes committed by Republicans against people and property, intended to demonstrate the truth of unfounded Francoist propaganda claims that the Rojos had assassinated hundreds of thousands of persons who did not support the July 18 1936 uprising, the frequently proclaimed 'Red terror'. These same archives contain reports of the multiple exhumations of those Caídos, following the victory. A typical record for Almadén, Ciudad Real, states:

- 21 August 1939, were exhumed and re-buried the remains of the following persons from El Viso, Cordoba, who were shot at km 17 on the road from Almadén to Saceruela during the civil war [12 are named].[59]

The record concludes by declaring the 'situation of persons accused by the Alamadén Municipal Authorities 20 February 1940', listing 37 individuals, 7 of whom are recorded as having been executed, 115 imprisoned, some charged in absentia and some freed. This and other records draw attention to the fact that local institutions, not just private individuals, also informed against the defeated, considerably exaggerating the facts as in this case, where 37 inhabitants of Almadén are jointly accused of having killed 5 persons.

The above is but a brief outline of the events of the Black Spring of 1939. It also illustrates how, in all of Spain, the machinery of the extermination program was prepared and controlled by the military. Everything in that great humanitarian catastrophe was military. One is reminded of the words of Felipe Acedo Colunga, a Francoist military prosecutor: '*We first have to disinfect the soil of the Fatherland. This is the task – sorrow and glory – that fate has entrusted to military justice.*'

4. The Church, at the root of the New Totalitarian State

Franco's so-called 'justice' was at the same time military, Falangista and ecclesiastic. The tripartite grouping of the military coup: barracks, casinos and church vestries, cannot be ignored or forgotten. Some authors have written about "The Church on Franco's side", but this needs to be rectified: the Church was not an adjunct of Francoism, nor was it a complement; it was an integral part of Francoism and one of the pillars of the regime. Logically, the Church acted in other ways, not overtly but instead as this institution did best: slyly, behind the scenes, in the confessional, from the pulpit, issuing bad conduct reports, through its sermons, chaplaincies in the prisons and in the multiple ways by which it influenced, supported and incited its flock.

Franco's principal ally could be found in the hierarchy of the Church. The Church helped Franco validate his military coup, justifying it by describing it as a crusade, more for foreign consumption than for domestic purposes, so that uncountable numbers of Catholics world-wide supported Franco. The Church hierarchy blessed Franco theoretically and judicially, quoting Canonic Law. They blessed him physically, saturating him in incense and raising canopies over his head as if he were the Holy Grail, saluting him with right arms upraised and finally, voting his being honoured with the Supreme Order of Christ in 1954. The Church prostrated itself before the supreme lawbreaker of the 5th Commandment, the proponent of his own Final Solution, the greatest war criminal in the History of Spain.

At the end of his life, the controversial Miguel de Unamuno who, whatever his faults, was possessed of a great intellect, commented on the blood pact between Franco and the Clergy, describing it as a stupid regime of terror in an African, pagan and imperialistic military manner. Referring to the shooting of individuals without due process of law as unjustified murder, Unamuno stated that there was nothing worse than the combination of the mentality of the barracks and of the church vestry, because traditional Spanish Catholicism was barely Christian. He predicted that the coming dictatorship would be the death of liberty and the dignity of Man. None of those who had emigrated, he said, would ever return to Spain; they would not be able to return, unless it was to live banished from their homes and reviled. "Poor Spain, poor Spain", he lamented.[60]

The Catholic Church, well entrenched in the eye of the hurricane, spoke more of Franco than it did Jesus Christ. It was euphoric, as Leopoldo Eijo y Garay, Archbishop of Madrid, one day told Franco in the Las Salesas Church that he had never burned so much incense with as much satisfaction as he did the day before him. Your Excellency".[61] The April 16 1939 front page of the *ABC* Seville newspaper, was covered with articles and photos of Franco's great victory parade, including one in which the dictator's silhouette stands out under a religious canopy, surrounded by priests.

The Church did the military establishment a great favour as it provided the Francoist regime with the doctrine that it lacked. The military launched this great adventure without any set project in mind unless it was the typical barracks rhetoric of order, discipline and harsh punishments. The military establishment arrived on the scene with an empty discourse that wanted for direction. Little by little, with the assistance of the Church, the Regime fashioned its discourse on a lot of Tridentine Catholic doctrine, a little traditional Calderonesque thought, some imperialistic notions and conservative beliefs, and a great deal of totalitarian dogma emanating from Rome and Berlin. The Church contributed with its congregations and impassioned masses, acting as if it were the great Spanish Fascist party (much more so than the Falange). This was how National Catholicism came to be founded.

Never was Spain so asphyxiated by incense and smothered by cassocks; not even during the darkest years of the Inquisition. By and large, the Church provided Francoism with the ideological leadership that it lacked, at the same time that the military took command of the practicalities of the repression.

The Church lay the table of Francoism with a wide range of retrograde material against the modernization of Spain, a modernization that had been counting on the first third of the 20th century to bring the country out of its state of underdevelopment. The Church weighed in with a Manichaean vision of the not unexpected social and political confrontation, seeing demons everywhere with every strike or slightest demand on the part of the workers. Anyone who expressed the least disagreement was branded by the Church as Godless. This was its eternal paranoia against heresy, that it countered with the threat of the rack and the pyre in the background. The bishops brandished the flag of reactionary Spanish thought with a bigotry that abhorred liberalism, constitutionalism, modernity, laicism, freethinking, and every new social theory introduced during the 'damned' 19th and 20th centuries. [62]

As Moreno Gómez said earlier, the Church continuously prostrated itself before the Dictator as much as Franco turned to the providers of holy water to legalize his military coup. The best example of this was the pomp and circumstance of the Church's consecration of the Caudillo in Santa Barbara Church, Madrid, May 20 1939, at the same time that the Law of Escapes was being liberally applied in the towns and villages of the Centre and South of the country.

Nineteen bishops, led by Cardinal Gomá, received Franco on the stairs of the church. Leopoldo Eijo y Garay, Bishop of Madrid-Alcalá, handed him the silver aspergillum so that the master of lives and properties could dip his fingers in the holy water and cross himself. Next, Franco and his wife entered the church under a majestic canopy, flanked on all sides by bishops, whilst the organ blared the monarchist anthem. Not in modern times had there ever been such pageantry. The highpoint of the celebration was when the Dictator placed his 'bloody' sword on the alter to the Christ of Lepanto, whilst monks from Silos Monastery who were also taking part, intoned arcane antiphonies from the Middle Ages. Franco, who could only manage to pronounce half a dozen clear lines in a row (public speaking was not his strongpoint), declared that this sword "had heroically vanquished the enemy of Truth in this century". The ceremony ended with Cardinal Gomá blessing him before God and History.

The following day, the newspaper *Arriba* interpreted this ceremony as the simultaneous reincarnation of Julius Caesar, Charlemagne and Emperor Carlos V, in the person of the Caudillo. The day before, another reporter, Ernesto La Orden, had dedicated a series of rhymes to that day's parade, in the style of the *Song of the Cid*. Even poor don Rodrigo found himself enmeshed in the Francoist delirium tremens. This is what Hilari Raguer, a monk from Montserrat, called the "debauchery of National Catholicism". [63] The Church, prostrate before its new idol, the new golden calf.

In Cordoba, the Church hierarchy, lacking a local Franco-like personage, had for some time bent over backwards to honour Colonel Bruno Cascajo, the Military Governor of the province, a leader of the coup and the perpetrator of the genocide in the city. The Church's worship of the regime is illustrated in an October 1 1936 photograph published by *Diário Azul* showing Bishop Adolfo Pérez Muñoz, surrounded by canons of the church, giving the Fascist salute as they leave an official reception in honour of a Francoist celebration. [64]

During those dark days of October, there was no doubt as to the Church's approval of Colonel Cascajo, as Bishop Pérez Muñoz publicly congratulated the brave saviour, a General by popular acclaim, who with a certain hand at decisive moments was entrusted with a heaven-sent mission that he accepted without reservation, defeating, as if he were another courageous and heroic David, the Red Goliath in Cordoba (…).[65]

It was not only the bishops who praised of the winner of the civil war in those days of victory when church bells rang out everywhere. The supreme leader of the Church himself, Pope Pius XII, sent Franco his own messages of congratulations:

- "…Our fraternal congratulations for the peace and victory with which God has deigned to crown the Christian heroism of your faith (…). This nation chosen by God has just shown this century's followers of materialistic atheism, outstanding proof that the eternal values are above everything else."

This was the first of two messages Pope Pius XII sent Franco in 1939, no greater proof of the Church's blessing of a war criminal, leader of a Fascist regime, instigator of a river of blood and a vale of tears. Not a single word of forgiveness or reconciliation. On the contrary, a call for 'justice for the crime'. Yet, when the other European Fascist regimes were defeated in 1945, Pope Pius XII had no qualms in declaring that there would be no peace until there was charity and forgiveness, sentiments that he did not extend to the Spanish defeated in 1939.

All the clergy, from the highest member of the Church hierarchy down to the lowest parish priest, with very rare exceptions, were at the service of the Dictator. The parish priest became yet another local authority, such as when new Francoist municipal officers were invested, this was in the presence of the parish priest as well as the local military commander and the head of the Guardia Civil. The ubiquitous good conduct references (especially 'bad' reports) had to be certified by the parish priest. Rather than engaged in their roles as managers of Divine Affairs, priests became executives and supervisors of the repressive machine. The summary records of the military courts also contained certificates issued jointly by the victorious tripartite: the head of local Guardia Civil, the Mayor and the parish priest. Again, the barracks, the casino and the church vestry ruled hand-in-hand.[xvi]

[xvi] Moreno Gómez consulted many of these summary reports in the Pozoblanco Judiciary Archives regarding indictments for Political Responsibility, that today are filed at the

The Church made remarkable statements regarding good conduct certificates. The Archbishop of Santiago de Compostela, Tomás Muñiz Pablos, issued a circular September 14 1936 according to which it was scandalous that a priest might save a parishioner's life by issuing a favourable report, not that he could virtually sentence him to death with a negative one. He further instructed his priests to abstain from giving certificates of good religious conduct to anyone who belonged to a Marxist organization and in all cases, to certify behaviour 'diligently, without any further deliberation, without contemplating any kind of human sensitivities.'[66] It was well known that a negative report (does not go to mass, for example) implied the execution of the individual, and so it frequently happened.

Military and ecclesiastic authorities did not conceal their collaboration and greeted each other warmly when participating in public events. The clergy attended political acts as honoured authorities and the military occupied front row seats during religious acts and ceremonies. Funerals, numerous and performed with much pomp and circumstance in the days following the victory, were held exclusively for the victors' Caídos. The Catholic Church never again prayed for the defeated, yet it has continued praying for Fascists for more than half a century. When November 20 1941, a great funeral mass was celebrated in Cordoba at San Pablo Church, for José Antonio Primo de Rivera, officiated by the Bishop in the presence of all the authorities. The Bishop himself led the funeral party to the Cross of the Caídos at the La Malamuerta tower. There, clergy, military and Falangistas, shouted the usual Vivas! and raised their arms in the Fascist salute, whilst singing *Cara al Sol* until they were hoarse.

The matter of crucifixes in public places, a subject that was fiercely debated during the Republic, a democratic regime that tried to anticipate the separation of the Church and State, that which is the norm today, became a burning issue. Crucifixes were hung all over the place. Not only in school classrooms, but in the most unexpected places, including City Hall. In the latter, religious paintings of the Sacred Heart of Jesus, a typical Jesuit memorial, were commonplace. One city hall unanimously deliberated that the image of the Sacred Heart of Jesus should be exhibited with all solemnity

---

Cordoba Provincial Historic Archives. The immediate post-war summary reports contained a high percentage of death sentences. He consulted them when they were kept in Pozoblanco, despite some opposition from the archivist who told him that from then on he had to forget these matters. To which Moreno Gómez replied that without a doubt, he meant that that one must forget them now, so as to re-write history later. Moreno Gómez' research was becoming a never-ending obstacle course. Francoism, that wrote its own fallacious history, embellished with bells and whistles, has always been opposed to the defeated writing theirs. Power against memory.

at City Hall, to make amends for the sacrilege committed in that house by the Marxist Horde and make it clear that the New State desired to inspire the Spanish people with the sacrosanct rules of the Christian Religion and to shelter all its subjects under the protection of the Sacred Heart of Jesus.[67]

The above text brings many surprising reflections come to mind: one, that sacrilege may be committed in a church but not in City Hall; two, that Francoism talks of subjects, not citizens; and three, that it is not up to the Municipality to preach the Christian Religion. All of this is politico-religious bunkum, something that was never preached in Spain, not even under the Inquisition.

In Montilla, the crucifix returned to preside over the Meeting room at City Hall October 1936. On the same day, crucifixes were blessed for all the schools, as were the ones that the women who worked in the Soup Kitchen were required to wear. December 1938, blessed crucifixes were given to every soldier. November 1936, when a teacher requested that an illustration of the Sacred Heart of Jesus be solemnly hung in his house, the entire National Catholic retinue went to celebrate the event. The famous archpriest Luis Fernández Caso, in an inflamed oratory, took advantage of the occasion to exhort everyone to do the same in their homes as it was time that the Sacred Heart of Jesus reigned over everyone, everywhere. It was no longer only schools that were turned into monasteries, but entire municipalities.

In most Cordovan municipalities, the religious image that had been enthroned still hangs on walls. The process of dismantling Francoism has been extremely slow, in accordance with the parsimonious spirit of the transition. Even today, this image still hangs above the councillors' seats in Pozoblanco City Hall.

These images also hung on the walls of premises belonging to the Falange, such as Post Offices and factories like the Electro Mecánica. Accordingly, May 7 1942 the local press followed on with an article that the Electro Mecánica celebrated its anniversary with a mass and the solemn hanging of the image of the Sacred Heart of Jesus, a formal act attended by the municipal authorities led by the recently retired genocide Cascajo and Félix Romero Menjíbar, secretary to Bishop Adolfo Pérez Muñoz.[68]

Clerical harassment targeted three groups in particular: all children in general, the prisoners who packed the jails, and humble people in the countryside. In other words, against the social base that had supported the Republic. As far as poor children and children of the imprisoned went, one and the same where poverty was concerned, they were placed under the auspices of the so-called infamous Social Welfare program where they were fed but primarily, brain-washed. Each roll of bread was accompanied by a class in religious doctrine in preparation for their First Communion (actually, mass Christening services for children of 'Rojo atheists'). They were taught numerous New State martial hymns: *Cara al Sol, Falange, Requetés*, etc., ending with *Cantemos al Amor de los Amores*. This was all a premeditated and perfected plan for indoctrinating (i.e., 'disinfecting') the children of the Rojos, upon whom it was impressed that their parents were 'lost sheep', sinners who bore all the hallmarks of Hell. Democrats were fodder for the devil; Fascists were not.

The Church forced its way into and controlled the private and public lives of the entire population. All civil registry marriages were declared null and void. The Church issued fire and brimstone ultimatums for church weddings, stating that it considered civil registry marriages as no more than sinful ordinary cohabitation. At the same time, it organized a wave of mass christenings as under the New State, if a child was to have any kind of right he had to have been baptized.

The press was a good reporter of National Catholicism harassment. One headline in the *Diário Azul* stated that 23 marriages of persons remaining in the Red zone were celebrated and 40 children received the sacrament of baptism in the town of Espiel.[69] This was followed by another headline reporting 63 marriages and 150 baptisms in a single day in Villa del Río.[70]

After each christening, parish records erased the 'pagan' or proletarian given names and replaced them with names from the Church-approved list. Many names under which children had been christened according to left-wing tradition or European laicism, such as Libertad, Aida, Lina, Germinal, Jaurel, Bebel, Floreal, and so forth, were viciously eliminated. For example, the last four had been used to christen the sons of Socialist mayor of Villanueva del Duque, Miguel Ranchal; the children were renamed Miguel, Juan, Antonio and José, respectively.

A notorious case of the religious coercion and manipulation of children was recorded in Montilla, December 1936, when Ágnela Zafra, a ten-year-old girl, was forcibly christened with her teacher as godmother, followed by a celebration in her house. Ágnela was the daughter of the great Socialist leader and ex-Member of Parliament, Francisco Zafra Contreras, who had been taken in handcuffs to Baena where he perished in a mass execution of more than one hundred defeated. One of his other children, her brother Francisco, was shot in Cordoba. Àgnela's christening and First Communion a few days later, was considered quite a coup for Montilla's National Catholics.

It is presumed that similar, long forgotten, cases occurred all over Spain. Let us continue in Montilla. Socialist Rafael Baena Cruz, imprisoned in Montilla jail, was promised that he would be saved from imminent execution if he agreed to marry in the Church. The poor man accepted and archpriest Fr. Luis Fernández Casado, celebrated the wedding. As soon as the ceremony was over, Rafael was taken away and executed. A few days, the archpriest callously christened Rafael's three children.

Fr. Casado did not rest in his mission of redeeming children of Rojos. He christened the three children of another Socialist leader, José Gama Rodriguez (executed in July 1936). He warned Antonio Luque and his wife Rosa Gómez who had married in the civil registry, that they should remarry in the Church if they wanted their daughter to be admitted to school. Another, no less rabid parish priest, Fr. Rafael Castaño, forced Manuel Aguilar to baptize his daughter so that she could attend school. Elsewhere, Araceli González, who had spent the war in Jaén and whose brothers Juan and Manuel were imprisoned in Mauthausen, where they died, had no sooner returned to Montilla after he was released, than he received the visit of several 'virtuous' young ladies (Sunday school teachers, daughters of famous landowners and winemakers in the region), who warned him that he had to baptize his children if they wanted to attend school and receive food cards and vouchers for municipal benefits.[71] Pure and simple religious blackmail.

Holy Sunday (Sunday after Corpus Dei) May 26 1940, 18 Republicans were executed in Villanueva de Cordoba just before the ceremonial religious procession. One of these was Eugenio Jurado, a high-ranking member of the PCE, who left a daughter named Aida. She was soon included in the group of children who were to be forcefully christened. The Sunday School teachers who prepared them acted as godmothers to the Rojo children as the Church did not allow family members who were 'contaminated' by Marxism to do so. Eulia Santos was godmother to little Aida who was rechristened Isabel and her original name erased from the records.

In practice, those who were destined to be killed and their families were subjected to all kinds of religious coercion. Antonio Cordoba Gálvez, 28 years old, was executed November 1939. He was already on his way to the firing squad when he was forced to marry in the church and rechristen his son Lenin Cordoba Polonio to Antonio forthwith. Even the few letters the condemned to death were allowed to write, were manipulated by the prison chaplains. Carlos García Herrador, who was executed in Cordoba June 28 1941, was forced to dictate his letter of farewell to his wife and daughter, to the prison chaplain Fr. Alfredo, a Carmelite. As the chaplain wrote what he felt like, it appeared more like a letter from a nun than from a Republican facing imminent death. The priest wrote that Carlos insisted that he forgave [his executioners] with all his heart and he wanted his wife to do the same, and that he had a message for his daughter to the effect that she should be educated in the Christian faith. It was important for the executioners to have the family of their victim forgive them, otherwise one day they might attack them in a fury of revenge.

The Church's involvement in the conflict of christenings and Church weddings pre-dated the civil war when, during the Republic, many employers would only give jobs to those who had been married in the Church. In 1936, with the coup, the dispute went much further and in towns that came under Fascist control, several people were shot solely because they had only married in the registry office. As the Church has, as have other religions, always been obsessed with matters involving sex, priests, in Cordoba capital and elsewhere, drew up blacklists of individuals who had not been baptized or married in the Church, or who may have had a clandestine love affair. Added to these, any perceived breaches of the 5th and 6th Commandments provided fodder for the lists that another priest, Fr. Ildefonso Hidalgo, presented to Don Bruno Cascajo. This Nero-like Lieutenant Colonel of the Guardia Civil was responsible for the genocide in Cordoba, the city that he drowned in an incessant blood bath.

Post-war, every vestige of laicism was eliminated without second thoughts and the church wedding became compulsory; no excuse or pretext was accepted. Church regulations were published in the Official Government Bulletin as were long lists of forbidden behaviour as in the matter of dances, the length of a woman's skirt, short sleeves, movie theatres (lights were placed in the back rows to prevent temptation), and prostitution during Lent.[xvii]

Another anathema of the Church during Francoism was the observance of pagan celebrations, such as Carnival.[72]

Government of the Nation. Ministry of Governance.

DECREE of January 12, 1940 confirming the absolute prohibition of Carnival celebrations.

As the so-called Carnival celebrations have been banned for several years and there being no reason for changing the said decision, the Ministry has decided to maintain the ban and to remind all Authorities under this Ministry of the absolute prohibition of the observance of such celebrations. Madrid, 12 January 1940. SERRA SÚÑER

No matter how tight the Church's control on the everyday lives of the Spanish people, its power over Education was even more intransigent, to the extent that schools were run in an almost monastic manner. Christian

---

[xvii] Also during the Republic there was less tolerance of extra-martial behaviour. 'Anti-prostitution crusades' were also organizedby conservative civil authorities.

doctrine was a major course subject, as was Sacred History, and teachers were required to organize all kinds of devout, activities. Classes began and ended with prayers. Pedro Cantero Cuadrado, Archbishop of Zaragoza, praised the 'Christian and Christianizing' work of the Ministry of Education by declaring that coeducation was banned in Secondary and Primary schools; Crucifix reappear, private libraries were purged, assistance was given to ecclesiastic universities and chapels were built in Catholic universities and schools of higher education, proof that the Ministry was no longer the bastion of laicism and now served Catholic Spain."[73]

Although children and students were favourite targets for the Church's religious brainwashing, its activities in the Francoist jails were of considerably greater concern. The prison universe was the basic theatre of operations for the Francoist repression, the focus of actions against the physical integrity of the defeated and against their moral fortitude. If the physical integrity was handled by the military and the Falange (punishments, torture, and firing squads), the Church took care of the ideological repression (brainwashing, re-Christianization and 'disinfection' of 'dissolutionary', i.e., democratic, ideals) through coercion and the forced imposition of religious practices.

Some ten years after the re-establishment of Democracy in Spain, the position of the Benedictine Abbot of the Valle de los Caídos sanctuary (and likewise, of almost all the clergy and doubtless the military also) continued to be clearly pro-Francoist and opposed to all the humble homages to victims of Francoism. Not long ago, the Laín Entralgo family gave Moreno Gómez a letter dated August 23 1986, that the Benedictine Abbot Manuel Garrido Boñano sent to Fr. Pedro Laín Entralgo, reproaching him for participating in the inauguration of a monument to the victims of Francoism in Dos Hermanas, Seville, August 1986. He reprimanded Fr. Pedro for extolling the so-called Rojo sovereignty, whilst they burned churches, imprisoned a multitude of persons and assassinated many thousands of innocents solely because they were priests, members of the clergy (monks and nuns) and practicing Catholics.[74]

After thirty years of Democracy, a young priest serving in the Valle de los Caídos, briefly replied to some opinions asked of him in a 2009 television documentary:[75]

- What does Franco mean for Spain today?

> "He is an example for those who govern us and an example for the Spanish and for Catholics. And this must be taught and well taught, without changing things. When history is changed, it is no longer history; it becomes a story." ~

- Who is changing history?

> "Today it is politicians who are doing so, and the media, and the schools. Many people tell me "Look, father, I had the best years of my life during the days of the Caudillo". And others tell me: "I only discovered that we had been living under a dictatorship two years after Franco died, when they began to say so. I lived under a dictatorship for seven years and unfortunately have not been able to live under it for longer.""

These opinions are not only those of this priest. The tentacles of National Catholicism still flourish today. Suffice to mention the ongoing integrationist activities of another priest, Fr. Ángel David Martín Rubio, the so-called 'historian' of Badajoz who continuously promotes his unacceptable ideas in his personal Blog on the Internet.

To conclude this brief description of the Church's role during the dark and very complex world of Francoism, one should take a look at how this was seen in some Catholic sectors throughout Europe at the beginning of the civil war. Of special note is the exemplary case of an academic who had served as a canon of Cordoba cathedral during the 1920s. Fr. José M. Gallegos Rocafull was a brilliant scholar, professor of the San Pelagio Seminary and later professor at the Universidad Central de Madrid, where he was when war broke out. He did not delay in expressing his rebuke of the military coup and his support of the Republican cause. October 12 1936 in Madrid, Fr. Gallegos Rocafull and a fellow academic, Fr. Leocadio Logo, published a manifest entitled *Palabras cristianas* [Christian teachings], where these learned scholars cite Papal and church texts in their condemnation of the uprising:[76]

— *"The Church will never stop teaching the respect and obedience due to the established power…"* Collective declaration by Spanish bishops 20 December 1931.

— *"…the Church has always condemned the doctrines and the men who rebel against the legitimate authorities."* Pope Leon XIII, *Au milieu.*

— *"The truth is that a few men have burdened the shoulders of the innumerable multitude of proletarians, a yolk that is very little different to the one of the slaves."* Pope Leon XIII, *Rerum Novarum.*

— *"The economic organization violates the true order when capital enslaves the workers."* Pope Pius XI, *Quadragesimo Anno.*

Bolstered by this baggage of authoritative ecclesiastical pronouncements, the Cordovan canon stood up to public opinion, speaking strongly against the coup and in favour of the Government, the only clergyman in Spain who dared to do so. Gallegos Rocafull travelled across Europe during the war, noting the for and against swinging of clerical opinions regarding the Spanish case and that these were by no means unanimous." [77]

He was particularly scandalized by the fact that priests were going to the front bearing arms, with a revolver tucked in their belt. Once again, the Spanish Church followed the Pope's lead in supporting his policy in all ecclesiastical matters, whereby infantrymen, in the Medieval manner, could be compared to Archbishop Turpin in *La Chanson de Roland*, a swordsman who with a few blows of his sabre charged against more than four hundred Saracens. During the days of the Francoist victory and the National Catholic paraphernalia, Gallegos wrote that he was pained by this abandon, this hard-heartedness, this loathing of the defeated, so alien to Christian charity. [78]

From Paris, Gallegos Rocafull was informed that Irish Jesuits were beginning to object to the actions of the Spanish clergy and had published statements such as the following one, in their magazine *The Messenger of the Sacred Heart*, to the effect that the real cause, albeit an occult one, is that the war was undoubtedly the social injustice condemned by the Popes." [79] Jesuit General Father Leodokowski's response was rapid and furious as he rushed to the pulpit to tell the Irish to shut up. As always, 'the reasons of high politics' that are always 'dishonourable' when they are not rotten and pestilential. [80]

In March 1937, Gallegos Rocafull met with Jacques Maritain, one of the great representatives of French Catholic existentialism who greatly impressed him with his modesty, his sincerity and his sweetness that conveyed a profound and solid spiritual life. [81] In turn, Maritain, in his prologue to Mendizábel's work on the Origins of the Spanish Tragedy, refuted the assumption that what happened in Spain was a Holy War, that it was by excellence temporal and that all war implied political and economic interests, greed of the flesh and the blood. [82]

Regardless, the Spanish Church sank into this can of garbage up to its thighs. In his 1938 book *Les grands cimitières sous la lune* [The great cemeteries under the moon], Georges Bernanos, another notable French Catholic Existentialist, gave the most tremendous tongue lashing ever to a group of clergymen, a literary expression to the shocking crimes that Francoists were committing in the Canary Islands. [83]

Whilst travelling in Europe September 1938, Gallegos Rocafull attended a homage to François Mauriac who had strongly expressed his disgust at the violence wielded by the insurgent rebels that June, in the French newspaper *Le Figaro*. In that article, Mauriac said that the assassinations committed by the Moroccan troops who had pinned a Sacred Heart to their robes, that the systematic purges, the cadavers of women and children left behind by German and Italian aviators at the service of a Catholic leader who claimed that he was a soldier of Christ, all of that was a horror at another scale.[84]

Rocafull was also impressed by the words of another famous French Catholic philosopher, José Bergamín, who also spoke at the homage to Mauriac, when he stated that Christ was not at the orders of any general nor of any dictator and that furthermore, that the priests and monks who were assassinated, as well as the victims of the summary judgements and secret executions and the innocents machine-gunned on their doorsteps, were equally entitled to the love and mercy of Christ.[85]

Clearly, opinions in Europe, opinions were far from unanimous regarding Franco. The Patriarch of Lisbon, Cardinal Cerejeira, criticized the excesses of the 'political Catholics' in Spain, remarking that they did not understand the meaning of Christ. They were working consciously or unconsciously to de-Christianize Catholicism.[86]

None of the above drew the fury that followed the Archbishop of Zaragoza, Rigoberto Doménech's Medieval message blessing the violence, in which he said that violence was not carried out in the service of the municipality, but legally, to the benefit of order, the Fatherland and Religion.[87] As Hillary Raguer pointed out in his book on the Church and the Spanish Civil War, quoting Southworth: "It was in Spain, during the civil war, that the union between the Catholic Church and the Fascist movements was sealed with blood."[88]

Gallegos Rocafull's opinions did not go unnoticed by the 'hierarchy of the 'Crusade', who considered that he was Cordovan although born in Cádiz. As early as 1937 the Bishop of Cordoba, Adolfo Pérez Muñoz, suspended him *a divinis*, but it was not until the 'Triumphant Year' of 1939, by which time Gallego Rocafull had fled to Mexico, that the Bishop of Cordoba's wrath exploded.

Bishop Adolfo, such a keen displayer of the Fascist salute when standing next to the genocide Cascajo, accused him of promoting the Rojo Marxist revolution, when what Gallegos Rocafull was actually supporting was the constitutional Government of the Republic. The Bishop sent the following message to Mexico, formally disbarring Rocafull from the Church:

"You are hereby barred, with a perpetual and unlimited suspension of every kind; that is, not only *a divinis* but also *ab officio et beneficio,* including all the distributions and administration of assets you have benefited from under Canon Law 2222, for your enormously serious and highly scandalous transgression of paragraph 1 of Canon 141 through your spoken and written activities in favour and in defence of the Rojo Marxist revolution that the Pope and the Spanish bishopric have condemned."[89]

This infernal labyrinth was just the tip of the iceberg of reprehensible activities with which the Spanish clergy cloaked itself in its synergy with the Dictator. Moreno Gómez addresses other aspects of this, when he discusses the numbers of executions, the microhistory of the prisons, the pestilent world of denunciations, the manipulation of children and the unholy maelstrom of the purges.

5. Religious manipulation of children

To begin with, some background data is essential. Many poor children, sons and daughters of the imprisoned, were scattered across a multitude of reception centres and for whom there is no exact data. These centres belonged to or were controlled by the Social Welfare authorities, religious organizations in towns and villages, charity soup kitchens for children of all kinds, and so forth. The few available statistics refer to children of the imprisoned, but only of those prisoners who came under the Redemption of Sentences through Work regime, of which there were few, very, very few. The official report to the government on these children, the 1943 *Memoria,* indicates that 9,050 children of prisoners were taken in during 1942 and 12,042 in 1943.[90] Furthermore, the Regime enacted another key measure (Law of March 30 1940), by which all children over the age of three years had to be removed from the prisons. These children were taken away by truck (in Saturrarán, Amorebieta, etc.) and in many cases, their mothers never heard of them again. Finding them, if at all possible of course, was made more difficult by the Law of December 4 1941, which legalized the Church's changing their names.

The ensuing reality was these children and many, many more, filled religious schools, convents, hospices and orphanages, all of which were under the tutelage of the Catholic Church, thus providing the favourite grounds for the Church and National Catholicism's work in the ideological repression of the defeated through their children. The children of the defeated who were taken into religious schools and welfare institutes that provided them with perfect 'Dianas' with which to shoot arrows of re-education and propagation of the victorious ideology. Mónica Orduño's research into the Catholization work of the Welfare Authorities [91] shows that in addition to data regarding baptisms, First Communions and church weddings, there was a separate section devoted to the number of religious vocations sent to the Seminary. It is also interesting to note that children of Rojos are recorded as more frequently enrolled in religious institutions, convents and seminaries than in public schools.

Juan Caunedo Domínguez' excellent documentary *Sombra, niebla y tiempo* [Shade, fog and time] for the Madrid Forum for History, relates two cases in those days when parents were imprisoned and their children frequently placed in a Seminary or convent. The first one is the mother's story:

"A mother was allowed to see her son who had come to visit her. He was about twelve years old, which means that he had been removed from the jail (and his parents) because he was more than three years old. He was wearing a cassock, the uniform for seminary students. During the entire visit, the woman held her tongue and held it well, but when she returned to the cells, she exploded in anger - they had killed her husband and turned their son into a priest. Children were dressed as priests and nuns when they were taken to visit their mothers in prison and they were taught that they had 'to pray for all the sins of their parents'. Although the intent was to break down a family and deconstruct that family's offensive ideals, all they achieved was to deconstruct a political ideology." [92]

Another witness from Gijón reports on similar religious manipulation she was subjected to as a child:

"I was taken to a religious school in Oviedo. After eating, we said an *Our Father* in thanks for the food we had received and another for 'His Excellency the Head of State, Lord of the Armies'. When we prayed for our father and mother we had to add 'kill them Franco'; when I refused to pray, the nuns would force me to pray alone if I wanted to go to recreation. When we went into the town, we stood out and people jeered at us and called us 'the hospice girls'. The nuns would punish us by making us kneel on dried chick peas and hold out our arms in a cross, and they would take our morning and afternoon snack away from us. They wanted me to become a nun in Pelayos, as another girl there had done; on Sundays we went to Mass there, so we could see her cloistered behind the grills, praying. They were determined that I should become a nun but all I wanted was to go home to my grandmother's."[93]

The above witness' brother (both people were charming people from Asturias whose names escaped Moreno Gómez - if there was a fault with the documentary it was that it did not sub-title the names of those who spoke; it only listed them briefly at the end), was sent to a Jesuit school in Gijón, as they did in those days when they tried to recover control of the orphans of the civil war through religious brainwashing.

Montse Armengou and Richard Belis produced a magnificent documentary *Los niños perdidos del franquismo* [Franco's forgotten children] for Barcelona television, [94] provides additional details regarding the forced religious vocation of prisoners' children with personal memories similar to those reported in Caunedo's documentary.

Teresa Morán, speaking with the great moral strength typical of Republican women, remembers that Santis' husband and two guerrillas who were with them were executed and she was taken to Ventas prison and condemned to death but her sentence was later commuted. Occasionally, some relatives would bring her news of her children who had been sent to different schools. One day she was called in to the visiting room. What a surprise! What a rare event! When she got there, there was her eldest son, dressed as a priest, accompanied by a priest who was one of his teachers., just as they came from the Seminary. She entered the room and saw her son dressed as a priest and… what can I say? Traitors! She shouted. 'How could you, they killed your father! This is the worst thing I could ever imagine. Seeing one of my sons dressed up like a priest, accompanied by one of those who murdered his father and have now taught him to hate him!"

Around 1942, four girls from El Viso de los Pedroche were 'netted' and taken to a convent in Barcelona, among them, the sister of the young guerrilla José *Rios* Murillo. The latter and his father had fled to the mountains mid 1941 but there is no information regarding their mother. We have no idea why the four girls were taken from this village. Perhaps to punish their parents.

As National Catholicism was determined to increase the number of its followers, the Church resorted to a massive campaign for religious vocations and by the end of the 1950s, seminaries were bursting at the seams. Most vocations came from humble families and from those whose left-wing parents had, or had not, been converted by the Church's constant pressure on every aspect of their lives. Juan A. Bustos Casado, one of many members of the Communist Party but of no known political activism, was shot June 12 1940 in Villanueva de Cordoba. He confessed to Fr. Marcial and asked him to look after his children. One of his sons, Gaspar, was sent to the Seminary and he is still a practising priest in Cordoba.

Not all Rojo children entered the church, however. Manuel Rubio, whose father Antonio Rubio Cobos from Pedroche was executed March 26 1940 in Villanueva de Cordoba was taken to the Salesian Seminary, where he remained for several years and completed a very high level of academic education. He had no vocation for the priesthood and left the seminary and became a teacher in a private school in Villanueva de Cordoba, where Moreno Gómez was one of his students. A history of the religious vocations of the children of Rojos who were either imprisoned or executed, would be very extensive and interesting, although it is sadly too late to undertake the necessary field work. Too much time has passed to discover what needs to be known. Spain's everything except exemplary, revolutionary 'Transition' has destroyed our memories and our History.

The Church's first great channel for preaching religion to children (and also in part, to their relatives), was the Falangista welfare institutions that were served by a great many priests and nuns. The Francoist media contributed with its stories of the food rations the soup kitchens provided, but most especially by publicizing the welfare institutions' support of the Church's campaigns for *en masse* Christenings, communions, confirmations and church weddings. Between 1939 to 1940, the Madrid Social Welfare Institute was the venue for 9,872 baptisms, 6,642 First Communions and 1,116 church weddings. There was a total of 24,513 christenings in all of Spain in 1940.[95]

There were no bounds to National Catholicism's harassment of children. This was a new, surprising doctrine, that was forcibly imposed on the minds of children who came from Republican, worker, and lay backgrounds, and who had never heard of such things. The theories of God's punishment, the fire and brimstone terror of Hell and similar things had a major impact on the minds of children in Welfare Institutions, as we can see in Ernesto Caballero Castillo's extraordinary *Memoires,*[96] extracts of which are published in Appendix II.

During those years, the Church had all kinds of ways to impose its authority and customs by the force of coercion. Labourers, if they wanted to be hired by the Señoritos, had to declare that they were Christians and attend Sunday Mass on the days when they were in the town. All marriages had to have been celebrated in the Church.

The Church's second great channel for converting Spain was the missions. When National Catholicism declared that Spain was a Mission country, the principal religious orders went to all the main towns throughout the country organizing missions. The towns and villages of Cordoba province were given a good dose of this proselytizing. The Jesuits were the favourite Francoist religious order. Even its name – Company of Jesus - was militaristic in nature. Next came the Dominicans, the Company of Preachers, created at the beginning of the Inquisition to convert the French.

Ernesto Caballero describes the first of three missions which appeared in Villanueva de Cordoba in 1943 or 1944.[97] These were young Jesuit priests intent on Christianizing every left-wing individual who was still alive and not yet imprisoned, as well as his relatives and the relatives of those who had already been executed. The imprisoned were Christianized in the jails.

The second mission in Villanueva de Cordoba arrived at the end of March 1954. In addition to novenas, confessions and mass communions, schoolchildren were sent down the streets in processions, carrying small saints and waving Vatican flags. This was the work of the Dominicans who turned the entire town's routines upside down so that everyone could attend dawn rosary prayers and other religious observances.[xviii]

The last mission in Villanueva was in Spring 1961, under the Jesuits, and it was more elaborate. By brainwashing the children, the Church knew that it had its best guarantee for the future. Schoolchildren put on plays in the town square, illustrating the seven sacraments. As a rule, children were given leading roles in almost every religious celebration. Everything was directed at the masses and everyone attended *en masse,* which illustrates the Church's enormous capacity for mobilizing entire communities.

6.   National Catholicism at war with Education.

Right from the early days of the military coup, the Church collaborated with the terrible crusade to purge civil servants and employees of the most different kinds of enterprises, of non-believers in the Francoist regime. For example, Banesto employees in Cordoba had to go to the military authorities and ask them to endorse their positions. Teachers, of course, were included in this kind of general purgatory directed at eliminating anyone who might have lukewarm feelings towards the Glorious National Movement; it was a search for unwavering support. When the Nationalists captured a town, Republican municipal policemen and employees were forced out of their jobs en bloc and

---

[xviii] In 1951, a Dominican came to the town to lead a novena and he attracted a young man to the Order, Pedro León Moreno. He was said to be the son of a Rojo, but quite the contrary, his father was a Francoist municipal policeman. He earlier served as a missionary (Honduras, Venezuela…) and he brought needy people from Latin America to Seville so that the Order could finance their studies. Moreno Gómez recently spoke with him and he got the impression that he was a very high-ranking member of the Order.

many were sent on the road to the cemetery. These jobs would be filled, as spoils of war, by the insurgents and their supporters.

The Law of February 10 1939 introduced the purging of civil servants. The same year, the Law of August 25 1939 decreed restrictions to all *oposiciones*[xix] and applications for public employment, while it reserved 80% of all jobs for select supporters of the Regime: war wounded, ex-prisoners of war, orphans of Caídos, and similar. The remaining jobs were for supporters of the Cause. The defeated were totally excluded. Purging of the press was declared May 24 1939; anyone who wished to retain his job had to sign a statement declaring his reaction to the events of July 18 and obtain sworn references of good behaviour and other requirements. The Order for the purging of doctors was dated October 6 1939. Lastly, came the purging of members of other professions such as lawyers and football referees.

Despite the general purging of the country, it was the teaching profession that would suffer the most. In 1936, the Church and Franco battered Education with the greatest purge in Spanish history, one that had no equivalent with that which was going on in other professions. This was reactionary Spain and the Church's great crusade against teachers in general and had much to do with the ensuing cataclysm. There is much to be found in this respect in recent studies that must be consulted, especially the work of two Morentes: Morente Valero (Granada) and Morente Diaz (Cordoba).[98]

That teaching was the first professional class that the supporters of the coup called to order in Cordoba city, is highly significant. July 3 1936, by order from Colonel Cascajo, several teachers in the capital were urgently summoned to report to the new Mayor, Salvador Muñoz Pérez. In his office, the Mayor reproached them for being responsible for the dissemination of Marxist propaganda in the schools and he ordered them to hang a crucifix in each classroom and to teach religion, as reported July 24 1936 in the *Guión*, a newspaper whose Director, Antonio de la Rosa, was a passionate member of the extreme right wing. As these teachers left the office, they were arrested and soon afterwards executed by a firing squad: Agapito de la Cruz, Enrique Fuentes Astillero and Juan García Lara. Many more were later sacrificed as the barracks, the casino and the church vestry joined forces in their persecution.

This was a monstrous and terrible inquisitorial process that one finds impossible to believe ever happened. This was not a persecution in the manner of the ancient sackings of the 19th century; it was more than just a purge. This was the case of a much more profound crusade: the Church's persecution of

---

[xix] Competitive public examinations required for employment in the civil service, state teaching positions, etc.

heretics; the clergy's violent retaliation against laicism; a settling of political scores. A persecution along the line of European fascist anti-culture.

The burning of books that marked the beginning of the IIIrd Reich, also occurred in Cordoba. Goebbels' declaration "When I hear the word culture, I immediately put my finger on the trigger of my gun," became the byword of Nazism, of Francoism and of Fascism in general. In Seville, when an elderly, 72-year-old lay teacher José Sánchez Rosa was arrested by Falangistas, he was placed on a mattress on the back of a truck that was taking him to be executed, because he was ill, surrounded by his books. When the military assassinated Federico García Lorca, Franco destroyed an icon of Republican genius and culture. Likewise, in 1936 the multicultural literary circle of Cordoba was destroyed when Francoists murdered its most distinguished members: the poet José Maria Alvariño, poet and bookseller Rogelio Luque, sculptor Enrique Moreno, music professor Aurelio Pérez Cantero, and many more. Clearly, this crusade against the teaching profession was no more than another chapter in the eradication of culture in Fascist Europe. 'Darkest Spain' was back with its destruction of culture, modernity and freethinking. More than a purge, which it also was, it also possessed the persecutory nature of European totalitarianism, a feature that cannot be ignored.

Francisco Morente Valero also commented on the striking similarities between the Italian Fascist and the Francoist Schools of thought. In both cases, Education had to be converted into a propaganda instrument for the Regime. By eliminating or punishing teachers, the Francoist were not instigating a class war, but a war of ideologies, a religious war and a war against culture.

There was a common denominator to the persecution of culture, teachers and books: an ideological and a religious war, whose features are still apparent today. One such example is seen in Amenábar's movie Ágora (2009), depicting Christians in the IVth and Vth centuries, who in a flood of fanaticism led by Saint Cyril of Alexandria, razed libraries to the ground destroying all of Alexandria's ancient knowledge, and immolated and excoriated Hypathia, the astronomer-philosopher. Clearly, the 1936 religious war was not the first time that the Church moved like a tsunami against books and teachers, as it also did during the Inquisition.

Manuel Morente Díaz described the purging of books and libraries in Cordoba, in detail.[99] In Moreno Gómez' earlier book on Francoist genocide (2008) he mentions some of Don Bruno's neurotic proclamations against books. The Nazis did the same, May 10 1933, when they built a huge pyre of more than 25,000 books, under Goebbels' approving eye. In Cordoba capital, the birthplace of sages such as Seneca and Maimonides, there were several pyres of burning books during the early days of the military coup. At first, it was Falangistas who burned the books, the kiosks and bookstores in the capital. Soon afterwards, the Carlistas also built a pyre. Privately-owned libraries, such as the one belonging to Antonio Jaén Morente on Calle Juan de Mena, were seized and burnt on Las Tendillas square, as they did those belonging to Dr. Vicente Martín Romera, Francisco Azorín, Eloy Vaquero, and so many other Republican scholars.

In 1940 a fanatical Jesuit who preached at several missions in Cordoba capital, wished to celebrate his inquisitional passion with another burning of books in Las Tendillas square, books taken from piles in the La Corredora square. At the end of 1939, several other Jesuit missions in Puente Genil organized another burning of books. José López Cavilán, who was a child at the time, describes one of those Nazi-like pyres as a great fire in Compañia square of an impressive pile of books in front of the chuirch. The parish priest had mobilized all the neighbours to bring books for the pyre and fear did the rest. It was intended as a public show of hatred of culture that the Church approved of. Never since the days of Almazor had so many books burned in Cordoba as when Bem-Abi-Amir destroyed Alhaquem II's 400,000-book library, burning everything that did not have a religious content. The Francoist scene was repeated several times.[100]

The anti-library persecution almost led to the execution of Carmen Guerra, the Director of the Cordoba Provincial Library. The Catholic newspaper *El Defensor de Cordoba* heartily fuelled the Francoist demand for the purifying destruction of books to eradicate the bad seed, the poison, the tools for disseminating dissolutionary ideas and the vehicles of modernity and laity in Spain.

The Seville Purging Committee, with branches in Cordoba, was created under the tutelage of four types of authorities: military leaders, Falange, Church and the Catholic Association of Fathers of Families. In Seville, according to Morente Díaz, one director was Antonio Domínguez Ortiz, for the Falange, and Manuel Gómez Rodríguez, a teacher at the Seminary, for the Church. In Cordoba, Canon Félix Romero Menjíbar represented the Church.

As books and culture were destroyed, so were mountains of teachers. In 1936, the Francoist so-called Nacional Defence Junta began by decreeing the removal of all teachers who had leftist ideas, for which purpose it ordered military commanders and the Guardia Civil to make the appropriate inquiries. The Purging Committees of Teachers came into action at the beginning of 1937 with the implementation of the State Technical Junta Decree 66 of 8 November 8 1936 (BOE November 11 1936). In addition to the persecution and the removal of teachers, the initial visual symbol of the process was the reintroduction of crucifixes in the schools.

Whenever a school was left without a teacher, the parish priest took his place. Later, army corporals or officers or members of the Catholic Action, would be instructed to do so. The open, modern, lay or liberal Republican school was erased from the face of Spain, as it became militarized, or beatified (what today we would call a Koranic school). Freethinking disappeared under Franco and the bishops.

Although the purging of Teaching was part of the overall program for the repression of the working class, it had an added feature, the ideological repression against the schools because of pressure from the Church. The New Totalitarian State demonized the Republican school and proposed to strip it immediately of all modern, lay, or European influences (Voltaire, etc.), of Krause philosophy and the Free Teaching Institution principle, in other words, of all democratic, workers' and equalitarian ideals. Franco himself, who lacked even a minimum idea of what education was, proclaimed in 1937 that the new school would be based on three principles: patriotism, the absence of all foreign influences, and Catholic values. He was particularly obsessed with vilifying the modernity that the Free Teaching Institution represented, declaring that it furthered the "pedantic and pseudo-intellectual promotion of every anti-Spanish action in matters of culture and teaching".[101]

Spokespersons for the Confessional State such as the Archbishop of Zaragoza, did not mince their words when making antediluvian declarations regarding matters of teaching and education, as did Minister of Education José Ibáñez Martín (1939-1951), in 1943 when he asked how could a teacher who does not know how to pray, shape the soul of a child. That is, the said, fundamental problem of Spanish education.[102]

As José Casanova so ably described them, priests were nothing else than talking heads who also bequeathed a rosary of anti-modernistic declarations, of heated praise of Saint Joseph of Calasanz pedagogy and sovereign idiocies regarding the training of teachers and basic problems of education.[103]

The greatest tragedy of all was the mass murder of teachers and professors during the first months of the military coup and of some during the post-war period and a few more who died of starvation in prison. During the first days of the insurrection, the instigators of the coup suspended the salaries and jobs of 54 Cordovan teachers. September 15 1936, incited by the Catholic newspaper *El Defensor de Cordoba*, the military government fired every teacher who belonged to the FETE[xx] union whilst meanwhile firing squads were busy in the cemetery. Moreno Gómez' research and Manuel Morente Díaz's extraordinary work, point to the fact that many more than 30 public school teachers (and some private teachers) were executed then. All crimes are repugnant, but murder of teachers is the nastiest of all.

[xx] *Federación Española de Trabajadores de la Enseñanza* – Spanish Federation of Education Employees.

Moreno Gómez is reminded of the son of Claín, the writer, Leopoldo Alas Argüelles, Rector of the University of Oviedo, who was taken hostage by Nationalist General Aranda soon after the military coup. Despite international petitions for his release, Claín was executed 6 p.m., February 20 1937, in the Oviedo prison patio. Again, military savagery such as seen in Rome and Berlin. Also, the appalling murder of Federico García Lorca, icon of Spanish Letters, at the hands of the most rotten right-wing element in Andalusía. Like these, there were so many, many more…

True, some teachers were also fired from their jobs in the Republican zone at the time, but more for social class reasons regarding who they were, not because of their profession. On the other hand, Francoists all over Spain shot teachers, solely on the excuse that they were poisoning their students by sowing 'dissolutionary', i.e., democratic, ideas. Table 2 provides a descriptive list of some of the teachers slaughtered in fascist Cordoba, based on Morente Dias' lists and on Moreno Gómez' own research. (Table 2. Names of teachers executed in Cordoba or died later of other causes 1936-1948.)

Manuel Torralbo, a private teacher, and five other unfortunate companions certainly did not imagine the tragedy when they were arrested on the afternoon of June 7 1948. Nobody in the village has ever been able to explain the reason for that particular Francoist crime, except to suggest that some of these were left-wing sympathizers and had perhaps even belonged to the PCE. Manual Torralbo was teaching class in his school on Calle Navas when several Guardia Civil appeared and ordered him to send his students, big and small, home. Somewhat naïvely surprised, he asked: 'Will it be for long?' 'Yes, for some time.' they replied.

Together with another six individuals (including Catallina Coleto mother of seven, a humble hard-working woman, married to *El Ratón*, a member of the guerrilla) they were taken to the mobile headquarters at the Fuente Vieja schools where they were interrogated whilst the telephone never ceased ringing with calls to and from Seville and Cordoba. The Francoists were about to teach the defeated another hard lesson. Ángel Fernández Montes de Oca, Lieutenant Colonel in the Guardia Civil of Cordoba, gave the order. In the early hours of dawn June 8 1948, the unfortunate six were taken along the Villanueva to Adamuz road and just two kilometres later, at the first curve - the Los Almagreras bus stop, those innocents were robbed of their lives. Their cries and tears echoed in the silence of the night: Manuel Torralbo, aged 29, Catalina Coleto, aged 52, who left 7 orphaned children and four other men.

Nowadays, every time Moreno Gómez drives past that curve on the road to his family's country cottage in the village, he thinks of them. Others might not remember them, but he does. These words are written in memory of them, a memorial that is something more than just History.

So far, this has been an elementary synopsis of the crimes that were committed against Cordovan teachers. No matter how painful this overview of what occurred in Andalusia, it pales against the impact that the far-reaching Francoist crusade for purging the entire bureaucratic process would have on education throughout Spain. <u>Decree 66 of 8 November 1936</u> (published in the BOE 11-11-1936), created four committees, or Courts of Inquisition, charged with implementing the purge: A, B, C and D. The last one, D, was charged with purging Primary Education.

In Cordoba province, Committee D first comprised Irmina Álvarez, Assistant Director of the Teacher Training College: José Priego López, Head of the Primary Education Inspectorate: and, in addition to another member, Lieutenant Colonel Juan de la Cuesta, an ignorant lunatic who incessantly declared: "the teachers are very bad".[104] Irmina Álvarez, however, was soon replaced by Ángel Cruz Rueda, Director of the Instituto de Cabra, a Francoist to the bone who set up his private purgatory in the Instituto Provincial Góngora in Cordoba city. Another member of this provincial Court of Inquisition was Joaquín Velasco, Vice-President of Catholic Action, and whose father was Mussolini's official representative in Cordoba.

The lawful Director of the Instituto Provincial Góngora, Antonio Jaén Morente, was in Madrid on July 18, thus fortunately escaping certain execution had he been in Cordoba when the insurgents took over. In his absence, the Francoist faculty of the Instituto convened a shameful Court of Honour October 17 to strip him of his academic qualifications and expel him from the Instituto.[xxi] Their deliberation was later officially confirmed by decree from the Burgos Government barring Antonio Jaén Morente from holding any kind of academic or teaching position in Spain.

As far as all of Spain was concerned, Francisco Morente Valero's research shows that 20,435 purging indictments were filed in 14 Spanish provinces, that is against more than 80% of all teachers. Of those indictments, 75% were resolved in favour of the teacher and 25% were sanctioned in different ways: dismissal, absolute disqualification and/or loss of rights (2,021); suspension of job and salary or temporary disqualification (1,044); transfer to other locations (1,983); disqualification for administrative positions (608); other sanctions (235). In one town, Aguilar de la Frontera, as many as 20 teachers of both sexes were indicted; 12 of those sanctioned were female.[105]

---

xxi On 24 February 2016, the Instituto Séneca, heir to the Instituto Provincial, in an Extraordinary Meeting of the Faculty revoked the 17 October 1936 decision and formally reinstated Antonio Jaén, Full Professor and past-Director of the Instituto Provincial, as a member of the Faculty.

Those percentages agree with Manuel Morente's study of Cordoba, where of the 814 teachers in the 1936 census, 205 were indicted by the Liquidation Committee, that is, 25% of the total.[xxii] Morente cites an interesting case in Villanueva de Cordoba, where Vicente Pascual Soler, a famous teacher, was indicted in La Rambla where he had taught for some years, on the grounds that he was a member of the Socialist party. His case was later resolved in his favour. What is not generally known is that in May 1946, the lunatic military in Villanueva de Cordoba had included Vicente Pascual in an absurd raid where he and another 15 persons were handcuffed to each other, marched through the village and then imprisoned in Cordoba where they remained for a year until their cases were tried. After his release, Vicente swore that he would never return to that Villanueva gone mad. He remained in Cordoba, where he became Director of the well-known Academia Espinar.

To better understand the manner by which Francoists purged Education, it is worth recalling the individuals who denounced those who were indicted, in order of importance: 1) the military and the Guardia Civil; 2) members of the Church; 3) sundry local residents who toadied to the Regime; 4) the municipalities, who actively collaborated in the repression on the side of the Francoists; 5) and curiously, in some out-of-the-way places, the Falange. One enthusiastic accuser of teachers was Fr. Paulino Seco de Herera, parish priest for San Nicolás in Cordoba city, who was very well known in the literary circles organized by teacher and poet Rafael Olivares Figueroa. The latter, who wrote the prologue to the well-known book *Canciones morenas* about martyr José Maria Alvariño, was able to escape into exile but was not forgotten by the parish priest, who in a damning report described the poet as 'notably extravagant'.

In the specific case of 144 Secondary School teachers and similar professionals, denunciations were filed against 82, that is 57% of the total.[106] Finally sanctioned, 44, or 31%.

As to the catalogue of accusations against the teachers and professors, aside from accusations of a political nature (followers of Marxism, Socialism, Communism, supporters of the Frente Popular, or leftist sympathies in general), the most curious were accusations of a religious nature, which bordered on the grotesque: middling believer, indifferent, not seen in church, has no religious ideals, indifferent to religious practices, distanced himself from the Church during the Republic, anti-Catholic ideas, atheist, doubts the existence of God and traditions of the Fatherland, criticizes the Company of Jesus in a book, does not allow his students to kneel when the viaticum (last rites) pass, does not kneel during processions, May 1936 refused to kneel when a procession was passing, etc., etc. As a result, idiocies like these

---

[xxii] Manuel Moente Díaz, op. cit., p. 358.

which lacked in consistency or any semblance of truth, brutally cut short the professional and family lives of many teachers, honourable men and women possessing indispensable culture. The destructive whirlwind of a culture in the hands of European Fascism converted Spain into a cultural wasteland from which, possibly, it has not recovered nor will ever recover from.

The number of calamities that fell upon Education as the authors of the coup did their best to demolish an entire generation of dedicated, irreplaceable teachers, is so vast that it is difficult to grasp. Likewise, the countless number of teachers who, notwithstanding pain, misfortune and heartbreak, refused to be broken, as illustrated by the following stories.

Ángel Carmona Jiménez, whom the coup caught in his school in Cordoba, went to his village, Montemayor, when he heard that Modoaldo had been executed. From there he walked to the Republican zone where the FETE charged him with organizing schools for children who had been evacuated to the North of Cordoba province. He then enlisted in the fight for the defence of Madrid until a hand grenade amputated his right hand. Thus mutilated, he went to France where he organized children's camps. In the middle of 1940 he decided to return to Spain where Franco received him in the Miranda del Ebro concentration camp from which he was released and permitted to return to his village, under house arrest. He was eventually able to rebuild his life in Cordoba and in Barcelona but he was never allowed to return to teaching.[107]

Another famous teacher from Montemayor, who lost his right arm, Alejandro Cabello Sánchez returned on a stretcher on the point of death, to France where he had trained. Once recovered, he went to Hungary where he was graduated in Agronomy in Budapest, then to Cuba where he obtained his PhD in Biological Sciences from La Habana University. He taught at both these institutions.

This section concludes with some deeply moving texts by Antonio Jaén Morente regarding the cataclysm that befell Cordovan Education. During the war he published *Estampas da Guerra* [Postcards of the War], a four-page leaflet that was published in Valencia by the National Council of the Izquierda Republicana.[108] One of the texts, entitled *Marruecos, una escuela sin maestro* [Morocco, a school without a teacher], is an elegy to Antonio de Ontavilla, a teacher in Alcázarquivir, Morocco:

> "Ontavilla was in the bloom of youth, 25 years old. He had a big heart. Republican ideals, left of the left. He spoke easily and his pen was fair and informative. A fighter of the kind who, like so many others, hearing treason germinate in the mouths of the Fascist crowd, sent warnings to Madrid calling for help. Therefore, no sooner did we win

the elections in February, he openly asked for the removal of certain members of the military whose names he indicated. He had to flee to Tetuán, as his life had been threatened."

Whilst Ontavilla was on home leave visiting his ailing mother in Galicia, the war broke out. Denounced by local Francoists, he was captured and returned under guard to Tetuán. Antonio Jaén's description of the prisons in Alcázarquivir and the schoolmaster's ordeal is horrific:

"The makeshift prisons in the regular army barracks were packed with men who supported the left, that is, anyone who had had any contact with the Frente Popular, who were tied to the troughs. Ontavilla and his companions were savagely beaten by the very Arabs that he had taught and were now fighting on the side of Fascist Spain (…) He was marched along the streets of Alcázar, hands tied and guarded on either side by two Nationalists, followed by the crowd yelling and shouting insults… During a halt in this terrible procession, he was stopped in front of the door to his own school, where his guards called out to the children: 'Come and look at your teacher!'

Then came sham justice: the court martial. The children of his school placed some posters on the street corners on which they had written 'Reprieve and Pardon' and it is said that some mothers and fellow teachers shouted this appeal in the streets. It was September. Dawn was breaking. The female Spanish teachers who had accompanied the children during this new ordeal, could not restrain their tears. A little before dawn 4 September 1936, in the last hours of his captivity, Antonio de Ontavilla managed to give someone a message for me: "If you are saved, say goodbye to me forever." The messenger arrived late, but he arrived. I received both the messenger and the message. Teachers of Spain, record this in the chronicles of Spanish Education's great martyrdom. Take note of 'The passion and death of Antonio de Ontavilla, teacher'. Ontavilla's grave is unmarked; no headstone bears his name. On a day that October, the students without a teacher, timidly walked through the gates of the cemetery. In the children's hands, flowers from African fields."

Immortal writings by Antonio Jaén, in a Ciceronian style worthy of those times and a living homage to the teachers who were martyred by Spanish fascism.

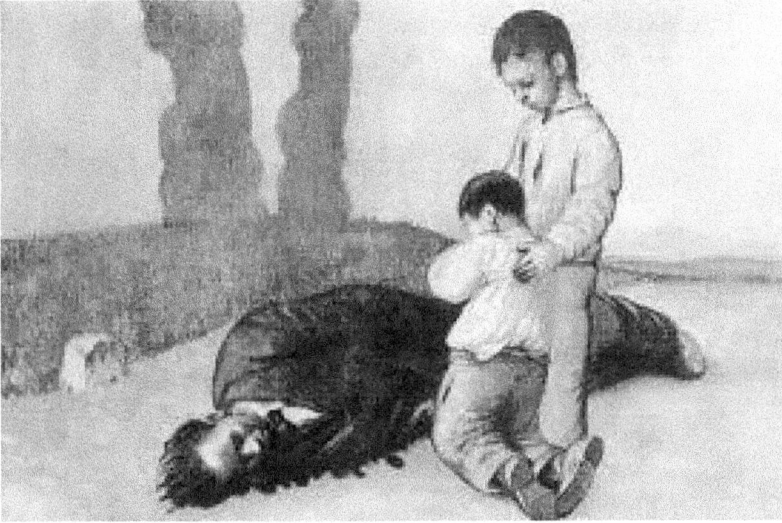

"The teacher's last lesson"
Pen and ink drawing by Alfonso Daniel Castelao.

Lastly, Moreno Gómez attempts, yet again, to impress upon the reader, the tragedy that pushed Spanish education to the edge of the cliff, by quoting another of Antonio Jaén's extraordinary texts, entitled *Galicia mártyr. Estampas de Castelao* [Martyrized Galicia. Sketches by Castelao].

The above pen and ink sketch of a fallen teacher and two children looking down on him, by this Galician artist and politician, is one of many by which Castelao used his art to denounce the cruelties of the Francoist regime. Entitled 'The teacher's last lesson' Moreno Gómez concludes this section with a last, heartfelt text by Antonio Jaén Morente:

> "Fascist Spain has become a great necropolis of teachers. In every region they have been the favourite target, because they were masters and seed of the Republic...
> How I weep for you, Juanito García Lara, teacher, President of the FETE, assassinated in Cordoba... If you could only see 'The Last Lesson', you would recognize yourself. It is your last lesson also. Thus you gave it, executed by firing squad against the white walls of the cemetery in Cordoba, and like you, Antonio Reina, and Agapito de la

Cruz, and Enrique Fuentes, and Modoaldo Garrido, and Augusto Moya, and ... I do not want to continue.

The list from Cordoba, like these *estampas,* is torn from my heart, from the depths of my pain... The scythe of death no longer harvests the fields; it digs up the earth, opening holes. Death sows the seeds. Buried today, they will germinate tomorrow."

Antonio Jaén Morente, Valencia, 1938

Endnotes for Chapter II

1   International Criminal Court, *Legal Texts and Tools*. Article 7(e). Consulted on the Internet at:https://www.icc-cpi.int/NR/rdonlyres/ADD16852-AEE9-4757-ABE7 9CDC7CF02886/283503/RomeStatutEng1.pdf

2   Ángel Viñas. *En el combate por la historia* (In the fight for History). Barcelona, Pasado & Presente, 2012, p. 20.

3   Antonio Elorza. "Genocides". In *Hispania Nova* (Online Contemporary History Magazine in Spanish) at http://e-revistas.uc3m.es/indLex.php/HISPNOV/index. Number 10, 2012..L

4   Eric Hobsbawn. *Interesting Times: A Twentieth-Century life.* Spanish translation. Barcelona, Critica, 2002, p. 72.

5   Pedro Pascual, "Campos de concentración en España" (Concentration camps in Spain). *Historia 16*, Year XXV, number 310, February 2002.

6   Idem. "Campos de concentración en España y Batallones de Trabajadores" (Concentration camps in Spain and Forced Labor Battalions). Minutes of the Congress on Concentration Camps and the Penitentiary World in Spain during the Civil War and Francoism. Barcelona, Crítica, 2003, pp. 359 et al.

7   Javier Rodrigo. *Los campos de concentración franquistas, entre la historia y la memoria.* (Francoist concentration camps, history and memories). Madrid, Siete Mares, 2003, 221. This number is surely greater if one takes into account the great many men who were taken prisoner after the battle of Teruel and the disaster in the Lower Aragon province.

8   Joan Llarch, *Campos de concentración en la España de Franco* (Concentration camps in Franco's Spain). Barcelona, Producciones Editoriales, 1978, p. 80.

9   Javier Rodrigo, op. cit., p. 366.

10 Pedro Pascual. Minutes of the Congress… op. cit., p. 366.

11 Francisco Moreno Gómez. *Cordoba en la posguerra (La repressión y la guerilla, 1939-1950).* Op. cit., p. 41.

12 José Ángel Delgado Iribarren. *Jesuitas en España* (Jesuits in Spain). Madrid, Studium, 1956, 235. Quoted by Joan Larch, op. cit., p. 41.

13 Antonio D. López Rodríguez, op. cit., pp. 167 et al.

14 Miguel Gila. *Y entonces nací yo. Memorias para desmemoriados.* (And then I was born. Memories for those who have forgotten). Madrid, Temas de Hoy, 1995. In Isáis Lafuente. *Esclavos por la patria. La explotación de los presos bajo el franquismo* (Slaves for the Fatherland. Exploitation of prisoners under Francoism). Madrid, Temas de Hoy, 2002, p. 142.

15 Anontio D. López Rodriguez, Ibid.

16 Miguel Regalón Molinero. Personal testimony sent to Moreno Gómez from Valencia, 31 August 1984. These men are all since long gone. The historian is left with the satisfaction of having saved this account of their sufferings. Not everyone forgot. Many managed to talk about them.

17 Juan Pulido Cantador. Several interviews by Moreno Gómez in Villanueva de Cordoba, 1983.

18 Miguel Regalón Molinero, Ibid.

[19] José Maria Carnicer Casas, written testemonial sent to Moreno Gómez from Reus, Tarragona, October 19, 1987.

[20] Idem.

[21] Arcángel Bedmar, *Los puños y las pistolas* (Fists and revolvers), op. cit., p. 102.

[22] Arcángel Bedmar, *Los puños y las pistolas*, op. cit. p. 102.

[23] Antonio D. López Rodríguez. Ibid., p. 201.

[24] Ángel David Martín Rubio. http://desdemicampanario.es/autor/angel-david-martin-rubio/

[25] Antonia González & Pablo Ortiz Romero. *Memoria y testimonio del campo de concentración de Castuera* (Memory and witness account of Castuera concentration camp). Minutes of the Congress on concentration camps and the world of the penitentiary in Spain during the civil war and under Francoism, op. cit., pp. 240 et al.

[26] Pozoblanco Municipal Archives.

[27] Antonio D. Lopez Rodríguez. Ibid., p. 256.

[28] Ibid., p. 266.

[29] Olof Palme. 1975. Quoted in *El final del silencio* (The End of Silence). Documentary by Mª Carmen España, 2011.

[30] Julián Casanova. *La Iglesia de Franco* (Franco's Church). Annotated edition, Barcelona, Crítica, 2005, p. 277.

[31] Founded in Cordoba in 1936 as the official organ of the FET-JONS and published until 1941. Predecessor of today's Diário de Cordoba.

[32] Ibid., 11 June 1939. p. 7.

[33] Ibid., 15 June 1939. p. 12.

[34] Ibid., 23 June 1939. p. 3.

[35] *ABC* Seville, April 23 1939.

[36] Ibid., 12 May 1939.

[37] *Diário Azul* Cordoba, 10 December 1939.

[38] Ibid., 21 December 1939.

[39] Ibid., 21 December, 1939.

[40] Ibid., 27 December 1939.

[41] Ibid., 5 January 1940.

[42] Ibid., 16 October 1940.

[43] Ibid., 7 November 1940.

[44] Ibid., 19 September 1941.

[45] Francisco Moreno Gómez and Juan Ortiz Villalba. *La masonería en Cordoba* (Freemasonry in Cordoba). Cordoba, F. Baena, 1985, p. 254.

[46] Francisco Moreno Gómez. *La resistencia armada contra Franco* (Armed resistance against Franco). Barcelona, Crítica, 2001. This book deals with the entire phenomenon of the guerrillas in Cordoba and other provinces in the Centre-South of Spain.

[47] Ibid., pp. 45 et al.

[48] Ibid., 583 et al.

[49] *Boletim Oficial Provincial*. Cordoba, January 1 and August 1 1940.

[50] Francisco Moreno Gómez. *El genocidio franquista en Cordoba.* (The Francoist

genocide in Cordoba.) op. cit., p. 545.

51   Antonio Ramos Palomares. Eye-witness testimony to the author. Almodóvar del Rio, 1982.

52   Eduardo de Guzmán. *Sócrates Gómez, de la derrota a la represión*. (Sócrates Gómez, from the defeat to the *repression*.). *Tiempo de Historia*, number 62, January 1980, p. 16.

53   Peter Anderson. Conference at the Universidad Complutense of Madrid 11 November 2011. LAuthor of *The Francoist Military Trials. Terror and Complicity, 1939-1945.* Routledge, London, 2009.

54   Árcangel Bedmar González. *La Luz Sepultada* (The buried Light). Publication of the I Congress on Historic Memory, Aguilar de la Frontera, 27 September 27 -October 7, 2006, p. 65.

55   *Cordoba*, 4 November 1941.

56   Juan Luis Torralba. Email to the author 4 November 2013.

57   Feliciano Delgado. *Diário Azul*. Cordoba, 13 August 1939.

58   Francoist Decree of 26 April 1940. Reproduced in *Fuentes para la Historia de la 2ª República, la Guerra Civil y el Franquismo* (Sources for the History of the Second Republic, the Civil War and Francoism): at http://fuentesguerracivil.blogspot.com

59   L. M. Montes Oviedo. "70 años después. Ley de Memoria Histórica" (70 years later. The Historic Memory Law.) *Feria y Fiestas*, Alamdén, 2009. Magazine kindly sent to Moreno Gómez by Ángel Hernández Sobrino.

60   Julio González Gil "El último testimonio de Unamuno" (Unamuno's Last Will). Uploaded to Youtube 2 November2007.

61   Ramón Serrano Súñez. *Entre el silencio y la propaganda, la historia como fue*. (Between silence and propaganda; history as it was). *Memorias*, Planeta, Barcelona, 1997, p. 272. Quoted by Julián Casanova, op. cit., p. 19.

62   Manuel Álvaro Dueñas. "Por derecho de fundación: la legitimación de la represión franquista" (By rightful foundation: validation of the Francoist repression". In Mirta Núñez Diaz-Balart et al, op. cit. p. 69.

63   Hilari Raguer, op. cit., p. 399.

64   *Diário Azul*. Cordoba. 3 October 1936. Quoted by Francisco Moreno Gómez in *Cordoba en la posguerra. La represión y la guerrilla, 1939-1950)* (Post-war Cordoba. Repression and Guerrilla, 1939-1950). Cordoba, F. Baena, 1987, p. 35.

65   Francisco Moreno Gómez. *La Guerra Civil en Cordoba 1936-1939*. (The Civil War in Cordoba 19361939). Cordoba, 1985.

66   Hilari Raguer, op. cit., p. 212.

67   Minutes of the Villanueva de Cordoba Municipality, 19 December 1939.

68   *Cordoba*. 7 May 1942.

69   *Diário Azul.*. Cordoba. 16 October 1939.

70   Ibid. 29 March 1940.

71   Arcángel Bedmar. 'El nacionalcatolicismo en Montilla y Lucena durante la guerra civil (Nationalcatholicism in Montilla and Lucena during the civil war). In *La Luz Sepultada*, Aguilar de la Frontera, Sept.-Oct., 2006, pp. 77-78.

[72] B.O.P.C. *Butlletí Oficial del Parlament de Catalunya* (Official Bulletin of the Parliament of Catalonia). 23 January 1940, reproducing the *Boletín Oficial delEstado* of 13 January, Year V, number 13.

[73] Julián Casanova, *La Iglesia de Franco* (Franco's Church), op. cit., p. 318.

[74] Abbott Manuel Garrido. Valle de lo Caídos. 23 August 1986. Letter to Fr. Pedro Laín Entralgo.

[75] Marisa Paredes and José Luis Peñafuerte. *Los caminos de la memoria.* (The paths of memory). Documentary movie, 2009. Can be dowloanded free, in Spanish, from: http://cinepeliculasflv.com/21524-los-caminos-de-la-memoria-online-peliculas-gratis-hd-espanol.html.

[76] José M. Gallegos Rocafull. *La pequeña grey. Testimonios religiosos sobre la guerra civil española.* (The small congregation. Religious Testimony on the Spanish civil war). Barcelona, Península, 2007, pp. 211 et al.

[77] Ibid., p. 203.

[78] Ibid., p. 199.

[79] Ibid., p. 85.

[80] José Luis Casas Sánchez. *"La memoria histórica del exilio republicano. El caso del canónigo Gallegos Rocafull"* (The historic memory of the Republican exile. The case of Canon Gallegos Rocafull". In *La Luz Sepultada,* op. cit., pp. 47 et al.

[81] Gallegos Rocafull. Ibid., p. 88.

[82] Ibid., p. 91.

[83] Ibid., p 169.

[84] Ibid. p. 183.

[85] Ibid., p.. 181.

[86] Ibid, p. 198.

[87] *Heraldo de Aragón.* 11 August 1936. Cited by Julián Casanova, op. cit., p. 16.

[88] Cited by Hilari Raguer, *La pólvora,* op. cit. P. 28.

[89] José M. Gallegos Rocafull, op. cit. p 206.

[90] *Memoria que eleva al Caudillo de España y a su Gobierno el Patronato de Redención de Penas por el Trabajo, de 1943* (Report from the Board of Trustees of the Reduction of Sentences through Work Group for 1943, to the Caudillo of Spain and his Government). Madrid, 1944.

[91] Mónica Orduño Prada. *El Auxilio Social (1936-1940). La etapa fundacional.* (Social Welfare (1936-1940). The foundation). Madrid, Librería Libre Editorial, 1996, p. 263.

[92] Juan Caunedo Domínguez. *Sombra, niebla y tiempo* (Shadow, fog and time). Documentary by this free-lance producer and director for the Madrid Forum for Memory. The author was unable to obtain any additional information.

[93] Ibid.

[94] Montse Armengou & Ricard Belis. *Los niños perdidos del Francoism* (Franco's forgotten children]. Award-winning television documentary, Televisó de Catalunya, Barcelona, 2002.

[95] Ángela Cenarro Lagunas. "Historia y memoria del Auxilio Social de la Falange" (History and memory of the Falangista Welfare Institution.). In *Pliegos de Yuste,* numbers 11-12, 2010.

96   Ernesto Caballero Castillo. *Vivir com memoria*. (Living with memory). Cordoba, El Páramo, 2001, pp 66 et al. Son of Julián Caballero, ex-Communist Mayor of Villanueva de Cordoba, who at the time of these events was a guerrilla commander in the North of Cordoba province.

97   Idem., p. 67.

98   Francisco Morente Valero. *La Escuela y el Estado Nuevo. La depuración del Magisterio Nacional (1936 - 1943)* (The School and the New State. The purging of the national teaching professions (1936-1943). Valladolid, Ámbito, 1997. and Manuel Morente Diaz. *La depuración de la enseñanza pública cordobesa a raíz de la Guerra Civil* (The purging of public education in Cordoba as a result of the Civil War). Cordoba, El Páramo, 2011.

99   Manuel Morente Diaz. *La mala semilla. Depuración de libros y bibliotecas en Cordoba.* (The bad seed. Purging of books and libraries in Cordoba). Cordoba, ECO magazine, number 8, 22 June 2011.

100 José López Gavilán, *Aquellos duros tiempos. Anecdotario,* Cordoba, 2004, p. 135.

101 Manuel Álvaro Dueñas. op. cit.

102 Ibid., 319.

103 Idem.

104 Morente Díaz, op. cit. p. 276.

105 Rafael Espino Navarro. Asociación para la Recuperación de la Memoria Histórica de Aguilar de la Frontera, *La tiza roja* (Red chalk), published on the social media.

106 Ibid., 469.

107 Luque, op. cit., 234.

108 Antonio Jaén Morente. *Estampas da Guerra.* [Postcards of the War]. Valencia, Izquierda Republicana, 1938. Moreno Gómez has three sets of *Estampas*, kindly given to him by Manuel Toríbio García, Cordoba historian and biographer of Antonio Jaén Morente.

III

CRUSHING THE VANQUISHED (B) – COURT MARTIALS, TORTURE AND EXECUTIONS

THE UNRECORDED SLAUGHTER IN ANDALUSIA: ENFORCEMENT OF THE LAW OF FUGITIVES – APRIL/MAY 1939. THE FARCE THAT WAS MILITARY JUSTICE: Proliferation of Military Courts Martial. Widespread wave of denunciations and false witness statements. Unbridled torture. MILITARY TRIBUNALS AND COURTS MARTIAL: Itinerant and standing military tribunals. Courts martial. Examination and assessment of sentences. False rhetoric and arbitrary procedures. Some leaders who survived.

> *In exterminating one third of the male population in Spain, we shall cleanse the country and get rid of the proletariat..."*

> Lieutenant-Colonel Gonzalo de Aguilera,
> to John Whitaker, Chicago
> *Daily News* War Correspondent, 1936

The unrecorded slaughter in Andalusia: Enforcement of the Law of Fugitives April/May 1939

When the expression *extermination* in this study, it refers to the Francoist interpretation of what it believed was an 'essential extermination', that is, the annihilation of everything and everyone that Franco's regime considered most evidently represented the Republic's social base and its elite.

In all the studies of the Francoist repression, one has yet to find an author who has paid due attention to this subject. Academics today still pay little or no heed to this unusual phenomenon of post-war Spain: to the wave of extra-legal summary executions that the victors perpetrated in April and May 1939, as well as the multiple summary executions in the concentration camps, another matter regarding which still little or nothing is known.

The Centre-South of Spain, the last region to fall into the hands of the insurgents, was further subjected to an additional extra-legal form of indiscriminate slaughter, what the people called *paseos* [walks] and reacted to with a terror similar to that which they felt during the early days of the insurgency. It was as if the unlawful Nationalist wartime proclamations, supported by Francoist public opinion, were again being applied as the law of the land. Undoubtedly these schemes were not apparent to everyone, although we hear of frequent references to an earlier euphemistic *Law of Fugitives*, a traditional tool of repression, whereby a person was shot without further ado, usually in the back, an execution justified on the grounds that 'the prisoner was attempting to escape'. This stratagem was activated with great enthusiasm at the end of the war by the euphoric victors and it would again emerge, in an out-of-control manner, during the so-called Triennium of Terror (1947-1949).

The application of the Law of Fugitives, as soon as victory was declared, was in line with the victors' first punitive objective, the implementation of actions to be served as a bloody aperitif paving the way for the bureaucratic dealings of so-called Military Justice. The victors were loath to wait for due process of law; they wanted to teach the defeated a quick 'cleansing' lesson. This would indicate that although due process began to be legislated in February 1937, the swift enactment of legislation to substitute the military's wartime proclamations was not of great importance to the victors. Besides, everyone knew that this legalization was a farce because whenever the regime was in a hurry, it resorted to extra-judicial shortcuts and direct elimination, as it did between July 18, 1936 and February 1937. Observance of due process of law was ignored in April and May 1939 and later, again during the 1947-1949 Triennium of Terror.

The fact that the 1939 the Law of Fugitives was applied throughout the Centre-South region, in almost every town and village that was finally occupied by the insurgents, demonstrates that this was not a spur-of-the-moment, improvised series of actions, as some writers have said, but rather that it was an intentional, clearly programmed, planned and carried out objective.

The records tell us, for example, that in Villarroledo, Albacete, these crimes were perpetrated without due process of law in the Los Barreros region, although there appears to be no detailed study of this. There is, however, more detailed information for some villages in outlying regions of Extremadura, near Badajoz.

In Villarta de los Montes, for example, the new Falangista Mayor, Carlos de Rivas Molina, who had already held this position during the two previous dark years of the insurgency, ordered an immediate cleansing of the town. Speaking from the Town Hall balcony, he told the townspeople that whilst the Nationalists had the balls to win the war, they now had the balls to clean up the town.[1]

He really meant it. 16 May 16, 1939, without waiting for a military tribunal and not beating about the bush, he ordered a raid against 23 individuals from Hoya de Fernando, who were to be 'taken for a walk', the infamous paseo[i]. The next day at dawn, the prisoners were removed in two groups from the garage-cum-prison in which they had been held. The first victim was Republican ex-Mayor, Julián Molina, an ordinary breeder of goats, who had earlier strived to prevent any kind of violence in the village. No matter. The right-wing supporters of Franco were determined to wipe the slate clean of all Republican office holders, authorities and other leaders, just because of who they were. They then turned to relatives, friends, neighbours, as we see in this case where the raid included two of the ex-mayor's brothers: Aurelio and Lisardo. Julián Molina's son Honorio was also scheduled to be shot but he managed to escape and flee to the mountains. Julian Molina's wife Marciana Merino died in Mérida jail and one of their daughters, Eleonor, died at home after being subjected to grievous torture. That is how Francoism decimated entire families and why, for this and so many more reasons, we speak of 'extermination' in this book.

In Talarrubias, still in Badajoz province, in one of these raids out May 17, 1939 the prisoners were taken for a paseo to Cuesta de la Escalera on the banks of the River Guadiana. Killed were a Republican Guardia Civil, Vicente Montalbán Prieto, a Justice of the Peace, Ángel Fajardo, several ex-town councillors, two or three ex-municipal policemen and several others. Their bodies were left where they fell, unburied, at the mercy of the wild animals. Ignacio Cendrero was killed later, his body was tied to a donkey and paraded around the town.[2]

There were similar cases in every village in the region: Navalvillar de Pela, Casas de Don Pedro, Fuenlabrada de los Montes, etc. There were so many that Ángel David Martín Rubio, pro-Franco Church historian, could not avoid talking about these paseos in his work,[3] curiously referring to data from the Causa General investigation archives.[ii] He mentions that regarding Esparragosa de Lares, the archives note two burials in May 1939, in La Horca farm, in some very deep trenches and in Peloche, two burials in the field of individuals whose names he was unable to determine but who were

---

[i]   At noon, late afternoon or at night, a knock on the door would announce the arrival of a truck with soldiers to take a person out for a walk, or *paseo*. Execution usually followed by the roadside or in the jail at dawn the next day.

[ii] The *Causa General*, or General Cause, is the name of an extensive investigation by the Ministry of Justice in 1940, regarding the 'criminal acts committed throughout the country during the Rojo rule'. These archives can be consulted on the Spanish Archives website at www.pares.mcu.org.

150

definitely disaffected with the National Cause, had enlisted in brigades of Rojo volunteer militia and were executed when this village was liberated.

Also, that in Fuenlabrada de los Montes, there is an indication of 17 initial executions by firing squad when the village was liberated. These are said to have died of 'acute haemorrhages caused by a traumatic agent unleashed by soldiers belonging to the military police.' These individuals had been arrested by the military, and generally speaking all were, before and during the Glorious Uprising, extremely prominent individuals who were disaffected from the Holy Cause, and had also been directly or indirectly involved in the murder, imprisonment and seizure of persons of authority in this village.

Jacinta Gallardo's research in Badajoz province villages[4] confirms the harsh reality of the consequences of the victory suffered in Cordoba capital and province. When Villanueva de la Serena was occupied by Nationalist troops in the summer of 1938, the first bloody tribute to the Cause was the summary execution of 59 individuals. 50 villagers were victims of the Law of Fugitives in 1939: 30 in April and 20 in May. A ceremony honouring the 300 persons assassinated by Francoists in this village was celebrated October 20, 2012. Of these, the deaths of only 125 are recorded in the municipal Civil Registry. This gives the reader an idea of the failings of the Civil Registry offices in all of Spain, a feature that has been more than demonstrated in numerous published essays and articles.

A recent article by Agustina Merino Tena[5] provides additional significant data regarding Villanueva de la Serena. Earlier, Jacinta Gallardo had managed to calculate that 110 persons had been executed: 93 men and 17 women. At first, Agustina Merino was able to document as many as 282 executed: 259 men and 23 women. In May 2012, further research produced a new total: 291 executed, plus an additional 27 whose actual fate was unknown. Later again, 318 victims in all, plus 18 also sentenced to death and executed on unknown dates, for a sum total of 336. Considering that this was a tiny village with a population of only 15,000, the total number of executions is appalling.

One cannot overstate the extreme importance of this research and the overwhelming weight of the conclusions, as ongoing research into the Francoist repression continues to bring new data to light by which the numbers are constantly corrected upwards. This is a difficult historiographic undertaking and an increasingly important one for which there will be no end as long as there are attempts to determine all the resting places of the Republican fallen and, with their identification, reduce the number of *disappeared.*

In Navalvillar de Pela, at least 68 are known to have been taken for a paseo, force-marched to the tune of the victory. There were many more 'irregular' victims on various dates, some because of reprisals during the persecution of disaffected fugitives. In her report, Jacinta Gallardo lists up to 141 victims in this village, of which 103 were sentenced in an 'irregular' manner, *manu militari*, and only 38 by a court martial. One individual from Navalvillar taken for a paseo on May 14, 1939 was the Republican ex-Mayor, Lorenzo Gallardo. An additional 33 victims fell under the Law of Fugitives in April and 35 in May 1939.

In Orellana la Vieja, 63 were taken for a paseo in 1939: 9 in April and 54 in May. Such a mass raid was repeated in Peña del Mentiero May 13 (48 men) and May 14 (6 women). Under the excuse that the arrested were being transferred to a prison in Puebla de Alcocer, three trucks were filled with prisoners; the third truck was stopped on the orders of the parish priest, Fr. Ramón Cordero, and the prisoners were executed on the side of the road. That night, Falangistas ran all round town hunting down the relatives of the victims and the imprisoned and beating them with sticks, thus adding to the terror by which they ruled the townspeople. In 1941, at the Las Gargáligas farm, Juan Cerro and his wife Brígida Ruiz Sierra were arrested because they were suspected of being in contact with freedom fighters. She was shot under the Law of Fugitives and he was 'made to disappear' in the neighbouring hills.

In Don Benito, which had already suffered so much in 1938 (191 victims, summarily executed without due process, including several dozen women), Jacinta Gallardo lists 61 victims under the Law of Fugitives in 1939: 46 in April and 15 in May. Their cause of death is officially given as an 'act of war', although this occurred in April 1939, long after the end of the war. In all, Francoists executed 309 persons in Don Benito, of which 49 were women.

Juan Casado Morcillo, who had served as Civil Governor of Badajoz province, with headquarters in Castuera since March 1937, is another who 'disappeared' under the Law of Fugitives. His grandchildren recently contacted Moreno Gómez for assistance as their investigations into the circumstances surrounding his execution and place of death had led to naught. They only knew that he was arrested by Nationalist troops in Calzada de Calatrava, from where he was taken to Don Benito prison. May 10, 1939, their grandmother was given her husband's clothes but no details. He was presumably executed in Castillo de la Encomienda.[6]

Historians and academia must stop ignoring the events of the April and May 1939 Black Spring. This period needs to be studied in greater detail. As shown, the entire Centre-South region of Spain that was the last to fall to Franco, was forced to make a first blood tribute to the victors, in the form of extra-legal post-war summary executions. In the small village of Chillón, Ciudad Real, local Falangistas and military observed that although a first lesson was being taught to all the town and villages and that 'they were not finished'. Some months after the end of the war, June 2, 1939, 9 prisoners from the jail were chosen for a paseo, mostly farmworkers and people of no political importance, but including Manuel Puebla, a schoolmaster (another victim of the crusade against teachers) and Bernardino Gallego, a 17-year-old youth. The prisoners were taken from jail at dawn in several vehicles and told that they were being transferred to Almadén. When they passed the El Contadero farm (outside Almadén) they were executed. 3 June 3. News of this crime against humanity spread rapidly. When the relatives of the deceased reached the locale, they found their bodies partly buried and eaten by wild animals.[7]

Proof that the pack of hounds of victory thirsted for blood and that this occurred throughout the Centre-South region, is the case described earlier in Chapter 1 regarding the slaughter of the 50 sailors of the Republican fleet, executed on board their ship 14 April 1939 as the Francoist Admiral Moreno was bringing the Navy back from Bizerte, Tunisia, to Cádiz.

The peculiar hypothesis that all post-war executions were the outcome of lawful summary procedures is totally incorrect. During the post-war period orders were also given, in an irregular and arbitrary manner, for extra-legal executions, the so-called paseo. The application of the Law of Fugitives is well documented in the territories that were the last to fall to Franco, most specifically, in the north of Cordoba province, as recorded in the orders and communications that the military authorities sent to the Civil Registry. In all these documents, there is a profusion of the following stated cause of death: 'shot whilst attempting to escape from the guards who were accompanying him/her'. Again, we note the Francoist Regime's older and the newer, even more forcible, use of terror.

There was nothing improvised in this latest burst of terror; it had been carefully planned for the period following the victory, as was the terror that was unleashed at the beginning of the coup in 1936. The lists of those who were to be taken were prepared at Military Police Headquarters and the executions were carried out by a unit of soldiers led by an officer under the orders of the local Military Commander. These units worked in close collaboration not just with the Military Police, but also with the support of the civil authorities and the Falange, who officially represented the local 'Information' or 'Purification' Committee.

In Los Pedroches county in Cordoba province, the first implementation of the repressive plan, the so-called 'bloody aperitif', was directed from Pozoblanco, especially in April 1939. Some of those executed from the townships in this county were listed twice: once in Pozoblanco and again in their respective hometowns. This was the case of 6 individuals from Villanueva de Cordoba, 6 from Villaralto and 2 from El Viso. It appears that all who were arrested were taken to Pozoblanco, where the Military Police and Falangistas took care of eliminating them.

Bartolomé Cabrera Peralbo tells us of his personal involvement in the first raids in Pozoblanco when he was taken by a couple of soldiers to the Party prison where he occupied the next to the last cell on the left, at the entrance, with seven others. Every evening at 8 p.m., a truck came to the door of the jail and waited with its engine running and they would hear the bolts being drawn from the doors of other cells from where they removed prisoners whose names were on a list. In April, his brother-in-law, Domingo Sánchez Redondo, was one of the chosen and to this date his family have had no further news of what happened to him, other than that he fell under the Law of Fugitives, like so many others.[8]

Although the above is an approximate idea of the extra-legal repressive actions that occurred throughout Spain during the Black Spring of 1939 as part of the first 'cleansing' operation, before the numerous courts martial began to act, these were more in the nature of isolated, improvised incidents. In the Centre-South region of the country, however, finally occupied at the end of the war during the Victory Walk, when curiously, these paseos took place during the afternoon, at noon, or at nightfall, and ended either in a roadside ditch or in the local cemetery.

The repressive phenomenon itself was much more widespread and not always under the guise of a paseo. The means employed were more brutal and ruthless. Máximo Castro, who had belonged to the local War Committee in 1936, was one of the first 13 individuals executed in Pozoblanco. All testimonies regarding Rufino Fernández *El Poleo* Alcaide agree that he died from a beating. Gaspar Jiménez was killed just because he was engaged to Tomasa Díaz, the Director of the female branch of the Young Socialists-JSU, a young twenty-year-old girl who was executed in October after unbelievable humiliation and torture. Sebastián Márquez Romero, a nineteen-year-old from a well-to-do family, who was never forgiven by the Pozoblanco Falangistas for having spent the entire war in the Republican zone, was executed April 13.

Francoist disrespect for its victims knew no bounds – Nationalist Corporal Rejas, from Triana in Seville, was frequently heard singing during the executions in Pozoblanco. The first allegations, jokingly known as 'paper kites of death', were often signed by a Salesian priest, Fr. Antonio Do Muiño. This was the true face of victorious Francoism, not the aesthetic visions blurred by the fog of the passage of time that those involved still attempt to present today.

One of the first residents of Torrecampo to be imprisoned in Pozoblanco, where he was executed, was José Romero Moyano, President of the local branch of the Spanish Socialist Workers Party-PSOE. Acisclo Romero Luque, another resident from Torrecampo, was taken from the fields where he was watching his goats and taken to Pozoblanco. A humble peasant belonging to the UGT, he was denounced by a right-winger from his village (Antonio Cantador) because when the latter was imprisoned in 1936, Acisclo who was serving as a guard at the jail, did not let him go home to sleep at night. His daughter, when going to see him in Pozoblanco jail, arrived at the same moment that he was being taken to the cemetery in a truck. He was executed in Pozoblanco April 15, together with Miguel Romero Vila who for a time had served as Mayor of Torrecampo during the war. Acisclo left ten orphaned children with no more of a Last Will and Testament than these lines that he was able to get to his wife, written on a piece of paper he had hidden in a bit of bread:

> "I am accused of crimes that I did not commit in addition to stealing the cape that covers the statue of the Virgin, that I stole blankets and bedspreads from houses, and dozens of silver forks. Lies, all lies. The greatest lie of all, was Antonio's complaint. We will never see each other again. Resign yourself and continue to watch over our children. Don't tell anybody about this paper."[9]

The list of the first victims of the Law of Fugitives in the Pozoblanco and Los Pedroches municipalities in April 1939 was obtained from the following sources: Civil Registry for Pozoblanco and neighbouring townships, Pozoblanco Registry of Cemeteries, research for my 1987 book, Gabriel García de Consuegra's book and numerous unclassified notes that Fernando López from Pozoblanco, lent me.[10] In total, 101 individuals were slaughtered under the Law of Fugitives and the repression (some of them due to the savage beatings received), in the Pozoblanco region, almost all in April 1939. (Table 3. Victims of the Law of Fugitives March/April 1939. Pozoblanco, Villanueva de Cordoba and neighbouring townships.)

Attention is drawn to the number of 'unknown' entries for this period in 1939, which is how the above burials are identified in the Book of Burials. On the other hand, the deaths recorded in the Civil Registry appear to indicate a greater involvement of the military as these individuals are recorded as executed in the cemetery, whereas the references to 'unknowns' state that they died in the gutters and in the countryside, thus indicating that the latter were presumably the work of civilian vigilantes or Falangistas. The Law of Fugitives would return to Cordoba during the Triennium of Terror (1947-1949) and whenever Francoists were in a hurry or when a crushing action against the disaffected population was desired and the formalities of military tribunals considered as no more than so many bits of paper.

Number of victims of the Law of Fugitives in the Pozoblanco region by town

Pozoblanco (identified 14, unknown 34)	48
El Viso	10
Torrecampo	9
Villanueva de Cordoba	11
Villaralto	3
Villaharta	3
Hinojosa del Duque	2
La Granjuela	2
Adamuz	1
Santa Eufemia	1
Villanueva del Duque	1
Montoro	1
Conquista	2
From outside the province	13
Total	**101**

In total, 101 individuals were slaughtered under the Law of Fugitives during the repression in the Pozoblanco region, almost all in April 1939.

This first bloodshed in the north of Cordoba province also occurred in the entire recently-occupied Centre-South region of the country: Northeast Badajoz, Toledo, Ciudad Real, Albacete, Cuenca, Guadalajara, etc. There are, however, very few studies to provide the exact number of those who died from torture and the Law of Fugitives. With victory, the lives of the defeated became totally worthless. Massive imprisonments, general humiliation, weeks of starvation, the Law of Fugitives, paseos and savage beatings were their fate.

The following is an example of a report sent by local Military Police Headquarters to the Civil Registry, giving the names of individuals killed under the Law of Fugitives:

"To the Municipal Judge of Pozoblanco

As required by the Civil Registry records, I hereby transmit the list of individuals from your town who died as a result of the wounds they suffered when attempting to escape from the guards attached to these Headquarters. Their names are entered in the margin of this report.
May God watch over you for many years.
Pozoblanco, 25 April 1939. The Year of Victory.
Sergeant (illegible) on behalf of the Senior Captain."

Names entered in the margin:
Antonio Herruzo Cejudo, age 26
Máximo Castro García, age 28
Diosdado García Cruz, age 49.[11]

Several cases were recorded for Villanueva de Cordoba during Black Spring 1939 such as that of Benito Pozuelo Regalón, aged 28, died from torture April 7 officially from pulmonary congestion but most probably from torture, and that of Captain Gabino Cabrera Expósito of the Garcés Batallion, who committed suicide because of the beatings and torture, recorded Apri 24 The description of Miguel Hertas Caballero's ordeal in Villanova de Cordoba, which led to his death May 23, is of particular interest as it describes an a-too-typical nightmare in Spain:

Miguel Hertas Caballero had spent a month and a half in Valsequillo concentration camp, obtained the required good behaviour references, was released and returned to his hometown where he was almost immediately re-arrested. It appears that José *Laurentino* A. Díaz' widow, a woman who spent her time falsely accusing individuals, had denounced him. What had happened was that the day that Republican forces counter-attacked and re-captured the town from the Nationalists in 1936, some members of the Republican volunteer militia had found Laurentino, a wealthy landowner, hiding in his house on Calle Real. They took him and the parish priest to Plaza Laguna del Pino where they shot them both. Although those responsible were miners from elsewhere (Puertollano), Laurentino's widow still accused Miguel Huertas of having been seen on Calle Real that day. That was enough. To make matters worse, he was a communist and in 1936 had gone to Madrid where he enlisted as a volunteer in the 5th Republican regiment and spent most of the war fighting. Miguel Huertas did not resist his first savage beating. Mortally injured, he was taken from La Preturilla prison to

157

the hospital where, according to the Civil Registry, he died some hours later from a 'cerebral haemorrhage'.

There was much talk in Villanueva about the killing of a group of six prisoners April 20. When that morning their relatives went to the prison with their breakfast, Fructuoso, the municipal policeman, told them that they had gone to Pozoblanco to make their statements. But the prisoners were already dead, executed outside the town at the beginning of the road to Conquista, next to the second group of water tanks, where they were buried. This is one of the many unmarked mass graves that still exist in Cordoba province. At least three of the victims (Juan Huertas, Diego Montoro and Juan Pedraza) were killed because of the widow Díaz's accusations that on the day that her husband was killed, somebody saw them on Calle Real at the time that he was taken from his house. (This was not surprising, as that day, all the working men in town were out on the streets.)

Of the above, the victim that people still talk about today was Manuel Cruz *El Picachos* Cole to, aged 25. He was accused of being a deserter, because although the war caught him doing his military service in the Francoist forces, in Cádiz, when the troops passed through the El Muriano region, he took advantage of this to cross over to the Republican zone. Furthermore, apparently some years earlier he had had an argument with a powerful local Falangista, Diego *El Chunga*, the person who would be responsible for Manuel's ordeal. At the end of the war, he was arrested in Torrenueva, Ciudad Real, and sent to a concentration camp where he remained for a few weeks. He was released April 18 and returned to Villanueva with this wife, Isabel González Jurado. As she said,[12] they arrived at 10 p.m. and the next day the Guardia Civil (led by El Chunga) came to arrest him and take him to the infamous La Pretuilla prison. There, they beat him viciously, cut off his testicles and applied all sorts of torments. They kept him alive during the night just to make him suffer. When he was taken to be executed at dawn the next day, he had almost bled out from the amputation of his genitals.

Now for all those who today continuously speak with fervour of 'psychological support' to relatives of victims, do stop and remember how it was in those days. Whilst Juan Pedraza, one of the above victims, was still in the realm of the living, a municipal policeman, Emilio *El del Lunar*, went to his house, grabbed Juan's daughters and put them to work as servants in the houses of local Falangist's and other bastards.

There are at least three cases of the Law of Fugitives in Hinojosa del Duque. In the case of one of those, Pablo Gómez Leal, executed at the age of 18, the Civil Registry indicates he died in La Cutierr. An email Moreno Gómez recently received from one of Pablo's nephews, following a notice he had posted online on the *Todos Los Nombres* project website, states that

Falangistas shot him at the door of his home, just because of his kinship with two local leftist leaders, his brothers Antonio and José, *Los Vidal*, both of whom were also executed.[13]

Names that will remain forever unknown are those of the 'disappeared' prisoners who were taken and summarily executed *in situ*, in the Valsequillo, Los Blázquez, La Granjuela, Cerro Muriano and other provincial concentration camps, and in Castuera. There are numerous testimonies that in all these camps, prisoners were plucked from their huts and shot.

In Castuera, there was a continuous procession of trucks leaving the camp, packed with prisoners on their way to their execution. Castuera eye witnesses have told us that a hut that also functioned as a chapel was an anteroom to death as those who entered it were never heard of again. All of this reinforces our belief that the true dimension of the Francoist genocide shall never be totally quantified. The Francoist authorities did an excellent job of getting rid of all the camp records and other documentation. A totalitarian system, we know, not only engages in the physical elimination of persons as it takes pains to erase all evidence of this elimination.

The farce that was Military 'Justice'

"There were 100 of us in our cell; there are only 73 now.
Dear foreign comrade, we three are also sentenced to death
and we shall be executed either tonight or tomorrow.
You, however, may survive; if one day you are free,
you must tell the whole world of how we were killed here,
just because we wanted freedom, not Hitler."
Signed: Three Republican Guerrillas

Letter written on a little ball of paper that the condemned men in the next-door cell managed to send to Arthur Koestler, March 11, 1937, Sevilla prison.[14]

1.   Proliferation of Military Courts

The Francoist regime's first great purge of the social base of the Republic (genocide, purely and simply) that began July 17 1936, was enforced with no more rule of law than the fledging insurgent government's wartime decrees, the so-called *Bandos de Guerra*.[iii] One hundred thousand persons were exterminated by Francoism on the basis of those decrees alone.[15] As far as Andalusia is concerned, it was only in February 28 1937 that ex-Republican General Queipo de Llano, presumably on orders from Burgos, decreed the abolition of his wartime decrees and introduced the subject of preliminary pre-trial hearings and the intervention of military tribunals. (Of course, 'military justice' is to Justice, what military music is to Classical Music; in other words, nothing.) All the military governors of the provinces under Queipo's command were sent the following telegram:[16]

> "All authorities within my jurisdiction are hereby ordered to abstain from directing the application of my wartime decrees in which the ultimate sentence is imposed; they must henceforth follow the legal procedures indicated by the military Legal Advisor and gather the greatest possible amount of evidence against all the detainees so that the urgently re-established courts-martial may rapidly proceed with the due sentencing. Receipt requested."

Theoretically at least, Queipo's wartime decrees ceased to exist March 1937 when the military courts became fully operational. We must remember, however, that the Francoist courts were already functioning in 1936 in a few exceptional cases such as those involving loyal members of the military, Republican authorities and other influential individuals. Still, when it suited Francoism it resorted to shortcuts to eliminate persons, without any fear of reprisal or due process of law, by means of unlawful arrests and raids and the extra-legal application of the Law of Fugitives.

This was the scene for the events of the Black Spring of 1939, and the pre-trial hearings of hundreds of thousands of individuals indicted on military grounds. In Madrid alone, at the end of 1944, 128,000 hearings or indictments are recorded, almost all collective. More than 300,000 persons were investigated, according to data on file at the First Military District Archives, Madrid. If to this sum, one adds the numbers for all the 9 Military Districts, the total is quite simply, horrifying and difficult to accept. In Cordoba province alone, more than 26,000 individuals were indicted in 1939; 37,000 in 1940; and so on afterwards. The closer we come to computing

---

[iii] The crucial *Bandos de Guerra* were:
National Defense Junta decree of July 28 1936, approved as Decree number 79.
Decree of August 31 1936.
Decree from General Franco number 55 of November 1 1936.

the multitude of Spaniards who were tried by Francoist courts, the more astronomical the numbers.

The first thing that strikes historians is the proliferation of courts martial in 1939. All the victorious military considered themselves as being on duty and following orders when they sent people to the firing squads. Today, we are baffled at the thought of where did so many high-ranking officers come from to enforce the victory and, as magistrates, apply Franco's justice against so many defeated compatriots. The whole of Spain was filled with military judges, military magistrates, military tribunals and courts-martial. Franco mobilized the army and the Guardia Civil for his *final solution*, the definitive, physical and moral extermination of all Spanish Republicanism. The armed forces became the Dictator's Pretorian Guards. Persons were executed without any fear of reprisal, they were tortured without exception, there were mass imprisonments, individuals were starved to death, all the 'disaffected' (including many who were neutral) were made to bite the dust as the widespread wave of terror came into being. This is no exaggeration; that is exactly how it was. It was the final solution for the program that had been started in 1936. If anyone still doubts this, Moreno Gómez recommends that he read, *Testimonios de mujeres en las cárceles franquistas* [Testimonies of women in Francoist jails][17], and after studying this Bible of Francoist repression, he might speak with some knowledge of the facts. When a biased historian does not listen to the victims (the so frequently despised oral sources), the rest is no more than tuneless music in his ears.

The entire repressive machinery was in the hands of the military legal system, beginning with Queipo's wartime decrees in 1936, and following the victory, with the courts martial. Furthermore, as military justice is not very good at making distinctions, everyone was accused of the crime of military rebellion, in accordance with the Code of Military Justice (articles 237 et al., namely articles 86, 287, 288 and 289). This code was complemented by a maelstrom of repressive legislation, which indicates that not only did the wave of repression not diminish with Franco's victory, but that it grew and grew until it was a sweeping, all-inclusive attack against defeated Spain.

The general post-war repressive program was structured according to a wide range of major legislation:[18] the Law of Political Responsibilities (February 9 1939); Law for the Repression of Masonry and Communism (March 1 1940); Laws for the Security of the State (July 12 1940 and March 29 1941); Law amending the Crime of Military Rebellion (March 2 1943); Decree-Law on Military Rebellion, Banditry and Terrorism (March 18 1947); Law of Public Order (July 30 1959); Decree on Banditry and Terrorism (September 21 1960); and Law 15/63 creating the Court of Public Order (TOP). As Captain Díaz Criado at Queipo de Llano's General Headquarters stated, the purpose of all this legislation was: "So that thirty years from now, not a soul will remain alive". How distant these barbaric laws were from the 'fair and wise laws' of the 1812 Constitution

As the military coup itself was illegal, its repressive legislation was tainted from the onset. Furthermore, it fell into the ridiculous aberration of so-called 'reverse justice', that is, the insurgents who led the coup condemned as rebels all those who had remained loyal to the constitutional government and were opposed to the military coup – the Glorious Movement as they called it. International jurisprudence has not taken this type of reverse justice seriously, nor given due consideration to the tragic implications of this way of thinking. Likewise, if Francoist legislation was corrupt from the beginning, much worse was the jurisprudence that regulated the courts martial whose farcical nature has been pointed out by everyone who has studied the matter. Franco's so-called military justice was a farce in terms of the pre-trial investigations, a travesty of due process of law in the way it accepted denunciations and unsubstantiated accusations, a disgrace regarding the crimes allegedly committed by the defendants, and a shambles as to how the courts martial handled the proceedings. Procedural guarantees shone by their absence.

The Francoist legislation was only repealed by the Spanish government thirty-two years after the death of Franco, under Law 52/2007. At the same time, Article 3 of Law 52 reversed the rulings of the Francoist courts and the sentences of the courts martial, declaring that they were illegal because they were 'fraudulent in form and substance'.

As everything and everyone came under military Francoist justice, one could say that civilian jurisprudence went on holiday for almost forty years. Even the theft of a bag of acorns could be considered as an act of military rebellion if, to this crime, the prosecution added the charge of having giving a handful of acorns to a guerrilla. Spain had become a military barracks, similar to the Italo-German model, and the sole project that the Nationalist military always had in mind from the very beginning of the coup, with one difference. It was both a barracks *and* a convent, because the Church worked hand-in-hand with the Regime as it also stoked its own fire.

With victory in their hands, Francoists were faced with the massive task of organising the trials for more than 280,000 prisoners that they had arrested during the first year of the National-Syndicalist Revolution. Ten provisional Inspectorates, in addition to the existing ones for the military regions, were created, as well as a multitude of military courts that found themselves totally overwhelmed during the first three post-war years.

An idea of the intensity of the repressive furore can be seen by the fact that in Cordoba, no less than 20 special military courts were set up in the capital and another 15 throughout the province, where they worked feverishly, especially in the surrounding hillsides, the last area to be occupied. Added to these, were the numerous Political Responsibility Courts and the Courts for the Persecution of Fugitives. (Table 4. Lists of Military and Special Courts in Cordoba capital and province.)

The Military Courts for important towns also covered smaller neighbouring towns and villages: Luque and Valenzuela in Baena; Nueva Carteya in Montilla; Fuente Pamera and Hornachuelos in Posadas; Espejo in Castro del Rio; several neighbouring towns and villages in Pozoblanco; Pedroche, Torrecampo; Adamuz, in Villanueva de Cordoba, and so forth. There were Temporary Military Courts in Baena, Bujalance Hinojosa, Montilla, Montoro, Obejo, Punte Genil, Villaviciosa and some other towns, but these are difficult to identify.

In Barcelona city, 10 military courts were created at the beginning, and another 15 in the province. In Malaga, no less than 67 military courts were operating (city and province). In Cartagena, the Francoist Naval authorities created an unspeakable number of military courts of their own: 57. Alicante was served by 22 military courts (8 in the capital and 14 in the province), just to mention a few examples in the country. The operating costs of the Military Courts were borne by the town and city councils in which they were located, as were the meals and other expenditure for the courts martial.

An Examining Magistrate responsible for updating the individual case files, presided over these courts. Pre-trial hearings were held *in camera* because lawyers were not involved, nor was there any reason for them as the accused were only permitted to say a few words in their defence during a court-martial, let alone during the examination. The Examining Magistrate was assisted by a secretary and a clerk. Also at the Judge's orders were civil, Falangista, military and Guardia Civil staff who would 'facilitate' the accused's declarations, whips in hands. This does not mean that all the so-called evidence was obtained by beatings, but there were a great many vicious beatings as we shall see. Torture was such an essential part of the committal proceedings that it was the rare pre-trial hearing that was not accompanied by some savage torture of the accused.

The Examining Magistrate, almost always a member of the military, or a Francoist affected magistrate or attorney, was often appointed from amongst persons whose families had suffered or been victims in the days of the fight against the coup, and who sought revenge. Those who also thirsted for the blood of the defeated and who lacked all scruples had a whole future before them. The Examining Magistrate, who himself usually had personal victims to revenge, was both judge and jury. These judges were contaminated by their own interests in the cases before them and when called to do so, rarely decried the charges they were examining. Besides, few accused or their families would ever dare question or appeal a magistrate's ruling.

The committal proceedings were rushed summary proceedings, without any formalities or due process. In a same committal dossier, there might be a document stating that the accused was a militant Communist; another document stating that he was a militant of the Izquierda Republicana; and yet another stating that he was a militant Socialist. The information was usually unsubstantiated as it was usually based on unproven declarations or accusations. In other cases, presumption was the rule: everyone had been involved in strikes during the Republic, therefore everyone was guilty of 'extremely bad behaviour' at the very least.

The kinship of Examining Magistrates with right-wing victims was apparent in quite a few cases in Cordoba province, but this did not always work in the accused's favour. Such was the case of the attorney from Pozoblanco, Juan Calero Rubio, who had been appointed Judge of Military Court number 11 in Villanueva de Cordoba. Although he had lost a son-in-law during the revolt against the uprising in his town, the Judge was able to escape to the Francoist zone with the help of some left-wingers, including the barber Manuel Fernández Contreras. When the barber was arrested during the post-war repression, although the Judge acknowledged that Fernández had helped him escape to the 'other' side, he never forgave him for not having saved his son-in-law and did nothing. to prevent Fernández' execution.

If Francoism placed these magistrates at the vanguard of the killing machine, it was because they were individually known to lack the minimum sense of clemency or humanity. Juan Calero from Villanueva de Cordoba was one of the most despised and immoral and cruel of these. Arriving in Villanueva as a Military Judge in the first days after the victory, he sowed terror in a jail that was packed with men and women prisoners from Villanueva, Pedroche, Torrecampo and Adamuz. Not only did he organize numerous pre-trial summary hearings that dictated several death sentences, he also initiated a program of beatings and torture that still haunts the townspeople, beatings that he himself joined in. In 1940 he fell into disgrace with the Regime for beating a priest, but the exact reason for his final disgrace is unknown. Some say that it could be because he ordered the execution of the Head of the Post Office in Villanueva, Misael López Díaz, whose family included a Francoist soldier who managed to get his sentence reduced. Whether it was because of this or some other misdeed, the fact was that Calero had done something terribly wrong and decided to end his life with a fatal dose of poison August 28, 1940, aged 53. His evil doings were many indeed, such as asking the daughters and wives of the condemned for sexual favours in exchange for saving the lives of their loved ones. According to a relative's testimony, it was said that he asked Juan Escoriza Segura's daughter for sex but still executed her father. To Moreno Gómez' knowledge, the judge never saved anybody and I have not heard that any woman agreed to his demands.

Demetrio Carvajal Arrieta, a Clerk of the Court who had been appointed Mayor and local head of the Falange of Pozoblanco as soon as it was occupied by the Francoist troops, was responsible for his own reign of terror in the Cordoba capital military courts.

In Rute, Bernabé Andrés Jiménez, Captain in the Military Corps of Justice, was a member of several of the courts martial most responsible for sentencing the accused to death. For example, in the first of his involvements in Baena, May 20, 1939, he sent the famous workers' union leader José *El Transío* Joaquín to the wall. In another court-martial in Puente Genil in which he intervened, Antonio Romero, a distinguished sexagenarian, recognized icon of Republicanism, past Mayor of Puente Genil on two occasions during the Republic, totally unaffiliated with any anarchical event or political movement, was sentenced to death by strangulation. After several tragic interventions involving this Francoist magistrate, Andrés Jiménez was appointed Judge in Aguilar de la Frontera and from there, to the Cordoba capital courts. His bloody curriculum elevated him to the benches of the Spanish Supreme Court and eventually, to being honoured by the Regime with the Great Cross of Saint Raimundo of Peñafort. His portrait continued to hang in the assembly hall of the Rute city council until 2005 when it was removed after an eloquent citizens' protest organized by Pascual Rovira. This image is now in Moreno Gómez' Black History Archives.

In Baena, we also note the family relationship of the military judge and right-wing victims of 1936, when the War Inspectorate of the Army of Operations in the South appointed right-wing Manuel Cubillo Jiménez to the position of Examining Magistrate. A man possessed of a fanatical and fervent desire for vengeance after losing his wife and three sons in the anarchist killings at the San Francisco asylum, he ensured that practically nobody connected with the left survived the wartime and the post-war repression. In this, Cubillo was assisted by Luis Cordoba García, Secretary of the Baena city council.

In Castro del Rio, there also was a kinship between the military judge Manuel Criado Valenzuela, who also served as Secretary of the city council, and right-wing victims of the fighting in 1936, when both his father-in-law and a brother-in-law were killed in battle. This judge, was further assisted in keeping the people of the village in line, by his Falangista brother-in-law Pedro Luque.

Cavalry Colonel Carlos Palance y Martínez-Fortún from Lucena presided over several courts that sentenced the accused to death.[19] Born in the village of Jauja (Lucena), he was the prototype of the great landowner and a rabid anti-Republican after he had numerous run-ins with the Lucena city council September 1931, because of his treatment of his farmworkers. In 1936, he was one of the leading conspirators of the military coup in Cordoba. Not only did he represent the perfect union between the agrarian oligarchy, the judiciary and the military, his hatred of the Rojos was fuelled when one of his brothers, Fernando, was shot in Guadalajara, a victim of the so-called Red Terror. Such individual characteristics were always of particular interest to Franco when it came to filling judiciary positions, as they were the perfect guarantee of an implacable and vindictive repressive action, devoid of any scruples.

A remarkable case of a Francoist Examining Magistrate was that of José Aparicio de Arcos, from Aguilar de la Frontera, who was posted in Montilla where he sentenced quite a few Republicans to death. What is peculiar in this case is that his brother Rafael, an eminent lawyer and a leading figure of Cordovan Socialism who held several top positions during the Republic, was executed in Cordoba capital by Fascists during the summer of 1936. The ideological abysm that separated the brothers was tragically typical of Spain in those times.

One of the military judges who specialized in trials against people from Posadas, was lawyer and wealthy landowner Fernando Sepúlveda Courtoy, a ruthless individual at whose farm Nationalist General Varela stayed whenever he visited Cordoba. A fanatical Falangist, he was an intimate friend of the appalling Don Bruno and the bloodthirsty Prosecutor Rafael de La Lastra y Hoces, whose rabid harangues, the highly controversial 'tirades of Don José', are described ahead.

Amid the general furore, however, some court officials kept a degree of common sense. José Espina Almansa, an attorney who had been a PCE candidate to city council in the 1931 municipal elections (how the world turns…), retained some embers of his ideals and was influential in lessening of some of the sentences given to important Communist leaders, such as Adriano Romero Cachinero and Alfredo Caballero Martínez. Curiously, considering that José Espina had been a member of the Abril Masonic Lodge in Posadas during the 1920s, it is a wonder that he escaped being purged by the Francoists, even that he was able to serve as the secretary for a military court.

The substance of the committal proceedings was based on three sources: the declaration or interrogation by the Guardia Civil, information from the Falange, and the number of real or bureaucratic, almost always false, accusations or allegations. In the case of the Guardia Civil declaration, the life of thousands of people depended on the mood of the local commander. For example, in the case of one of the most distinguished residents of Pozoblanco, Bartolomé Fernández, ex-Major of a Volunteer Militia Regiment and as circumspect, respected and professional an individual as any, the Guardia Civil concluded that, because he was an individual who, because of his actions and bad behaviour, was considered a danger to the Regime and society. This report was signed by the morose commander of the post, Andrés Arévalo García. Still, by some happy quirk of fate he was not executed, as in the judicial circles of the time, prisoners were classified as belonging to one of three groups: affected, disaffected and dangerous. The latter were almost inevitably doomed.

The second source of information was the report from the Falange Department of Information and Investigation (SIIF). The reports from the local branches, the *Junta Local de Información*, also played a major role in the lives of thousands of individuals. As an example, the case of another accused from Pozoblanco, Ventura Redondo Fernández, reads:

> "This is a person with left-wing ideas, although we cannot specify the party to which she belongs. At the beginning of the Glorious Movement, she joined the Red Corps of Carabineers as a volunteer and therefore she is considered disaffected with our Cause. [signed illegible] For God, Spain and the National-Syndicalist Revolution. Viva Franco! Viva Spain!"

The number of contradictions between reports on a single individual show how frequently there was a total disregard for the truth, as the slightest indication of accuracy shone by its absence. An example of this are the evidentiary reports presented at the 1945 pre-trial hearings of three volunteer militia from Villanueva de Cordoba. The Guardia Civil report regarding one, José *El Lobito* A. Cepas, states: "Was a Communist and participated in the arrests of individuals who were later shot." The Falange report says: "Belonged to the Izquierda Republicana" and adds the more serious crime: "participated in assassinations".[20] Noticeably, the Falange reports went straight to the jugular. In effect, the Falange killed many more people with its reports than it did with its revolvers. The same can be said of the Francoist Guardia Civil, whose reports were more lethal than their rifles.

The third source was civilian denunciations and, frequently, reports from the parish priests. The latter are almost always present in the files of those indicted under the Law of Political Responsibilities, but less often in more conventional trials. Even so, in all cases the reports from the clergy were of great import and were also responsible for thousands of lives. Sometimes, the priest simply wrote the damning words: "I do not know the accused", implying that this person never went to Church and as such, there was sufficient reason for his arrest. What a disaster: condemned to death because he was a leftist and, to add insult to injury, because he was an atheist as well!

Many priests became so deeply involved in this maelstrom of extermination that they informed on matters that were none of their business and well beyond their religious obligations. Fr. José Armario, parish priest in Morón de la Frontera, turned to gossip to write the following report on an accused: "Having been duly informed, I can say that Pedro *El Carabinero* García Flores, a metalworker by trade, was an eminent member and activist of the CNT in this city, that he made bombs and threw them against the Guardia Civil barracks and participated in the attack on the same, August 26, 1939. The Year of the Victory."[21]

These accusations were totally false. García Flores had left for Ronda when the war broke out and that was all. So much for priests and the 8th Commandment (Thou shalt not bear false witness). As far as the 5th Commandment is concerned, I could only make cynical remarks in the light of the orgy of bloodshed.

2. Widespread flood of denunciations and false witness statements

The Francoist regime decreed a *General State of Denunciation* as if it were an emergency measure and promoted it through the media with mantras such as: "It is everybody's duty to report every indication against the Marxist Horde". Every Falangista, just because he was one, was required to present denunciations, so many denunciations per person. Every right-winger was also expected to follow suit. During the first months of 1939, the Falangista daily paper in Mataró, as did the press all over the country, repeatedly published articles encouraging denunciations with headlines such as: "Franco's Justice needs and asks all Spaniards to cooperate." The same newspaper later insisted: "We remind and encourage all people of their obligation to cooperate with the execution of Justice".[22]

Denunciation was the spark that triggered the motor of the extermination machine. For an individual to be considered 'worthy' by the New State, nothing better than to offer himself as an informer. Right-wingers who did not present denunciations were considered 'neutrals', as if this were a sin by omission. The state of generalized denunciation entailed a far-reaching objective: extending this complicity and collaboration to the Regime's entire social base. This collaboration, more rural than urban, was an important factor in ensuring cohesion within the Regime, and this cohesion was rewarded with high marks for loyalty and unwavering allegiance. This way, the victorious base became full members of the Movement as they contributed to the great nation-wide cleansing and extermination operation. This is in keeping with repressive regimes the world over who have always looked to integrate their followers in their task of general repression by means of denunciations, rumours, gossip and whispers, with falsehood as the main ingredient.

In the Spanish case, some civilian accusers attempted to withdraw their allegations when they saw the very serious and unjust results, but they were so threatened by the authorities that they gave up trying. What's more, allegations from authorities, almost always very vague and clearly false, were often changed by the Examining Magistrates, with terrible consequences for the accused,

In reality, Falangists and unconditional supporters of Francoism cooperated with the regime in its arbitrary use of denunciations as a tool with which to ensure the great extermination or macro-cleansing of dissenters, staging farcical pre-trial hearings and proceedings hose result was decided upon beforehand. A remarkable case w of the capricious use of allegations and total disregard for the truth, was Juan Cantador Zamora's court-martial May 24, 1940. The entire case against him was based on Luisa Doctor, a 1936 widow's presumed allegation. When she was asked in court whether she recognized the accused, Juan Cantador, to everybody's surprise she said no. The judge then asked the widow why she had accused him of having killed her husband, to which she replied: "No sir, Judge Juan Calero must have misunderstood me. What I said was that he was known as one of Juan Elías' kindly tenants." The ensuing situation was ridiculous. The Court repeatedly threatened the widow in an attempt to force her to retract her statement, to no avail. Manipulation of the allegation was obvious, but putting the record straight was of no use either as Juan Cantador was still executed in Cordoba September 12 1941. Clearly, his elimination been decided beforehand and the faked allegation was just for show.

Moreno Gómez wrote the distinguished professor Vicente Pascual Soler, director of the Academia Espino in Cordoba city, regarding this particular and other cases and this is what the professor replied: «A career Examining Magistrate, Juan Calero Rubio from Pozoblanco and well-known in Villanueva, substantiated the charges against the accused. This representative of so-called Francoist justice took his job seriously with the collaboration of a typist and a couple of henchmen who would torture the accused. With such persuasion, the magistrate obtained the accused' signed confessions that were considered evidence enough to justify the sentence that had previously been decided upon for each case.'[23]

The dark world of informants and accusations encouraged by Francoism is surely the most foetid and nauseating illustration of the character of those responsible for so-called Francoist justice. Their route down the moral sewer is the most stinking, sometimes ridiculous, always tragic, path ever have imagined.

As previously mentioned, the first allegations that were examined usually were the reports from the Guardia Civil and the Falange. In addition to the bizarre examples described, there were some equally peculiar situations influenced by National-Syndicalist thought in Montilla. Here, as in every town and village, local authorities received a multitude of requests for information from concentration camps, forced labour battalions, etc. A sample of the answers from Montilla informers is a true anthology of the nonsensical. As everywhere, prisoners were accused of 'bad or extremely bad moral behaviour.' Membership of or association with a leftist political party, trade union, service in a civil or military position was classified as 'undesirable social political behaviour' or 'without shame'. One accused, Aurelio Casas Cordoba, was also charged with being an 'atheist from birth'.[24]

Faced with this flood of denunciations of supposed crimes and outrages, it is useful to look at some data to determine what actual percentage of prisoners could actually be guilty of the supposed 'blood crimes' with which everyone was also accused. There is some data that helps illustrate this. According to the 1937 *Memoria de la Inspección de Campos de Concentration y Prisioneros,*[25] the number of Franco's prisoners that year was 106,822, classified A, B, C, or D, (D, being those accused of civil crimes). Of the total number of prisoners, only 2,282 were accused of specific crimes: seizure of property and registers, burning of religious images or sacrilege, and, of course, blood crimes. Of those executed, only 2.13% were accused of common law crimes and not all of these were blood crimes.[26] The accusation 'was involved in assassinations' was the joker in the pack that was used in most of the cases that received the death penalty. During their trial, the only thing those unfortunate individuals could say before they were executed was that the accusations were false. It served no purpose. Everything had been decided, and well decided, beforehand.

One lethal accusation by Francoist justice was that the prisoner had served on a local War Committee. When accused of this, nobody was safe. *Causa General* records clearly illustrate the purpose of this stratagem as they include detailed lists of all the leaders of working people in a town or village. Each list identifies twenty to thirty individuals who are accused of having belonged to a town's War Committee, when in actual case, it never comprised of more than five or six people, including the town Mayor.[27] In Bujalance, for example, there is a list of more than twenty individuals. There are dozen names on the Santa Eufemia War Committee list; El Viso, more than 15; Dos Torres, more than 13; Pedroche, almost 30; Villaralto, 20; Fuenteobejuna, 12; Villaviciosa, 13; Villa del Rio 17; Montoro, almost 20; Hornachuelos, 33; and so forth. The fake Committee lists reported in the Causa General records were nothing more than blacklists of individuals slated for execution.

If in a town some crime had allegedly been committed against one or more right-wing individuals, every Republican in the town was accused of having taken part in the crime. These are the collective denunciations we find in both in official reports and in allegations from private individuals. Here again, the specialist data is the Causa General records. It is well understood that the real purpose of the Causa General investigation was, in addition to searching for foundations of a Francoist martyrdom, to collect the reports and denunciations that were submitted to it by Mayors, Falange Information Service, Guardia Civil, Municipal Police, Courts and other sources. The Causa General files represent a repertoire of allegations in a town, based on which the investigators drew up a list of the most notable leftist individuals in the town and on the basis of which those individual's who were on the respective blacklist were accused of being collectively guilty of the alleged crime(s).

This is what occurred in Posadas, for which a list of 87 right-wing victims in 1936 concludes with the accusation and the statement 'all the accused have been imprisoned or executed'. In Cardeña, with 4 right-wing victims, the Causa General accused no less than 22 farmworkers, 'all who belonged to the left wing in the town'. The Causa General also collected accusations from private individuals, such as the one filed by Elisa Gallardo Velarde, from Pedroche, against 22 persons for the murder of her husband in July 1936. One of the persons on her list was Alfonsa de la Remonta, whom she also accused of taking religious pictures home to burn to cook the stew.

Attempting to analyse the repertoire of allegations and accusations found case files is tricky. To dare to draw the profile of an accused based on what appears in his file is dodgy because although one can read what the Francoist machinery states, one cannot know what an accused might have said, because he was never allowed to speak in his defence. A recent publication in Madrid, *Los fusilamientos de la Almudena* [The Almudena executions] by Manuel Garcia Muñoz is totally misleading. The author gives a list of individuals executed, accompanied with an extract of the accusations against each one, many of which are clearly invented. The result is astounding instead of providing a list of judicial victims, it looks like a list of devils, terrorists and thieves. To make matters worse, the author attaches the derogatory nicknames that Francoists liked to give everybody. This is intolerable. In addition to being a historical aberration, the entire work is offensive, purely and simply because the majority of denunciations and accusations were false, especially because we have no idea of what version of the events the victims could have given had they been permitted to speak.

An example of how the denouncers' omnipotent powers enabled them to become virtual owners of lives and property, occurred in Madrid. Agutina Sánchez Sariñena, whose husband was killed in the war, lived with her mother-in-law, Josefa Perpiñán. A neighbour of theirs who coveted their apartment, made a double denunciation in two separate courts, falsely accusing both women of having been leaders of the *Checa[iv]* on Calle Fomento, when neither had ever heard of that street. They were tried in two court-martials, January12 and 17 1940. Agustina managed to be released. Not so her mother-in-law who was executed July 24 1940, despite the fact that it was proven that she had spent the entire war far from Madrid, in Denia, Alicante.

Another example from Madrid shows how when Francoists could not locate an individual they were hunting, they would content themselves with a relative and make him pay. Hilario Collado, a farmer from Santa Olalla, Toledo, where his son Eugenio Corruco appears to have killed a baker in 1936, was imprisoned in Madrid. As Eugenio had fled to the mountains in 1939 and they could not find him, the Guardia Civil arrested his father instead and sent him to Madrid to be tried. The Mayor from his home town sent a nasty report in which he stated that Hilario encouraged his son Eugenio to murder Juan Sánchez, the baker. The Mayor had invented the bit about the father encouraging his son and it was that which led Hilario to the grave. In the court martial, the prosecutor blew the facts out of proportion as usual, stating that: "The accused encouraged his son Juan Sánchez to murder the baker from that town, and in effect he died because of this encouragement."[28] In other words, the baker did not die because Eugenio was supposed to have shot him, but because his father supposedly encouraged him to do so, when the poor man was probably more involved in tending to his goats at the time. Yet another example to show how anyone one who still doubts that Francoist justice lacked even a modicum of credibility, is incredibly naïve.

On the other hand, there were many cases of fanciful accusations that carried the death penalty where the accused escaped the death penalty for one reason or another. Such was the case of Miguel Hernández who was sentenced to death for being a writer and poet of the revolution. He was not executed simply because Vicente Alexandre and other literary notables appealed for him *in extremis*. The result was the same, unfortunately, because

---

iv Communist police headquarters in Madrid at the beginning of the insurrection.

172

Miguel Hernández ended up dying in prison of starvation and deprivations. Another whose death sentence was commuted was Antonio Buero Vallejo, the playwright, who despite having been arbitrarily accused of being an active Rojo propagandist, managed to escape from falling off the edge of the judicial cliff by remaining in prison until 1946 when he was finally released.

A case in point from Reus, Tarragona, illustrates the frivolity of Francoist denunciations and accusations, for which there was only one reality: the trials were a total farce and case files were only created as cover-ups. On this occasion, Falangistas wanted to get rid of Ferrán Fontana Grau, an outspoken author and playwright. Failing a specific accusation, he was indicted on the grounds that he was "the author of several plays of a revolutionary nature and tendency, that he directed several of these in Reus theatres; that he also wrote verses of the same nature and tendency, such as the one entitled *Canción de retaguardia* [Song from the rear-guard], a poem that sums up the charges he is accused of." The prosecutor asked for 20 years in prison but the court martial sentenced him to death. He was executed August 8 1939 in Pilatos prison, Tarragona.[29]

On the other hand, many allegations were attributed to a case arbitrarily because there was such an avalanche of dossiers, such huge numbers of prisoners and accused, that it was humanly impossible to put any order in the allegations or judiciary inquiries received or asked for. The entire Francoist bureaucratic sector was in total chaos and the only clear objective was that people had to be eliminated in one way or another and the more, the better.

Take the case of Francisco Copado Sánchez, of Villanueva de Cordoba, who was sent under arrest to be tried in Valencia. A chauffeur by profession and a communist of little importance, he was nevertheless a candidate for the firing squad because in his pre-trial hearing, it was alleged that he was known to handle dynamite and that in this capacity he had been involved in the left-wing revolt in the town. All of this was false and Copado's wife did everything she could to save him. Maria discovered that Juan Fernández had denounced him, but when she spoke with him he assured her that he had nothing against Francisco. He just happened to be at the Headquarters when he was told to sign the accusation because the Court needed two signatures. He agreed to accompany the Copado family to the Examining Magistrate Juan Calero and withdraw his accusation. The judge rose to his feet angrily and furiously accused the family of dithering. Terrified at the outburst, Juan Fernandez kept quiet. Actually, someone else was responsible for Copado's demise. His accuser, Manuel Rodríguez Moreno, stated without proof, that he had heard rumours that Copado was seen on the streets the day of the revolt. Nothing specific, just insidious allegations.

It is worth looking at this case a bit closer, to see just how the dark world of the informants worked. It also so happened that Francisco Copado was first cousin to Fr. Bernabé Copado, SJ, the famous Jesuit chaplain to the Nationalist Redondo Unit conscripts. Copado's wife decided that she should go to this cousin and enlist his help in obtaining her husband's release. Francisco responded to Maria's plans in a letter from Modelo jail in Valencia, in which he praises her attempts at getting his release although he is resigned to his fate as he is aware that his demise was pre-ordained.[30]

As it turned out, Maria had no time to travel to Málaga or do anything else, because two days later, January 11 1939, Francisco was executed in Paterna, Valencia, cemetery. There had been no commutation or review of his sentence. The pre-trial hearing that he mentions in his letter had nothing to do with his Jesuit cousin, who did go to Villanueva. The hearing was convened based on nothing more than a petition for Francisco's release, signed by one hundred right-wing and apolitical persons. The document was sent to Valencia but it was accompanied by an insidious notation from Mayor Gregorio Pedraza who stated that the petition was a fraud and that many of the signatories were not right-wingers, but leftists. With a stroke of his pen, the Falangista Mayor destroyed all of Maria Copado's efforts and anything his Jesuit cousin might been able to do had he so wished.

Francoist justice was not just a farce, a staged performance, or a display of vindictive rancour. Even worse, if this was possible, the allegations and accusations on which many of the sentences were based clearly indicate the extreme retroactivity of the emotions involved, as many accusations centred on events that dated back not just to 1934 but much further back, as far as 1931. The purpose was clear: the Republican system was not just to be demolished, it had to be purged and with it, the entire social base that sustained the Republican regime. Demolish the system, demolish the base. This was "the work – the nightmare and the glory – that destiny required of military justice" in the words of Felipe Acedo Colunga, a military prosecutor and one of the Spanish war criminals who should have been allocated a seat at the Nuremberg trials.

Contrary to some authors, Moreno Gómez prefers never to use the word 'revolutionary' to describe the actions of those who fought against the military coup. The people who fought against the coup, Republicans, did not initiate a revolution; they acted in defence of the Republic, in defence of democratic Spain.[v] If there was a true revolution, it was the National-

---

[v]   Whenever Moreno Gómez refers to Republicans, he is almost always speaking of the population of southern Spain, because he is an expert on the *Hispania ulterior*, south of the River Ebro, not on *Hispania citerior*, the region north of the River Ebro.

Syndicalist and National-Catholicism's involvement in the military uprising. These were the true revolutionaries, those who lay Spain flat on its back. The idea of a revolution was constantly promoted by Falangistas and the regime's propaganda that bandied the idea of a left-wing revolution to scare the population, promote hatred of the disaffected and justify the military insurrection. European Fascists of the day were so terrified of the presumed leftist 'revolution' that they went wild with their attempts to destroy the existing democracies, and Spain suffered greatly the consequences of that insanity. One is reminded of Estaban Ibarra's famous words: '*A ghost is running around Europe*'.[vi]

The menu of allegations and accusations, extracted from more than half a thousand proceedings Moreno Gómez consulted at the Pozoblanco District Court, 1987, is extremely revealing:

- The <u>most lethal accusation</u>, punishable by death, was having 'belonged to a War Committee'.

In the early days of the uprising, trade unions and other civilian groups raised regiments of volunteer militia to supplement the Republican regular army. Although untrained fighters, they proved to be excellent soldiers and fighting men. These units were each commanded by a War Committee, usually civilians, who organized the units, appointed officers, obtained weapons and supplies, etc., and were considered dangerous 'revolutionaries' by Franco's Regime and its supporters.

- The <u>second most serious accusation</u> was 'exhibits extremely bad conduct', in other words, was a leftist or had been a militant in a workers' party or a trade union (Izquierda Republicana, Unión Republicana were included here).

This extremely bad behaviour included having participated in strikes or demonstrations as long ago as 1918. Just what did the Regime want to

---

[vi] Ibarra, Esteban. "A ghost is running around Europe, the specter of xenophobic populism who dangerously feels the totalitarian tsunami that wants to destroy historic democratic achievements, especially those toward universal human rights. The new extreme right continues its long marche against the institutions in all European countries, encouraging intolerance and hate, contaminating parties and democratic institutions across Europe." Ibarra's statement regarding 21st century xenophobia, is nonetheless reminiscent of what was occuring in Spain during and after the civil war. *Xenophobia in time of crisis.* Madrid, 24 March 2011. Posted by cristobalgomez and downloaded from https://movementagainstintolerance.wordpress.com/.

175

achieve with all these retroactive declarations of terrible conduct? No more nor less than to penalize all those who were involved in the entire trajectory of the trade union movements since their inception. The destruction of the unions was at the heart of the military coup's objectives.

- Likewise, there was a <u>third class of allegations and accusations</u> that had grave consequences for those whom they described as: 'stood out as a 'propagandist' for the left' during the war or, more seriously, before the war. Along the same lines but much, much worse, was 'has spoken at meetings or was a spokesperson for the Frente Popular'. Having served in any public position during the Republic and before, was a serious crime, even it was only having been elected town councillor or a member of the Country Council. Woe to anyone who had ever been elected a Member of Parliament.

If the above were prime targets of the Francoist judiciary, high officials – mayors, governors, officers in the Republican Army, political commissars and suchlike - were particularly hated. In the concentration camps, the classifying Juntas graded all these leaders and local authorities as Class C criminals whose destiny was cannon fodder for the firing squads.

- The <u>fourth class of allegations and annotations</u> in the case files of those who took up arms and fought for the Republican cause. 'Enlisted as a volunteer in the militia' was intolerable and counted as an immovable aggravating factor. Having 'belonged to the Corps of Guerrillas of the Republic' and been 'involved in sabotage' were firmly proclaimed serious offences. As almost nobody accused of these allegations escaped death, many of these 'children of the night' fled to the mountains.

- Lastly, a series of <u>less specific </u>allegations added to the above list of crimes, allegations and accusations with more specific military and political connotations, there was a series of less specific allegations:

  - 'was a friend of Marxists leaders;'
  - 'participated in some kind of anti-clerical action': burning of churches and religious statutes, insults to the clergy, that which they called profanations, and similar acts. There are numerous photographs of protestors in Málaga wearing chasubles and surplices, which led many to the firing squad.

Other peculiar accusations were levied against honourable Republicans who had absolutely nothing to do with any kind of violence but who the Regime demanded should be removed from the scene. Examples of these are:

'is vain', 'insulted the Generalissimo', or simply, 'is a danger to the Glorious Movement', or a plethora of cases bearing the surreal accusation: 'left town and did not avoid bloodshed.'

Equally bizarre, an apparently positive declaration in favour of an accused, such as 'saved the life of a right-wing person', could be twisted into something lethal, such as when one prosecutor argued that: "If the accused saved one person, two things must be considered. Was he a very influential person? If so, if he saved one, why didn't he save them all?" This is what happened to Joaquín Pérez Salas, who protected many right-wing individuals and used this argument in his defence at his court-martial. It did him no good. He had forgotten that there was no excuse for his having been a member of the Republican military. He was executed in Murcia.

When it came to women, the choice of denunciations and accusations was equally peculiar:
- 'is influenced by her husband's ideas or is married to a leftist;'
- 'supported the *Socorro Internacional Rojo;* [vii]
- 'incited men to take up arms;'
- 'carried the flag in demonstrations or has embroidered a Republican banner;'
- 'organized plays to raise funds for the *Casa del Pueblo* or the Peoples' Army;'
- 'was a militant member of a leftist political party or organization;'
- 'participated in creating registers, in seizures or testified in a lawsuit against somebody from the Right;'
- 'spoke against the National Cause' and so forth.

The entries in women's case files go far beyond the known boundaries of stupidity, such as in the case of Eustaquia Encinas Olmo[31] who was accused of 'talking with Marxists', 'participated in demonstrations against the imprisonments', 'bore false witness against Lucas Díaz Fernández who was murdered during a bombing'[viii] and lastly, 'the parish priest says he does not know her', in other words, she never went to mass. Very bad. She was sentenced to 12 years in prison for 'gossiping'.

Moreno Gómez studied numerous Causa General (CG) and other case file containing examples of the above allegations and the unacceptable manner by which these have been processed. A few of the more notable, from

---

[vii] International Red Aid, an international service organization created by the Communist International in 1922 as a kind of political Red Cross.
[viii] Actually, he was a Francoist who was killed by the Nationalist Air Force when it bombed Pozoblanco.

Pozoblanco, Villlanueva de Cordoba and other Cordoba province towns, as recorded in the respective CG files, are described in some detail.

Some of the CG case files bear the notation *educated*, which was especially grievous. As far as Francoists were concerned, such an accusation was fundamental to its repressive orgy as the regime believed that the uneducated masses were influenced by their leaders and by distinguished individuals whom they charged with swindling and twisting and poisoning the minds of the workers. Involvement in any cultural activity, especially teaching, was considered by the Francoist courts as a major aggravating factor. Franco, in his daily confirmation of death sentences, almost never commuted the sentence of anyone whose file bore the indication 'educated'. Schoolteachers and members of the *Centros Obreros*[ix] were regularly sent to their graves. Cordoba courts were no exception to the rule. "Death to the intelligentsia!" shouted the generals and the Falangistas who were against all forms of education for the lower classes. "*We don't want men who study, just bullocks who work.*"[32]

If the tragic story of Antoniuo Varo, whose story is told in Appendix II were not enough, his son-in-law, Enríque Ramírez Dópido, Head Postmaster of Pozoblanco, was less fortunate. Despite the fact that he was imprisoned by the insurgents from July 23 1936 to August 15 in the afternoon, after the town surrendered to the Nationalists, according to what he himself wrote in an appeal, his accusers fabricated another lot of false allegations for which he was arrested:

- 'was one of the crowd who took members of the right-wing on *paseos*';
- 'inspired and was morally responsible for the excesses committed by the Red committees';
- 'ordered the arrest of Moisés Moreno Castro and was responsible for his execution';
- 'acted as the go-between for the besiegers of the town', etc.

Just when Enrique hoped he was going to be released, the train for Valencia on which the oft-mentioned Moisés Moreno travelled, had already left. Enrique Ramírez was unable to clear himself of the mountain of lies.

[ix] Workers' Community Centres.

When April 3 1940 his appeal reached the "magnanimous Caudillo", Franco simply wrote *enterado*[x] on the file. Enrique Ramírez was executed in Pozoblanco April 12.

To this additional tragedy, the victors added the economic ruin of Antonio Varo's family and business associates, as the Falangistas were not content to be left empty-handed when there were assets to be seized. Enrique Ramírez and his father-in-law Antonio Varo were owners of a flour factory in Fuentes de Andalusia, in partnership with José Madueño, whose story also appears in Appendix II. The latter's house, the finest in Pozoblanco, was seized by Antonio Calero, the leader of the Falange. Other Falangistas confiscated the flour factory. Antonio Calero also bought and paid Enrique Ramírez' widow peanuts for an orchard. Another example of how the elimination of persons was not solely fired by the Fascist cleansing furore, but that it was also fed by greedy locals.

During the Black Sprin of 1938, there was an avalanche of reprisal allegations and accusations in Pozoblanco from relatives of right-wing victims, not just of the fifty who had been killed there August 1936, but also of the more than one hundred who were sentenced by the Republican People's Court in Valencia, most of whom were executed in Paterna in September 1936. Causa General records state that 25 Republicans were accused by relatives of 61 right-wing victims, including:

- Socialist Antonio Baena (executed) was accused by relatives of at least eight right-wing victims, all from outside Pozoblanco and absolute strangers to him. Yet there was not a single accusation against him from the relatives of some 55 right-wing victims in that town.
- Communist Bautista Herruzo de la Cruz (executed), was accused by relatives of another eight victims, especially of the Muñoz Cabrera brothers and the oft-mentioned Moisés Moreno.
- Another Socialist Mayor of the town, Rafael Rodrigue *Tres Cuartas* Redondo (in exile in France), was accused by relatives of four victims.
- Elias de la Cruz Gutiérrez (also in France) was accused by relatives of six victims.
- Assorted individuals from Pozoblanco whom we know were unconnected to any kind of violence, such as Antonio Varo, Mayors Rafael Rodriguez and Antonio Márquez, among others, were nevertheless accused by many relatives of right-wing victims.

---

[x] *Enterado:* noted.

In Belalcázar, as in many other townships, the municipal archives contain copies of the multitude of daily reports that the Francoist Mayors signed, as requested by the military courts. During the first months of the Regime, the courts continuously sent the mayors urgent requests for information regarding everyone they considered a Rojo and the mayors responded with totally negative information and allegations, truthful or not. Following is an example of one such report for Alfonso *Sincolor* Paredes Medina, the great freedom fighter from Belalcázar, who had already been sentenced to death but had managed to escape from prison and flee to the mountains where he led a large group of Republicans who had also fled. His end is a mystery; he disappeared and nothing more is known of him.

> "I, the undersigned Mayor, by virtue of my office, am honoured to make public the following information:

> ALFONSO PAREDES MEDINA is an individual with left-wing ideas and an active propagandist of the same. When the Glorious National Movement began, this individual fled to a farm named Malagón, where there was a concentration of Marxists from that town. He joined the Rojo column that assaulted and occupied the town August 13 and 4 1936, committing all kinds of murders and arrests and was seen in the patio of Federico García-Arévalo's house during the morning of August 13 1936. He engaged in plundering properties and he went off to join the Rojo Army, in which he remained until the end of the war, when he was arrested. He later escaped from the Hinojosa del Duque jail in which he was imprisoned.

> In witness of the truth of these accusations against this individual (signed)

> Manuel Escribano Medina, Mayor, Belalcázar, March 12 1940."[33]

The municipal reports, an 'official' variation of the allegations and accusations, were added to other reports from the local heads of the Falange and the Guardia Civil, the parish priest and private citizens. All these were filed together with the accused's statement (always obtained after a good beating). In the town of Belalcázar, among those who appear to have signed the greatest number of private denunciations were members of the Delgado

Gallego right-wing family and the head of the municipal police, Fernando Ballester Tobajas.

It is difficult to get to the truth of each event because to do so, one must listen to both sides, which is all but impossible as so many years have passed since then.[xi] Furthermore, we are faced with the well-oiled extra-judicial mechanics of a repressive program that caused the death of many innocent men, without any due process of law or even the minimal legal proceedings that would make it possible for historians to obtain a clear image of the facts.

Undoubtedly, the great majority of post-war victims can be attributed to reasons of an exclusively political nature and not to a desire to purge all those who were alleged to have committed presumed crimes of blood. Nobody should be surprised at this conclusion, given that the thousands of those who were exterminated by Francoism behind the lines of battle during the three years of the war, were also killed for political reasons and not on the basis of any lego-juridicial criteria of any kind. The carnage in Galicia, León, Zamora, Valladolid, Burgos, Logroño, Navarra, Zaragoza capital, Canary Islands, Ceuta, Melilla, Cordoba capital, etc., etc., did not obey any judicial criteria, it was spurred on purely by the political motivation of an extermination programmed by the authors of the military coup.

Many members of the Frente Popular who did their very utmost to prevent all kinds of violence, were killed in an arbitrary and cruel manner for political reasons alone. As far as Cordoba province is concerned, a few names immediately come to mind: Miguel Rachel (Mayor of Villanueva del Duque), Pedro Torralbo Gómez (Provincial Deputy from Villanueva de Cordoba), Francisco Dios (Captain Paco, from Villafranca), Eduardo Bujalance (Deputy, from Hornachuelos), Antonio Baena (from Pozoblanco) and many, many more.

Obviously, the Francoist repression was not looking for the simple cleansing of individuals allegedly responsible for blood crimes. Likewise, the military courts never showed any interest in the truth, simply because the principle objective was the ultimate dissolution, not to say extermination, of the Republican social base and the Republic's civil and military leaders, at the same time that the rising pillars of the New Regime were cemented with violence and terror.

During the post-war period, in towns where there had earlier been attacks on right-wingers, mostly by individuals who were inflamed with indignation

---

[xi] The entire dark world of denunciations in Pozoblanco can be consulted in the *Causa General* documents, in boxes for Cordoba, National Historical Archives, Madrid. The Judge examiner of the Causa or his collaborators did a considerable job of obtaining exhaustive details regarding the multitude of allegations. This document appears to begin in Pozoblanco September 18 1941.

against the military coup, those events, the work of a minority, were used as a pretext for the execution of hundreds of Republicans, including hundreds of innocent people. This occurred in Baena where the tragic killing of right-wingers in the San Francisco refuge, the work of only a handful of people in reprisal for the slaughter, by Francoists, of hundreds of workers in that town the same day, was used as a pretext for executing hundreds of working men, both during and after the war. In the same way that in Spain today, when there is talk of the Francoist killings, latter-day Francoists wave the flag of the Paracuellos massacre by communists November 1936, to shut people up. The same is true regarding the case of the San Francisco Refuge in Baena, where Francoists continue to refuse to admit, let alone accept, their cold-blooded execution of 700 leftist townspeople in reprisal for 80 right-wing victims. Sadly, shut-your-mouth exhortations work very efficiently against those who are searching for the true historic memory.

3. Systematic torture

Torture is one of the most heinous crimes against the dignity of Man. Raphael Lemkin who, in his studies on genocide first called this a crime against humanity as he included torture in the same group of *Acts of brutality by which an individual is wounded in his dignity.*[34] The crime of torture as a crime against humanity is defined in Article 7 of the <u>Statutes of the International Criminal Court</u>, Item 4. This humiliating crime was included in <u>The Nuremberg Trial Proceedings under Crimes Against Humanity</u> (August 1945) : namely murder, extermination, enslavement, deportation, and *other inhumane acts* committed against any civilian population, before or during the war, or persecutions on political, racial or religious grounds." (Article 6.A.c).

To the list of Crimes Against Humanity, the Charter of the International Court adds: 'Leaders, organizers, instigators and accomplices participating in the formulation of execution of a common plan or conspiracy to commit any of the foregoing crimes are responsible for all acts performed by any persons in execution of such a plan. In Spain, it was the authors of the insurrection (military, Falangistas and Church) who were responsible for those crimes, yet to date, none of these three groups has asked for forgiveness, as did the perpetrators of the crimes of apartheid in South Africa. As for the Church, its proclivity for violence dates back through the ages, not just to the days of the Inquisition, but even further back, to the 5th century A.D. when St. Cyril drove the Jews out of Alexandria.

So-called justice under Franco provided the same persona guarantees as did the Inquisition. Likewise, that ancient form of Church justice was based on torture, as were the Francoist judicial military proceedings, even though trial by torture was abolished by the 1812 Constitution. If the first punishment against the defeated had been a general imprisoning in jails and concentration camps, torture was the first rung to Franco's hell and justice. Every case file that Moreno Gómez was able to consult, without exception, provided information obtained by torture in the ante-room of all the suffering that was to follow.

Francoism triggered that which could be described as the horrendous storm of a general state of torture. The brutal methods of torture practiced by the Inquisition pale in comparison to those applied under Franco, particularly after his victory in 1939. There was less torture during the war, as the regime appeared to content itself with mass executions by firing squad – the macro cleansing of the first stage. In the post-war period, however, there was an explosion of a vindictive neurosis, the malicious desire to punish the defeated before execution, the application of absolute cruelty, the total contempt for the individual. This was not, as Moreno Gómez stated earlier, simply revenge for behind-the-lines and battlefront right-wing victims. It was so much more: vengeance against those who had opposed the immediate triumph of the insurgents, who had resisted the coup and who fought in defence of the democratic government. For the victors, opposition to the Glorious Movement was an unpardonable affront, an insult to the Church that, together with the Berlin and Rome regimes, had blessed the insurgency. There could be no pardon for the defeated fighters who had taken up arms in defence of some democratic freedoms that Francoists looked upon as being of no more interest than a pile of sodden papers on the altar of totalitarianism.

Francoism justified torture on two beliefs: the impunity of the victors and the necessary demonization and dehumanization of the defeated. The great conditioning factor was the generalized belief that the victors enjoyed absolute impunity for their actions. This is what Baltasar Garzón, wrote in his book *El alma de los verdugos* [The soul of the executioners][35] and so eloquently explained in his interview on Radio Argentina in 2008. [36]

> "Who were these men who, after kissing their children as they left their homes, went to work as exemplary employees, torturing and murdering political prisoners?... People have become convinced that they were ordinary people, who at a given moment in time went beyond the barrier restraining perversion that Man also carries within him, and if once he has passed this hurdle, cannot stop...

(for the simple reason of political disagreement) … That, associated to the climate of impunity… When this situation disappears, when he no longer holds the reins of power in his hands…. is when cowardice appears, there is a hiding, a non-acceptance/recognition of the facts."

As regards the belief in the need to dehumanize the defeated, this assumption could be attributed to the Catholic Church. Throughout History, this holy institution has been a master in degrading the image of the heretics, the heterodox or, in our case, the dissenting Republicans. The Church vilified them, demonized them, declared them to be abominations and dehumanized them. From then on, all barbarities were possible.

For the repression and torture to reach a maximum level of efficiency, during 1939 when systematic torture was most brutal, the regime began by ensuring that the cruel and savage punishments were first enforced in every imprisoned person's hometown, where hatred and calls for revenge would stoke the general fires of political vengeance, before those who had been arrested were transferred to prisons in the capital cities. It was not unpremeditated. Well into the 1940s, the idea was that the euphoria of victory would feed a sadism embellished with the most perverse accusations so that the defeated individual would suffer the full weight of the purge where people knew him. Later, when prisoners were transferred to provincial prisons, they stood out less as individuals although the threat of brutal beatings and unbridled attacks by those who wielded the rods, always hung over their heads

Systematic torture, especially widespread during 1939-1940, was another of the great post-war differences compared to the repression of Republicans in 1936, when extra-legal raids were carried out with some celerity and only rarely involved the added sadism of torture. (There was, however, a precedent for the military's use of torture when, in 1934, right-wing government troops savagely repressed the miners' uprising in Asturias. Several military were later tried for 'the Asturias excesses'.)

There were three types of torture. The first, shock or vindictive torture, seen in the towns in 1939, a violent reaction on the part of Nationalists triggered by anger repressed during the war and personal hatreds, as well as revenge for the sufferings of right-wingers. The most savage beatings were given by guards with whips and rods in the jails or when Falangistas went into the municipal holding cells and kicked and slapped the prisoners or took some outside and beat them unconscious. One way by which the victors, who were often drunk, celebrated their victory.

Then there was the judiciary torture, applied during the instruction of a summary procedure, when the accused was beaten in the presence of the Examining Magistrate, on his orders. Again, nothing was improvised or uncontrolled. The declarants often ended up unconscious from the blows. If an accused fell to the ground, he was roused with buckets of water and again beaten, until he made his 'voluntary' statement. The imprisoned, when they were called to 'make statements', that is, to be interrogated, trembled with fear. When they returned to their cells, they were frequently so battered as to be almost unrecognizable. When they could, their comrades tried to cure their wounds with water mixed with salt and vinegar. More often than not, the unfortunate prisoner never made it back to his cell.

The purpose of judiciary torture varied: to compel the accused to sign the record which many refused because of the number of lies that were included, although after a good dose of 'syrup of the lash', they ended up signing whatever was put in front of them; to get an accused to confirm that he had practiced the crime for which he was charged; to force him to give the names of friends of neighbours who might also be involved; and to get a prisoner to speak and provide some kind of information. Falangistas, local right-wingers, municipal police, Guardia Civil and all kinds of 'volunteers' participated in carrying out this judiciary torture. There was no doubt that this torture was institutionalized as an integral part of the judiciary mechanism. Seventy years later, in 2011, ex-prosecutor Carlos Jiménez Villarejo correctly described certain active members of the Supreme Court with shady pasts, then in their eighty years of age, as torturers' accomplices.

The accused were led from this world under a mountain of denunciations and false accusations, that they signed as true under the duress of the 'law of the lash'. Although in 1939 no one believed that a condemned man could ever protest the false accusations, this was occasionally possible in 1940 when we find case files for some condemned, in which they express their unhappiness at the false accusations and the beatings they received. Arcángel Bedmar describes the case of José Tarifa Galvez who sent a letter to the Cordoba Wartime Court of Appeal on July 20 1940, from the Castro del Rio jail, requesting a review of his case on the grounds that: "All this is totally false, because I was forced to say this in the Guardia Civil barracks after I was beaten with a lash."[37] It didn't do him any good because the Francoist avenging angels paid no attention to such trifling details. August 6 1945, another prisoner declared to the Baena Examining Magistrate that he "neither confirmed nor amended the declaration he had made to the Guardia Civil in Baena, on the 31st of the previous month, because although he recognizes his signature on the document he is shown, he signed this under duress. That the statement he wrote was dictated by the magistrate as his, but he was forced to sign it and four blank pages of paper as well'.[38]

Confirmation that torture was an approved and widespread practice is present in the instructions that, in the mid-1940s, the Regime sent to the prisons telling them to lay off the mistreatment, not because they were concerned with the prisoners, but because they were afraid that details of their actions would be reported outside Spain. The Director General of prisons sent a most private and confidential circular August 4 1944, stressing the need to avoid mistreatment; as that instruction was generally ignored, he sent another circular November 22, also with little effect.

In third place, there was the police torture, the kind that the National Corps of Police practiced at police headquarters in capital cities and important towns. Police torture was much more refined than other kinds in that it involved the use of electric current and all kinds of torture contraptions, that also resulted in a number of deaths. More techniques inherited from the Church's Holy Inquisition. Little by little, police torture became the dominant instrument of terror, especially when in 1942 the Minister for the Government Blas Pérez enthusiastically dedicated himself to fine-tuning the Regime's terrible police policies that were aimed less at the events since 1936 and much more at any clandestine outbreaks of political unrest.

There is something, however, that must be made clear: although police torture prevailed in the capitals, in the towns and countryside, it was the Guardia Civil, under the orders of Camilo Alonso Vega, who during the three years 1947-1949 – the Triennium of Terror - went much, much further, launching a program for the renewed application of the Law of Fugitives with such force that in all of Spain, more than one thousand persons (160 in Cordoba alone) were executed by the extra-legal paseo, without due process of law.

Lastly, a fourth kind of terror that we could call *maintenance torture*, was routinely employed by the Guardia Civil in villages where they had their rural headquarters, throughout the post-war period. This was not a very refined form of torture, mainly beatings with rods, lashes, slapping and punching, as well as some cases of hanging the prisoners by their wrists and other practices to make them talk. There were two very specific objectives to this torture. One, the persecution of escapees and the more or less severe punishments inflicted on relatives of the escaped or of guerrillas who were presumed to be in contact with their kin, and country folk in general. Sometimes, a person was beaten to death and some were hanged. The second objective was the *paso de lista,* or the posting of a list at the door of the jail in the evenings. All those whose names were on the list, described as Rojos, included the sons (even children) and relatives of guerrillas, and especially *libertos,* prisoners who had been released from jail or were out on parole. Every afternoon, some of those were chosen for a session of beatings, just to remind them who were the victors and who were the defeated.

Parallel to the 'official' mistreatment of prisoners, the phenomenon of drunken Falangistas visiting the jails at night-time to beat the inmates was widely known throughout Spain. Similar behaviour by Falangistas and young supporters of the Regime is documented in the prison of Aldeanueva de San Bartolomé.[39] We also know that in Quintanar de la Orden, Toledo,) they crushed the inmates' feet to prevent them from escaping.

As Moreno Gómez already observed when he spoke of the concentration camps, the reality of torture was a new descent into the hell of the Francoist repression. As he proceeded with his investigation of the tragedy of Francoist mass torture, he was eventually driven to the deepest levels of this hell, into the cesspits of society. In Cordoba province, many townships suffered terribly: Puente Genil, Palma del Río, Posadas, Castro del frequently refer to Río, Bujalance, Villaviciosa, Fuenteobejuna, Hinojosa, Pozoblanco and Villanueva de Cordoba. If he centred his research and comments on Villanueva de Cordoba and its outlying townships, it was because it was here that he was able to obtain the greatest number of eye-witness accounts in the town considered by Franco to be the most important nucleus of Communism in Andalusia.

Painful as it was, his investigation brought with it an extraordinary retrieval of the facts, numerous personal testimonies and the occasional finding of a notarized act of Francoist cruelty and extermination that would have otherwise remained in oblivion. He was able to come close to the truth of what had happened both during and after the end of the civil war by interviewing survivors and relatives and people who knew the victims personally, although he was unable to confirm much of what he learnt from official documents or Civil Registry records. Recording the testimonies of survivors was essential as it would have been naïve to think that the oppressive Regime would keep an official record of the torture. After all, nothing new can come to light if all that we do is simply affirm that in defeated Spain, the defeated were massively beaten by the victors.

The following monographs, that I have grouped around the villages, towns and cities of Cordoba province where these events occurred, are a sample of the personal testimonies collected these reported in greater detail, together with the Causa General case number when available, in the Appendixes. For decades, the victims who managed to survive and their families have lived in enforced silence and it is time that History is allowed to speak for them. The individual stories of these unsung heroes must be told to substantiate this proof of the Francoist reality and, by helping recreate the Historic Memory, offer some form of closure to Spain. Some accounts are paraphrased.

Those who today attempt to sweeten the pill of the past and who persist in denying the facts must be prevented from supporting the current allegation that what went on under Francoism was little more than some friendly rough and tumble between individuals of different opinions. Does anybody still doubt that the purpose of the purge was to exterminate everyone who had formed the social base for the Republic?

During the early post-war period, the preferred method for interrogating prisoners was beatings and whippings. The more aggressive, or refined, methods of the political police were not applied until later years.

Marcos Ana, the poet who was arrested in 1939, reported that in those days, the methods were very brutal, not very refined: they just beat you ferociously. Many who fell into their hands just died. But in the end, the third time round, you just lost consciousness and the torture ended. The second time around, in 1943, it was much worse.[40]

Puente Genil

In Puente Genil, where almost a thousand Republicans had already been murdered by troops from Africa under General Antonio *Castejón* Espinosa in the first days of August 1936, those who escaped that attack suffered yet another flood of repression after the fall of Málaga in February 1937. Many were captured and taken to Cordoba, to a new wave of executions. Clearly, despite the wartime genocide in Puente Genil, the Francoists were not satisfied with the results so they continued with the bloodshed in the immediate post-war period with mass arrests of all those who returned from the Republican zone (the system of vigilance in the Station was continuous). The most savage torture was applied to the returnees and there was a new slaughter of the defeated. Rafael Bedmar Guerrero, who managed to survive the mistreatment he was subjected to, provided a heart-rending description of his ordeal and the sufferings of his fellow prisoners.[41] (Appendix I)

Few went quietly when they were arrested during the victors' maelstrom of arbitrary violence. José Mora Valencia, a socialist railway worker who had been the Chairman of the local War Committee, was beaten time after time until he was finally executed April 24 1940, as was another distinguished socialist, Justo Deza Montero, who had been a Frente Popular councillor and also a member of the War Committee.

In Puente Genil we note 39-year-old local blacksmith Grancisco Palos Gálvéz' desperate resistance as he was ready to make those who came for him pay heavily for his life. November 16 1939, two municipal policemen (Jose Palos Ramírez and Juan Mendoza Calvillo) went to Francisco's house, intent on arresting him. Warned that they were coming, he was waiting for them in his living room where he disarmed them easily as they entered, then killed them with an iron bar. They were soon followed by a group of Falangistas led by Mayor Jesús Aguilar, revolver in hand, who shot the defiant Republican.

Baena

The survivors of the July 28 1936 brutal massacre in Baena at the hands of the Nationalist troops from Africa under Eduardo Sáenz de Buruaga, suffered the usual reprisals levied at the prisoners of war and in the immediate post-war period, at the defeated who returned home. These reprisals were aggravated by the Baense bourgeoisie's unabated eagerness to obtain revenge as they launched themselves like hyenas against the defeated. As occurred elsewhere, the bourgeoisie remained behind the scenes, furthering their ends by hiring civilian vigilantes, thugs who openly arrested people and beat them liberally with sticks.

There was no escaping the beatings and torture. All the prisoners were systematically beaten in the Guardia Civil barracks during their interrogations. One survivor testified as to how they beat him on his back whilst he knelt on a stick. José Padillo Marín, a member of the Zarabanda family and another survivor, was tortured as he hung from his arms until, broken, they allowed him to die in hospital. His father Agustín and his uncle Manuel were also executed.[42]

The townspeople of Baena still remember the sadism of José *El Moraíto* Rabadán, a Falangista prison guard who delighted in throwing the food that relatives brought the prisoners down the toilet. Other notorious persecutors, enflamed by the *vox populi*, were Manuel *El Conde* Rojano, Antonio *Faroles* Morales, the guard *Papafritas*, the municipal policeman Amador de los Ríos (who before the war had been arrested for murder), Pascualito *El Sacristán*, Rafael *Cordelillo* Santiago, Cristóbal *El del Bacalao*, to name but a few. The last two of these had defected from the Republican CNT and in their savagery, excelled the Falangistas with whom they sought to gain brownie points. The bourgeoisie-hired thug arrangement was not a trivial relationship: it presumed the delegation of power and an extension of complicities. This could be found all over Spain, where the upper class delegated their power to this group of henchmen, sleuths or killers for hire, fully confident that they would obtain optimal results. To this day in Andalusia, there is an oral tradition that the Señorito's foreman is always much more cruel than his boss.

Castro del Río

Francoism had a special mission in Castro del Río, a region where Cordovan trade unions and the CNT had considerable influence. The townspeople sadly remember that prisoners held in the town jail or in the Convent of the Nuns were brutally beaten when they refused to answer searching questions such as: "Who were those in the square on the day that the Guardia Civil barracks surrendered?" or "Who were those who went to the El Garabato farm?" There had been right-wing victims in 1936 in both locations where local gangs of hoodlums such as the *Gallito*, the *Blanca*, the *Potrilla* and others acted as executioners.

In his research of the events in Castro del Rio, historian Francisco Merino writes about how sometimes a prisoner's shattered body could not survive the beatings, which is how Juan Rojano died July 26 1939. Others would return to their cellmates, dragged by their tormentors, bleeding from their mouth, nose and ears. Felipe Aguilera Arroya was thrown into a latrine, where he died an inhuman death. The beatings went on for months. The unfortunate recipients, semi-conscious from the blows they had received, would utter the first names that came to mind when they were interrogated, even if the accused were innocent. In this way, every day new working men were arrested and they swelled the list of the condemned."[43]

Also according to Merino, an inmate only known as *El Moño* died because of torture and another, Miguel Márquez, was tormented with nails before he was shot by firing squad. The appalling treatment of the defeated often led to suicide or to desperate attempts to escape, sometimes successfully, sometimes not so, with tragic results. One extremely unlucky individual, Andrés *El Colorín* López, was discovered as he had everything ready for his escape from the Castro del Río jail. He was shot in the act and all the prisoners were forced to march past his body. Another, nicknamed *Sobraguisos*, escaped from the jail through the roof but he was later captured on a neighbouring farm and shot.

Bujalance

No description of the repression in this small town would be complete without mention of José Moreno Salazar, a freedom fighter who fled to the hills after the war to join the Los Jubiles guerrillas. In addition to the book of memoirs he wrote in 1985, he also wrote Moreno Gómez with details of how prisoners were treated in Bujalance.

"Prisoners were packed in the Party jail on Calle Zarcos, and behind it, where they set up the Military Headquarters where they were tried and tortured and taken to be shot at dawn by a firing squad, against the cemetery walls. Many of these executions were attended by a prostitute, so-called *La Pepilla*, whose lover had been executed in 1936 by the people's volunteer militia.

The worst tortures, however, were carried out in Calle de Las Cadenas at the Guardia Civil headquarters; the most sadistic of all the Guardias Civiles is the one whom I frequently mentioned in my book of memories, a man by the name of Requena. Civilians also tortured many prisoners, namely Falangistas such as *Praíto*, Marcelino *El Carcelor*, someone called Ríos, especially the last one who became famous as a blackleg during the years of the Republic, during strikes. Killed by beatings - I remember someone called Trigueros who left the Guardia Civil headquarters dead; and in my memories. Never forgotten, Francisco Milla's mother and sister who were beaten to death by Requena and who died in my arms, when I was imprisoned in the Hospital."[44]

Fuenteobejuna

In Furenteobejuna, Claro González returned home April 18 19939 and the next day was already imprisoned in the City Hall building's improvised jail. The beatings were terrible and they had no other medicine than salt and vinegar to heal their wounds. They lived between beatings and hunger. Felisario Cidoncha, another inmate who was cruelly tortured, was shot by a firing squad August 4 1939.[45]

Villanueva de Cordoba (also Valle de Pedroche, Adamuz and other outlying townships).

Enforcing Francoist law in Villanueva de Cordoba were: corporal José Martínez Galiániz (head of the local Guardia Civil post), Lieutenant Leopolodo Mena (SIPM Lieutenant), Captain Ignacio Pizarro (local military commander), and the infamous Judge Juan Calero Rubio. Added to this cluster of Francoist judicial and para-legal officials, was a clutch of henchmen and followers eager to thrash the imprisoned defeated: low-class rabble with guns tucked in their waistbands, hired thugs and staunch supporters of the landowners who hired them. Relatives of right-wing victims of 1936, such as Pepe Delgado, Pedro Serrano and Vicente *Salado* Muñoz also participated in the torture, seeking revenge. Although the tormenters included several landowners who were also known as staunch Francoists, some such as Matías *Malaleche* Pedraza had no relationship whatsoever with any right-winger who had suffered in 1936, quite the contrary. The latter's father, Dionisio Pedraza was in fact protected by the loyal militia because of his excellent relationship with working men during the Republic.

A selection of the eye witness accounts from survivors of this climate of violence and torture, especially in the outlying towns, is included in Appendix II, Volume 3 of this book. They describe the two tpes of mistreatment already discussed: vindictive beatings and sadism by Falangistas, and the judiciary beatings, during the pre-trial hearing interrogations, especially meted out to those who had been freed from a concentration camp then re-arrested as soon as they returned to their hometowns.

Moreno Gómez has certain knowledge of at least five prisoners who died from torture between 1939 and 1940 in Villanueva de Cordoba. Three, in particular, died from torture in 1940, whilst the Spanish Legion African troops were garrisoned in the town and the surrounding countryside. The first of the three victims, Juan Fernández Moreno, aged 54 years, was beaten savagely for no apparent reason at Legion Military Headquarters and left to die on a bit of waste ground August 24 1940. Likewise, two days later, Juan *Horozco* Cantador Cachinero. October 16 next, the Legionnaires killed José Huertas Valverde by forcing water down his throat through a tube, until his throat was ripped by the aggression.

The number of individuals responsible for the brutalities committed in Villanueva de Cordoba is never-ending. Already mentioned is Matías Pedraza, the landowner, who led the night-time visits by drunken Falangistas to the local jail, where he amused himself by stepping on the inmates, lashing at them with his riding whip or with willow canes, and according to a witness, throwing their lunchboxes with food that they contained at their heads, always with bursts of laughter, insults and threats. When those who were most persecuted - Francisco *Beatas*, Eugénio *Palmera*, Lopez *El Dinamatero* Ibañez, one *Cucharas*, and others became unconscious, they were taken out to the patio where they were left on the floor to recover, until the next night.

An unforgettable event in Villanueva that was often mentioned by eye-witnesses, was the night when the Falangistas entered Fuente Vieja jail for some entertainment and, to please the Señoritos, prison guard El Tiraor ripped Francisco Illescas' ear off. This unfortunately inmate had served in 1936 as a guard over right-wingers who had been arrested, among them El

Tiraor, who was now getting his revenge. Several surviving fellow inmates remember that night as one of the most dramatic in the jail.[46]

Far too often, the desire to arrest and punish the great number of Republicans meant that many individuals were arrested for either unknown or totally futile reasons. Pedro Molinero, ex-activist of the Unión Republicana, a thoughtful and careful individual, whom Montero Gómez interviewed several times at the beginning of the 1980s, was arrested in 1939 for unknown causes. On other occasions, allegations of childhood disagreements as in Antonio Pedraza Garcia's case, or simply having stood as a prison guard during the Republic, were sufficient cause for imprisonment.

Blas Arévalo Carbonero, brother-in-law of Nemesio *El Floro* Pozuelo, the Communist leader was denounced by *El Tiraor* and by Roque *Castilla*, because the latter's son had been arrested by the Civil Government, apparently when Blas was standing guard over right-wing prisoners. Apparently, the young man was handed over to a guerrilla group and he was killed near Cardeña. In 1939, the victors tried every means to determine exactly what had happened, without success. Blas knew nothing about it, so could confess to nothing despite brutal torture. According to his family, "he was beaten so badly he didn't even let his own children hug him". This poor man, who had no notable political role, was executed without any specific charge and without any proof of his having committed a so-called blood crime. This was not unusual, because as Moreno Gómez said earlier, of the 106,000 imprisoned in 1937, only 2.13% had actually committed any kind of civil crime.

It is presumed that matters were similar in 1939. Cecilio Ruiz, a socialist, was aged 55 when he was arrested by Diego El Chunga, accused by the Falangista Lara, and executed. He was not a leading politician, but he had also stood guard over right-wing prisoners in 1936.

Not infrequently, many years after the events, when relatives of executed disaffected heard of Moreno Gómez' research, they made special trips to speak to him, sometimes just in an attempt to ensure that what happened to their father, brother or uncle should not go unrecorded nor their memory unforgotten. Often, these surviving relatives were the sons and daughters of a deceased who, as children, suffered untold horrors they could not fully comprehend at the time. This was the case of José Torralbo Rico, Antonia Sánchez Cerezo and Cataina Cantador Romero, whose stories are reproduced in the aforementioned Appendix II.

As they proceeded to cast their net as far and wide as possible and sow terror in the towns and villages, Falangistas cooked up a variety of schemes to serve as a pretext for raids among people of little or no political significance. In summer 1939, there appeared some posters in Villanueva proclaiming

"Viva! Negrín[47] is returning to Spain," a fanciful creation of the Commander of the municipal police, Bartolomé Berenguer. This 'joke' in bad taste cost José Luna Mata no less than 30 years in jail and numerous beatings:

> "They took me to the barracks and began the interrogation. First, they took my jacket off. They sat me on a stool and several Falangistas stood behind me. Before they asked me anything, the beatings rained down on me. "This is the welcome," they said. That is what it was. They then interrogated me regarding the posters, and I denied having painted them or even seeing one, which was true. The beatings returned and continued for a couple of hours. Several times I fell to the floor from the blows, where they kicked and stomped on me. When they saw that they could get nothing from me, they hung me from my wrists and continued whipping me until I lost consciousness. When I regained consciousness, I was soaking wet from the bucket of water they threw on me.
>
> The interrogation ended and they took me to Fuente Vieja prison. There were more than 500 men there. The women's jail was also packed full. My comrades came to tend to my injuries and they said: "You were lucky. When we removed your shirt, your skin did not stick to it. They didn't beat you all that much." They massaged me with vinegar, which is all that they had. We repeated this operation every day for the comrades who came from the barracks, from headquarters or after suffering the night-time attacks of the Falangistas. I can prove that the bodies of many comrades were live flesh, after their skin had peeled off after sticking to their shirts."[48]

Everyone Moreno Gómez interviewed in Villanova remembered that the week of October 12 to 19 1939 was particularly horrific in terms of the victors' increased brutality, especially when Juan Calero was the Examining Magistrate at Military Court 11. The ex-prisoners called this the 'tragic week' because almost all of them were re-interrogated at La Preturilla and at Military headquarters. Sebastián Gómez' testimony[49] is significant in that it confirms that military judges took part in the beatings.

Judge Calero, taking it upon himself to act as both judge and jury, often wielded the lash. In doing so, he ushered in a post-war administrative reign of terror under a totally militarized justice that was wholly dependent on and subject to Franco's totalitarian regime. Antonio Rubio Cobos, for example, was tortured until they broke an arm and several ribs because he refused to sign the statement written by Judge Calero. He was executed March 1940. His young son Manuel Rubio was taken in by Francoist 'benefactors' and pressed to commit to a life in the Church at the Salesian Seminary. Instead, he abandoned his studies when he was well advanced in his training and became a celebrated teaher at the Villanueva Public School where he was Moreno Gómez' first teacher.

A similar story of a Francoist military judge participating in the torture and immersing himself in a whirlwind of hateful actions, was recounted by Francisco Poyatos, an eminent Cordovan attorney who witnessed a court martial in Cordoba against 19 prisoners, as part of Examining Magistrate Gregorio Prados' Court. He was the only trained career attorney present there because the others were all active military officers. The pre-trial hearing was interrupted for a break, after which the magistrate turned to one of the accused, from Belalcázar, and scolding him shouting: "So you are what's-his-name!", physically launched himself against the accused, slapping him in the face.[50]

Prisoners from Pedroche were also taken to Villanueva de Cordoba jail and it was there that Falangistas from their town would go to beat them up. Francisco Romero Cachinero told me of a man from Pedroche (or Torrecampo), whose name he could not recall and who was beaten to death in Villanueva jail.[51] Miguel Regalón later identified him as a fellow from Pedroche, whose surname was Regalón, like his, who was caught with a razor. They beat him so savagely that he died the next day.[52]

Falangistas from Torrecampo were accustomed to travelling to Villanueva to torture fellow townsmen who were imprisoned there, although it is true that the Villanueva tormenters, quite content to torture everybody they could lay their hands on, did not require any help from outside. For example, they savagely beat people from Torrecampo such as Sebastián Luque and his son, as well as Ricardo Ranchal, whose nails they pulled out, among other ordeals. One of Manuel Luque's worst tormentors was a right-winger called *El Colodro*. All these unfortunate men from Torrecampo ended their lives in front of a firing squad.

As an example of those who managed to survive the appalling abuse, Moreno Gómez earlier told of José García *El Perica* Coleto, who managed to escape from a line of prisoners 1939 and fled to the hills swearing that one day he would kill his tormentor, Fructuoso *El de los Dientes* Reyes. The oppressors in Villanueva were so enraged when they heard of this, that in revenge they carried out a major raid in the town to punish as many individuals as they could, taking their prisoners to the Guardia Civil barracks where they beat them mercilessly. According to statements from his family, one of these, Acisclo Cruz Villarreal, was beaten unconscious then dumped outside on the street, at the door to the barracks, from where his family picked him up.

Cordoba

The events in Cordoba capital prison were no less heinous, as we hear from Rafael González Roldán regarding his uncle Manuel González de la Fuente. As Franco had proclaimed that 'anyone whose hands were not stained with blood could return in peace', his uncle returned to Spain where he as arrested and imprisoned. Not only was he frequently beaten in the jail, they also took him from the jail to the Guardia Civil barracks, hung him from his ankles, and left him unconscious. Rafael, who was also imprisoned in the same jail, remained by his side all that last night, wrapping him in a shroud and praying for him, until the next day they took his uncle out and buried him, ignoring his relatives who were waiting to receive his body at another door.

Moreno Gómez was unable to find any official or Civil Registry records for the above person nor regarding Juan Sánchez Cabrera from Villa del Rio who, according to José Merino Campo's testimony, died from being beaten with rods in the Cordoba Provincial Court. As the whereabouts of their remains are still unknown, they are considered as 'disappeared'.

Pozoblanco

The following cases that have all the appearance of death from torture, although the usual euphemisms for the cause of death were entered in the records. Nonetheless, Montero Gómez' experience over the years regarding the customary treatment of prisoners, the lack of specialized medical care for their wounds, as well as numerous individual testimonies, indicates that such cases may not always escape the 'clinical eye' of the historian.

- In Peñarroya-Pueblonuevo, Dionisia Alcántara Calvo, 'due to a collapse', according to a report from the Judge Advocate, December 16 1939.
- In Pozoblalnco, Gervasio Martinez Hidalgo, from 'epileptic attacks', according to a report from the Military Police, September 3 1939.
- In Pozoblanco, Juan Álvarez Pozo, from Hinojosa, from 'cardiac asystole', according to a report from the Military Court, October 14 1939.
- In Pozoblanco, David Cuello Amadeo, from Alcaracejos, from 'acute endocarditis', according to a report from the Military Court, December 17 1939.

- In Pozoblanco, Rufino Fernández *El Poleo* Alcaide, 'died attempting to escape from the guards who were leading him', although actually he died from torture April 25 1939, as confirmed by witness statements.
- In Bujalance, Pedro Alcaraz Mira, from 'cardiac arrest' May 22 1940, according to the Civil Registry.

During the first days of the terror, a leader of the reprisals in Pozoblanco, Corporal Rejas, commander of the Military Police headquarters in Costanilla del Risquillo, was noted for his cruelty. Interrogations and the consequent beatings took place in the so-called Palace and at Las Monjas school. Captain Bautista Herruzo de la Cruz of the Pedroches Battalion was one who suffered the most. After each session, several men had to carry him out, dripping with blood and unconscious. The Falangistas had decided that he had informed against the right-wingers from Pozoblanco who were imprisoned in Valencia, many of whom who were shot in September 1936. Rafael, son of the intellectual Antonio Porras, was also sorely beaten in Pozoblanco prison after he was brought under arrest from Madrid. Although he was tried in Pozoblanco and found not guilty of the charges against him, his enemies denounced him again and again until he was finally returned to Madrid where he was executed May 19 1943. Pedro Villarreal's sister testified that he was carried from the sessions 'bloodied like Christ'. The same punishment was meted to Francisco *El Endeble* Díaz Pastor, according to statements from his widow. Although Moreno Gómez was reliably informed that Severo Garcia Gonzalvo was brutally tortured until he died, the records state that he was executed November 29 1939.

Dos Torres

Ordinary citizens who were caught committing small thefts in the countryside (mainly acorns and olives) and were continuously vigorously persecuted by the agrarian bourgeoisie and the Guardia Civil at their orders, were often object of beatings, an endemic evil in the rural world. During the post-war, the number of such thefts went through the roof because of the dreadful widespread poverty. The victims of these severe punishments were most often women (also some young men) whose husbands were imprisoned and who had nothing to eat in their homes. The masters of the public order not only punished these women with the lash, but they also stripped them naked, shaved their heads, forced them to drink castor oil and put them to work sweeping streets, to cleaning military headquarters and private Falangista homes. In Dos Torres, women were frequently subjected to a usual form of fascist entertainment: stripped naked, they were marched down the streets and forced to sing *Cara al Sol*, until they reached the Dos Torres Casino, where Señoritos laughed at the show.

In Dos Torres, the Panzurrine brothers, both communists, together with Pedro *El de la Filomena* and *El Trapero*, were tied to a window of their mother's house so that she could be sure to hear everything, and there they were savagely beaten. Afterwards, a 2nd Lieutenant in Dos Torres, ordered their execution on the pretext that they were in cahoots with others who had escaped to the hills. This was in July 1941.

Belmez

Vicente Blanco, a leading communist, was one of the brutally mistreated in Belmez. A curious fact was that during the sessions of torture it was not only the usual local tormenters who participated in the beatings but also several right-wing women who hammered him with nails and other stabbing objects. He was later executed in Cordoba.

Almodóvar del Río

Antonio Ramos Palomares', an anarchist leader from Almodóvar del Río, the story of what happened to him after he was released from the army, when he returned to his hometown after the Republican defeat, is reproduced in Appendix II.[53]

Montilla

Arcángel Bedmar, historian of the Cordoba Campiña region, refers to cases of torture in Montilla as a widespread phenomenon common to all Francoist prisons[54]. Francisco Cordoba Gálvez was beaten, hanging from his arms, until he lost consciousness. Emilio Montoro Delgado was tortured by a Guardia Civil corporal in the Military Court building. Rafael García Espejo was continuously beaten and during one session they tore off his moustache. Manuel Ruz Aguilar was tied to a fig tree and beaten non-stop. Antonio Pérez Lao arrived in prison with a broken leg and despite that, they still beat him. He died, from the punishment, shortly after he was released in 1943. His father had been executed six years earlier. The same author reports the oral testimony of Francisco Carmona Priego, from Montilla, when in the Worker Soldiers Disciplinary Battallion of Cerro Muriano, Cordoba, he witnessed a sergeant breaking an inmate's back by beating him with a pickaxe handle. That pickaxe handles were often used for beatings was not unusual, especially when prisoners were working in the countryside outside the camps, as Antonio D. López stated regarding a case in Castuera when the guards "broke the handles of the pickaxes as they smashed a prisoner's ribs".[55]

Elsewhere in Spain

The above examples are from Cordoba province, but what of the events in the light of the general panorama of Francoist torture in all of Spain? To Moreno Gómez' knowledge, such a monographic compendium has not yet been published in Spain. It is of course essential that one obtains the testimony of the victims themselves and not base one's account solely on Francoist written documentation as it would be naïve to think that the oppressive Regime would keep an official record of its actions. Nothing new can come to light if all that we do is simply affirm that in all defeated Spain, the defeated were massively beaten by the victors. Here are a few such accounts for the region outside Cordoba province.

Navalvillar de Pela, Badajoz

In Extremadura, as in Cordoba province, many defeated who were freed from Castuera concentration camp were re-arrested as soon as they returned to their hometowns. This happened to Valentín Jiménez Gallardo and to several residents of Navalvillar de Pela, Badajoz. They were re-arrested, beaten and imprisoned in Puebla de Alcocer jail from where they managed to escape and flee to the hills.

Santiago de Compostela

Casimiro Jambonero's memoires of his experience in Santiago de Compostela prison, in his book *Diary of a Republican Soldier*, are similar accounts of the mistreatment of prisoners elsewhere. After dinner, some guards from Labacolla came to remove one of the inmates who had been arrested with him and he and his fellow inmates did not know why or where they were taking himhim. At the end of the day, he returned from Labacolla and they saw that everything they had imagined did occur: his face was totally misshapen from the blows he had received, his head was swollen and he had been badly beaten all over his body."[56]

Puerto de Santa Maria, Cádiz

Cordovan Rafael Sánchez Guerra, imprisoned in Puerto de Santa Maria (Cádiz), met a fellow prisoner in the infirmary who had served as a Guarda de Asalto in Valladolid. When he commented on his fellow inmate's pitiful physical condition, the latter replied:

> "You see me like this now, because when these bastards' movement broke out, I was arrested by the Falange and taken to one of their unofficial jails where they broke my back

with their beatings. I lay between life and death for several days and I have had the incredible bad luck of surviving. My brother, poor soul, was more fortunate because when they were beating his back with sticks, they smashed the bottom of his skull and he died instantly."[57]

Málaga

In his book *Diálogo con la muerte*,[58] Arthur Koestler, Hungarian-born British journalist and war correspondent, wrote several monographs illustrating the Francoist treatment of prisoners that he witnessed when he was arrested in Málaga February 8 1937, the day that the city fell to the Nationalists. During the week that Koestler was imprisoned in Málaga, before he was transferred to another prison in Seville mid-February 1937, he again had a chance to be dumbfounded by Francoist brutality.

Moreno Gómez mentioned several cases when prisoners went crazy and totally lost their minds because of their sufferings and he will mention a few more later on. For the moment, however, a personal experience of his father's in Villanueva de Cordoba around 1940 and that he, Alfonso Moreno Zamora, told him by chance in 1995. One day, the Guardia Civil ordered my father and Miguel Gutiérez Marín, both of whom were not much more than 20 years old at the time, to take some cattle from the Los Pobos fields to the Guardia Civil barracks in Montes de Adamuz. Halfway there, for no apparent reason, Miguel began to sob and he cried non-stop for several hours but there was nothing that his father could do to console him. The Guardia Civil's order had been a last straw and it was only much later that his father discovered what was behind it all.

In those days, the young Miguel Gutiérrez was a close friend of Juan *Hebrero* Caballero Coleto, who escaped to the hills at the end of the war. They had agreed that Miguel would take him food to a hidden spot and the guerrillas would collect it come night-time. Unfortunately, the Guardia Civil got wind of this. They called Miguel to the barracks and beat him within an inch of his life. The young man went mad and never recovered. Never, during all those years, never anybody, not even Moreno Gómez' family, had ever told him why it was that Miguel Gutiérrez had lost his mind, even though they lived next door.

Undoubtedly, the legal framework can be studied at any time. Not so the recovery of the facts and the memories of the victims and their relatives. Far too much time has passed. This is what academia and historians should have done during the years of transition, instead of dedicating themselves to developing the art of 'disremembering'. Ángela Cenarro, Professor of

Contemporary History at the University of Zaragoza, has commented on how historians should proceed with their research into the legal framework. She stresses that if they limit themselves to enumerating the subhuman onditions to which thousands of anti-Francoist prisoners were subjected during those days, they run th risk of getting lost among so much misery and desolation, without adding anything to the knowledge of the legal and institutional framwork.[59]

Moreno Gómez did descend into the misery of prisoner torture but he did not get lost. On the contrary, as he expanded his field work, as he sank even deeper into the abyss of pain and suffering, he became increasingly aware of the importance of the researcher's duty to study the legal and institutional framework in order to discern the true historical facts. More so in the case of the Francoist legislation of the 1940, where the demagogic rule of redemption, its altruistic decrees and regulations, hypocritical social welfare programs, represented nothing more than worthless pieces of paper for a propaganda that had nothing to do with the reality; worse still, that concealed it. What Ángela Cenarro said is all very true, but at the end of the day, she concluded that Francoism said one thing openly, to the public gallery, whilst it acted in a totally different manner when it came to the punishment and extermination of the defeated.

Moreno Gómez cannot protest too much at the sovereign stupidity of a recent newspaper article by the much admired and highly commended Antonio Muñoz Molina, to the effect that the people of Spain have always happily spoken openly about the things that happened during the war and that the idea that there was some kind of enforced silence about the events was a total myth created by foreigners. Molina's declaration that all that was said about there being 'two Spains' was absolute garbage and that the significant factor of the war was not the actions of the people who acted in all consciousness, aware of what was at stake. Instead, the activities of the thoughtless, irresponsible and amorphous people, that stupid thing called 'third Spain', those who were forced to go and fight and who did not give a damn for whatever it was that they were supposed to be fighting for.[60]

So much for Muñoz Molina's inspired analysis of the platitude that *nobody likes to go to war*. One's mind boggles…

Today, we are again far too often faced with the twisted tendency of certain intellectuals from the 'progressive' intellectuals who believe that they are possessed of the gift of happily rising above all extremes, disseminators of equidistance and authors of false revisions of the facts. Those whose work is coated with the varnish of a post-modern, banal and superficial - to the point of nausea - aestheticism and whose view of the History of the civil war and its aftermath apparently lies halfway along the road between Gila's War[61] and Berlanga's La Vaquilla.[62]

Military Tribunals and Courts Martial

"The 40,000 executed by the firing squads during the Commune guaranteed sixty years of social peace."

José Calvo Sotelo, leader of the *Renovació Española* and the *Bloque Nacional*, speaking in Parliament, referring to the example of the Paris repression in 1871).[63]

Linguistically, in English – as opposed to Spanish - and *de facto*, it is difficult to distinguish between the expressions 'Military Tribunal' and 'Court Martial'[xii], particularly when it comes to the composition and proceedings of both under the farcical Francoist rule of law and the organized repression that ruled the country. Before the Regime passed the Decree on Banditry and Terrorism (September 21 1960) and Law 15/63 creating the Court of Public Order (TOP), all offenders were considered bound by the Francoist military rule of law, regardless of the nature of the offense of which they were accused.

If one can be permitted a linguist *nuance,* one might say that the so-called Military Tribunals were regarded as Higher Courts, whose Judges administered, not usual military justice with due process, but a repressive and vengeful, considerably more vicious and speedy justice, ruling as if from 'on high' as both judge and jury, on the basis of summarized reports of interrogations by Examining Magistrates who also, in countless courts martial, handed down sentences. In actual fact, it was these courts martial, often presided by the very same judges and with the same composition but technically on the next rung down the administrative ladder, that provided the public face of Francoist justice. Magistrates dedicated to speedily prosecuting and sentencing groups of prisoners, rather than individuals, non-stop and on the basis of summary proceedings and interrogations, in a desperate attempt to keep pace with the astronomical number of accused whose trials overwhelmed the entire court system.

[xii] In Spanish>English<Spanish, Military Tribunal is the reciprocal translation of Court Martial and vice-versa.

1.   Itinerant and Standing Military Tribunals

To the multitude of military tribunals created especially for the great purge and cleansing of Republicans during the post-war period as part of the Regime's programmed extermination (35 courts in Cordoba province: 20 in the capital and 15 in townships; Málaga 67; Alicante 22; Cartagena 57, etc.), we must add the mass creation of other military courts of law. It would appear that the principal occupation of the victorious military in 1939 and following years, was the appalling mission of handing down death sentences (the only accepted sentence) right, left and centre, thus sending thousands of men and quite a few women to the wall, and serving the Dictator in the foulest manner possible, the annihilation of their own countrymen.

That is how victory was administered, with a great campaign involving the extermination, punishment, harassment and exclusion of the half Spain that had been defeated, a campaign that exhibited a typical Fascist characteristic of invoking of the ghost of the revolution, Fascism's *raison d'être*. Not only was the Regime's program typical Fascist purging of possible revolutionaries, it also was the repression of an entire class of activists for workers' rights, of trade unions and left-wing political parties, all of whom suffered the most brutal punishment in all their history. This was the genocide of an entire sector of the population for social and political reasons. A genocide that was triggered by the military coup in 1936 and that spread throughout the country in 1939 with the end of the civil war.

The sequence of events was as follows. Once there was a sufficient number of indictments or pre-trial hearings in the standing military magistrate courts, a date was set for prosecuting the accused, usually collectively. Itinerant military courts of law were created and they were sent to large towns in the province of Cordoba, to examine and rule on the summarized files of those who were scheduled to be tried by the notably farcical courts martial. The courts that went to the towns often travelled from one to another, whilst those in the capital were more permanent in nature and they usually limited themselves to receiving the lines of prisoners pre-destined for 'the only sentence'. The itinerant courts worked intermittently, that is, whenever they had enough cases to rule on. Two or three times a month they went from town to town, beginning with those where the most number of cases were waiting to be prosecuted: Castro del Río, Bujalance, Puente Genil, Baena, Peñarroya, Hinojosa, Pozoblanco, Villanueva de Cordoba, etc. The cost of accommodating and feeding the courts was paid for out of the municipal budgets (hotels, meals, telephone calls, and so forth, for which there are numerous invoices in the Minutes of the sessions books.)

A Military Tribunal was composed of a Presiding Judge (the highest-ranking officer), three (sometimes, two) Members, a Rapporteur, a Prosecutor and a Public Defender (the lowest-ranking officer). Seven in all, all serving military, except when there was an exception and the role of Presiding Judge was given to some local magistrate in recompense for his 'undisputed supporter' of the Movement. Evidently, there was 'military justice' and 'justice' that depended on the victor's extermination program.

On the date of this writing, there still are some Francoist magistrates wearing judges' togas who were promoted to high judicial positions, especially during the days of the TOP (Court of Public Order). However, as the transition period proved to be the cover-up that was expected, none of these magistrate was, or has been, asked to explain his muddy past.

Moreno Gómez obtained details of the composition and activities of quite a few Military Tribunals in Cordoba province by consulting several summary reports of cases in the press, even though the press very rarely reported details as the Cordoba *Azul* did the composition of the court that sat in Baena on May 20 1939: [64]

20 May 1939	Baena
PRESIDING JUDGE	
Coronel Evaristo Peñalver, Guardia Civil	
Members	Captain Enrique Vilches
	Captain Rafael Mariscal
	Captain Baltasar García Valdecasas
Rapporteur	Bernabé Andrés Perez Jiménez
Prosecutor	José Ramón de la Lastra y de Hoces
Public Defender	Lt. Fernando Moreno González Anleo
Also present: the Judge Advocate for the Army of the South	Lt. Coronel Ignacio Cuervo

Sometimes, as in this case, the Judge Advocate for the Army of the South, Lt. Colonel Ignacio Cuervo, was also present.. The scenario was typical of every trial in Baena. Manifestations of solemnity, before and afterwards, always in response to the official desire to conceal the details of the great Francoist massacre of July 28 1936. On that occasion, several hundred unarmed men lying on the ground in the town square, were individually executed with a single shot to the head, one by one, by Lieutenant Pascual Sánchez Ramírez of the Sáenz de Buruaga Guardia Civil. One of many crimes of genocide that should have been tried before a Spanish Nuremburg. As they escaped the massacre in the town, a group of any anarchists killed 81 right-wing prisoners held in the Asilo de San Francisco.

The *Azul* described the frenetic activity of the above Tribunal as "having acted with extraordinary diligence in administering Justice and after recently judging crimes committed in Bujalance, Castro del Rio and Posadas, the Court returned to Cordoba Saturday 20th in the early evening."[65]

Waving metaphorical banners recalling the events in the Asilo, the great landowners of Baena and their entourage still today continue to express their desire to suppress all mention of the Francoist massacre. In Baena, everyone is involved in the cover up and if mention of that fateful date comes up, they quickly change the subject to what happened in the Asilo. Not a word regarding the Francoist massacre in the square. This attitude has become so pervasive that when a few years ago, a German film team went to Baena to make a movie of the Francoist massacre (for whom Moreno Gómez was engaged as a specialist advisor/consultant) the local powers that be, so-called 'democratic' authorities included, made their work so difficult, their lives so very impossible, that the Germans abandoned their project and left. To this day, there still is no other kind of law in Baena than the law of the great landowners and olive-oil producers.[xiii]

The Baena Tribunal, presided by Evaristo Peñalver and embellished by the spectacular oratory of Prosecutor José Ramón de la Lastra (a latter-day version of *Fray Gerundio de Campazas*[xiv]) sat in September 1939 in Puente Genil, where the eminent Antonio Romero, ex-Republican Mayor, was condemned to death by garrotte. Another frequent member of this court was the tireless Torquemada from Rute, the aforementioned Bernabé Andrés Pérez Jiménez. Captain of the Judge Advocate General's Corps, his 'blood' achievements were so appreciated that he was promoted to the position of Supreme Court Judge. He also intervened in numerous courts martial in Baena, Puente Genil, Cordoba and elsewhere.

The Tribunals were put to work very early on in post-war Pozoblanco, beginning May 28 1939. Lieutenant Colonel Rafael Carbonell Morand,

---

xiii When Moreno Gómez' book *La guerra civil in Cordoba* was published in 1985, in which he related the Francoist horrors that were committed in Baena, this implacable bourgeoisie set out to find an author to write a counter-book. They still have been unable to find one. Arcángel Bedmar, in 2008, put a full stop to the subject with a new book along the same lines as Moreno Gómez', *Baena, roja y negra* [Baena, red and black], op. cit.. The Socialist Mayor timidly attended the launching of Bedmar's book; the local neonazis boycotted it. Democrary is still not widespread in Spain.

xiv Fictional hero of a mid-18th century novel by José Francisco de la Isla y Rojo (*Historia del famoso predicador fray Gerundio de Campazas, alias Zotes*) depicting a typical preacher who used high-faluting, often offensive, illogical and ludicrous language when addressing his congregation.

Lieutenant Colonel Rafael Mora Sánchez and Commander Ramón Navarro de Cáceres were the first presiding judges. Juge Mora also presided over Tribunals in Villanueva de Cordoba, with some variations in the composition of the Court. It is curious that a same military officer acted as a Public Dexcerpt for the efender in some Tribunals and as a Prosecutor in others. At the same time, those who acted as Public Defenders were usually the lowest ranking officers.

Except for the Presiding Judge, the rest of the members appeared mostly interchangeable from one court to another. The rulings or sentences decreed by the Tribunals were of the maximum severity, almost always condemning the accused to the 'ultimate' or 'only' penalty. A lower sentence of Life Without Parole or thirty years, was considered a special favour.

In November 1939, Commander Francisco Ferrán held Court in the mountains of Cordoba 1936, where he presided over the Tribunal in Pozoblanco. In 1940, the most active Tribunal in th Sierra mountain region (the Campiña was subject to less 'avenging justice' pressure because much of the population had already been massacred in 1936), was presided by Coronel Luengo Benítez, one of the leading Cordovan Fascists, founder in the capital of the Nationalist Battalion of Cordoba Volunteers, in 1936, and whose fighters later entered many towns in the valley of the Guadalquivir, spitting blood and spitting fire in the days of the wartime genocide.

This Court arrived in Villanueva de Cordoba 1 April 1940, intending to hit hard on the famous communist stronghold of Villanueva, the so-called Red Town, where it proved to be especially vindictive and ruthless against eminent communist leaders. Severe sentences were handed down from April 23 to 27 and from April 30 to May 4. May 1, Militia Captain Pedro Torralbo Gómez, past communist city councillor and Provincial Deputy was sentenced to death. A little more than a year lataer, in June, he and several others died in a mass execution in Cordoba cemetery. In June, Judge Luengo Benítez continued his repressive judicial activities in Pozoblanco and again in Villanueva. March 14 1940, Judge Ricardo Rivas Vilaro presided over the Villenueva de Cordoba Tribunal.

Lastly of the many Tribunals that sat in Cordoba capital, the February 5 1941 one was presided by the recently promoted Judge Aguilar Galindo, known for being a notable handliner hawk during the bloody hours of July 1936. He was also responsible for the genocide in Fernán Núñez, where row upon row of dead Republicans lined the gutters on the road to Cordoba.

5 February 1941	Cordoba
PRESIDING JUDGE	
Coronel Manuel Aguilar Galindo	
Members	Lt Diego González Rodríguez
	Lt. Francisco González Cáceres
	Lt. Filiberto Agregano Gasco
Prosecutor	Captain Luís Mendieta
Public Defender	Lt. Ignacio Alfaro Guzmán
Examining Magistrate	Lt. Antonio Corredor de la Cruz

As described earlier, the composition of the Tribunals was almost exclusively military and they were always presided over by a high-ranking officer, with only the very occasional presence of civilian magistrates. Court officials could be attached to one or another court, or change about, as they went about their repressive pilgrimage over the entire Sierra in 1939 and 1940, after which the headquarters for the purging were centred in Cordoba capital where all those who were arrested in September and October 1940 were taken.

2. Courts martial

The courts martial were the staged public face of Francoist justice. The first Francoist courts martial all over Spain began in May 1939. Every historian has qualified these staged events as 'judicial farces' hostile to those who were loyal to the constitutional Government. If the summary prosecutions already represented a multitude of fundamental defects and judicial abnormalities, including the application of mass torture, the courts martial added to the number of legal irregularities. Nonetheless, despite the present Democratic Government's repeal of the Francoist judicial legislation, it has been unable, nor has it dared or had the mettle, to rescind the courts martial sentences and these are still considered valid under law, after thirty years of democratic rule.

An almost daily post-war spectacle were the chains of prisoners tied to each other two by two, as they were led each morning from the jails to the place where the courts martial were held. In Cordoba capital, trials or courts martial were held in the Military Tribunal Hearings Building, Avenida del Gran Capitán number 4.[xv] In Madrid, the accused were taken in automobiles to Las Salesas. In other towns, they usually went on foot. In

---

[xv] Later, *Delegación de Hacienda,* or Tax Agency Delegation.

Cordoba province, the most picturesque places were chosen for these staged events. In Baena, it was the Theatre on Calle Alta, the venue for ostentatious legal farces, worthy of Valle-Inclán's pieces of theatrical nonsense such as *Los cuernos de don Friolera*[xvi]. It was here, to this theatre, that the non-violent and Messianic anarchist leader *El Transío*, was brought and exhibited as an *Ecce Homo* before a packed audience, to hear that he had been given three death sentences, to the raucous delight of the Baenense bourgeoisie present.

In Castro del Rio, courts martial were held in the Jesús Nazareno Hospital, except for the first one which was accompanied by special propagandist pomp at the Teatro Cervantes. In Pozoblanco, as in Montilla, Puente Genil, Peñarroya-Pueblonuevo and elsewhere, the venue for the farce was the City Council General Assembly Hall. In Hinojosa del Duque, trials were held in the main meeting room of the El Gato Casino, a bar on the main square. In Villanueva de Cordoba, chains of prisoners were marched along a considerably tortuous route through the city, from Fuente Vieja prison to the Torres events hall on Calle Concejo. All along this route, obviously extremely humiliating for the accused who were displayed as an example to the population, relatives would come out at the crossroads (mothers, wives with their children, etc.), in an attempt to catch a glimpse of their loved ones, for the very last time for far too many, all of which added to the prisoners' suffering.

The proceedings were open to the public. Whenever the accused had some standing as a public figure, the venue would be packed with a typical public: Falangistas, Señoritos, ladies from the bourgeoisie and especially, relatives of right-wingers who had died earlier, dressed in full mourning and demanding justice. Also present were the denouncers who reported the crime and the witnesses to the accusations. Witnesses for the defence, who very few called, did not dare to appear in the midst of such an extremely hostile environment. Occasionally, relatives of the accused would creep in timidly and stand at the back of the hall where they would shed silent tears at the fate that was about to be meted to their kin. In 1980 Moreno Gómez was able to obtain some valuable eyewitness testimony as to the nonsensical opulence of those trials and how, on the rare occasion when the crimes for which a person was accused were proven to be false, this was usually ignored and the prisoner would still be executed. Such was the case (and there were thousands of similar cases) of Juan Cantador Zamora, from Villanueva de Cordoba, whose daughter Catalina Cantador Romero attended his trial:

> "On 24 May 1940, [my father] was tried by the military court in this town and sentenced to death.

[xvi] "The cuckholding of Don Friolera". Today, the theatre is a venue for wedding receptions.

At the court martial, the prosecutor asked Luisa Doctor, the accuser, to point out which of the accused men sitting on the bench had killed her husband. The good lady said she did not recognize any of them and that she had heard nothing said about him. The Judge then asked the accuser if she had ever spoken to the accused, to which she answered that she might have spoken to him as she might have spoken to anyone.

Judge: Then, why did you say that he had killed your husband?
Accuser: No sir. Judge Juan Calero must not have heard me correctly. What I said was that it was someone from outside, one of Juan Elías' agents."[66]

The accusation was clearly disproved at the trial, but as these stagings were farces and the outcome had been already decided upon, the accused was still executed. When the prosecutor asked her father why he had signed a confession, he answered just like thousands of other accused: "I was beaten until I signed." The prosecutor then asked him, heaven knows why:

"Prosecutor: Were you ever beaten?
Accused: Yes sir. It would be impossible for me to name all those who beat me as I often lost consciousness. The examining magistrate himself beat me."

Catalina continued:

"When the court martial was over, my father was taken to Fuente Vieja prison. No sooner did he arrive there, that a 2nd Lieutenant, the Judge and José Higuera entered the patio and, in the presence of the other prisoners, beat my father until he lost consciousness. I could hear his screams from outside the building, on the street. From the day on which he was condemned to death until September 26 1940 when he was transferred to Cordoba prison, we never saw him again."

That was how Francoism 'tried' the accused and how many ordinary people died during the post-war period. This could be the subject for an entire treatise on the reality of Francoist justice, not just because of the tragedies, but also the ridiculous scenarios that Francoists staged to give an appearance of 'legality' to the extermination. Farce, nonsense, burlesque and spoofs, were some of the means the military employed. The above case clearly shows a) how it was by pure chance that an accused's innocence, not his guilt, was proven, but never to any avail; b) that the accused were tortured or beaten until they confessed; c) that relatives or friends of the prisoners were said to have made accusations that they denied or whose meaning was twisted by the Court to its advantage.

A distinctive feature of Francoist trials was their collective approach. It was a rare occasion when a court martial was convened for a single accused. Quite the contrary. The bench of accused was always occupied by several individuals, in greater or lesser numbers, all whose fate was decided in less than an hour. This administration of group justice was another affront to the individual defendants. The court centred its attention on the group of accused and not on the individual characteristics of any given prisoner. By grouping several cases, the court martial was politicized and promoted the desired depersonalization of the prisoners. The Francoist apparatus and the justice that depended on it only saw the accused as yet another clutch of Rojos, on whose extermination depended the security of the Regime. Examples of single individual trials were rare in Cordoba.

As soon as the accused had been seated in the courtroom, tied to each other two by two and guarded by Guardias Civiles and Falangistas, the Court took its seat on the podium and began the formal proceedings, with the expected results. The Rapporteur would read out a so-called summary for each accused and not the complete summary accusation. This summary condensed and simplified the accusations and the charges, without forgetting that these were summary accusations obtained by the examining magistrates after applying torture, based on manifestly false data obtained without the minimum due process of law and signed by an accused after he had been beaten and tortured until he confessed to what they had written in his stead.

Once the summary was read out and each accused's name was briefly mentioned, almost as if it were just another name in a list of prisoners in a jail, the prosecutor would ask the accused a few superfluous and redundant questions that never met the burden of proof, as he expanded or simply paraphrased that which had already been written in the summary accusation. Few witnesses for the defence were brave enough to appear. Nothing was proven and there were no amendments to the charges, little or no variation in the accusations or allegations. The courts martial decisions were not based on proof; the indictment was considered enough on its own and the only persons from outside who were allowed to speak were the accusers and the witnesses to the charges.

The Rapporteur and the Prosecutor limited their interventions to expanding certain aspects of the summary reports and to emphasizing the working-class connections of an accused and his 'extremely bad behaviour' – all the way back to the days of the Republic, and even earlier, since the days of the so-called Bolshevik triennium (taking part in strikes, demonstrations, embroidering flags, etc.), with special emphasis on any rank he may have held in the Republican Army. There was an evident insistence on these political and ideological features, rather than on determining the truth of the supposed commission of blood crimes. The courts martial were more interested in dispensing with anyone who might have committed a common blood crime so as to focus on purging the country of everyone who may have committed what was considered a political crime. In other words, the courts martial were no more than instruments for the political purging of the country of anyone who might be disaffected.

The highpoint of the trials was the intervention of the Prosecutor, who spoke aggressively, vehemently giving full rein to every available Falangist or National Catholic argument. In post-war Cordoba, none of the prosecutors could reach the heights of neurotic rhetoric as much as José Ramós de La Lastra y Hoces, attorney, Marquis of Ugena, grandson of the Duke of Hornachelos, wealthy landowner and ex-President of the Agricultural Association – the personification of the landed gentry and the decadent aristocracy, with all the vices of Spanish caciquism. Dom José's interventions in trials were notorious.

A partial transcription of one of these, a May 21 1939 article in the Cordoba *Azul*, gives details of the most infamous court martial in Baena, where the principal "anarchist" leaders of the town were eliminated. Judge Evaristo Peñalver, a Colonel in the Guardia Civil, presided over the court martial. After pondering the merits of Baena's 'heroic fight against criminal Marxists' (he may have been referring to the townspeople's violent reaction to the slaughter of several hundred unarmed men lying in the main square), Don José went on and on in this vein without this having anything to do with the accused on trial.

> "The Prosecutor continued with his brilliant allocution. He decried the arrival of the Republic, considering it the door that opened the way for Russian cruelty and criminality in Spain. The Republic served only the Masons and the Jews, and created the concentrated hate of the Army, alluding to Pemán's statement that 'The Levites were the damnation of Spain and the Army its salvation.'

211

He affirmed that everyone and everything were conspiring against Religion and the Army, the most fundamental and serious pillars of the Fatherland, the military and the religious, so perfectly defined by José Antonio Primo de Rivera.

The Frente Popular, with its Masonic and Jewish coercing agents, had as its sole mission handing Spain over to Russia. The Caudillo's, to whom all of Spain owes so much, mission was heaven-sent as he was entrusted by God with saving the Fatherland.

It now happens that the Marxists claim they are not Nationalists. Can there be anything more beautiful than this description, so that even the bad patriots are unable to apply it to themselves?

The Red beasts murdered 96 people in the San Francisco de Baena Convent. Corners, cloisters and rooms, filled with the pain of the tragedy. Killing for the sake of killing. They knew not what they were defending. He who said that the Rojos were defending themselves, did not know against what. The fact of the matter is that criminal instinct found the open dark door and murder was committed with satisfaction.

Spain is saved. The Sacred Heart of Jesus has fulfilled its promise. God watches over her. We now see those who obeyed like wild beasts, and those who beyond the frontiers enjoy a life of wealth and well-being. These did not hesitate to become criminals when they received their orders to do so.

The Prosecutor referred to the 1934 government banners, the ones that led to the events of 1936. This 1936 must not again happen. He asked for justice with serenity, his hand on his heart in obeisance of his duty.

He declared a welcome and praise to heroic Lieutenant Pascual Sánchez Ramírez, Military Commander of the town of Baena and its stalwart defender, who has already been honoured by the Generalissimo with the Military Medal. Men like these – he said – honour the Fatherland that gave them birth.

We, he added, represent Spain. Against criminal Marxism, the hammer and the sickle, the indignity and unconfessable designs of the ominous triangle, as opposed to our Cross of Redemption. 96 murders have left their mark on Baena, a city deserving of better luck, filled with bitterness and pain. He connected the deeds and monstrosities committed, signs of unheard of and horrible cruelty.

This is the time for exact, considered, inflexible justice. The deeds are covered under Article 235 of the Code of Military Justice and are punishable under Article 538.

At this point, the Prosecutor and the Court stood up. So did the public. It was a very emotional moment. In the name of the Caudillo, he asked for the death sentence for all the defendants."[xvii]

The newspaper headlined the ostentatious and grotesque May 20 1939 court martial in Baena: "36 death sentences for 20 accused". In other words, several accused were sentenced to death more than once. Once would have been enough. After this theatrical description, the press rarely printed this kind of report regarding other courts martial. It is presumed that the authorities issued orders for prosecutors and the press to be more discreet.

When faced with examples of forensic oratory, the court martials always supported the Prosecutor's conclusions and felt no need to change them based on the defence's succinct remarks. The possibility that a meek intervention from the military defender might influence the Court's decision was extremely unlikely, particularly with such meek requests for clemency "considering that we are living in times of strict and inflexible justice, but also of generosity and Christian forgiveness."[67]

The individual nature of each of the accused was totally buried amid the prosecutor's political ranting. As far as he and the Court were concerned, the accused were not tangible persons, just elements of the anti-Spain and of a perverse system (Republican democracy). This reveals basic features of the extermination machine: depersonalization and demonization of the defeated by treating them as objects and reducing them to the category of vermin. First demonize and then exterminate without remorse.

The figure of the Public Defender in the court martial was relegated to a marginal position. He was either a 1st or 2nd Lieutenant, rarely a Captain, who

---

[xvii] The journalist misconstrued or falsely reported many of the facts: the prisoners were anarchists (the usual Francoist description for anyone against the Regime, the disaffected), not Marxists, who were being tried and it was Francoists who described themselves as Nationalists, not the other way round; the number killed by the angry townspeople was 81, not 96, and not a single individual was proven guilty of this; 500 was the number of unarmed men executed by the Francoist Military Commander in Baena town square. The journalist appeared unaware that it was home-grown disaffected, not Marxists from Russia, who were being tried, unless he chose to spout the official Francoist line rather than speak the truth.

spoke timidly, briefly and even as if by rote. What could a military 'defender' say in favour of all those individuals described as monsters, over whose heads the gallows already hanged? The Public Defender's words were addressed to a collective, he made no reference to any individual prisoner. He limited himself to simply asking for a reduction of the sentence to a less drastic punishment, but frequently, not even that, just for the indulgence, clemency or Christian charity of the Court. His were purely pro-forma interventions that totally ignored individual accusations, without even the slightest hint that any of these charges had even been examined.

This latter observation regarding the lack of examination applied to prosecutors and timid public defenders alike. None ever showed the slightest desire to clarify the charges, either during the interrogations or during the trials. Nor was there any desire for clarification nor real desire to defend the accused. Such was the case in the Baena court martial that was adjourned for a break because another court martial was scheduled for 1 p.m. The records for this second court martial describe the actions of the defence in the following terms: 'The Public Defender, Lieutenant Bernal, after a few brief words, asked the Court's indulgence for the accused.' Just like Cicero in his defence of Milo or the poet Arquias.

Three days after the end of the second court martial against 7 accused from Valenzuela, *Azul* newspaper reported yet another example of the aristocratic prosecutor José Ramón de La Lastra's extravagant rhetoric: [68]

During this trial as in the previous one, the aristocratic prosecutor alluded to the Freemasons, a subject that was totally irrelevant to the cases on trial and totally unknown to the ordinary workers who were sitting on the bench of the accused. In the earlier intervention, the Prosecutor alluded to the 'hammer and sickle and the ominous triangle'. During his second intervention, he continued to spout the Regime's neurotic, obsessive ranting against the Masonic motto of 'liberty, equality and fraternity'. Both, references that had absolutely nothing to do with the rural world of a handful of anarchist working men.

The rhetoric of the trials was located on a totally different plane from that of the life of the accused, most of whom were farmworkers and labourers. The anti-Masonic obsession was a scarecrow that the Caudillo and the Church (especially the latter) constantly brandished, then and during the next forty years. In the Dictator's last, extremely brief declaration in 1975 at the Plaza del Oriente, he returned to the scarecrow when he referred to 'the Jewish-Masonic-Marxist conspiracy'. It was an obsession that would darken his death-bed, as all the ghosts of the past prepared to 'welcome' him from beyond the grave.

An especially dramatic moment during the court martial was when the Public Defender for the accused stood up to speak on their behalf in this totally hostile environment, as a court martial rarely allowed an accused the right to speak for himself. At the very most, the court gave the floor to only one accused to speak on behalf of all. What could one man say on his behalf or on behalf of them all? Here too, we see another form of depersonalization under Francoist 'justice'.

Whenever an accused managed the courage to say a few words, he almost always denied the charges against him, drawing attention to the false nature of the accusations. If the Presiding Judge replied that the accused had signed a confession, the prisoner replied that it was because he was beaten until he did so. Occasionally, from amongst those who sat on the accused's' bench, one heard a more eloquent voice, someone accustomed to speaking in meetings and in public. Inevitably, the Presiding Judge would immediately tell him to shut up.

In his book of *Memoires,* reproduced in part herein, Rafael Bedmar Guerrero reconstructs some of Prosecutor La Lastra's allegations at his trial in Cordoba Court October 25 1939 when Rafael spoke in his own defence. The Presiding Judge was the omnipresent Evaristo Peñalver:

In an undated document of memoires given to Moreno Gómez, Adriano Romero refers to his trials, one of the rare individual courts martial, perhaps because the accued had been a Member of Parliament and he was to be made an example.

> "The trial lasted three hours, something that was completely unusual, and at the end, when I was asked if I had anything to say, I stood up ready to speak some truths, but I was only able to say a couple of words before I was forced to sit down and the session was adjourned."[69]

In his memoires, he added that Juan Escribano, a friend of his who attended the court martial in the Cordoba Audiencia in 1941, reminded him that he also declared that he had been a communist since he had reached the age of reason and that the Court could only condemn me for that and not for any blood crime of any kind.

Everything that occurred during the trials was a grotesque travesty of traditional judicial procedures. Franco's typical military justice was no more than a pro-forma vehicle for eliminating the Regime's opponents, procedures where no one troubled to do any prior work to prove the charges, without any desire to clarify the events, that included the absurd intervention of the military Public Defender. In José Subirats' magnificent book of memoires,[70] he cites the bizarre case of a defender who asked for the death sentence for the person he was defending, during a court martial in Tarragona,[71] contrary to the Prosecutor's recommendation; the accused was led to the firing squad. Subirats also recalls his own court martial (August 10 1939), which lasted little more than thirty minutes and was over so quickly that the Rapporteur barely had time to read out the charges against the 15 accused.

The Judge Advocate's Court in Tarragona convened daily collective courts martial, one at 11 a.m. and another at twelve noon. Another farce, a sham, grotesque. After glancing over the indictments, the Court would convene a mini-council that would meet briefly and dictate the sentences on the go. The accused were swiftly despatched back to their prison with their death sentences under their arms, and then directly to death row where they were held incommunicado from the rest of the inmates.

Lastly, the remarkable relationship between the local oligarchy in each town and the Regime's judiciary apparatus was particularly noteworthy. The most unyielding local members of the right-wing and the Falange collaborated closely with the military judges both during the instruction of the summary proceedings and later, with the special Military Court that sat in their town for two or three days. In a great many cases, the Examining Magistrate and other officers of the Court were members of the local oligarchy, such as Judge Manuel Cubillo in Baena, Prosecutor de La Lastra in the capital, etc. In any case, those responsible for justice frequently asked for and always received support, advice and instructions from the local right-wingers.

In Villlanueva de Cordoba, for example, it is well known that the members of the military Magistrate's Court and the major landowners of the town met regularly in the house of the Sepúlvedas and in the Casino, meetings that were frequently attended by the Jesuit priest Bernabé Copado, S.J. On these and other occasions, those present fine-tuned the details of the repression, drafted the black lists, agreed upon the death sentences and decided on any possible combinations of or changes to the accusations that were levied against the defendants. When we examine the Francoist repression, at no time can we lose sight of the close collaboration between the military courts and the landowner bourgeoisie in southern Spain, along the lines of that which has been described as Rural Catholic Fascism.

3. Examination of sentences and appeals for clemency. False rhetoric and an arbitrary approach.

The possibility of a condemned person's appealing his sentence was not contemplated by the Regime until the beginning of 1940. Besides, in 1939 such a possibility did not exist for the defendants who were usually executed a few weeks after they had been condemned to death. Even when an accused had a very slight opportunity to defend his case during the court martial, he frequently found that all doors for any kind of an appeal for an examination of the procedure or a reassessment of his sentence had been closed. Furthermore, the accuseds' generally low level of formal education and the even lower level of literacy of any relatives who might help them outside the jail, proved to be a major barrier to any bureaucratic management of an appeal.

Of special note was the dedication of communist leader Matilde Landa, who in Ventas, Madrid, and Palma de Mallorca prisons devoted herself to drafting appeals for sentence revisions for her companions in prison. She was one of the great women of the Republic, with an impressive trajectory, who tragically took her own life in prison when she could no longer bear the Church's insufferable attacks against her.

January 25 1940, the Presidency of the Government issued an executive decree creating Provincial Committees for Examining Sentences (CPEP),[72] specifically to 'abolish, as humanly possible, any inequalities that might have occurred and did occur in many cases for various reasons, given the confusion resulting from the lack of uniformity of criteria to judge and punish similar crimes of the same gravity.[73] These were not beneficial measures from the totalitarian New State (as some historians have suggested), just simple measures to unify the procedures involving the geographic distribution of the numerous military courts throughout the country, as well as the two great classes of individuals sent to trial: military and civilians.

Civilians received the harshest sentences. This was never a question of mitigating the outcomes of the judicial procedures. Suffice to remember the variety of civilians who from the onset were excluded from any possibility of requesting an examination or review of their sentences.

The CPEP, invented for fine-tuning the repression with the excuse of the need to uniformize procedures, began operating in February 1940 and lasted five years until the committees were disbanded February 25 1945. They were followed by the Central Bureau for Assessing Sentences (CCEP) attached to the Advocacy of the Ministry of the Army. As these Committees were created by executive Decree from Franco's personal office they were, consequently, autonomous bodies that fuctioned independently of the judicial summary

217

proceedings and the military tribunals. Despite that, they strongly influenced the sentencing, which itself was a juridical irregularity under the very laws of the Regime that apparently did not even respect its own legislation.

The CPEP, according to Judge Juan José del Águila, was a hybrid body with an administrative structure and a so-called jurisdictional soul. In case of a disagreement between the Judiciary Authorities and the Judges Advocates, the cases were sent to the Supreme Council of Military Justice which resolved the matter behind closed doors, according to a Decree of June 3 1942.

Following the decree creating the CPEP committees in January 1940, the Minister of the Army, General Varela, later dedicated himself to issuing communiqués regarding the Assessment of Sentences, which were not published in the B.O.E. (Official Bulletin of the Army) and only added huge amounts to the judicial tangle, which became immersed in the most absolute subjectivity. To complicate matters relating to the CPEP and communiqués, the decrees were in violation of the Regime's own Military Code of Justice (1870) that in Article 176 stated:

> 'No military offense may be punished by a penalty that was not previously set by law for such an offense, before the date on which the offense was committed. The only sentences that will be examined are those imposed by the Courts as a result of a judicial proceeding.'

Juan José del Águila then writes:

> "It is clear that the new penalties (the ones established by the CPEP and the many communiqués) were determined after the fact, after the supposed crime had been tried and punished by the sentences from the Courts Martial, and that many of the standing penalties could not be applied by the Courts, as they did not meet the specific terms of the recently-created Committees for the Examination of Sentences."

The Regime's judiciary shambles aside, just who could appeal for a review of their sentences and who were affected by the wide array of exclusions? The January 25 1940 Decree contained nine instructions, some of which were truly amazing, such as the second instruction that stipulates that a committee may not discuss facts that havae been declared as proven and must limit itself to drafting a proposal, whether it agrees with the judicial decision or whether it deems it convenient to propose that a sentence be reduced or commuted;"

or instruction nine that further clarifies the role of the committees as being to draw attention to the politico-social and moral background of the accused or his personal behaviour 'before the Movement', or the impact of his actions for or against the National Cause'.

Clearly, the mission of the CPEP, far from introducing compassionate measures, was nothing more than a fine-tuned bureaucratic regulation to unify and typify every detail of the colossal machinery of Francoist justice, whilst retaining the severity of the sentences handed to 'qualified' disaffected and to a certain extent, separating them from 'neutral' disaffected and run-of-the-mill criminals. It is also important to remember that the mission of the CPEP only applied to cases directly related to the war, so-called military war crimes, and not to all post-war prosecutions for a variety of other reasons, namely, the 'ordinary conviction' of non-military individuals who as 'disaffected' civilians, nevertheless continued to attract the Regime's anger and for which they were equally severely punished.

By 1944, the CPEP committees impacted the sentences in 107,983 cases of ordinary convictions, of which 2,269 involved professional soldiers and 104,702, disaffected civilians or members of the militia. In other words, a quarter of everyone arrested by Franco. For some unknown reason, only 2,060 dossiers of the more than 30,000 convictions appealed in Cordoba, were examined. The CPEP was dissolved February 24 1945.

Despite the constraints on the condemned and their apparently hopeless situation, numerous prisoners attempted a new means of salvation - written appeals for some sort of clemency. Since 1939, those condemned to the 'ultimate penalty' searched within and outside the jails for literate individuals, preferably who also knew how to type, to help them submit their appeal, although, as we have seen, those appeals very rarely had a positive result. In the famous case of 'The Thirteen Roses', the night before the women were executed in Madrid, numerous written appeals were still being written and submitted but these were not even looked at or processed. Likewise, thousands of cases all over Spain. In all the examples of such appeals that Moreno Gómez found in Cordoba, when the condemned had a high political profile, the death sentences were carried out. Two examples of such appeals, in 1940, are addressed to the Judge Advocate for the Army in the province of Cordoba (those filed in 1939 were addressed to Lt. Colonel Ignacio Cuervo, Judge Advocate for the Army of Occupation, and in Peñarroya, Captain Francisco Casas Ochoa, Delegate Judge Advocate).

Eugenio Jurado Pozuelo, a prisoner from Villanueva de Cordoba who had been condemned to death, submitted a last-minute appeal which he wrote with the assistance of his brother José, ex-Mayor for the Lerroux Party.[74] The Delgado family and Juan Lucio alleged that Eugenio had testified to the charges against several right-wingers who were tried in Jaén, one of whom was Juan A. Delgado Fernández, whose brother Pepe Delgado, was Eugenio's principal accuser and who participated in the terrible beatings that he received:

If not actually ignored, his appeal was probably never heard, because just a few days later, Holy Sunday May 26, Eugenio Jurado and 18 others were executed at dawn. A few hours later, those responsible for their deaths participated in an ostentatious religious parade up and down the streets of the town.

Another such appeal, Ex-Captain of Militia Pedro *Cuadrado* Torralbo's, was also of little use although there was more time for it to be heard, as he was executed a year later in the Cordoba city cemetery. His family kindly gave Moreno Gómez a copy. The texts are of both this and Eduardo Pozuelo's appeals are reproduced in the Addendum, Volume 2.

Everything that Pedro Torralbo had written was true. Apparently, however, Pedro Torralba was unaware of the Regime's plans for the extermination. He was wasting his time claiming that his was a pacifying role, which it was, and that he was opposed to the crimes and the mistreatment of the prisoners. His problem was that he was a political leader and Francoism was liquidating every leader of a leftist political party, of a trade union, all Republican authorities and all commissioned officers in the Republican Army. The charges against him were false – which probably did not surprise the Regime. Another factor against Pedro was that he, the victim, had the audacity to ask the oppressors to declare his sentence null and void (they never did so; today's weak-willed democratic government has still not dared do so). The very most that Pedro might have hoped for was a commutation of his sentence. Nothing more.

Lastly, it was futile to hope that the totalitarian Regime would interview the witnesses for the defence and accordingly, revise the charges or make inquiries. The Regime almost never called witnesses for the defence, nor could it be bothered to do so. Furthermore, if those witnesses were not called during a court martial, it was even less likely that they would be called for a sentence review. Pedro, like other victims, was unaware that the trials were a sham and that there was no such thing as justice under the self-styled Francoist rule of Law.

Pedro Torralbo's life had been earmarked for liquidation during the Casino meetings and the outcome was decided beforehand. With or without denunciations and accusations, the simple fact that he was classified as a community leader (not just as an active member of a political party, but he had also served as a Town Councillor in 1931, Provincial Deputy in 1936 and

Captain in the Militia, all the qualifications for classification as belonging to Group C of outlaws), indicated that there was nothing that could be done. That was that. Pedro Torralbo fell under a hail of bullets June 3 1941 in Cordoba capital, after having first been sent to prison in Burgos where he suffered unmentionable punishments. That was the exterminators' usual practice.

4. Some leaders who were saved.

Despite the Regime's persecution mania, some leading Republicans still managed to survive after they were embroiled in the oppressive labyrinth, as Moreno Gómez was able to corroborate in some cases in Cordoba province. Luck, especially, made it possible for a few leaders amongst the mass of thousands upon thousands of prosecutions, to escape the ultimate sentence. Good fortune and the fact that their trials were postponed to a later date. There was no possible escape from the trials held in 1939, but as time went by, some holes began appearing in the net, as in the case of the Socialist Deputy, Eduardo Blanco Fernández from the mining region of Peñarroya, whose court martial was delayed to June 11 1943. Had he been tried earlier, he would not have escaped the death penalty.

According to Eduardo Blanco himself, his salvation was also due to the efforts of some right-wingers (not all were blood-thirsty), whom he had assisted during the war, namely Carlos Calatayud, Professor at the Instituto de Peñarroya, a very active traditionalist since before the war who owed his life to Eduardo Blanco when in 1936 he prevented the execution of the right-wing prisoners from Peñarroya-Pueblonuevo. Furthermore, on several occasions, he formally opposed the local War Committee's intentions, as he prevented attempts by outside militia, especially Jaén Militia, from attacking the jail. When Peñarroya was evacuated in October 1936, these prisoners were transferred to Ciudad Real and the majority survived. Nonetheless, meritorious acts were of little importance to the Regime when it was the case of a prominent individual. To have been a do-gooder was not enough. It was also necessary that nobody in the barracks, the casino or the vestry had decided on his liquidation and that there was no allegation or accusation of import against him. A whole set of miraculous events had to occur for a prisoner to escape death.

Eduardo Blanco was arrested in Ciudad Real at the end of the war. He remained there for a year and was later transferred to a jail in Peñarroya that had been set up in the old Miners' Union building, when the furore of the immediate post-war period had begun to die down a bit. From there, he was sent to Cordoba prison where he was tried by court martial, as he reports:

> 'I believe that the CEDA Deputy, Laureano Fernández Martos, intervened in my favour, as I was tried in Cordoba instead of Seville, where it would have all been much more difficult for the Court. The Prosecutor also was clearly in my favour and I was sentenced to thirty years. When I was asked which books I had read as a student, I replied Victor Hugo's, whose book *Les Misérables* I read when I was 16 years old, when I worked down the mines.
>
> In the jail, I was I immediately put to work in the Canteen, where I helped with the accounts. However, when I discovered some incorrect entries and tried to get to the bottom of the misbehaviour, I was transferred to Burgos at the instigation of some nuns who were stealing wine and watering down what was left.'[75]

Undoubtedly, Eduardo Blanco had to be blessed with a powerful 'helping hand' because the result of his trial was by no means usual or normal. His sentence reads:

> "The National Movement found him in Madrid, from where he went to Pueblonuevo during the first days of the war, where he later became a member of the Board of the Rojo Committee. In all the positions that he held, despite his extremely leftist ideas, as is repeatedly apparent throughout, the accused always appears to have acted in favour of right-wing individuals, opposing all criminal acts against them, such as those that a Committee of Rojos from Peñarroya attempted to commit against some right-wingers. IT IS THEREFORE DECIDED: THAT the accused Eduardo Blanco Fernández shall be condemned to the sentence of LIFE IMPRISONMENT…"[76]

Such a result was unheard of in courts martial during the immediate post-war period, especially because he also was a Frente Popular Member of Parliament, belonged to the local War Committee, was a founder of the Terrible Battalion and later, Civil Governor for Republican Cordoba. One cannot understand how it was possible that his case was not tried until mid 1943. The fate of the majority of the Republican leaders was much, worse.[xviii]

More challenging was the grim situation of Bartolomé Fernández Sánchez, founder and Commander of the Pedroches Battalion, Socialist from Pozoblanco, Major in the Mitia (September 14 1938) then Senior Officer of the Cartagena Base during the dark March 1939 days of the Casadistas,[xix] when he was arrested and imprisoned by the Nationalists. He, too, was tried by court martial very late in the day, March 16 1943, and sentenced to death. The principal obstacle to his defense was a denunciation against him by a local ruffian, José Plazuelo, who falsely accused him of commanding the squad the executed 18 right-wingers in Pozoblanco September 20 1936. On that date, Bartolomé Fernández Sánchez was actually in Madrid where he was negotiating the purchase of arms for the Pedroches Battalion. Besides, firing squads were always commanded by lower ranking officers, never Commanders and Batalomé Fernández had been the Battalion Commander since August 31 1936. He dedicated himself with determination to preparing his appeal.

The day after the sentencing, March 17, Bartolomé sent an urgent request to a right-wing friend, José Elías Cabrera Caballero, who had considerable influence in Pozoblanco, asking him to convince the local Pozoblanco authorities to lessen the accusations against him. He then approached a series of influential contacts in Sevilla and Madrid, in order to get a reduction of his sentence. Lastly, he was able to put together a portfolio of signatures of right-wing individuals who, during the Republic, had received favours and special attention from Bartolomé Fernandez.

This was the usual route taken by numerous condemned throughout Spain, with varying results. In addition to these measures, it was usual for a condemned's family to go into action, right left and centre, to collect signatures, recommendations, documents and other material in support of the appeal. During the post-war period, thousands of wives travelled from office to office, often subject to humiliations, as never before. Every effort, every request was directed at finding evidence to weaken the accusations and denunciations and the bitter milk of human kindness that permeated the

---

[xviii] Moreno Gómez was able to located Eduardo Blanco in 1981, in his house in south Madrid. He could not have more kindly given access to all the material that he was interested. Eduardo said that he was honoured by Moreo Goméz' research as this was the first time that anybody had interviewed him regarding his past history. He spoke of his existence and of his persona in a Socialist fora, where these faithful followers of the Transition policy of 'forget the past' one of the last survivors of the Frente Popular Parliament. Eduardo left them quietly, without a single gesture from his companions.

[xix] Supporters of Republican General Segismundo Casado who unsuccessfully tried to negotiate a surrender with Franco.

reports from the Falange, Guardia Civil, Mayor and other local authorities, as well as the parish priests who, in some townships, added as much fuel to the fire as they could. Bartolomé Fernández's wife also duly travelled to the Military Headquarters in Sevilla, as part of the so-called 'bureaucratic pilgrimage'.

Bartolomé Fernández's case was also favoured by a most unusual reference: that from the famous Republican Colonel Joaquín Pérez Salas,[xx] who took full responsibility and exempted Fernández of all blame for the crime he was accused of. This case is of particular historic interest and a copy of the letter Pérez Salas wrote to Bartolomé Fernández June 16 1939, when the gallows were already hanging over that great soldier's head is also reproduced in Volume 2. Pérez Salas was executed August 4 1939 in Murcia cemetery, having been imprisoned in San Julián castle and Jaime I barracks in Murcia.

Accordingly, 30 June Pérez Salas signed a declaration in favour of Bartolomé Fernández, in which he stated that he always followed his orders as is military practice, and that as his commanding officer, he assumed full responsibility for all Bartolomé's actions. This document, written when Pérez Salas had only a few days left to live, was unable to produce the desired effect because when it arrived at Military Court Number 16, unknown interested parties made it disappear. Yet another insight into the judicial farce of Francoist justice: the convenient disappearance of documents that could be favourable to an appellant whose fate had been decided beforehand. Despite everything, Bartolomé Fernández managed to save himself, because it took so long for his case to be tried and thanks to the help of some right-wingers who owed him a favour.

Chance and good fortune also enabled other important labour leaders in Cordoba to be saved, such as Adriano Romero Cachinero, from the large communist stronghold of Villanuva de Cordoba, belonged to the Central Committee and the Political Bureau of the PCE during the Republic, travelled to the USSR in 1933 and in 1936 was elected Frente Popular Member of Parliament for Pontevedra. The outbreak of the war found him in Almeria on July 18 when, after offering his services to the Civil Government, he contributed to maintaining law and order in that province. He commanded the 55th Brigade and held the rank of Major in the Militia on the Malaga front. At the end of the war, he was arrested March 11 by Casadistas in Ciudad Real and handed over to the Nationalists on the 28th of thet month.

[xx] Celebrated Republican Artillery officer who stood out for his actions during the Battle of Cordoba and his leadership during the victorious Battle of Pozoblanco in 1937 against the Nationalist troops of Queipo de Llano.

Adriano Romero remained in prison in Ciudad Real for a year. He was only called to make a declaration once, March 1940 when his case was claimed by a special judge from Cordoba and he was transferred to the old prison in the city. Again, all these delays were always beneficial to the accused. In this case, a new factor appeared in Adriano's favour: the judge's secretary was an old friend of his and in 1931 had belonged to part of a little-known communist candidacy to the municipal elections in Cordoba capital. This was José Espina Almansa, an attorney and influential professor. Not only had he had a connection with the PCE, and the CNT before then, but it is also possible that he was a member of the Abril Masonic lodge in Posadas. José Espina had been on the 1936 blacklists of those to be shot in the capital, but he was saved by the president of the Court. How and why José Espina became a supporter of the New State remains a mystery. The fact is, that José Espina, secretary to a Francoist Cordoba judge, saved not only Adriano Romero but also Alfredo Caballero Martinez who had been Provincial Secretary of the PCE during the war. The respective indictments were 'fixed' and the charges against them were toned down. According to Adriano's own testimony.[77]

The first conclusion that one reaches from Adriano Romero's court martial is that if the accused, as in his case, could sometimes refute the false accusations against him, this practically was never possible in trials from 1939 to 1941. This was also unlikely later. In this case, even after the false accusations were withdrawn, he was still condemned to death. This was in August 1941.

Adriano Romero would surely have been executed had it not been that two months after the trial, he was extended another lifeline in the form of a military attorney who pushed for a revision of his case on the grounds of the lack of evidence and failure of due diligence. This was most unusual. A new judge was appointed who took advantage of the requests from a Granada judge to hand over the case file, which took the prosecution out of the Seville jurisdiction where Antonio was in serious danger. He was transferred to Granada in July 1942.

In Granada, the military judiciary process was, as expected, identical. The Examining Magistrate did not even ask Antonio to make the customary declaration, he closed the case file without comments and handed the case over to the Judge for the court martial. One false denunciation, by someone named Maldonado Castillo from the Catholic Trade Union of Vélez de Benaudalla, implicated him in blood crimes in this town. Although he was able to refute this false accusation, this second court martial September 1943 sentenced him to death for the second time. Six months later, thanks to help from the Consul for Venezuela in Granada and the defence counsel's excellent work, his sentence was reduced to thirty years in jail.

Adriano Romero was finally released from jail on parole March 1946. Behind him, a long string of obstacles that he was able to overcome almost by good fortune alone. The numerous delays in the prosecution, his transfer to Granada in 1942 and the assistance of several influential individuals, made his survival possible.

Other eminent leaders must be added to the list of those who fortunately survived. Miguel Caballero Vacas, one of the founders of the PCE in Villanueva de Cordoba, several townships, Cordoba capital and Seville. His activities during the war were centred in Jaén. At first, he was sent to Puerto Real, Cádiz, concentration camp where he survived under a pseudonym among four thousand other prisoners. Later, at the end of 1939, he was sent to Rota, Cádiz, concentration camp. In 1940, he was transferred to the Los Barrios, Cádiz, Workers' Battalion where he was recognized and denounced by an individual from his home town and sent to jail in Algeciras, accused of promoting the death of Villanueva de Cordoba right-wing prisoners in Jaén (1936) and of being an agent at the service of a foreign power.[78] The Prosecutor was asking for two death sentences by hanging, when the well-known claims of a judge from Jaén resulted in his transfer to Santa Clara Convent prison July 1940. A new prosecution and back to the beginning. The claims from military judges from another judicial jurisdiction, with the consequent delays in scheduling the trial, were again of great benefit to the accused. Miguel Caballero did not appear before a court martial until the late date of November 3 1943, when he was sentenced to thirty years in jail.

Artillery Captain Francisco Blanco Pedraza, Colonel Pérez Salas' right hand officer in the defence of the Republican zone of North of Cordoba province, was another one of those who was remarkably saved, unlike his chief Pérez Salas. Attached since 1936 to the Cordoba front, he was noted for the accuracy of his canon fire. He commanded the 88th Mixed Brigade in 1937 and later, the 38th Division of the VIII Army Corps. In June of the same year, he was promoted to Artillery Major then Artillery Commander for the entire Army of Extremadura. In the end, all these senior military officers supported Casado's coup. The end of the war found him in Puertollano and it was a tragedy that fate made him lead the surrender of Puertollano to General Yagüe's troops 29 March 1939.

When he was arrested, Blanco Pedraza was sent to Cordoba prison. His case (number 25.419/39) was heard 28 September 1939 in the Artillery Barracks and he was sentenced to death. There he suffered the unbridled attacks of all his triumphant ex-brothers at arms, who demanded his head at all costs, as they did with Pérez Salas in Murcia. The speed of Blanco Pérez's court martial made everyone fear the worst, but in his favour was the fact that his brother Juan Rafael, a Falangista, had been a victim of the Republican repression in Madrid in 1936. Armed with this information, his mother urgently travelled to Burgos where she presented a single argument: 'The Rojos killed one of my sons. Are the Nationalists now going to kill my other son?' It appears that General Varela was moved because he recommended the commutation of his sentence effective April 1940. After several years in jail, the dedicated officer who had served so brilliantly in the artillery on the Cordoba front, Captain Blanco Pedraza, rebuilt his life in Madrid teaching mathematics.[79]

The following is a remarkable story, with which we conclude Volume 1 of Damnatio Memoriae – They Shall Not Be Forgotten.

Ex-Member of Parliament Martín Sanz Diéz, socialist, is one of those whom we could describe as one of the Cordoba capital 'moles': he was saved after living in hiding for eleven years. If he had not, he would not have escaped the cruelty of the Cordovan military. Martín Sanz was from Valladolid; he first worked as a tailor in Madrid then in Cuba during the 1920s, where he was politically active as a trade unionist, which is why the dictator Machado deported him back to Spain. Martín Sanz set up shop in Cordoba around 1930 and became totally involved in the political scene of the times, at the heart of the PSOE/UGT. He was elected Member of Parliament in 1931 but he did not run for re-election in 1933. When the insurgents invaded Andalusia and took Cordoba, he found himself in such a perilous situation that during the first weeks he hid in some friends' house, whilst his wife said that he had gone over to the Republican zone. He later returned to his own house. His grandson Luís tells his remarkable story.

> "My grandfather remained hidden in his own house, not only during the entire war but also, once it was over, until summer 1947 when he was discovered and denounced by a neighbour and arrested by the police. At that time, even though he was 74 years old and that eleven years had passed since the end of the war, he was held under Francoist law and imprisoned in Seville…
>
> I don't know what happened during his trial but he was sentenced and then sent to the Cordoba prison. By around 1949 he was already out of jail. From that moment on until he was almost 90 years old, he continued to work as a tailor in the workshop he set up in his house. He was a personal friend of Pablo Iglesias, whose numerous correspondence with him he bequeathed to the PSOE.

This information that I remember regarding my grandfather Martin I have, as you can imagine, because I know all this as my mother told it to my brothers and to me... I have not collected it all, for example the visits of the Francoist police to my grandfather's house during the war, and how, on one occasion, when they did not find him, they took my uncle Antonio who was only 13 or 14 years old at the time and kept him under arrest at the police station for some time... And how the family had to resort to a lot of ingenuity so that my grandfather could be operated on for a serious stomach ulcer, thanks to false documents and the generous complicity of several surgeons who were his friends.

Then there was the farce set up by the Guardia Civil the day they went to arrest him in 1947: the whole street was cut off and filled with uniformed guards, a huge number of armed vehicles, the amazement on the faces of the policemen who when they went to his house, instead of the 'dangerous Rojo' they had been sent to arrest, they were taking in an elderly 74-year-old who sported a long white beard...'[80]

Endnotes for Chapter III

1   Rufino Ayuso Fernández. Field work given to Moreno Gómez in 2002. An enthusiastic supporter of groups dedicated to recoverying the historic memory, he was a policeman by profession and died very young. Moreno Gómez refers to this research in greater detail in "Huidos, guerrilleros, resistentes. La oposición armada a la dictadura" (Fugitives, volunteer militia and freedom fighters. Armed opposition to the dictatorship.) In *Morir, matar, sobrevivir. La violencia en la dictadura de Franco.* (Death, killing and survival. Violence during Franco's dictatorship.) Collaborative book coordinated by Julián Casanova. Barcelona, Crítica, 2002, pp. 200 et al.

2   Vicente Fajardo. Short field work given to Moreno Gómez, a colleague of his at the Institute.

3   Ángel David Martín Rubio. *Paz, piedad, perdón... y verdad* (Peace, pity, forgiveness... the truth.) Madrid, Fénix, 1997, p. 249.

4   Jacinta Gallardo Moreno. *La guerra civil en La Serena* (The civil war in La Serena). Badajoz, Diputación Provincial, 1994.

5   Agustina Merino Tena. '*La represión franquista en Villanueva de la Serena (Badajoz'* (The Francoist repression in Villanueva de la Serena (Badajoz). In *Memoria Antifranquista del Baix Llobregat. El genocidio franquista en Extremadura*, number 12, 2012, pp. 93 et al.

6   Letter fro Nieves Casado Gómez, Madrid 5 April 1999, following the publication of Moreno Gómez' book *Victimas de la guerra civil* (Victims of the civil war). Madrid, Temas de Hoy, 1999.

7   Jerónimo Mansilla Escudero and Luís Miguel Montes Oviedo. *El crimen de El Contadero. Los nueve asesinados de Chillón – 3 de junio de 1939* (The crime of El Contadero. The nine murdered townspeople of Chillón – 3 June 1939.) Ciudad Real, 2009.

8   Bartolomé Cabrera Peralbo. Written testimony. Pozoblanco, 17 October 1986.

9   Letter shown to Moreno Gómez thanks to the kindness of Acisclo Romero Luque's family.

10 Gabriel Carcía de Consuegra, Angel and Fernando López López. *La repressión en Pozoblanco (guerra civil y posguerra)* (The repression in Pozoblanco. Civil war and post-war.). Cordoba, F. Baena, 1989.

11 Documents that in 1987 were kept on file in the Pozoblanco Court archives.

12 Isabel González Jurado and Agustina González. *A dos voces* (Two voices). Cordoba, 2011, pp. 37-38. In this book of memories, Isabel and her daughter describe all that happened, an event that is still well-remembered in the town today.

13 Antonio Gómez Cabello. Emails to Moreno Gómez January 6 and September 12 2007. Notice posted on the *Todos Los Nombres* Internet project, asking for information regarding the whereabouts of his uncle. Link: http://www.todoslosnombres.org/enlaces.

14 Arthur Koestler. *Diálogo con la muerte (Um testament español)* (Dialogue with death. A Spanish testimony.) Madrid, Amaranto, 2004, p. 180.

15 Moreno Gómez personally examined the application of the decree for his book *Víctimas de la guerra civil* (Victims of the Civil War). Madrid, Temas de Hoy, 1999, pp. 407 et al. This calculation of 100,000 killed by Franco between 1936-1939 only, is not an estimate, but a fully researched and documented total.

16 José María García Marquez and Miguel Guardado Rodríguez. *Morón: Consumatum est. 1936-1953. Historia de un crimen de guerra.* (Morón: Consumatum est. 1936-1953. History of a war crime.) Morón de la Frontera, Seville, Planta Baja, 2011, p. 259.

17 *Testimonios de mujeres en las cárceles franquistas* (Testimonies of women in Francoist jails). Huesca, Instituto de Estudos Altoaragoneses, 2004.

18 José Manuel Sabín Rodríguez. *La dictatura franquista (1936-1975). Textos y documentos.* (The Francoist dictatorship (1936-1975). Texts and documents.) Madrid, Akal, 1997.

19 Arcángel Bedmar. Lucena. op. cit., pp. 220-221

20 Case No. 128.712, Archives of Territorial Military Court I, Military Government, Madrid. Proceedings instructed by Col. Enrique Eymar. José A. Cepas *El Lobito*, and Alfonso Días *El Parrillero* were shot by firing squad 21 February 1946 in Madrid, in the same group as the famous Cristino García.

21 José Maria García Márquez and Miguel Guardado Rodríguez, op. cit., p. 351.

22 Josep M. Solé i Sabaté. *La repressió franquista a Catalunya, 1938-1953.* Barcelona, Edicions 62, 1985, p. 61.

23 Vicente Pascual Soler. Written testimony sent to Moreno Gómez from Cordoba January 19 1979, a short while before he died.

24 Arcángel Bedmar. op. cit., p. 104.

25 Minutes of the Concentration Camps and Prisoners Inspectorate.

26 Francisco Moreno Gómez. *Cordoba en la posguerra.* op. cit., p. 139. Moreno Gómez says that he reported that 15-20% were accused of crimes, which has proved to be an overestimation, as it refers only to those who were actually executed and not to the total number of imprisoned.

27 *Causa General* documents, Cordoba Archives. National Historic Archives, Madrid. Only documents for some of the Cordoba city courts are found here.

28 Emergency Proceeding of the Court, number 335 - Archives of the I Territorial Military Court, Military Governorship. Cited in Francisco Moreno Gómez, *Armed resistance against Franco.*, op. cit., p. 42.

29 These and other tragic examples can be consulted in J. Subirats Piñana. *Pilatos 1939-1941. Prisión de Tarragona* (Pilate 1939-1941. Tarragona Prison). Madrid, Ed. Pablo Iglesias, 1993. Cited in Francisco Moreno Gómez, *La represión en la posguerra*, op. cit., p. 312.

30 Francisco Copado Sánchez. Letter he wrote to his wife in prison in Valencia and shown to Moreno Gómez by his brother Afonso.

31 Causa General (CG) Case file 11,395/39.

32 Bravo Murillo, 19th century radical politician.

33 Document on file at the Belalcázar Municipal Archives.

34 Raphael Lemkin, Polish Representative to the V International Conference on the Unification of Penal Law, Madrid, Octuber, 1933.

35   Baltasar Garzón and Vicente Romero. *El alma de los verdugos* [The soul of the executioners.], Barcelona, RBA, 2008.

36   Carolina Gil Fonce. Interview with Judge Baltasar Garzón, 12 May 2008, on Radio Argentina. Can be downloaded at http://www.informam.nl.

37   Arcángel Bedmar. *Baena.* op. cit., p. 121

38   Idem.

39   José Manzanero, testimony, reported by the author in his book *La resistencia armada contra Franco,* op cit., p. 190.

40   Ana Marcos. *El País Semanal,* Madrid, 19 February 1984.

41   Memories of Rafael Bedmara Guerrero, from Puente Genil, discussed with Moreno Gómez during an interview in November 1981.

42   Arcángel Bedmar. Historian of the civil war in Cordoba province. Several publications.

43   Francisco Merino Cañasveras, *Castro del Río, del rojo al negro* (Castro del Río, from the red to the black). Terrassa, Barcelona, 1979, pp. 101 et al.

44   Letter to Moreno Gómez from José Moreno Salazar, from Osa de la Veja, Cuenca, dated October 13 1985. Book of memoires: *El guerrillero que no pudo bailar - resistencia anarquista en la posguerra andaluza* (The guerrilla who could not dance – post-war anarchist resistance in Andalusia). Silente, Ed. Victoriano Camas, 2004.

45   Claro González. Interviewed by Moreno G+omez in Fuenteobejuna, August 1979.

46   Told Moreno Gómez by Sebastián Gómez in Villanueva de Cordoba 7 August 1982.

47   Juan Negrín Lopez, Republican Prime Minister 1937–39.5

48   José Luna Mata. Unpublished memories. Consulted August 1982.

49   Testimony of Sebastián Gómez, Villanueva de Cordoba, 1982. Reproduced in Appendix II, Volume 3.

50   Francico Poyatos, interviewed by Moreno Gómes in Cordoba, 1982.

51   Francisco Romero Cachinero, interviewed by Moreno Gómez August 1983, Villanueva de Cordoba.

52   Miguel Regalón Molinero, letter sent to Moreno Gómez from Valencia, April 1986.

53   Antonio Ramos Palomares. Oral and written testimony, recorded by the author in Almodóvar del Río in 1982.

54   Arcángel Bedmar. *Los puños y las pistolas. La repressión en Montilla (1936-1944)* (Fists and guns. The repression in Montilla. 1936-1944) Montilla, Ayuntamiento, 2009, p. 105 & p. 143.

55   Antonio D. López Rodríguez. *Cruz, bandera y caudillo. El Campo de concentración de Castuera* (Cross, flag and caudillo. Castuera concentration camp.) Badajoz, Ceder-L Serena, 2006, p. 232.

56   Casimiro Jambonero, *Diario del soldado republicano Casimiro Jabonero* (Diary of Casimiro Jabonero, a Republican soldier). Ed. Victor M. Santidrián Arias, La Coruña, 2004, p. 107.

57   Rafael Sánchez Guerra, *Mis prisiones* (My imprisonments). Buenos Aires,

Alaridad, 11946, p. 210.

58 Arthur Koestler, *Diálogo con la muerte. Un testamento español.* (Dialogue with death. A Spanish testament.) Madrid, Amaranto, 1937, pp. 87-88.

59 Ángela Cenarro. "La institucionalización del universo penitenciario franquista" (The institulization of the Francoist prison universe), in *Una inmensa prisión* (An immense prison), Barcelona, Crítica, 2003, p. 134.

60 Antonio Muñoz Molina. "Guerreros deseanados" (Apathetic Warriors). *El País. Cultura. 13* October 2012.

61 *Guerra de Gila.* Caustic monologue by the comedian Miguel Gila Cuestas, where he, as a soldier, appears to have a phone conversation with 'the enemy'. *Is that the enemy speaking?* 2014. YouTube 17/08/2009 *https://www.youtube.com/watch?v=R7d4Aj4tFA4.*

62 *La Vaquilla.* Comic movie by Luís Garcia Berlanga, 1985. During the civil war, bored soldiers on either side of the Aragon front try to discover how to raise tmorale and depress the enemy. The Republican's idea of boycotting a local festival falls to pieces when both sides get involved in chasing a young cow (actually a bull) who had escaped from the village and had run into no-man's land....

63 Manuel Álvaro Dueñas, in *La gran repressión*, collective work, op. cit. p. 101

64 *Azul.* Cordoba, 21 May 1939.

65 *Azul.* Cordoba, 23 May 1939.

66 Cantador Romero, Catalina. Written testimony. Madrid, 1980. Sent to Moreno Gómez.

67 Minutes of the 15 June 1939 court martial in Pozoblanco against Luis Romero Cortés and other accused from Torrecampo.

68 *Azul*, Cordoba, 23 May 1939.

69 Adriano Romero. Undated, typed memoires, in his family's possession.

70 José Subirats. *Entre Vivències* (Memoires). Viena, 2003.

71 Ramón Alujas, June 12 1939. Ibid., op. cit.

72 Published in the *Boletín Oficial de la Provincia de Cordoba*, February 12 1940.

73 Discussion based on Judge Juan José del Águila Torres' presentation at the IX Congress of Contemporary History, Murcia, September 17-20 2008, entitled 'La jurisdicción militar de guerra en la represión política: Las Comisiones Provinciales (CPEP) y Central de Examen de Penas (CCEP), 1940-1947', 27 folios, Guadalajara General Military Archives.

74 Alejandro Lerroux y García. Spanish politician, leader of the Radical Republican Party during the II Republic. Prime Minister of Spain three times from 1933 to 1935.

75 Eduardo Blanco Fernández. 1981. Interviewed several times by Moreno Gómez in his home in Madrid.

76 Eduardo Blanco's private archives, consulted by Moreno Gómez in Madrid in 1981.

77 Adriano Romero's private family archives, consulted by Moreno Gómez thanks to the kindness of his brother Antonio. Also mentioned in his book *Eurocarrillismo y oportunismo* (Eurocarrillism and opportunism). Bilbao, 1984, pp. 99 et al.

78 Miguel Caballero. Interviewed by Moreno Gómez several times in Madrid from 1980 onwards, and consultation of personal papers belonging to him, by kind permission.

79 Brief witness accounts by his family who received Moreno Gómez at the Paseo de San Francisco de Sales, in Madrid, albeit somewhat unwillingly. Moreno Gómez published his biography in number 17 of the newspaper *Villanueva*, Villanueva de Cordoba, September 1981.

80 This testimony regarding the 'mole' Martín Sanz, written by his grandson Luís 24 May 2003, was very kindly given to Moreno Gómez by José López Gavilán, another of the men who suffered the extreme cruelty and arbitrary actions of Francoism in his home town, Espiel, and in Quintana de la Serena, where his father was murdered 18 September 1938. López Gavilán has published a small book of memories entitiled *Aquellos duros tiempos. Anecdotario* (Those hard times. Anecdotal accounts.) Cordoba, 2004.

Table 1. List of Francoist concentration camps housing ± 500 prisoners from La Rambla village in 1939

Campo de concentración de Alcalá de Henares
Campo de concentración de Albatera, Alicante
Campo de concentración de Alcoy, Alicante
Campo de concentración del Castillo de Santa Bárbara, Alicante (2)
Campo de concentración de la Plaza de Toros de Alicante
Campo de concentración de Almería
Campo de concentración de Teruel, Aragón (2)
Campo de concentración de Aranda de Duero
Campo de concentración de Guardiola, Barcelona
Campo de concentración de Horta de San Jorge, Barcelona (3)
Campo de concentración de Deusto, Bilbao (2)
Campo de concentración de Los Escolapios, Bilbao
Campo de concentración de Cáceres
Campo de concentración de Puerto Real, Cádiz (2)
Campo de concentración de Rota, Cádiz
Campo de concentración de la Plaza de Toros de Castellón
Campo de concentración de Ciudad Real
Campo de concentración de Daimiel, Ciudad Real (2)
Campo de concentración de Manzanares, Ciudad Real (4)
Campo de concentración de Puertollano, Ciudad Real
Campo de concentración de La Granjuela, Cordoba (3)
Campo de concentración de Valsequillo, Cordoba
Campo de concentración de Benalúa de Guadiel, Granada
Campo de concentración de Bucos, Granada
Campo de concentración de Padul, Granada (5)
Campo de concentración de Pinos Puente, Granada
Campo de concentración de la Isla de Saltés, Huelva
Campo de concentración de San Juan del Puerto, Huelva (3)
Campo de concentración de La Especia (?)
Campo de concentración de León
Campo de concentración de Lérida
Campo de concentración de La Aurora, Málaga (2)
Campo de concentración de Málaga (2
Campo de concentración de Miranda de Ebro (5)
Campo de concentración de Ronda, Málaga
Campo de concentración de Murguía, País Basco
Campo de concentración de Camposancos, Pontevedra (2)
Campo de concentración de Corbán, Santander (2)
Campo de concentración de Los Carmelitas, Tarragona
Campo de concentración de Reus, Tarragona
Campo de concentración de Manel, Valencia
Campo de concentración de Porta Coeli, Valencia (8)
Campo de concentración de Orduña, Vizcaya
Campo de concentración de Zamora
Campo de concentración de Toro, Zamora

Source: Jesús Maria Romero Ruiz. *Recuperación de la memoria histórica de La Rambla.* La Rambla, City Council, 2010.

Table 2. Teachers executed in Cordoba Province the first months of the coup or died later of other causes. 1936-1949

Name	Age	School	Date died	Cause	Place
Agapito de la Cruz López de Robles	42	President of FETE Cordoba	17 Nov 1936	Executed	Cordoba
Antonio Baena Moreno	34	Pozoblanco	17 Nov 1941	Exceuted	Cordoba
Antonio Martínez Gutieérrez	?	Public School No. 3	1 Aug 1936	Executed	Cordoba city
Antonio Mendez Gómez	34	Industrial Elementary	28 Sept 1936	Executed	Cordoba city
+ Antonio Molina Fuentes	25	City Councillor	30 July 1936	Executed	Cordoba city
Aurelio Pérez Cantero	27	Dir. Symphony Orchestra	8 Aug 1936	Executed	Cordoba city
Blas Gajero López	26	Montoro	9 June 1941	Executed	Cordoba
Eduardo Ruiz Yepes	26	La Rambla	16 Aug 1936	Executed	Cordoba
Enrique Fuentes Astillero	46	Instituto Seneca	20 Aug 1936	Executed	Cordoba city
Fernando Ferdández de Haro	55	Private. Villanueva de Cordoba	26 May 1949	Executed	Villanueva de Cordoba
Fernando Mata Povedano	?	Montemayor	26 Sept 1936	Executed	Cordoba
Francisco Dueñas Llergo	25	Pozoblanco	4 Sept 1936	Executed	Cordoba
Francisco Duque Iñiguez	41	Nueva Carteya	9 Apr 1937	Executed	Seville
+ Francisco Molina Fuentes	35	Puente Gentil	30 July 1936	Executed	Cordoba
José Gómez Cárdenas	41	Nueva Carteya	9 Apr 1937	Executed	Cordoba
José González Cantillo	35	Nueva Carteya	9 Apr 1937	Executed	Cordoba

José Pérez Arenas	33	Nueva Carteya	27 Dec 1936	Executed	Cordoba
Juan de Miguel Budia	23	Palma del Río	? 1936	Executed	Cordoba
Juan García Lara	29	Instituto Seneca	17 Aug 1936	Executed	Cordoba city
Juan Robles Relaño	28	Aguilar de la Frontera	Summer 1936	Disappeared	Aguilar or Cordoba
Manuel Camacho Parejo	61	Escuela Normal	2 Aug 1936	Executed	Cordoba city
Modoaldo Garrido Diez	41	Vistahermosa, Director FETE	10 Aug 1936	Executed	Cuesta del Espino
Pedro Aljama Siles	29	Fuenteobejuna	7 Oct 1936	Executed	Fuente-obejuna
Santiago Dionisio Gil Diaz	33	Fuenteobejuna	16 Oct 1936	Executed	Fuente-obejuna
Tomás Cortés Rodrígues	29	Priego	13 Aug 1936	Executed	El Tarajal
Adalberto Serrano Rodas	54	Peñarroya	?	Encephalitis	?
Antonio Fernández Carreiro	56	Villaviciosa	? 1939	Tortured	Linarea jail
Benito Cordobés Herencia	52	Espejo	6 Aug 1936	Presumed executed	Montilla
Galo Adamuz Montilla	45	Belmés, active member FETE	7 May 1942	Pneumonia	Cordoba
Juan Manuel Nacarino	63	Private teacher, Palm del Rio	16 Oct 1941	Uremia	Cordoba
Manuel Torralbo Cantador	?	Private teacher, Villanueva de Cordoba	? 1948	?	Cordoba

SOURCE: Moreno Gómez research; + Brothers; FETE – Union of Teachers

Table 3. Victims of the Law of Fugitives March/April 1939 Pozoblanco, Villanueva de Cordoba & Neighbouring Townships

Name, age, profession, where died/buried

POZOBLANCO CIVIL REGISTRY AND BOOK OF BURIALS

31 March 1939
> Tomás García García, 75, farm worker, Pozoblanco

6 April 1939 at 8 p.m.
> Manuel Linares Ruiz, 52, farm worker, El Viso
> José Ollero Sepúlveda, 47, farm worker, El Viso
> Cristino Cebrián González, 41, farm worker, Pozoblanco
> 2 Unknown. Mass grave.

7 April 1939
> Esteban Pérez Ruegón, 48, Villaharta
> Antonio Ortiz Arias, 58, Pozoblanco

8 April 1939
> 3 Unknown. Mass grave

10 April 1939 at 8 p.m.
> José Romero Moyano, 30, peasant, Torrecampo
> Felipe Madueño Orellana, 25, Villaralto
> Juan Serrano Tornero, 28, Pozoblanco (at 3 p.m.)
> Antonio Bociagas Ruíz, Santa Eufemia
> 1 Unknown, in Pozo del Concejo, Pozoblanco (Eulalia Grande's nephew)

11 April 1939, at 6 p.m.
> Gaspar Jiménez Cebrián, 25, manual worker, Villanueva del Duque

12 April 1939, at 4 p.m.
> Antonio Blanco Balsera, 51, miner, La Granjuela
> 2 Unknown. Mass grave.

13 April 1939, at 1 p.m. and 4 p.m.
>Juan Rísquez Ranchal, 25, farm worker, Torrecampo
>Francisco Romero Sicilia, 42, farm worker, Torrecampo
>Sebastián Marquez Romero, 19, shopworker, Torrecampo
>José Sierra Murillo, 32, farm worker, La Granjuela
>3 Unknown. Mass grave.

14 April 1939
>Antonio Conde Gutiérrez, 27, farm worker, El Viso
>Andrés Pérez Alamillo, 33, Torrecampo

15 April 1939
>Aciclo Romero Luque, Torrecampo
>Miguel Romero Vila, farm worker, Torrecampo
>Juan Puerto Zarco, 55, farm worker, Torrecampo
>2 Unknown. Mass grave.

16 Aril 1939
>Manuel Rodríguez Fernández, 23, Constantina

17 April 1939
>1 Unknown. Mass grave.

18 April 1939
>Manuel Gómez Carrillo, 53, El Viso
>Emiliano Jordán Obejo, Torrecampo
>7 Unknown. Mass grave.

19 April 1939
>Justo Casado Escribano, 56, Villaharta
>1 Unknown. Mass grave.

20 April 1939, at 3 p.m.
>Alfonso García Torrico, Villaharta
>Modesto Rubio Rubio, 21, Villaralto
>Rafael Luna Gómez, 22, Villaralto
>Antonio Muñoz Gómez, 24, Villaralto
>Paulino Sánchez Muñoz, Villaralto
>Manuel García García, Villaralto
>3 Unknown. Mass grave.

21 April 1939
Blas Risco Salazar, 49, Siruela (Badajoz)

22 April 1939
8 Unknown. Mass grave.

25 April 1939
Antonio Herruzo Cejudo, 26, Pozoblanco
Máximo Castro García, 28, Pozoblanco
Diosdado García Cruz, 49, Pozoblanco
Pedro Ferández Calleja, 30, Pozoblanco
Domingo Sánchez Redondo, 52, Pozoblanco
Manuel Rubio Garrido, 25, Pozoblanco
Diego Alcaide Porras, 34, Pozoblanco
Rufino Fernández Alcaide, 49, Pozoblanco (from torture)

28 April 1939
1 Unknown. Mass grave

VILLANUEVA DE CÓRDOBA CIVIL REGISTRY
(Moreno Gómez' note in brackets)

27 March 1939
Miguel Salado, 40, farmer, refugee from Amodóvar del Rio.
cause of death: gunshot wound in the precordial region
(Killed by two Moroccan soldiers before they raped the women on the farm)

1 April 1939
Pedro Capitán Moreno, 45, cattle breeder
Killed on his farm. (He was later found in a well).

8 April 1939
Benito Pozuelo Regalón, aged 28.
Died in hospital from pulmonary congestion (Tortured)

20 April 1939 at 4 p.m.
When trying to escape from their guards (according to Military Police Headquarters M., S. 8):
Juan Huertas Torralbo, 45, manual worker, Villanueva de Cordoba

Juan Pedraza Garcia, 44, businessman, Villanueva de Cordoba
Diego Montoro Luna, 66, cattle breeder, Villanueva de Cordoba
Manuel Cruz Coleto, 25, bricklayer, Villanueva de Cordoba
Sebastián Molinero García, 45, manual worker, Villanueva de Cordoba
Bartolomé Calero Sánchez, 46, manual worker, Villanueva de Cordoba

24 April 1939
Gabrino Cabrera Expósito, 37, blacksmith
Died in La Preturilla jail (Torture and suicide)

23 May 1939, at 5 a.m.
Miguel Huertas Caballero, 43, bricklayer
cause of death: cerebral haemorrhage (Tortured)

MISCELLANEOUS COURT RECORDS - Deaths

CONQUISTA COURT
12 April 1939
Juan Luque Moreno, 24, outside the village

MONTORO COURT
20 April 1939
Miguel Cañuelo Lozano, 30, baker, Marmolejo

VILLARALTO COURT
25 April 1939 in the outskirts of Pozoblanco
The 6 individuals listed earlier for Pozoblanco on the 20th of the month
Also Felipe Madueño Orellana, 24, manual worker, Villaralto;
recorded in the Pozoblanco Book of Burials
10 April at 4 p.m.)

EL VISO COURT
14 April 1939
José Aranda Murillo
Rafael Díaz Helvio

2 May 1939 – between Pozoblanco and Villanueva (by soldiers who were guarding them)
Manuel Teno González
Juan García Rubio

Marino Ramírez Moyano
Juan Muñoz Hoyo
Also José Ollero Sepúlveda and Manuel Linares Ruiz, recorded in the
Pozoblanco Book of Burials 6 April

ADAMUZ COURT
15 April 1939. Cause of death: gunshot wounds
José López Ayllón, farmworker
1 Unknown, farm worker.

HINOJOSA DEL DUQUE COURT
19 April 1939, in La Gutierra
Sebastián Martínez García, businessman, Hinojosa
Prudencio Garía Gómez, 50, retired Lieutenant, Santander
Pablo Gómez Leal, 18, manual worker, Hinojosa.

APPENDIX I

Written testimonies from prisoners regarding the first concentration camps at the end of the war and afterwards. Prison diaries and letters.

Descriptions of the journeys to the concentration camps and the terrible days that followed Castuera, Badajoz

<u>José Maria Carnicer Casas</u>, a Catalan from Reus, Tarragona, October 19 1987. Written testimony sent to Moreno Gómez October 19 1987 regarding his story that begins March 26 1939, when he is taken prisoner at the end of the war.

- "We drove through Alcaracejos without problems, but when we arrived at Villanueva del Duque we saw advance Nationalist troops entering the village. We were stopped a couple of kilometres ahead and told that we should go no further as Franco's troops had entered Hinojosa del Duque. We jumped off the truck and I went off on my own looking for our own troops, but I had not gone even one kilometre when on my right, I saw a column of Moroccan soldiers and on my left, some infantry. Obviously, IU chose the latter. In other words, I surrendered to the first group I found… to members of the 13th Volunteer Infantry Regiment.

  We took to the road. We arrived in the village of El Viso. I was left in a fenced-in yard where I remained for 6 days. I only had one meal during all this time. The rest of the time I had to make do with a little bit of bread… I and the other prisoners were near the rod and from there we watched truck after truck full of all kinds of armed men: Falangistas, troops, Moroccans, infantry. I was also overwhelmed by the number of priests and Guardia Civil who accompanied them. No wonder. It was three years since I last saw them.

  Every day we were told that we would be fed the next day… The camp was continuously filing up and hope for food decreased with every day that passed. One day we were told that we were to be moved to another camp. Four Guardia Civil arrived: two took their place at the head of the column and two at the end. We began walking. There were so many of us. That day we got as far as Villanueva del

Duque, some 14 kilometres distant. The next day they gave us a little bread and we continued our march. This time we went further – 31 kilometres to Peñarroya-Pueblonuevo where, we were put into a large yard; I think it was a flour factory. There were a lot of women at the entrance to the yard who threw us pieces of bread over which we fought ferociously.

The next morning, we started walking again until we arrived in La Granjuela. Again, that damn village. There, I first met Vicens de la Selva. The first thing he asked me was whether I had any tobacco. When I replied that I hadn't, he gave me a few small boxes. What a great guy. La Granjuela was a disaster: not a single house remained standing. Three times it was taken by the Nationalists and three times we took it back. We remained there ten or twelve days. We lived between four walls, with another fellow from Reus, one from Montroig, another from Cabra del Campo, another from Valls (called Gomis), another from Cambrils (called Sentís), another from the province of Lérida (called Florensa) and me. In the morning, they gave us a little bread and the occasional can of sardines for two people; sometimes, for a change, it was a can of tuna, but always for two people. To that, we added our own special stew. The fellow from Montroig would go out into the fields and bring some grasses that we boiled in a pot we had found and when they were well cooked, we ate them.

One afternoon, they told us that we would resume our march the next day as we were being transferred to another camp. They gave us our rations for the following day: a roll of bread and a can of sardines per person, but when had to happen happened. We had built up such a hunger that as soon as we returned to our 'hotel' we devoured all that we had been given. Then to bed, to wait for the next day and find out where we were going.

We set off very early. I cannot tell you exactly where we went. All I can say is that we became exhausted. We crossed some towns and villages and knocked on the doors of the houses, asking for a bit of bread. The only thing we received were words of consolation or the oft-repeated cry: *Sons of sorrow!* I think that we marched 50 kilometres that day. As if something was missing that day, it began to rain mid-morning. I walked with Florensa and I remember that whenever we stopped to sit a moment, one of us had to keep standing so as to pull the other up because our joints were no longer working on their own. Another memory from that day: as we marched through an acorn oak forest we foraged for acorns, like so many pigs. I don't know how many of us there were, but there must have been at least a thousand. That evening, we arrived at Castuera and that particular ordeal was over.

We were ordered to stay in the town and sleep on the streets and in the squares. It may seem impossible that we didn't all take off, but I believe that the thought never crossed our minds as the only thing we could think of was how to fill our stomachs. They told us that the next day we would be taken to the concentration camp and once we got there, we would be fed… I imagine that the fearful spectacle we must have presented the townspeople must have been quite disturbing. As you can imagine, we looked terrible. Wearing one shoe and one espadrille, washing any way we could, unable to shave, we must have looked extremely macabre.

Florensa and I squatted back to back in a corner and waited for the next day. At dawn, we left for the concentration camp. It could not have been very far away because I remember that we got there relatively quickly. We were each told the number of the hut that we were to occupy. With small door and large windows, there was very little living space per person as each hut was occupied by 80 men. We had to beg pardon to turn around. Also, we were unable to change clothes or shave during the entire time that we remained in the camp…

I am now going to talk about our infamous concentration camp. A very large yard. In the centre, some flagpoles where the flags of Spain, the Carlistas and the Falange waved. The huts were arranged around the yard. On one side, the kitchen. On the other, the latrines, which were no more than trenches that we had to dig beforehand… If we needed to go to the toilet at night, we had to call the guard and a soldier with a fixed bayonet would accompany us… And we were not even criminals! The campo was surrounded by a double row of barbed wire, a trench 3 metres deep ad 6 metres wide, then another double row of barbed wire. And finally, all around the camp, machine gun posts.

In the morning, at sunrise, reveille. We had to fall in immediately in front of our hut; if we didn't, the sergeants would enter through the windows and lash us with whips. Once we had fallen in, we were made to sing the set hymns: the hymn of the Legion, of the Falange and the *Orimendi*. We then left the camp, two by two: on one side of the gate there was a mountain of pickaxes and on the other, a mountain of shoves. There we remained until noon, when we returned to the camp to eat. Depending on the day, we got either cold or hot food. When it was cold food, we were given a small can of tuna. When it was hot food we went to get it, two by two, and were given a ladle of water and some chickpeas. In the evening, we got either cold or hot food, the opposite of what we had been given at lunch. As far as brad was concerned, we were given less than half a roll; every hut was allotted 30 or 35 rolls, but as there were 80 of us, we each got less than half a roll.

As far as personal hygiene was concerned, I can say that the whole time that I spent in Castuera we were never given any water in which to wash. As most of us had no razors, we just let our beards grow. As we couldn't wash our clothes, we were a mess. As far as bugs were concerned, in addition to being abundant, they were all kinds and colours. One of our pastimes was racing body lice.

When we first arrived at the camp, the guards were Falangistas. When we went out to work, there was a guard for every 8 prisoners. In addition to making sure that we did not escape, another one of their duties was making sure that we did not sleep on the job. These guards always carried rifles. A month or a month and a half later, the Falangistas were replaced by soldiers, and we all benefited from that."

José Maria Carnicer was able to leave Castuera well into the month of June 1939, thanks to a good behaviour reference his father and other persons were able to obtain for him. He had been interned for three months.

Miguel Cruz, from Villanueva de Cordoba. Interviewed by Moreno Gómez in Villanueva de Cordoba, Summer 1980.

- "The arrival of the Nationalist troops in Villanueva marked the beginning of mass detentions in the town, led by individuals such as Diego *El Chunga* Cachinero, Vicenti *Salado* Muñoz, Bartolomé *Berenguer* Cepas, Emilio *El del Lunar* and others.

I left for Castuera in the convoy that had been organized in the town for this purpose, April 20 in the afternoon. The previous convoys had been sent to Los Blázquez and Valsequillo. There were some 200 of us who were first taken to the bullring in Puertollano. From there, we were sent to Castuera by train. Castuera camp was bursting with prisoners, so much so that the commander had to be forced to accept us. Our names were recorded and then we began to suffer all kinds of punishment, privations and hunger. We were made to work digging an enormous 3-metre-wide trench enclosed

245

on either side with barbed wire. Improvised showers and building huts, each of which contained some 80 prisoners.

Juan – *El de la Loma*, one of those who managed to escape from town earlier when he heard they were looking for him, returned to Villanueva where, unfortunately, he was caught. Diego Ranchal, brother of the Mayor of Villanueva del Duque was also there with me. Another good companion was Pablo Agenjo, who was shot near Cardeña by the Guardia Civil, under the Law of Fugitives.

To be released from the camp, one needed good behaviour references from people of good standing in our home town. I was finally released after two months in the camp, with no more food than the bread roll and can of sardines that I was given when I left."

Francisco Romero. Interviewed by Moreno Gomes in Villanueva de Cordoba, August 1983.

- "An edict was published in Villanueva according to which everyone who had served in the Rojo Army had to present himself, without exception, excuse or pretext, for transportation to Castuera concentration camp. Several hundred of us did so and we were taken from Villanueva Station to Puertollano. There, we slept under the stars with frequent threats from the guards in case anyone should think of escaping.

  We left for Castuera and there we were received by the commander, who greeted us with an aggressive and insulting speech. The repression began in the camp. Many died there, either from the beatings they received from the Falangistas, from hunger or the cold, as there were practically no sheds. We managed to build ourselves a kind of hut with brush from the nearby hills."

From Valsequillo to Castuera via Los Blásquez

José Prats Martí

- "After two or three days in Valsequillo, we were taken (actually, we took ourselves) to Los Blásquez, to something that looked like a concentration camp. In effect, the village had been surrounded by rows of barbed wire, on either side of which there were two 7 x 8 metres dirt trenches that showed the footprints of anyone who attempted to cross them.

  One evening we were told that the next day we would be leaving for Castuera. The march was no joke; it was a 50-kilometre walk. In brief, 800 of us left, escorted by or under the custody of – or whatever you wish to call it - some 40 soldiers. Small groups of us were left behind along the way; they just could go no further as we were not given anything to eat and those who had managed to keep something, ate it all at the beginning of the walk. Around ten thirty that night, about 50 of us, guarded by four or five soldiers, arrived in the town of Castuera."

Valsequillo and La Granjuela, Cordoba

<u>Mariano Martín Sierra</u>. Unpublished memoires.

- "Valsequillo and La Granjuela were two villages that had been totally destroyed by the bombing; they were deserted by every inhabitant except the prisoners. The parts of the houses that had not totally collapsed served as refuges and we huddled in them like rats. I shred an attic with 12 men from Madrid, all of whom also were bakers as I was. The stairs to the attic were completely destroyed, so getting up there was a real circus act.

  The commander of Valsequillo was a 'good' Falangista who would frequently order the prisoners to fall in even though many could not even stand because they were so weakened by hunger. Two or three Falangistas, wearing their blue shirts, would walk between the ranks and start looking at us… The unlucky men who were chosen were called out of the ranks, taken away and we never saw them again…

  When I could get up early in the morning, I would go to the place where they threw some garbage; I ate whatever I could find or whatever others who had been there before me had left behin. Potato peelings, banana skins, the occasional mouldy acorn were, in that order, my first, second and third course."

[There was a changing of the guard in Valsequillo May 6 1939 and the Falangista commander was replaced by a militiaman. Martín Sierra was sent to the workshop.]

  "As letters arrived from everywhere, our work consisted, among other things, of opening them and sending them to the office. These frequently consisted of allegations and accusations against prisoners from various local authorities in each prisoner's home town, all of which put that prisoner's life at risk. This is where 'my job' began. In the absence of the commander, we would gather the accusations that we considered to be the most damaging and, very carefully, I would go outside and tear them up or burn them wherever I could, returning to my post of if nothing had happened."

Rafael Bedmar Guerero, from Puente Genil but interned in Higuera de Calatrava, Jaén, described his experience in his diary *Memorias de uma guerra.*
- "I presented myself to the Military Headquarters in Linares. They had a file on me that contained a good behaviour reference from persons of recognized standing but they only referred to when I had lived in Linares. I was sent to a room that was set aside for suspect individuals and was full of people. An hour later, our hands were tied together with wire and we were taken outside. When we left the building, we met with a convoy of trucks full of prisoners collected from other centres. We were put onto one of the trucks, crushed so tightly against each other that we could not move. The convoy took off down the middle of an empty road, flanked all around by armed soldiers.

  We had no idea whatsoever of where we were going. Continuing along bad roads, we rode a hundred and fifty kilometres until we arrived at a town that had been destroyed during the war., Higuera de Calatrava, located between two lines of fire. Only the church remained standing. We were shoved off the back of the truck and as soon as we landed, several officers beat us on our backs with their riding crops, urging us to move faster.

  As best we could, we removed the wires from our hands. We were crushed together in a building as if we were objects. We could not move and there was little air to breathe. Any toilet functions had to be made where we stood, stuck to each other. Several prisoners who were unable to survive the cruel treatment died. The next day we were taken out and our names were taken down at some tables they had set up on the street. As we left the table, some soldiers gave us a roll and a can with three sardines. Other soldiers led us to ruined houses that remained more or less standing.

  There was an attic in the prison that served as a torture chamber. Eight days after I was imprisoned, I was taken to this attic. An official sat at a table, a typewriter in front of him, and he was flanked by four other officials, riding whips in hand. There was a chair in front of the official who was writing and in the centre of the roof, under a metal beam, a wooden stool. Above the stool, hung some ropes and some wires. I was seated in front of the scribe and told: 'All right, we think this is going to end soon. You are going to tell us what we want to know. A friend of yours has made a statement. He says

248

that you accompanied the military patrol from Malaga and that you went to his house to arrest him; that they wanted to kill him on his doorstep but you interfered and you saved his life. Therefore, we believe that you are a person of some standing among the Rojos and so you must know who it was who killed Tom, Dick, Harry. Many of those responsible are here, imprisoned in the cells, and you are going to tell us who they are. So, begin singing and we'll finish quickly.'

I knew what to expect. I absolutely refused everything. If I were to turn in just one of comrades, they would make me talk, and talk, and later shoot me with them. When they saw that no amount of soft-talk could get me to talk, the guard who was interrogating me punched me in the nose and knocked me off the stool, onto the floor, blood pouring from my nose. Two other guards then picked me up. The one who was interrogating me asked: 'Have you had enough or do you want some more?' I continued to deny everything.

They then tied the rope around my neck with a loose knot and tied my hands with wire, made me stand on the stool and, when they were ready, asked: 'Make up your mind or you'll leave this room for the cemetery.' I knew that one way or another I was going to die and I preferred that it be this way. At least; I would take nobody with me. I continued to deny everything they asked. My tormentors got angrier and angrier and they pulled the noose and the wires tighter and tighter. I was almost hanging from my neck. A single ick at the stool and my body would be left hanging.

One of the tormentors took off one of my shoes and sock, got hold of my big toe with some pliers and pressed down on my toenail. He crushed it so hard that I felt my toe go numb. When my toe turned black, they removed the pliers. They then took some tweezers and, getting hold of my nail, pulled it so hard that all I felt was a strong electric shock that reached right into my brain. They did the same thing with my other foot and I almost went into shock. I couldn't feel my legs any longer; I felt pins and needles all over my body. I closed my eyes so I couldn't see their faces. They kicked my stool and I was left hanging like a sack of sand. One guard swung me back and forth. When my body swung towards the guard in front of him, the latter would give me a lash on my back with his riding crop. They did this forty or more times, back and forth, whip lash after whip lash... I stopped counting. I only felt as if my feet were being wrenched from my body.

They stopped once or twice and sat me on the stool. Always the same questions, but I could no longer hear a thing. I almost fainted.

Furious with my resistance, the guard who was in front of me kicked me in the stomach. I felt a large knot rising from my stomach and vomit coming into my mouth. My tormentor stopped and almost fell on the bloody garbage that littered the floor. Few seconds later, I lost consciousness.

When I opened my eyes, the jailor, with a bucket and cloth was wiping my body with watery vinegar solution. I was in a small cell, apart from the others. I don't know how I was taken to that place. My body shivered convulsively, I had a very high fever. I struggled between life and death for a week. Little by little, I got better. My physical strength once again enabled me to resist. No sooner had I recovered from the torture that I was taken from the small cell and put in amongst a hundred or more other prisoners. My comrades were horrified when they saw the scars that covered my body. They shook with fear as the thought that they, too, would be called to be interrogated.

When the time came to give me the food my mother had taken for me, the jailer threw it down the toilet to make the others think I had eaten it. They still discovered nothing. I hid the undershirt that I wore during the torture: pieces of skin from my back stuck to the cloth. I scooped out the crumbs from a loaf of bread that my mother sent me and returned it to her with the shirt hidden inside, so that the jailer did not see what I had done.

When my family discovered the mistreatment that I had been subjected to, my mother took that shirt and ran through the streets shrieking like a madwoman: 'Criminals! Murderers! Look what they have done to my son!"

We were divided into companies, and a leader was appointed for each one. Once the operation was over, a bugle called us to go to the square and listen to a speech by a colonel. For more than an hour, we were harangued by the colonel as he ranted about the wonders of the Glorious Movement and the marvellous Caudillo that God had miraculously sent us. We then had to fill out forms with our names, telling where we were caught by the Movement, political affiliation, etc. Naturally I wrote down what I saw fit.

Several days passed and we were put to digging a ditch, which I soon understood would serve as a mass grave. As the information arrived from the various hometowns, they called out those who had the worse references, shoved them into the basement at the command post (it filled up every evening), and the next morning took them out and shot them."

Excerpts from Prison Diaries and testimonials regarding conditions in penitentiaries of all kinds and especially the _sacas_[xxi].

Antonio Baena Moreno. Pozoblanco. Unpublished personal Diary of his experience in the local jail July 19 1940 – September 12 1940, before being sent to Cordoba. Sentenced to death by garrotte April 22 1940, executed November 17.

- 19 July 1940. Last night we entertained ourselves for a few hours playing cards, smoking cigarettes. I fell asleep at midnight and, as usual, woke up at the ill-fated hour. It appears that all is quiet and no saca is expected. The spyhole to the cell remains open… The danger is past!

  21 July 1940. Day of euphoria and optimism. As there are no sacas on Sundays, we can enjoy the luxury of a long siesta and at night, sleep without worrying.

  22 July 1940. Today marks 3 months since I was tried. Three short months! How much more human it would be for the sentences to be carried out quickly. Families would stop having to spend what they don't have and once it was all over, they might begin to accept the situation. Unfortunately, it appears that what they want to do is to cause the most possible suffering.

  26 July 1940. We were apprehensive all night. After we were locked down for the night, a companion assured us that a large saca was planned. We stayed awake all night, waiting for dawn. When I awoke, the fatal hour had almost passed. If I had been taken in that saca, I think I would have reacted as if it were a simple _paseo_. I was very tense and felt an Olympian hatred for my enemies. I have reached such a state that I am indifferent to whatever is going to happen to me. With every passing day, I am more and more convinced of the utter irrationality of these procedures.

  27 July 1940. Saturday. Two days of safety. Everyone is sleeping in total relaxation.

  6 August 1940. It seems there are rumours of a tragedy. This morning we all thought there was going to be a saca; a truck stopped by the gate at the fatal hour and many of us thought that our time had come. We were pessimistic all day. We have heard that several death

---

xxi A _saca_ was the removal of inmates from a jail cell around midnight, to be shot at dawn.

251

sentences were commuted to several years in prison and when this happens, this is always followed by executions.

4 September 1940. I woke up in the middle of the night while the light in the corridor went out; I thought that the dance had begun. I waited, patiently smoking a few cigarettes, until daybreak. The fatal hour had passed.

12 September 1940. The blow that some of us had been expecting, fell. This morning at dawn, three companions of ours were shot. It has hit us like a bomb… It was about four in the morning, almost two hours earlier than the usual fatal hour, when they closed the spyhole in the cell door, a sign that the saca was about to begin. The fact that it started so early led us to believe that it would be larger than usual and that many of us would be executed. We all thought that we would be one to have this terrible bad luck. Of the numerous sacas we have lived through, none caused such fear. Regarding two of the comrades who were shot, there were no serious accusations against one and the other was a kindly person by nature, incapable of harming a single soul.

When I awoke, the spyhole was already closed. I asked my cellmates, who were already sitting on six baskets, how long it had been closed – only a few minutes, they replied. Because of that, I endured a good couple of hours expecting it to open and to hear them call my name. You can never appreciate how relative time is in such situations. If it were not because we are used to suffering… two hours like this would be enough to age you a dozen years. All the same, when I went into the patio, the ravages of those two hours were etched on our comrades' faces. Everyone looked as if he was just recovering from a serious illness."

Arthur Koestler. Hungarian-born British war correspondent, captured and imprisoned by Nationalists after the fall of Malaga February 5 1937. Several monographs and extracts from his diary entitled *Dialogue with Death. A Spanish Testimony.*

- "I was taken to a large empty room. In one corner, there was a stool on which I was made to sit. Two Guardia Civil sat down in front of me, next to the door, with their rifles on their knees. We remained that way for some time.

   I then heard screams coming from the patio and a young man whose chest was bare and covered in blood was brought into the room. His face was battered, covered with cuts; for a moment I thought that he had been run over by an engine, Holding him up by the armpits, they dragged him to the other side of the room, screaming and moaning. The Faangistas who were dragging him spoke to him softly: 'Quiet man, we are not going to beat you any more.' They took him out through another door, closed it, and a few seconds later we heard the noise of beatings, slaps and kicks. The man screamed at regular intervals.

Then there were a few seconds of silence. I could only hear rapid, panting breaths. I don't know what they did to him during those seconds. He then screamed again, just once, an abnormally sharp cry; and finally, he was quiet. A little later the door opened and they dragged him across the room in which I was seated, to the patio. I could not tell whether he was dead or simply unconscious. I did not have the guts to look at him any longer. Later, a second victim passed through this room and was subjected to the same treatment; and then another.

■ "That night, when I opened my eyes, it was still not daylight; I had been awakened by a noise. I listened: someone was singing. He seemed to be very nearby. The man who was singing appeared to be in one of the solitary confinement cells across from mine. I sat up, and my heart stopped: he was singing the *Internationale*.

He was singing off-key; he was hoarse. Obviously, he was hoping that the other condemned men would join in, but nobody did. He sang alone in his cell, in the jail, and at night… I was hearing the Internationale being sung by a man who knew that he was about to die… He repeated the chorus two or three times, stretching it out so that the song would last longer. I stood up, went close to the door and, teeth chattering, raised my fist… and I got the feeling that everyone in all the cells around me were standing next to their doors, like me, solemnly raising their fists in a gesture of goodbye.

He sang. I could see him before me: unshaven, broken nose, tortured eyes… but none of us sang along with him: we were too afraid.

…About four in the morning, there was a noise in the corridor. A saccharine voice was reading out a list of forty or fifty names; some doors opened, then were slammed shut. The sound of steps, whispering, mysterious noises.

I then put my ear instead of my eye next to the spyhole. I could only discern the sound of a long line of men shuffling along the corridor, slowly, hesitantly, as if they were walking against their will. The sound of steps slowly disappeared. Forty or fifty men were walking to their death.

I lay down on my cot and asked myself if the singer was one of them, and whether they would be shot one by one or in groups; with rifles or machine guns…

I must have just fallen asleep when I was woken by the same saccharine voice that I had heard earlier that morning. This time it came through the bars of the window in the cell, from one of the patios that I had crossed when I was looking for Sir Peter. He read out twenty or thirty names. I couldn't count them exactly; the length and complexity of Spanish surnames confused me. On this occasion, all those who heard their names called had to answer 'present' and when someone didn't reply quickly enough, the saccharine voice burst out wearing. The guard then called out:

'Everyone in cell number 17.'

'Everyone in cell number 23.'

Koestler was transferred to Seville prison, where he lived in constant panic. There, in April, he befriended a young farmer who had been recently arrested.

- "He was taken prisoner ten days ago on the Almeria front and was sentenced three days later. He, like all prisoners of war, is accused of 'military rebellion'. As we walked in the patio, Nicolás told us about his trial before the Seville court martial. It lasted three minutes. The presiding magistrate read out the name of the prisoner, his place of birth, and the name of the place where he had been captured. The Prosecutor asked for the death sentence and added: 'I am only sorry that I cannot put this pinko in a cage and send him to Geneva before we shoot him, to show the League of Nations the kind of miserable individuals are its supposed defenders of justice and democracy.'

  …I offered to lend Nicolás a book but he said he couldn't read. He said he had hoped to learn how to read after the end of the war.

14 April, in the morning, Koestler looked for his friend in the Seville prison patio.

"Nicolás has disappeared. Rest in peace, Nicolás. I hope that it all happened very quickly and that they did not make you suffer too much. How little you were, small Andalusian farmer with slightly bulging, soft blue eyes, the eyes of the poor, of the meek."

Mid-April, Koestler again witnessed one of many sacas in Seville prison:

- "I had fallen asleep and woke up a little before midnight. In the dark silence of the cell, seeped in the nightmare of three hundred sleeping men, I heard a priest praying softly and the tinkling of a hand bell.

  A cell door opened, the third one on the left, on the same side of the corridor as mine, and someone called out a name. A sleepy voice asked: '*Que? Qué pasa? What's up?*' The priest raised his voice and rang the bell more loudly.

  In his cell, the sleepy man understood. At first, he just groaned then, in a muffled voice, begged: '*Socorro! Socorro! Help!*' They took him away. I could hear him yelling outside. Still, the distant sound of shooting was some time coming.

  Meanwhile, the priest and the prison guard had opened the door to the next cell; cell 42, the second one on my right. Again: '*Que pasa? What's up?*' Again, the praying and the hand bell. This prisoner was sobbing like a child. He called for his mother: '*Madre! Madre!*' Again: '*Mother! Mother!*' They took him away.

  They then went to the next cell. They called my neighbour, but he said nothing. He was probably awake and, like me, prepared. But when the priest finished praying he asked softly, as if he were speaking to himself, 'Why must I die?' The priest answered him with a few words, spoken solemnly but quite rapidly: 'Have faith. Death is deliverance.'

  They went on to the next cell. He was also prepared. He said nothing. Whilst the priest prayed, he began to sing the *Marseillaise* softly, but after a couple of stanzas, his voice chocked and he, too, began to sob. They took him away…"

- "Our hearing became miraculously acute. We heard everything. The nights on which there were executions, we heard the telephone ring at 10 o'clock. We could hear the guard answer. We heard him saying 'the same… the same… the same…' at regular intervals. We knew that the guard checked a name with each 'the same'. We did not know whose names were checked, not if one of us was on the list.

  The telephone always rang at 10. That left us to lie on our cots, waiting until midnight or 1 o'clock. At midnight or 1 o'clock, we could hear the strident ring of the night doorbell. The priest and the firing squad had arrived. They always arrived together.

  The sound of opening doors, the tinkling of the hand bell, the priest's praying, the shrieking calls for mercy, cries for mothers…"

The steps came closer down the corridor, they moved away, they came closer, the moved away. They stopped at the cell on one side, they went to another cell in another wing, they returned. The priest's voice always rang out clearly: 'Lord, have pity on this man; Lord, forgive him his sins. Amen.' We lay on our cots, our teeth chattering like castanets. Every night, we placed our lives on the scales and every night, somebody fell out."

19 April: "These past three days all the noises from afar were blanketed by the voice of a man who sobbed and called for his mother non-stop. His cell must have been near mine. Every time that I put my ear to the door I could hear him. I asked Ángel who was the man who did not cease crying. He is a militiaman, he said, who was sharing the cell with his brother but who has been alone since Friday night."

22 April: "I get this burning desire to murder that small, brown, fat priest who rings the hand bell every night."

25 April: "Sunday afternoon they brought another prisoner in and put him into my old cell, number 41. I watched as they brought him. He was very young, only about fifteen or sixteen years old. I heard a guard say that they would be coming for him that night. At that moment, the young man in cell 41 began banging on the door; he must have heard everything. 'I don't want to die!' he screamed. '*Madre! Madre!* Mother!* Help! I don't want to die! Help! Help!'

His cries echoed all along the corridor. The entire prison became uneasy. Confused, but clear, sounds came from all the cells. The young man kept yelling and they took him out of that cell and put him in some special solitary confinement cell… They had to call some more guards to help them.

A little later – before 10 o'clock ' the priest came down the corridor, probably to take the young man's confession. A guard called out for some brandy. At ten, the phone rang. I heard them answer 'noted' three times… It was not about 11 0'clock. I fell asleep. The next day I discovered that they had shot three prisoners before midnight. The young man had not shouted. They may have used the brandy to get him drunk."

Pablo Uriel. Zaragoza. Young doctor arrested in the autumn of 1936 and imprisoned in the General Military Academy prison at San Gregorio,

Zaragoza. Author of *Mi guerra civil*, book of memoires and frequently quoted by Moreno Gómez, reporting on sacas in that jail.

- "There was no singing at 6 p.m. At that time, every conversation flagged. Nobody paid attention to what was said because everyone was tense, trying to hear sounds from the workshop. At once, the entire prison acquired a single ear whose hearing was sharpened and particularly acute. If one thought that he had understood the noses that came from the workshop and he wanted to confirm his doubts, all he had to do was bang on the door to his cell. A soldier would soon appear: 'What do you want?' – 'I want to go for a pee.' – 'Not now. Nobody can leave his cell'

  This meant that the Falangistas were in the workshop, bringing with them their hateful lists, and that in the next few minutes five, six, maybe ten of us would begin their final journey. The silence continued until one heard the car engines speed away from the prison.

  The four of us I our cell were feeling the usual anguish. In the silence of the prison, we heard steps coming down the corridor. Immediately, someone touched the lock on our door. When the corporal opened the door, I could see four men standing there; the corporal was holding a sheet of paper but he was not looking at it. He looked at sergeant Sangrós: 'You're on the list; please come with me.'

  Sangrós did not appear surprised and he did what we least expected: moving automatically, from many years' habit, he shook each of our hands. As he walked to the door, he turned around: 'If any of you manage to get out of here, don't forget to go and see my mother. Tell her that I am only sorry for her.'

  We sat down, despondent and silent. The same question went round and round our heads. Who decided who would die? Why? Sangrós died without knowing shy. As we put the sergeant's papers in order, we took note of his mother's address in case one of us could visit her."

Another day, another of his cellmates was taken: Leonardo Navarro, a university student who was alarmed because he had seen one of his classmates, a rabid Falangista, arrive at the prison. His cellmates attempted to calm him down, but:

- "The lock turned in the door and the corporal called out: 'Leonardo Navarro, please come with me.'

Hearing this, Leonardo suddenly calmed down. Calmly, he looked at us with reproach, and pronounced the unexpected: 'See how I was right? I knew it, but you didn't believe me.' Then, quite simply and calmly, he removed his watch, gave it to us and walked out impassively and determinedly."

Yet another day, a Nationalist sergeant was put into Paulo"s cell:

- "He was from the Siguenza front, he had fought bravely and he swore that he had been cited in the Order of the Day for his valour. Two of his brothers had been shot in his hometown earlier and he had enlisted to avoid being also eliminated. He was ordered to present himself urgently to the Zaragoza barracks.

    At noon, there was some unusual coming and going in the prison: 'Everyone get into your cells! Hurry up!' As I returned to my cell from the patio, I saw the shape of an automobile in the shade and in the corridor, next to the workshop, some blue-clothed Falangistas… The door to our cell opened and the corporal told the Sergeant to go with him. The latter, not having any idea of what was awaiting him, got up cheerfully and followed the corporal without saying a word.

    The corporal later returned to get the sergeant's cape and he spoke frankly to those of us in the cell, appearing that he had to get something off his chest: 'It was a terrible scene. At the moment that the Sergeant was coming out in handcuffs, about to get into the Falangista's car, his wife arrived with a lunchbox of food. She went crazy and we had to calm her down in the workshop.'

APPENDIX II

Selected eyewitness accounts of violence and torture in the provincial townships

Villafranca de Cordoba

<u>Santiago Cepas Romero</u>. Released from Castuera concentration camp and rearrested as soon as he returned May 20 1939. Letter to Moreno Gómez from Valencia April 20, 1984.

- "I was working in the forge at Romero's home. May 20, 1939, I was arrested in my own home by two Falangistas armed with rifles, the so-called 'El del Lunar' and the other, 'El de los Dientes'. They said: 'Santiago, you have to come with us to answer some questions, then you can come back here.' That is what they told everyone.

    I was taken to La Preturilla. There I found quite a few Falangistas, an SIPM lieutenant, and a Guardia Civil called Medina. The lieutenant told me to sit on a chair without a back and to unbutton my shirt collar. Next, the soldiers who were on either side of me, rained beatings on me until they got tired. Meanwhile, Medina, typed away without asking me anything. At the end he told me. 'Sign here, and if you don't, you'll get another beating.'

    Some days earlier they had killed several prisoners by beating them with rods, one of whom was Gabino. Rafael Diéguez Montes, another prisoner, unsuccessfully tried to kill himself by throwing himself from the veranda onto the patio of the jail. He was taken to Burgos and later executed by firing squad in Cordoba

    The evening on which I was arrested, another ten or twelve fell: Isidro Díaz Luna, Miguel 'El Merino', Juan José Ventijera, Miguel Silva Jurado. We had all been brutally beaten. They smashed. Miguel Silva's toes by stomping on them. They tied Calixto Santos up because he stood up to them, and almost killed him. From La Preturilla, we were taken to the City Hall jail and from there, some days later, to Romo's house and, finally, to the Fuente Vieja Schools, from where we were taken to be court-martialled.

    In Fuente Vieja, many evenings Falangistas came to beat us. One of us who was most often beaten was Lope Ibáñez. The poor fellow was left half dead and we had to move him by dragging him along the floor on a blanket; he was covered with wounds. The guards threw buckets of water onto him to revive him. He was later executed by firing squad... The Villanueva beatings were our daily bread."

Miguel Regalón Molina. Describing his personal experience in 1939 before the end of the war. Letter to Moreno Gómez from Valencia, April 1986.

- "In Villanueva, a so-called Don Juan, the military judge, and a SIPM lieutenant, were two of the most sadistic individuals one can imagine. I never dreamt that there could be people who remained impassive as men fell beaten and bloodied before them, with nothing with which to treat their wounds or stop the bleeding.

  I didn't think that my body could resist the punching, beatings, kicks, being hit with rifle butts, and beatings with a fire tong. I was not allowed to speak during the interrogations. The only ones who spoke were the tormentors, on my right and on my left, two monsters dressed in military uniforms, all of which took place in front of a large crucifix and a group of Señoritos and Falangistas.

  When I fell to the floor unconscious, they would throw me into the patio. When I came to, I crawled on my hands and knees into the warehouse to join my comrades. In my case, I urinated blood, I lost consciousness three times from the beatings, my whole body was one swollen haematoma and my genitals were swollen from their kicks.

  At daybreak, several drunken men would come in with the sergeant of the guard, revolver in hand, and they would begin running on top of the men who were lying down, stomping on their heads and stomachs, under the pretext that they were taking a count of who was there. They then brushed us with a toilet brush covered in shit to show that we had been counted. Not content with such savagery, they took Eugenio Palmera, and me and others out to the patio, slapped us a stood us up against wall, pointed their revolvers at our chests and asked us whether we wanted to die facing them or shot in the back. The whole time they passed bottles of alcohol from one to the other until they left... until the next night.

  The little food and clean clothes that my family sent me were kept by the soldiers, until my family ran out of clothes to send. My life as an inmate, like that of so many others, was saved by miracle, as my file was marked 'dangerous Rojo'. When I was transferred from one prison to another my handcuffs were so tight that they cut my circulation and my hands turned black On one occasion I begged them, please, to loosen them a bit and they just tightened them even more. I spent several days without being able to move my wrists. I began to believe that I was alive by a miracle and even that they might kill me once and for all.

Before the interrogations, during which only the tormenters spoke, they made me pass through what they called the 'tunnel of laughter', which consisted in sending the prisoner between two rows of soldiers who beat him, slapped him, kicked him in the butt and more, so that when he got to the interrogation room he could not stand up. I remember two bastards there: one called Higuera and another Vigorra. This happened in the Fuente Vieja Schools.

In La Preturilla it was the Guardia Civil who took charge of the first interrogations, using the same procedures. There Pedro Juan El Chunga read out the charges, promising the prisoner that he would not be executed. Then they killed him.

In La Preturilla barracks, in the patio, on the left, there was a room or cellar with wooden beams and a pulley with a rope. The floor was covered with sawdust, stained red with blood that was also splashed on the walls. I was put in there but I was not hung. During my interrogation, when only the tormentors spoke, a group of individuals roared with laughter whenever we fell to the ground."

Francisco Romero Cachinero. Describes his passage through the Fuente Vieja Schools jail. Letter to Moreno Gómez from Villanueva de Cordoba August 1983.

- ■ "The Fuente Vieja group of schools was the most horrendous jai that was ever known in Villanueva, where hundreds of persons from Valle de los Pedroche, from Adamuz, from other townships, were tortured. A frequent major contributor to the torture was Matías Malaleche Pedraza, accompanied by a group of local political bosses who treated the inmates brutally.

  The inmates depositions were taken at the Guardia Civil headquarters, always in the presence of several Falangistas who told the Guardia Civil of the prisoner's importance and determined the extent of the beating given by a short, grubby soldier from Galicia who would stand behind the inmate, who was seated on a chair without a back, and beat him without pity until he fell unconscious.

  These statements were then sent to Judge Calero and the inmates were forced to sign everything that he wanted, or else... more beatings. The Judge's principal assistants were Pepe Higuera and Pepe Delgado. The scribe was Luis El Plancha. We also had to put up with the beatings from the Falangistas themselves. They

261

would come to the prisons, having drunk a bit too much, take the inmates they wanted, without any opposition from the prison guard, and beat them until they were exhausted. They threw buckets of water over the inmates to revive them. This is what happened to Crisóstomo Marcelina Romero Badia and to José El Papel, two of several soldiers who crawled back to the cell where they remained many days in bed without being able to move. The one who did the most beating was Pedro El Chicorro Muñoz Ruiz and who was known for his violence."

Sebastián Gómez. Speaking of the Fuente Vieja Schools jail and the notorious Judge Juan Calero, during an interview with Moreno Gómez in Villanueva de Cordoba August 7 1982.

- "It happened in Fuente Vieja jail, I believe in Summer 1939. Matías Pedraza and others, including El Tiraor, arrived and the latter shouted: 'Pay attention, those whose names I shall now call out: Francisco Sánchez Muñoz, Antonio El Piñon, Juan El Ramo Antonio Caado, Pedro Torralbo, José Maria Sánchez and Francisco Illescas. It was about midnight. First, he slapped Piñón, then Beatas, but the latter threw a can of olives at El Tiraor and they spilled all over his head whilst Matías Pedraza burst his guts with laughter. El Tiraor continued, now beating Illescas and saying: 'I am going to leave you with a souvenir for the rest of your life', he tore a piece off Illescas' ear with his teeth and stomped on it.

  It was a dissolute, cruel and uninhibited environment that the victors created around the defeated. One day, Matías Pedraza violently slapped José Jurado, ex-Mayor for the Radical Party during the Republic. This was an act of vengeance by Matíaz Pedraza who one day had been fined by the ex-Mayor because of some scandal involving prostitutes. Clearly, many of the worst civilian acts of violence during the post-war period were acts of revenge for personal reasons."

- "October 19 1939, Juan Calero came to Fuente Vieja to interrogate Francisco El Villaralteño Rubio Gómez, who had been arrested. When Francisco appeared before him, the Judge turned to the right-winger Pedro El Ché Benito and handed him a lash saying: 'Come on! Avenge your father's death!'

  Although Pedro Benito was reluctant to do so and as the Judge insisted, he hit him only twice with the lash. Juan Calero stood up, furious, tore the lash from his hands and launched himself against the prisoner with a rain of blows, knocking him to the ground. Calero then stood over him and began to kick him. Two soldiers came up to help the Judge; one stood on Francisco's head and another on his stomach."

Pedro Molinero

- "Emilio El del Lunar came to arrest me and I was taken to the Guardia Civil barracks in La Preturilla, which also housed the SIPM headquarters. When I arrived, there were more than 40 right-wingers present – rich men, Falangistas and accusers. Some of them had been arrested in Jaén or Totona during the war and others were accusers because of the death of some relative. Nevertheless, when I came in, most of them left, probably because I was not considered to be all that important a prisoner.

    After I made my deposition before the SIPM lieutenant, Guardia Civil Corporal Galiánaiz immediately came and stood next to me and it was he who beat me the most. Also present to punch me and wield their ships were the Muñoz Fernández Salado brothers, two soldiers and some others.

    The whole business of my making a deposition was to force me to sign a declaration that I had belonged to the local War Committee, but as I denied it, they beat me. One rich guy added a codicil to the supposed declaration: 'This is the person who handed our farms over to the workers', because I had been a member of a collective of small landowners. Generally, the great names of the oligarchy did not show their faces there, although they were in direct contact with Judge Juan Calero.

    After spending some time in City Hall jail and in the house on Calle Conquista, I had to attend a second inquiry by the Military Court in the Lauriano House. There they read the declaration they had previously written and continued to insist that I had belonged to the War Committee. Roughly speaking, the accusations were all the same for everyone had participated in the taking of the town, had belonged to the Committee, had spoken against right-wingers, and so forth. Assisting Judge with the declarations were Luis El Plancha as recorder and Francisco Madueño. The beatings were given by two officers, a 2nd Lieutenant of Artillery and another 2nd Lieutenant from a Regular regiment. The latter, El del Gorro Colorao later became tragically famous as Teniente Pepinillo who sowed terror in Espiel and ended up committing suicide.

The principal figure was the examining magistrate, Judge Juan Calero Rubio, whose greatest explosions of rage appeared when he felt the inmate was not receiving enough of a beating.

In summer 1939, the inmates were transferred to the Fuente Vieja Schools. That Judge went there from time to time, accompanied by the terrible Lieutenants, to take declarations. I cannot forget the horrendous beating of José Escribano whom they wanted to sign an admission that he had participated in shooting 21 Nationalists. Fortunately, Escribano was exceptionally able to get them to remove that accusation, and he survived. Miguel Carabinas Cabezas, Juan Lorenzo Cucharas Cantador and many others were also brutally beaten.

Antonio Chaparro. Interviewed by Moreno Gómez in Villanueva de Cordoba, 1981. He had served as a prison guard in the Preturilla barracks.

- "One of the worst torturers was Bartolomé Berenguer Cepas who had been appointed head of the municipal police and who reached the rank of sergeant during the war. One day I saw him in action with corporal Caiániz, under the orders of Leopoldo Mena the SIPM Lieutenant. They brought in a prisoner when I was on guard duty and made him kneel with his hands tied behind his back. They accused him of having taken a pot-shot at Torrico and whenever he corrected them or denied something, the lieutenant gave a signal and they beat him non-stop.

  At one moment, he begged for some water from a pitcher that was nearby, but in the pitcher there was nothing else except dirty water and cigarette butts. They left him in a coma. When they too him to the hospital they dressed him in a new shirt because the one he had been wearing was so bloody it had stuck to his back and they had to cut it off. I believe he died in hospital. This unfortunate inmate had served in 1936 as a guard over right-wingers who had been arrested, among them El Tiraor, who was not getting his revenge."

Antonio Pedraza García. Denounced by Pedro 'Sangento Chicorro' Muñoz because the two had fought each other when they were boys. His son Bartolomé Pedraza recalls a moment in his childhood. Revenge ran deep.

- "No sooner was my father taken to jail, that he received terrible beatings that broke three ribs. The ones who beat him were Juan Lucío, Pepe Delgado, Miguel Higuera's sons, the Falangista Lara and El Chicorro. One day my mother tried to talk to my father through a window that gave onto the street but at that moment a lieutenant came out of the building and ordered my mother to strip naked. On another occasion when I went up to the top floor of the house on the Calle Conquistador to see him, Falangistas who were there kicked me down the stairs."

Francisco 'Curro Beatas' Sánchez Muñoz. Member of the Izquierda Republicana executed May 17 1940. Report from his daughter **Antónia Sánchez Cerezo**, Villanueva de Cordoba 1983. (Francisco Sánchez' farewell letter from prison to his family is reproduced in Volume 2.)

- "At the end of the war, my father tried to escape to the hills to join Julián Caballero, but whilst at the El Minguillo farm he was betrayed by his nephew Mateo Sánchez and he was arrested then and there. My father was taken for interrogation many times, always getting the same beatings. He had been a member of the local War Committee, but he also saved many right-wingers, such as Alfonso Fernández, and he was able to prevent others from setting fire to Dionisio Pedraza's house, whose son Gregorio was Mayor at the time. The one who beat him the hardest was Miguel Higuera's son, Pepe.

  The first beating he received was given him by the scandalous Berenguer, who beat him until he lost consciousness. When the Falangistas heard that my mother, Agustina Cerezo, was publicly complaining about the way they were beating my father, they ordered her to go to La Preturilla and, in her presence, gave my father another savage beating. They sent her away with the warning 'Now go round telling people that we are beating your husband'.

  When my brother Francisco tried to say goodbye to Father, they told him to take 50 pesetas and they kept the money, made him wait all day, but in the end, he was still unable to bid him farewell. After he was executed, my mother asked for my father to be buried in a niche in the cemetery. She was told to take 60 pesetas to pay for the niche. She had to sell her sewing machine to get the money, but they kept it and my father was buried in the mass grave."

Pedro 'Cuadrado' Torralbo Gómez. High-ranking member of the Communist Party, served as a Captain in the famous Garcés Battalion for which he was executed after the end of the war. His son **José Torralbo Rico**'s story of visit to his father in jail is harrowing.

- "We went to the square because we knew they were interrogating my father, hoping to see him. There, a member of the public took only me by the hand and led me into the City Hall. The jail was on the left as you go in. There was a thick wooden door and behind it, another one of wire netting. I was just a child, but they opened the doors and let me in so I could see my father. It was horrible: a pile of men, leaning against each other, semi-conscious, vomiting and bleeding.

Among them – I can't forget it – I saw my father sitting on the floor, his back against the wall, legs stretched out before him and his head fallen on his chest, bleeding from his mouth, from his ears, from all over his body. Today I understand what that man must have felt when he saw me, if he even saw me, because I remember that they took me out immediately... His tormentors were Francisco El Tiraor, assisted by Berenger, Pedro El Barbero Serrano, and others."

Juan Cantador Zamora. A totally innocent man caught in the Francoist circle of torture and death. This is his daughter **Catalina Cantador Romero**'s story.

- "From the day after the war was over until April 17, my father had to present himself daily at the Court by order of the Judge. On that date, finding that he had not committed any crime, the Judge suspended the order for his arrest and set him free.

  <u>May 10 1939</u>, at midnight, Vicente Salado and a soldier arrived at his house and took him to La Preturilla, where he was tortured and afterwards informed that there was an allegation against him. He was tortured so savagely that strips of skin from his back stuck to the shirt he was wearing. He was allowed home.

  Two days later, he was again taken to La Preturilla where he was again beaten in such a barbaric manner that, because his screams could be heard from the street, they closed the road to traffic. When I took his breakfast to the jail the next morning I could confirm that he was unable to move because of the beating he had received. He went home. The next day, he was back at La Preturilla and again suffered a new beating.

  I, his daughter, who from the street could hear my father's terrible screams, am telling you this. How I saw how Bartolomé Capas (head of the municipal police= come outside sweating, with a whiplash in his hand, and go back in with a case of what appeared to be beer. I also saw the following individuals, among others, leave the building: Vicente Salado, Francisco Tiraor, Diego El Chunga, Pepe Liñán, Miguel Fernández and Fuctuoso El de los Dientes. The son of Rojas, from the tavern in the square, stood guard at the door of the building.

From where I stood t the door of Morales' home, I could see how the priests who were in the church poked their heads out through the vestry door each time they heard a scream, closed the doors and windows tight, never saying a word or making the slightest gesture of disapproval.

May 24 1940 my father was tried by the military court in this town and sentenced to death. At the court martial, the prosecutor asked Luísa Doctor, the accuser, to point out which of the accused men sitting on the bench had killed her husband. The good lady said she did not recognize any of them and that she had heard nothing said about my father.

The Judge then asked the accuser if she had ever spoken to the accuse, to which she answered that he might have spoken to him as she might have spoken to anyone. He then asked her why she said he had killed her husband. 'No sir', she replied. 'Judge Juan Calero must not have heard me correctly. What I said was that it was someone from outside one of Juan Elías' agents.'

The Prosecutor asked my father why had had signed a confession and my father replied that it was because he was beaten until signed. The Prosecutor then asked him whether he was ever beaten. Again, my father replied that yes, he had and that it would impossible for him to name all those who beat him as he often lost consciousness. The examining magistrate himself had beaten him.

When the court martial was over, my father was taken to Fuente Vieja prison. No sooner did he arrive there, that a 2nd Lieutenant, the Judge and José Higuera entered the patio and, in the presence of the other prisoners, beat my father until he lost consciousness. I could hear his screams from outside the building, on the street. From the day on which he was condemned to death until September 26 1940 when he was transferred to Cordoba prison, we never saw him again."

Antonio Ramos Palomares. From Almodóvar del Rio. Soldier returning after the defeat.

- "After we reported in 1939, at first it appeared that our tormentors had some consideration for the defeated, but when a little time had passed, when it appeared that no-one else was turning himself in, they [Francoists] began with their interrogations. As we swore that each one of us would be responsible for his acts and that no one would accuse anybody of anything, they began with the mistreatment and the punishments.

There was the case of Ángel Plazuelo Lozano, who had been a guerrilla sergeant and who they wanted to give details of the services he had rendered in the Rojo zone and the names of the companions who had fought with him, but he remained faithful and was tortured to death. He was immediately thrown down a well to simulate a suicide and the next day they took his body to the cemetery in a garbage truck.

From then on, all of us were continuously beaten. They divided us into two groups: one in the Santo Hermitage (the larger one) and another in the Trades Union building. In November, they thought that one of us had escaped, something they could not prove, and because of that they held us incommunicado. We were beaten and tortured at all hours. In my case, my comrades ha to feed me for more than fifteen days because they had destroyed my arms during the sessions of torture."

APPENDIX III

Court Martial Prosecutor José Ramón de La Lastra y de Hoces' comments in a court martial; rebuttals, appeal statements, requests for assistance

Baena Court Martial May 20 1939, excerpts of which are reported in the Cordoba *Azul* newspaper May 23.

- "**Prosecutor José Ramón de La Lastra y de Hoces** began by stating that the most serious feature of the tragedy was that a criminal fury was raging through every town and across every field in the province. He resisted the desire to analyse the horrifying events described.

    Referring to one of the accused, he began: 'Cristóbal Díaz Borrego, aged 6, accompanied his father to the Casa del Pueblo. At the age of 12 he had become a socialist republican. That father, instead of giving his son a Christian education, instead of guiding him along the paths of culture, allowed him to go to places where hate and resentment came together, he opened the road to where his son would later go to commit crimes of this nature, crimes that would bring him close to the gallows. That father taught him how to hate God and not to love his Fatherland. The responsibility of his having done so should weigh like a slab of stone on his conscience. This is a painful and terrible lesson for those who do not supervise their sons with true love, who do not instil in their souls the virtues of men, as opposed to the instincts of wild beasts.

    To think that one can throw three fellow men alive, into a bonfire, and that one can stuff another person's mouth with a burning rag when he called for his mother in the hour of his anguish and torture, is horrible. And that this is done in the name of liberty, equality and fraternity is doubly monstrous. The dastardly Republic has made us witness these inhuman vandalisms. Those responsible for these dramas do not deserve to live, neither inside nor outside of Spain.

    I stand before the Court to ask for justice. We must remember Pradera the martyr's words: 'The life of a criminal is worth nothing, when compared to the life of the victim.' Our Caudillo the man who providentially has saved the Fatherland with his magnanimous heart, has offered his pardon to those whose hands are not besmirched with blood. But that promise is also a promise for justice to be applied to those who have blood on their hands. Given these facts, I have only one word for the accused: Since you have not known how to live as Christians, know how to die like those who do not behave like men.

On behalf of His Excellency, the Head of the Spanish Government, I as for …

[The sentences this Judge always asked for were death, by firing squad on by garrotte, or by both.]

Rafael Bedmar Guerrero. Testimony in rebuttal of **Prosecutor José Ramón de La Lastra y de Hoces'** allegations at Rafael's trial in Cordoba Court October 25 1939, when he spoke in his own defence. Presiding Judge: Evaristo Peñalver.

- "Don José de la Lastra began his speech as follows: 'President, gentlemen of the Court! What you have here is the scum of society. This is the Marxist rabble that we must remove from every town in Spain. Everyone here will say he is innocent, but who killed our priests? Who burned our churches? Who killed our lawmakers? How many of ours have fallen for God and for Spain! The blood of our finest asks for Marxism to be exterminated from our society.'

  He concluded his lengthy discourse, one directed at the emotions of the Francoist cause, with these last words for the presiding Judge: 'President, gentlemen of the Court: all the accused are guilty of high treason against the Fatherland, al their hands are sullied with blood, all prefer to make a fist rather than extend an open hand, all are Marxists and for all of them, without exception, I ask for the sentence of death. I have spoken.'

  The officer who was acting as Public Defender limited himself to asking the Court for clemency for the accused. Turning to us, the Presiding Judge, declared: 'As we know beforehand that you will all say the same thing, let one of the accused stand and speak for all.' Not even one did so. So, he turned to me and said: 'You, the youngest, stand up and speak on behalf of your companions.' The guard who was standing behind me indicated that I had to stand up.

  I began: 'Sir, I was only 16 years old on July 18. I did not think that by putting myself at the service of the legal Government of the Republic I had committed an act of high treason. I have served the Spain that you all one day swore to defend. If I had burned churches, as I am accused of doing, which is not true, I would have destroyed buildings of stone, but you are destroying human buildings.

Mr. President: Have we been permitted to see an exact information of everything we have been accused of? Have we been allowed to appoint our own defence? How is it possible to condemn innocent men who were not permitted to prove their innocence? How, seated in front of a cross of Christ, can you apply the same methods that were used by those who crucified him?'

The presiding judge slammed his gavel on the table and shouted out in anger: 'Enough! This session of the court is adjourned.'"

Examples of rebuttals, statements of facts, appeals

Eugenio Jurado Pozuelo. From Villanueva de Cordoba. Appeal against death sentence filed May 9 1940.

- "Dear Sir,

    Eugenio Jurado Pozuelo, aged 33 years, married, carpenter by trade, born and resident in this town at number 13, tried March 13 in this town by court martial that condemned him to the 'ultimate sentence', respectfully presents to Your Excellency, for your consideration, the following comments regarding certain statements that are recorded in my file:

    1. As I was in the fields on July 18, the date on which the Movement began, I had no knowledge of it until the 19th at 3 p.m., which is when I returned to the town. I remained at home or nearby, without anybody asking me to do anything until the 22nd, when I was ordered to leave the town by the Evacuation Committee. I duly set off with my wife and a niece to a farm some 15kms distant from the town, having spent the night on the way in a shed belonging to road workers in the place called Custea del Jaro, together with Alfonso Tintorero, Francisco Serrano and his wife.

    The next morning, as we attempted to continue our move, we were stopped by a truck driven by Arturo Díaz López and occupied by several individuals armed with rifles who forced me to abandon the women who accompanied me and return to a place near the town called La Zorrera, where there was a camp of armed Rojo men and where several members of the right-wing were being held under arrest. I protested vigorously against the mistreatment of some of them and I was listened to, as Juan Pulido Díaz who was one of them, can testify.

    I remained in that location and near the camp from the 23rd until the morning of the 25th, during which there was an attack against the Guardia Civil barracks and the town was retaken [*sic.* by

271

Republicans], events in which I took no part, precisely because I was elsewhere, as I have stated.

On the morning of the 25th, once the fighting had ceased, entered the town by the street on which my parents and I lived, accompanied by Pedro González Valle and a brother and a nephew of his. We separated at the door to right-wing leader Diego Romero Rodriguez' house, without bothering or asking anybody for anything, even though we noted that he was hiding. I returned immediately afterwards to my parents' house.

2. When I went to the Totana Communists, which I did, not for the reasons given at my trial that I wished to aggravate the situation of the right-wingers who were arrested there, but just because I wanted them to do what they could for one of my brothers who had been arrested and who, despite everything I tried to do for him, was still sentenced to 30 years in prison.

3. I was later appointed to the War Committee but after all the bloody events that occurred in this town; I only remained as member for a fortnight. I was appointed Director of the Electrica in this town and was replaced by somebody else to the said Committee.

4. I joined the Communist Party in 1931, the year in which the party became legal and I had no position of any responsibility until well before July 18.

5. I always did what I could to assist right-wingers avoiding as much unpleasantness and trouble as I could to Cristobal Arellano, Diego Romero, Diego Higuera Díaz, Andrés Cabrera Valero, Francisco Ochoa Ortega and José Benítez Caballero. It is totally false that my declarations in Jaén harmed the accused, as Basilio Villarreal and Sánchez Gómez said. Proof of this can be obtained from Blas Carbonero and Bartolomé Torres and others who will speak for me.

Given all the above, the truth of which I swear to by al that I hold dear, that this represents all my actions. It causes me great pain to think that others who were much more extremist that I, have been sentenced to 30 years in jail, whilst I was condemned to the maximum sentence under the Law.

I beg Your Excellency to take all the above into consideration and ask for confirmation of what I said, if you should consider it appropriate, so that my sentence might be lessened.

A favour that I hope I have deserved from Your Excellency, on whose life God might shine for many years to come, for the good of Justice.

Eugenio Jurado Pozuelo
Villanueva de Cordoba, May 9 1940."

Pedro 'Cuadrado' Torralbo. Villanueva de Cordoba. Appeal filed June 29 1940. Ex-Militia Captain, executed one year later, June 3 1941 in Cordoba.

- "Dear Sir,

I, PEDRO TORRALBO GÓMEZ, aged 40 years, married, weaver by trade, resident in this town at Calle Egidio number 23, interned in the prison of this town and submitted to an emergency summary court martial by this Party's Military Tribunal, respectfully presents the following to Your Excellency:

WHEREBY May 1 last [1940], I was tried by the Military Tribunal and as requested by the Prosecution, was condemned to the maximum sentence on the grounds that, under the terms of Article 238 of the Military Code, I was guilty of having adhered to the military rebellion.

The charges laid by the representative of the Law and the subsequent request for the maximum sentence were motivated, without any doubt and I say so with all due respect, to a defect in the summary information that was presented to the Court, given that there re missing elements of information which had they been included in the charges, would have meant that the Prosecutor's arguments and conclusions would have been different and always more beneficial to the undersigned petitioner. The following information was missing from my case file:

FACTS

1. It is not true that I took part in the taking of the towns of Valle de los Pedroches as a Militia Commander. I never held that rank and nobody can say that I participated in that battle in ay of those towns because I was not there nor was I a member of the Rojo militia who went there, as I can prove with witnesses (Miguel Camacho Illescas, es-resident t Calle del Plazarejo).
2. It is also false that I took part in the attack on the Guardia Civil barracks, as I was elsewhere and not in this town when that occurred, as Juan Vacas Captain, prisoner in this prison, and Diego Camo Rico, Miguel Camacho Illescas (both members of the right-wing) and others who were detained can attest to, and furthermore, I attempted to stay with them to ensure that nothing would happen to them.
3. When I arrived at Fuente Vieja square, where two people died and several were injured, the events had already taken place,

as Juan Gómez Calero (Calle Conquista), Juan José Fernandez Moreno (Calle de Herradores) and others who were wounded there can attest to. They can also confirm that I was threatened by death y someone from out of town called 'El Trapero' who pointed his gun at me because when I arrived at the place where these events had occurred, I said that those responsible were murderers and strongly condemned what they had done.

4. Julián Caballero, the Mayor at the time, ordered me to La Charquita, where the Guardia Civil and several other countrymen surrendered, to prevent, if I could, any bloodshed. In the first place, I did not participate in the fighting there, because that was not my mission and in the second place, the fighting was over when I arrived there. Soon after the Mayor and other members of the Frente Popular took charge of the detained and took them back to town along the Pedroches road to Villanueva de Cordoba. I returned along the road to Torrecampo to search for my family which was in Dehesa de Navauenga, and I did not return to town until the next day when I discovered that almost all those who had been detained at La Charquita had been shot.

5. I strongly deny all moral and material responsibility in those murders. I was, at all times, against such occurrences, as Juan Camacho Castillo, imprisoned in this jail, and others can attest to and in fact I wrote to the Frente Popular condemning that which was going on. Seeing that this was not working, I suggested that Juan Camacho Castillo should call a meeting of the Communist Party, which he did, and I repeated my condemnation of the crimes that were being committed, describing them as murder. Faced with my opposition and that of others, such s Juan Camacho, we were able to get many to react and more than a few took our side until we all agreed that nobody should be killed. I firmly believe that if there had not been the intervention of individuals who were strangers to the town, we would have managed to enforce the agreement we had just reached.

6. My actions and behaviour towards the members of the right-wing was to protect them as much as I could, as can be proved by José Liñán (Calle del Torno) and by Pedro Cano Rico (Calle de la Preturilla), in whose case, when I discovered that they were looking to arrest him, told him to remain hidden in the house in which he was until I could come and get him out without danger. Nobody can say that I arrested anybody, that I pillaged any house, that I molested anyone with words or deeds, as I never was an

organizer or member of the War Committee. Likewise nobody can say that I was ever seen with that Committee, not even at a distance, because I found its actions totally repulsive.

I BEG YOUR EXCELLENCY to read the above, to reflect upon my account and after considering everything that I have said, nullify the sentence to which I was condemned and order the revision of the indictment. This is the justice that I hope to obtain from the high principles advocated by Your Excellency, on whose life God may shine for many years to come.
Villanueva de Cordoba, Military Prison
June 29 1940
Pedro Torralbo

ADDRESSED TO THE CORDOBA JUDGE ADVOCATE
Names of witnesses, written in the margin: Casildo Cabezas, Juan Cantado Díaz, 'Vizco' Zurita, José Liñán (Calle del Torno), Pedro Gómez Calero (Calle Contreras).
Also written in the margin: Manuela, have somebody type this for you and send it to me so that I can sign it. Kisses to the children. With my love, your husband, Pedro Torralbo."

Adriano Romero. Villanueva de Cordoba. Important pre-war labour leader in Cordoba. Belonged to the Central Committee and the Political Bureau of the PCE during the Republic, Frente Member of Parliament for Pontevedra, fought as a Major in the Militia. Arrested March 11 1940 in Ciudad Real but not tried by court martial until August 1941 in Seville when he condemned to death. Retried September 1943 in Granada by a second court martial, was sentenced to death for a second time. Thanks to the efforts of several influential individuals, six months later his sentence was reduced to thirty years in jail.

- "José Espina told me that my indictment was not yet finalized and that it contained some very serious accusations and if the case was quickly taken to trial there was a risk that I would be speedily liquidated, but if I let it rest, which was the best thing to do, it might one day be taken down rung or two. We agreed that he would gradually work on this."

A whole new year passed during which he was able to gain some time, until there was a change in judges.

- "My dossier was closed, just as it was, and given to a Plenary judge so that I could be informed of the charges against me. I was alleging that

275

the case had not yet been prosecuted and that the serious accusations that were made were false, and I asked that a series of witnesses be interrogated to corroborate my affirmations.

The judge told me that what I wanted would need six months to process and he could not agree to my request, which led me to understand that he had been ordered to proceed... Consequently, I was also not interrogated. Finding myself in the worst conditions, without any witnesses nor any documents in my defence, I was taken to trial by count martial in August 1941...

This first court martial was also remarkable, because as I was very well known in Andalusia for my political activities, they wanted to give the people of Cordoba the idea that I was being tried in a Court of Justice. Contrary to the custom by which defendants were tried in groups, I appeared alone before the Judge. The Prosecutor, who had long worked for that Provincial Court and who knew of my activities before the war, presented a very detailed description of my political activities, that I never denied.

As I knew that I would not be allowed to speak at the end of the trial, I adopted the tactic of defending myself during the interrogation stage in order to destroy all the non-political accusations against me, to wit: of having served as Secretary of a People's Court that tried and sentenced to death the Guardia Civil who rose against the Government in Villanueva de Cordoba, my birthplace; of having organized a Column Unit in Almeria with which I disembarked in the Port of Motril. Both these charges, under Article 37 and 28 of the Code of Military Justice, were penalized by death on the grounds of military rebellion and leader of a rebellion.

As these charges were so obviously false, I had no trouble rejecting them. I could not have participated in the said Court because on that date I was on the front line in Granada. The Column that I was accused of organizing was organized by the Almería Military Headquarters and I only took command of it after it had disembarked.

The Prosecutor, after making a long and detailed report on this could no longer justify the charge of military rebellion, asked the Court to adjourn so that he could organize his notes. When he returned, he presented another report in which he modified his conclusions, stating that he could only accuse me f 'supporting the rebellion', which required a sentence of life imprisonment.

When the Court returned, I was condemned to death, on the grounds that during the court martial I had shown that I was the same enemy as always."

Letter from Colonel Joaquín Pérez Salas to Bartolomé Fernández. Letter written June 16 1939 from Garay Barracks, Murcia prison, in reply to Bartolomé Fernández' request for assistance with his own appeal. Pérez Salas was executed August 4 in Murcia.

"Murcia, June 16 1939

To Bartolomé Fernández, Cartagena

My dear friend,

From the first days of April, I have tried by every means available to me, which naturally were not very many, to find out how you were doing. I had earlier tried to get you out of Murcia, which I was unable to do because your arrest almost coincided with mine. In mid-April I thought I heard your name called on a list in the San Julián patio, where people replied to their second surname; but I could do nothing – I was incommunicado – please confirm whether you were there.

On the 17th I was transferred to this place and again I tried to find out about you but I could not find anyone who could give me any news. Today, I finally got a letter from Cifuentes, whose whereabouts I also did not know, where it appears that you are there to where I am writing.

In addition to my natural interest in getting news from you, the reason I decided to bother you was to offer to do anything that I can to help you. If you need, or for any reason are interested in, a declaration from me, always in agreement with the truth that I believe in and that you deserve, you must tell me as soon as you can, with details of what you need and to where I should send my statement. It may appear more logical for such declarations to be submitted indirectly, rather than at the request of the interested party, most especially in cases such as yours, where by telling the whole truth the declarant is doing the greatest favour. Even so, I did not wish to do so without first telling you, because it would be simpler and more effective if you could tell me exactly which points could be of greatest interest in my declaration.

Of course, as I said earlier, everything that one can declare regarding you, in respect of the truth, must be in your favour; but I must again strongly insist that it is far best that, for me to do so, you must at least in part tell me what it is you wish me to declare and to whom I should address my declaration.

I believe that you did very well, as I did, even though you had, s I did, all types of means at your disposal to avoid these small bothers, precursors of other greater ones. At least, one way out is to confess to the accusation of a crime that neither you nor I committed, regardless of whether others believe us or not, and to accept the punishment, no matter how severe it is, as in my case with the full knowledge that we did our duty.

I resume that you have heard of Castro's march, regarding which I have heard no more since March 29, which is not surprising If you have any news about any of our friends from Andalusia, I would like to hear it.

I await your reply so that I can work in the way that you ask of me and, meanwhile, please receive a warm hug from your friend,

J Pérez Salas.

Garray Barracks.